Is There a "Battle

realize that Murray Harris cannot [ignore Geisler] and that his position does merit support. His position is certainly within the bounds of orthodoxy and he is right when he says, toward the end of his volume in response to Norm Geisler, that "there is no Battle for the Resurrection."

James Montgomery Boice, Tenth Presbyterian Church, Philadelphia

Neither inerrancy nor orthodoxy can be used fairly as an "open sesame" that will automatically settle intepretive debates. Evangelicals must awaken to the fact that belief in a high view of Scripture and a belief in the central truths of the Gospel do not insure unanimity on every interpretive point nor the uniform adoption of the traditional exegesis of all scriptural passages—especially those that deal with questions such as those Professor Murray J. Harris's book poses. To use this division of the house on matters of interpretation as the occasion for introducing suspicion and doubt regarding one's orthodoxy or one's doctrine of Scripture is to fail to remember how widely equally convinced inerrantists disagree on such things as the mode of baptism, the practice of charismatic gifts, the doctrine of election, and the type of church government Scripture teaches.

Walter C. Kaiser, Trinity Evangelical Divinity School

The serious student of Scripture will read this excellent book with great interest. Dr. Harris brings fresh insights to the historic doctrine of Christ's resurrection. His analysis will stimulate thoughtful discussions among scholars, clergy, and laity. The reader may or may not find himself in total agreement with the writer, but I guarantee that his approach to this crucial historical event will broaden and deepen our understanding of the resurrection phenomenon. Dr. Harris's commitment to the reliability of Scripture required his total integrity in exegeting and piecing together the biblical data about Christ's resurrection. This book has challenged my own thinking and helped me understand in a greater way the complexity of the data and the miracle of the resurrection. I am happy to commend this book to you for your further understanding of the reality of the bodily resurrection of Jesus Christ.

Thomas A. McDill, President, Evangelical Free Church of America

The whole church benefits from the necessity laid on Professor Harris to prove his orthodoxy in the matter of resurrection—Christ's and ours. This is a clear, warmhearted book, impeccable in scholarship and inspiring to read. Resurrection questions are not easy, and not all readers will agree with Professor Harris on every detail, but Harris is undoubtedly in the main stream of resurrection faith, and there is no more thorough treatment of the questions currently in print.

James I. Packer, Regent College

Harris presents the most thorough and scholarly treatment of the biblical teaching concerning resurrection from an evangelical perspective for more than a half century. His study will serve as a standard text for many years to come and will be of interest to every serious student of the New Testament.

W. Ward Gasque, Eastern College

From Grave to Glory

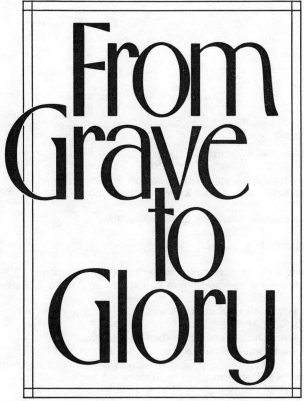

From Grave to Glory

RESURRECTION IN THE NEW TESTAMENT

Including a Response to Norman L. Geisler

Murray J. Harris

Academie Books
Grand Rapids, Michigan
Zondervan Publishing House

From Grave to Glory
Copyright © 1990 by Murray J. Harris

Academie Books is an imprint of Zondervan Publishing House,
1415 Lake Drive, S.E., Grand Rapids, Michigan 49506.

Library of Congress Cataloging in Publication Data

Harris, Murray J.

    From grave to glory : resurrection in the New Testament :
including a response to Norman L. Geisler / By Murray J. Harris.
      p.   cm.
    Includes bibliographical references.
    ISBN0-310-51991-8
    1. Jesus Christ–Resurrection–Biblical teaching.
2. Resurrection–Biblical teaching.   3. Bible. N.T.–Criticism.
Interpretation, etc.   4. Geisler, Norman L.–Views on resurrection
in the New Testament.   I. Title.
BT481.H324   1990
232'.5–dc20   90-32252
                                       CIP

Edited by Lori Walburg and Leonard G. Goss

Printed in the United States of America

90 91 92 93 94 / AK / 10 9 8 7 6 5 4 3 2 1

CONIVGI AMANTISSIMAE

HOC OPVSCVLVM

QVOD IPSA SEMPER FOVEBAT

D. D. AVCTOR

ANNO SALVTIS MCMXC

CONTENTS

PART ONE:
RESURRECTION IN THE NEW TESTAMENT
RESURRECTION BEFORE CHRIST

THE RESURRECTION OF CHRIST

PART TWO:

A RESPONSE TO DR. NORMAN L. GEISLER

——Abbreviations——

BAGD	*A Greek-English Lexicon of the New Testament and Other Early Christian Literature*, by W. Bauer; ETr. and adapted by W. F. Arndt and F. W. Gingrich; 2d ed., rev. and augmented by F. W. Gingrich and F. W. Danker. Chicago/London: University of Chicago, 1979.
BDB	*A Hebrew and English Lexicon of the Old Testament* based on the lexicon of W. Gesenius as tr. by E. Robinson; by F. Brown, S. R. Driver, and C. A. Briggs. Oxford: Clarendon, 1953.
BDF	*A Greek Grammar of the New Testament and Other Early Christian Literature*, by F. Blass and A. Debrunner; ETr. and ed. by R. W. Funk. Chicago: University of Chicago, 1961.
DCG	*A Dictionary of Christ and the Gospels*, 2 vols., ed. J. Hastings. Edinburgh: T. & T. Clark, 1906–8.
ed(s).	editors(s), edited, edition
et al.	and others
ETr.	English translation
GK	*Gesenius' Hebrew Grammar* as ed. and enlarged by E. Kautzch; ETr. rev. by A. E. Cowley. Oxford: Clarendon, 1910, 2d ed.
GNB	The Good News Bible. The Bible in Today's English Version. New York: American Bible Society, 1966, 1971, 1976.
Goodspeed	*The New Testament. An American Translation*, by E. J. Goodspeed. Chicago: University of Chicago, 1923.
JB	The Jerusalem Bible. New York: Doubleday, 1966, 1967, 1968.
LSJ	*A Greek-English Lexicon*, by H. G. Liddell and R. Scott; ed. by H. S. Jones et al., 2 vols. Oxford: Clarendon, 1940, 9th ed.

LXX	Septuagint
MH	*A Grammar of New Testament Greek*, by J. H. Moulton. *Vol. II. Accidence and Word-Formation*, ed. W. F. Howard. Edinburgh: T. & T. Clark, 1919–29.
Moffatt	*The Moffatt Translation of the Bible*, by J. Moffatt. London: Hodder, 1935.
MT	Masoretic text
n.	note
NAB	New American Bible (1970)
NAB[2]	New American Bible. Revised New Testament (1988)
NASB	New American Standard Bible (1977)
NEB	New English Bible (1970)
NIDNTT	*The New International Dictionary of New Testament Theology*, 3 vols., ed. C. Brown. Grand Rapids: Zondervan/Exeter: Paternoster, 1975–78.
NIV	New International Version (1983)
rev.	revised, revision
RSV	Revised Standard Version (1952)
SB	*Kommentar zum Neuen Testament aus Talmud und Midrash*, by H. L. Strack and P. Billerbeck; 4 vols. München: Beck, 1922–28.
TCNT	Twentieth Century New Testament (1904)
TDNT	*Theological Dictionary of the New Testament*, 9 vols. ed. by G. Kittel and G. Friedrich; ETr. by G. W. Bromiley. Grand Rapids: Eerdmans, 1964–74.
tr.	translated, translation
Turner	*A Grammar of New Testament Greek,* by J. H. Moulton, *Vol. III. Syntax,* by N. Turner. Edinburgh: T. & T. Clark, 1963.
Weymouth	*The New Testament in Modern Speech*, by R. F. Weymouth. London: Clarke, 1909, 3d ed.
Zerwick	*Biblical Greek Illustrated by Examples*, by M. Zerwick, ETr. by J. Smith. Rome: Pontifical Biblical Institute, 1963.
ZPEB	*The Zondervan Pictorial Encyclopedia of the Bible*, 5 vols., ed. by M. C. Tenney and S. Barabas. Grand Rapids: Zondervan, 1975.

Abbreviations of Dr. Geisler's writings are as follows:

"Bodily"   "The Apologetic Significance of the Bodily Resurrection of Christ," *Bulletin of the Evangelical Philosophical Society* 10 (1987): 15–37.

"Battle"   "The Battle for the Resurrection," *Fundamentalist Journal* (March 1989): 12–15.

"Physical" "The Significance of Christ's Physical Resurrection," *Bibliotheca Sacra* 146 (1989): 148–70.

"Flesh"   " 'I Believe . . . in the Resurrection of the Flesh,' " *Christian Research Journal* 12 (1989): 20–22.

Battle   *The Battle for the Resurrection* (Nashville: Nelson, 1989).

——— FOREWORD ———

The doctrine of the inerrancy of the Bible assures believers that we may have total confidence in God's revelation to us in the Bible; it does not mean, however, that we may have total confidence in our particular interpretation of that revelation. Nevertheless, it is discouraging to note how frequently evangelicals make the methodological mistake of confusing the assurance of the truthfulness of the Bible with the assurance of the correctness of traditional interpretive positions. All too many believe that to question the latter is equal to doubting the former.

In a world where rapid change and flexibility are more to be counted on in everyday existence than the verities of truth itself, uncertainty in the area of interpreting some passages of Scripture appears to many to be the last straw. Instead, they argue that we should leave nothing open or unsettled, for it will only invite more of the spirit of modernity. And to make sure that nothing comes loose, some argue that we should equate all hermeneutical options with the doctrine of inerrancy, thereby guaranteeing consistency and certainty for all interpretations of Scripture.

But neither inerrancy nor orthodoxy can be used fairly as an "open sesame" that will automatically settle interpretive debates. Evangelicals must awaken to the fact that belief in a high view of Scripture and a belief in the central truths of the Gospel do not ensure unanimity on every interpretive point nor the uniform adoption of the traditional exegesis of all scriptural passages—especially those that deal with questions such as those Professor Murray J. Harris's book poses. To use this division of the house on matters of interpretation as the occasion for introducing suspicion and doubt regarding one's orthodoxy or one's doctrine of Scripture is to fail to remember how widely equally convinced inerrantists disagree on such things as the mode of baptism, the practice of charismatic gifts, the doctrine of election, and the type of church government Scripture teaches.

Nevertheless, our former colleague and diligent defender of the faith, Dr. Norman L. Geisler, appears to be falling into just such a methodological trap. He alleges that Dr. Murray J. Harris holds to views on the resurrection of Christ that are both unorthodox and unbiblical. Notice that he refuses to charge Professor Harris with being "heretical"; he only faults him with being "unorthodox." Unfortunately, whatever nuance or distinction Dr. Geisler may make in charging the one, but not the other, will be lost for most of his reading public.

So serious is this alleged departure from the norms of orthodoxy that Professor Geisler charges the institution where Professor Harris teaches (Trinity Evangelical Divinity School) and its sponsoring body (The Evangelical Free Church of America) with mishandling their numerous inquiries (as were required by the tenure procedures of the denomination and the seminary) into all such matters. The implication seems to be that these officials were less than candid with the Christian public and decided to look the other way when one of their own needed to be put under discipline rather than given tenure.

To read Dr. Geisler's articles and book, and to listen to the radio program interviews he has given, one would conclude that the Trinity administration, its faculty, and The Evangelical Free Church of America have allowed one of its teachers to deny the bodily resurrection of Christ. But that is the mischief of this long three- to four-year episode. Professor Harris affirms ". . . simply and unambiguously: I believe, and have always believed, in the bodily resurrection of Jesus Christ from the dead, and also in the bodily resurrection of believers. . . . [T]he same body of Jesus of Nazareth that had been placed in the tomb after his crucifixion was raised from the dead on the third day. . . ."

"So what is the point of the debate?" you will ask.

It will perhaps come down to this basic question: Could Jesus be visually seen over the period of the forty days between his resurrection and ascension, or did he appear at intervals during those forty days with the same body that went into the grave, although now transformed?

"Why," many will query, "is it important to answer this question? It does not appear to be all that determinative as a central article of our faith. In fact, it seems to be more speculative in nature than foundational for building theology!"

For Dr. Geisler it is necessary to argue that the resurrected body of Jesus be readily available for all to see during those forty days after the Resurrection lest the crowning miracle that validates the truthfulness of our Christian faith be subtly equated with some prestidigitation, i.e. some sleight of hand that says, "Now you see it; now you don't." It might leave some with the question whether the resurrected Jesus was real or merely whimsical.

Dr. Harris has responded using biblical, rather than philosophical or apologetical categories. One of his pivotal passages is Acts 10:40: "God . . . granted that He [Jesus] should become visible." Accordingly, whenever Jesus appeared after his resurrection, it was due to the fact that God was allowing Jesus temporarily to come into visibility. Dr. Harris feels he is bound by the text of Scripture; he may say no more and no less!

"But does Professor Harris," you might counter, "deny that the glorified Jesus is still 'in the flesh'?"

No, Harris answers; Jesus did not cease to be fully human when he arose, for Scripture teaches that "in Christ there dwells the whole fullness of deity *in bodily form*" (Col 2:9, emphasis added) and that the one mediator between God and man is "a man, Christ Jesus" (1Ti 2:5) in his resurrected form.

What we have here, then, is a classic problem of two levels of discourse. One person, the philosophical systematician, is arguing from the logical implications of what it means to be fully man: the resurrected Christ must have a material, physical, fleshy body of the same substance as his pre-resurrected body. To say less is to impugn some categories of orthodoxy and to deny many traditional interpretations of Scripture. The other is arguing from precise biblical vocabulary, refusing to say more than what is said in Scripture: the same Jesus that went into the grave came forth as the resurrected Christ, but because of enhancements, he now has a "glorious," "powerful," "spiritual," "heavenly," "eternal" body "from God."

The reader will not need to be reminded that Professor Harris does not intend to argue that his understanding of the Resurrection is the official view of Trinity Evangelical Divinity School or that there are no other positions on the nature of the resurrected body represented on the faculty. In fact, the variety of positions is only an illustration of one of the strengths of Trinity: unity on the essentials of faith, with diversity in the areas where we have less or little biblical evidence— until we all arrive at the unity of the faith (Eph 4:13).

This debate and the resulting treatise in your hand are more than a tempest in a teapot; they are an exercise in forming and shaping theological models. More may be learned from the debate than simply who is right (or closer to the truth) and who is wrong (or further from the truth). In the providence of God we might just learn more about these issues: how to shape the questions we put to Scripture; what are the limits of our own extrapolations from Scripture; how can we listen more carefully to what a fellow believer is saying in areas where we do not have as much biblical information as we might wish for without charging one another with being unorthodox; and how deep is the "mystery of godliness," i.e. that Christ appeared in a body, was vindicated by the Spirit, was seen by angels, was preached among the nations, was believed on in the world, was taken up in glory (1Ti 3:16).

Walter C. Kaiser, Jr.
Senior Vice President of Education
Academic Dean
Professor of Semitic Languages and Old Testament
Trinity Evangelical Divinity School
February 1990

—— INTRODUCTION ——

Right at the outset, let it be said simply and unambiguously:

*I believe, and have always believed, in the bodily
resurrection of Jesus Christ from the dead, and also in
the bodily resurrection of believers.*

That is, by God's miraculous act, the same body of Jesus of Nazareth
that had been placed in the tomb after his crucifixion was raised from
the dead on the third day and transformed, so that the tomb was left
empty and the risen Lord appeared in person to his disciples over the
course of forty days and is now at the right hand of God in his
immortal "body of glory." At the End, believers too will be raised
from the grave in spiritual bodies to enjoy eternal life in the presence
of God.

Over the past three years there have appeared four articles and,
most recently, a book entitled *The Battle for the Resurrection*
(Nashville: Thomas Nelson, 1989), written by Dr. Norman L.
Geisler, Dean of the Center for Research and Scholarship, Liberty
University Graduate School of Religion, Lynchburg, Virginia. This
author alleges that the view I hold regarding the resurrection is not
biblical or orthodox, and that the institution at which I teach, Trinity
Evangelical Divinity School, and its parent body, The Evangelical
Free Church of America, have mishandled their enquiry into my
views in that both groups have officially declared my views on the
resurrection to be well within orthodoxy and the Free Church
Doctrinal Statement.

What the present volume seeks to do in part 2 ("A Response to Dr.
Norman L. Geisler") is to show that my view is both biblical and
orthodox, and that the present controversy is a remarkable paradox
in view of the fact that in 1985 I championed the cause of

conservative Protestants in Britain and throughout the Commonwealth in writing a response entitled *Easter in Durham* to the Bishop
of Durham (England), in which I defended the orthodox view of the
bodily resurrection of Jesus against the nonbiblical view of the
bishop. What is more, the faculty of the Divinity School, the board of
directors of the Divinity School, the ministerial of the Free Church,
and the General Conference of the Free Church have each affirmed
that my view of the resurrection is completely orthodox, whether
shared by them in every particular or not.

In part 1 ("Resurrection in the New Testament") I shall sketch
some of the main views of the afterlife held in the pre-Christian era.
Then I shall review the New Testament evidence for the resurrection
of Christ in order to show its secure basis as one of the best attested
facts of ancient history, its unique character as an unparalleled and
unrepeatable event, and its theological significance for Christ himself. Finally I shall discuss the perpetual relevance of the resurrection
of Christ for believers and nonbelievers alike. The book, therefore, is
not merely a defense against groundless accusations that have been
leveled against a teacher of the New Testament and the officers of an
evangelical seminary and denomination, but also, and principally, a
positive restatement of one of the central truths of the Christian faith,
the triumphant resurrection of Christ from the grave and its
permanent and universal implications.

As they stand, parts 1 and 2 are independent. Part 1 is much
broader than part 2 in the topics discussed, but obviously there is
considerable overlap since both deal with issues relating to resurrection. A certain amount of repetition has been inevitable, but this has
been kept to a minimum so that the person who reads the whole book
will not be frustrated by a sense of déjà vu. In general, part 2
discusses specific issues in detail, whereas part 1 encompasses the
whole field of resurrection.

I have sought to keep the text free of technicalities wherever
possible, but since part 2 is a response to certain charges that have
been made, some specialized discussion is unavoidable there.
Usually, however, detailed discussion and the necessary documenta-
tion are found in the endnotes.

There are several indications that *The Battle for the Resurrection* is
directed primarily against Trinity, the Free Church, and myself.

(1) In his dedication of the book, Dr. Geisler credits Dr. Robert D.

Culver with bringing this issue to his attention. They were colleagues for six years (1968–74) at Trinity, where I have taught for eleven years (1967–68, 1971–78, 1986–present). Dr. Culver left Trinity at the end of 1974 and Dr. Geisler in 1979.

(2) There are only three evangelicals named in the book as propagating erroneous views regarding the resurrection: Dr. George E. Ladd (who is no longer alive), whose book on the Resurrection appeared as long ago as 1975; Dr. Glenn Hinson, whose book on the life of Jesus was published back in 1977; and myself, whose volume on resurrection and immortality, entitled *Raised Immortal*, appeared in 1983 in the U.K. and in 1985 in the U.S. Ladd's views are discussed in detail in two pages, Hinson's in two, and mine in eight. But elsewhere Dr. Geisler cites my work on some twenty-two occasions.

(3) Dr. Geisler's general discussion of "Lessons to be Learned" from this controversy draws on his observation—at a distance—of recent events at Trinity and in the Free Church. When he says "schools" or "institutions" or "a well-known school" he is referring principally to Trinity. It is left to Dr. Culver in the Foreword to make this unambiguous.

(4) Dr. Geisler's second sentence under "Drawing the Line in the Battle for the Resurrection" refers to "some evangelicals" who claim that my view is orthodox.

If Prof. Geisler's recent book had contained no reference to Trinity and the Free Church, I would have ignored this most recent attempt he has made to state and critique my views, as I already have for the past three years. But when a well-known theological institution and an international denomination have been reluctantly drawn into the controversy because of charges leveled against them, I feel that my silence must be broken.

Of course the particular exegetical views expressed throughout this book are mine alone, and in no case should they be understood as necessarily representing any official view of Trinity Evangelical Divinity School or of The Evangelical Free Church of America. I know that some of my colleagues at Trinity do not agree with my exegesis of some of the biblical passages discussed in this book; indeed, some would espouse a position that is probably nearer to Dr. Geisler's than to mine. But unlike Dr. Geisler, they all respect my right to hold a different interpretation on certain debated exegetical points, and none regards my views as heterodox. As for Dr. Geisler's own views on the Resurrection, I do not regard them as unbiblical and unorthodox. They are possible interpretations of the scriptural data but are certainly not the only views that conform to Scripture and orthodoxy.

I am most grateful to Trinity's Academic Dean, Dr. Walter C. Kaiser, Jr., for contributing the Foreword.

Unless otherwise indicated, the translations of ancient texts and Scripture are my own. In some sections of the book I have made considerable use of material from my earlier work, *Raised Immortal,* which is now out of print. Permission has been kindly granted by the JSOT Press of Sheffield University (UK) for the use of material (in Chapter 4) that first appeared in *Gospel Perspectives. Vol. 6. The Miracles of Jesus.*

Many friends, including colleagues and students, have kindly read various parts of this manuscript and offered helpful suggestions. They are too numerous to name, but I remain indebted to each of them. Two typists have worked diligently and efficiently to enable this relatively prompt response to Dr. Geisler's recent book; I am very grateful to Ruth Jones and Dana Anderson. Richard R. Snyder gave valuable help in preparing the indexes.

Those who wish to go directly to the heart of the controversy should begin by reading section A of chapter XXI on the "Spiritual Body" and the final chapter (XXII) entitled "Reflections on the Controversy."

The reader will not be surprised to learn that the writing of some portions of part 2 was not a pleasant task for me. On the other hand, to write part 1 was a sheer delight. What more exciting topic is there in Christian theology than the resurrection of Christ and its many consequences? Reflection on this lofty theme—or rather this exalted Person—thrills the mind and elevates the spirit. It broadens our spiritual horizons, prompts our devotion to God, and strengthens our motivation for Christian living. May this meager offering achieve some of these effects in the reader.

PART ONE

RESURRECTION
IN THE
NEW TESTAMENT

*God raised him from the
dead and gave him glory.*

1 Peter 1:21

**By his power God raised
the Lord from the dead
and will also raise us up.**

1 Corinthians 6:14

*We rejoice in our hope
of sharing God's glory.*

Romans 5:2

Resurrection Before Christ

— I —

The Afterlife and Resurrection in Egypt and Greece

Long before the advent of Christianity, people entertained hope of a life after death. For some it involved the mere prolongation of physical life in new surroundings, while for others it consisted of an ethereal existence, free of the body. As a backdrop to our discussion of resurrection in the Old Testament, Intertestamental Judaism, and the New Testament, it will be illuminating to sketch two representative pre-Christian views of the afterlife and "resurrection"—the Egyptian and the Greek—that roughly correspond to the alternatives mentioned above. Later, in chapter XVI, we shall compare the Egyptian, Greek, and Jewish traditions with the Christian tradition, in order to highlight the distinctives of Christian teaching about the afterlife.

A. Egypt

Our knowledge of ancient Egyptian views of the afterlife comes mainly from three sources: (1) the *Pyramid Texts*, inscribed on the interior walls of pyramids, were composed by the priests of Heliopolis and reflect views held during the Old Kingdom period (2800–2500 B.C.); (2) the *Coffin Texts* belong to the Middle Kingdom (2134–1786 B.C.); and (3) *The Book of the Dead*, a collection of spells, in its earliest form dates from the Old Kingdom (5th Dynasty, c. 2600 B.C.), although our more complete manuscripts date from New Kingdom times

(1550–1250 B.C.). We should not be surprised that, covering such a lengthy period (more than 1400 years), Egyptian views of the hereafter did not remain uniform but became somewhat complex and confusing, although some development is clearly discernible.

Any view of the afterlife is closely related to one's view of the nature of human beings; eschatology always reflects anthropology. In general terms we may say that the ancient Egyptians believed that human beings had two material parts and two nonmaterial aspects, although they were a psychosomatic unity. The *heart* was the vital organ, but also, as "the god in a man," functioned somewhat like a conscience. The physical *body* was essential for all life, whether before or after death. One of the incorporeal aspects of man was the *ba*, the life-breath. After death the *ba* became an entity independent of the body but always closely associated with it, and so in art it was represented as a human-headed bird perched near or in the tomb. The other incorporeal aspect was the *ka*, the personality or genius, a type of "double" of the living person, to which the dead person became joined. The *ka* inhabited the *ka*-statue in the tomb and was pictorially represented by two upraised human arms. If appropriate mortuary rites were performed, a deceased person was transformed into a glorified being, a "shining" spirit, an *akh*, who was equipped with everything necessary for a happy life in the Field of Rushes. Symbolically the *akh* was represented by the crested ibis.

The *Pyramid Texts* purport to testify to the destiny of the pharaohs alone but in the course of time they afforded safeguards in the afterlife not only for the nobility but also for more ordinary people. There were two main alternative conceptions of the destiny of the deceased pharaoh. The "solar hereafter" involved passage to the sky to accompany Ra, the sun-god, in the movement of his solar boat across the heavens by day and through the netherworld by night before "rising" each day in the east. Alternatively, the dead king journeyed to the underworld in the far West, where the "great god" Osiris reigned, and where life continued as on earth, but always with bountiful harvests, plentiful shade, and consummate pleasures. By the time of the New Kingdom these two views of the afterlife were sometimes combined, so that Ra was the sun by day and Osiris the sun by night prior to rebirth or resurrection.

From the beginning of the Middle Kingdom, the worship of Osiris dominated the religion of Egypt. Legends about Osiris vary greatly, but he was thought by some to have been a historical figure from the East who led a prehistoric invasion of nomads into the Nile delta. After he had ruled the Egyptians beneficently and taught them the arts of civilization, his brother Seth killed him by trickery, and finally his body was cut up into fourteen parts and scattered throughout Egypt. His sister-wife, Isis, collected and reassembled the parts and used the magic of Thoth (the god of writing and reckoning) to resuscitate him, so that he became lord of the netherworld. Consequently, what Egyptians feared was not the benevolent Osiris who was incarnate in each pharaoh but the judgmental Osiris who determined the fate of the souls of the dead.

The rites for the dead, at first performed only on the pharaoh, were later applied to Egyptian nobles and then to the common people. The same basic pattern of mortuary ritual was practiced for almost 3000 years, down to the fourth century A.D. In essence these magical rites, with prayers addressed to Ra (the chief of the gods and primary god of the sun) and Osiris himself, sought to transform the dead person into a double of the divine Osiris who would then have a share in this god's life after arriving in the underworld. There it was hoped that he would be absorbed into the rhythm of the universe in which Osiris, as the god of vegetation and regeneration, symbolized the renewal of life through the river Nile. But to be transformed and mystically identified with Osiris through solemn rites, the dead needed to be preserved from physical disintegration in the same way that the deities

Isis, Nephthys, Horus, and Anubis had worked to preserve the body of the deceased Osiris. Provided the body was eternally preserved in a recognizable form, the spiritual counterpart of the body would also remain intact forever. Hence they evolved the elaborate procedure known as "mummification."

In the earliest days the primitive Egyptians were buried in pit graves in the sands of the desert where in zero humidity the corpses would be naturally preserved for centuries. But they came to realize that if bodies were elaborately wrapped before burial, or particularly, if they were placed in tombs as opposed to sand, they tended to decay much more quickly. So, in one sense, mummification was a substitute for the natural processes of preservation available in the sands of Egypt.

Egyptian techniques of embalming remained similar during the almost 3000 years (c. 2600 B.C.–A.D. 300) that mummification was practiced. In its most developed form, there were several clearly defined stages in the seventy-day procedure. (1) The body was desiccated by coating it with a drying agent called natron. (2) After the brain had been extracted and discarded, the internal organs (but not the heart) were removed through an incision and certain of them were separately preserved in four limestone canopic jars (liver, lungs, stomach, intestines). (3) The body cavities were cleansed and stuffed with linen soaked with resin, or with bags of natron crystals. Alternatively, during the 21st Dynasty (1085–950 B.C.) at least, the embalmed viscera might be replaced in the empty chest and abdomen. (4) The skin was anointed with a sweet-smelling lotion to restore its suppleness and then coated with molten resin to preserve its form. (5) Finally, over a fifteen-day period the body was bound with layers of bandages and wrappings, accompanied by the prescribed magical spells. In early days the face of the mummy was covered with a mask of painted cartonnage (a combination of linen and plaster), but later the whole mummy was encircled in cartonnage.

Further protection against the ravages of time was afforded by the coffins in which the mummies were placed, and also by Egyptian tombs which were called "houses of eternity" and were designed to preserve and honor the deceased, to prevent spoliation by robbers, and to house or depict in drawings the furnishings and nourishment needed to guarantee survival. But before the mummy was placed in the tomb, a magical ceremony called the "Opening of the Mouth" was performed, in order to restore to the embalmed body the faculties lost in death. What Horus had done for his father Osiris, the officiating priest now did for the deceased: by touching the eyes, nostrils, and mouth, the dead person was enabled to see, breathe, and receive food.

It is in the *Coffin Texts* and especially in *The Book of the Dead* that the idea of postmortem judgment most clearly comes to expression. Typically, the judgment scene is depicted thus. The jackal-headed mortuary god Anubis brings the dead person into the great Hall of the Two Truths and sets him before Osiris, the Lord of Eternity, who is seated on his throne with Isis and Nephthys in attendance. Anubis weighs the heart of the deceased in judgment scales against an ostrich feather, the symbol of Maat (Truth or Justice). The heart is almost hypostatized, for it can bear independent testimony against its owner. The divine scribe Thoth, Master of the Balance, records the fateful verdict. If goodness has made the heart light, the dead person is permitted to enter the Osirian Fields in the West. But if the heart is not right with Maat, the dead person is devoured by the fearsome Ammut ("eater of the dead") who ominously crouches nearby.

In spite of the efforts of the Heliopolitan priests to perpetuate and popularize their view of a "solar hereafter" associated with their god Atum-Ra, it seems that a distinctly Osirian view of the hereafter prevailed in Egypt. The highest good for the dead person was to be preserved physically and therefore also spiritually, so that through the necessary magical mortuary rites his personality or spirit (*ka*) could be transformed into a superhuman or glorified being (*akh*), become one with Osiris, and enjoy a continuation of earthly pleasures in the realm of Osiris in the Field of Reeds, located in Duat, "the abode of those who are faultless."

How are we to describe this hope? Not as physical resurrection, for the embalmed body remained in the tomb, the "house of the *ka*," although the afterlife was thought of in concrete, physical terms. Moreover, since Osiris was always represented as a mummified god, ritual identification with him in death cannot properly be deemed resurrection *from* the dead. The realm of the dead was always the dead man's home, even if his soul was able to move about freely and assume appropriate forms. Perhaps we might describe the Egyptian hope as the return of the *ka* into the mummified body, or the transformation of the person, or even the resurrection of the spirit, as the *ka* became an *akh* and thus gained immortality.[1]

B. Greece

Whenever mention is made of the Greek view of the Beyond, we all tend to think of the immortality of the soul, and not without reason, given the widespread influence of Platonism on Western thought. But to imagine that there was a uniform Greek view of immortality—the Platonic—is misguided. Just as the Greek concept of immortality did not spring to life fullgrown but emerged over a period of time, so in the history of this doctrine among the Greeks there was both variety and development.

We may delineate four main stages in the development of the Greek doctrine of immortality in the pre-Christian era.[2]

1. The Homeric poems

In the Homeric epics, the *Iliad* and the *Odyssey*, the "souls" of the dead in Hades are called "idols," shadowy representations of once-living persons. Only those people guilty of great offenses are punished in Tartarus, and only divine heroes are wafted away to the Islands of the Blest. Since the soul is bound to the body, when the body dies the soul is snatched away in the expiring breath. The term *psyche* ("soul") is generally applied to a person at and after his death rather than before, and has no relation to a person's intellectual functions during life. All that really survives a person's physical life is his reputation, for these ghostly "doubles" in Hades lack any consciousness and so are without mental activity or will.

2. The Orphic religion

Orphism was an effort to reform the rites of Dionysiac worship. The chief impetus to a development of the doctrine of the soul from the eighth to the sixth century B.C. were the rituals of the Orphic religious brotherhoods. When the worshiper wholly devoted himself to the wild processions and frenzied dances of these Dionysiac rites, he gained a sense of "standing outside himself" (Greek *ekstasis*, which gives us our word *ecstasy*) and of being identified with divinity. This ecstatic experience, in which the devotee felt temporarily liberated from the limitations of time, space, and embodiment, naturally gave rise to a conception of the hereafter in which, permanently separated from the body, the soul would enjoy the bliss of endless communion with the god whose rites had been celebrated on earth. Typical of Orphic religion was belief in the essential divinity of the soul and the view that embodiment was the exile of the soul from the society of heaven. Such sentiments were summed up in the celebrated Orphic pun, *soma sema*, "the body is the tomb (of the soul)" (Plato, *Cratylus* 400C).

3. Plato

If belief in the eternal survival of the soul was based on religious intuition in Orphism, it gained intellectual respectability at the hands of Plato.[3]

According to Plato the soul is tripartite, having three forms or functions (not material parts): the rational, the spirited or courageous, and the appetitive (that pertaining to the desires and affections). These three he compared to a charioteer (reason) and two unequally yoked horses, one good (courage) and one bad (bodily desires) (*Phaedrus* 246A–D). In its rational or divine element, the soul is preexistent (*Timaeus* 69–70) and eternal (*Republic* 10.611B) and so prior to the body. The body has dealings with the mutable, physical world, but the soul has relations with both the phenomenal world and the unchanging ideal world. Yet there is interaction between the body and the soul. The soul can rule bodily desires, but bodily vices or inferior physical education may adversely influence the soul (*Timaeus* 86B). If in fact the body has in any way ruled the soul and polluted it by sensual pleasures, the soul must pay the price in successive rebirths. After death, the soul must do penance for earthly misdeeds in an intermediate state of bodilessness, before rebirth in a minimum of three further incarnations (*Phaedrus* 249A) with a period of 1000 years between each birth (*Republic* 615A; *Phaedrus* 249A–B). Such purification (*katharsis*) ultimately leads to a withdrawal from the cycle of rebirth and the whole material realm, and it enables the soul to "regain its wings" by entrance into the invisible realm of the divine in the everpresent now.

In works that come from the period of his maturity, Plato adduces five arguments to prove that the rational soul or the rational "part" of the soul is immortal—the argument from opposites (and from reminiscence), from affinity, from "forms," from indestructibility, and from motion. Few philosophers today are convinced by any of these arguments, but one argument in particular has exercised a great influence on subsequent discussion, viz. the argument from affinity or from the simplicity of the rational soul. A sketch of this argument will give the flavor of Plato's method of reasoning.

All visible and material things such as the body are composite and therefore are able to be dissolved into their constituent parts (at death in the case of the body). But the invisible and incorporeal soul is more akin to the class of things that are unchanging, eternal, and indissoluble, than to the visible and material realm that is doomed to perish, for it finds peace in contemplating the imperishable realm of eternal ideas and its nature is not to serve but to rule. Its affinity to the invisible, eternal realm shows that it is uncompounded and so imperishable. It is inconceivable that the soul perishes at death since the body itself remains intact for some time after death (*Phaedo* 78B–84B).

Did Plato believe that the soul in its totality was immortal? And was that immortality personal? It would appear that he regarded only the rational "part" or function of the soul as deathless and indestructible,[4] for the two lower functions (the "spirited" and the "appetitive") could hardly be exercised when the soul was incorporeal. He implies that the incorporeal soul has personal consciousness and retains its self-identity (*Republic* 611A). It was the considered judgment of E. Rohde that "for Plato the Souls live on as they had been in the beginning—individual beings conscious of themselves in a time that has no end and is beyond all time. He teaches a personal immortality."[5]

4. Aristotle

Aristotle distinguishes three types of living organism that share in the "principle of life" (*psychē*, "soul"), viz. vegetable, animal, and man. All three types are dependent on nourishment and all experience growth and decay. Thus they all possess the nutritive or vegetative soul. All animals have the sensitive or appetitive soul in that they experience sensation and feel desire. But only man has the rational soul with its power of thinking and intellect (*nous*), although the human soul embraces the powers of the lower souls (viz. the appetitive soul shared with animals and the vegetative soul shared with animals and plants). Aristotle reserves immortality and eternality for "active intellect" (*De Anima* 415A), the active operation of the *nous* by which potential intelligence ("passive intellect") becomes actualized. However, since the faculty of memory belongs to the passive and perishable part of the intellect (*De Anima* 408B), the disembodied and immortal "active intellect" will, it seems, lack self-consciousness, individuality, and continuity with earlier bodily existence. What survives the death of the individual is the impersonal reason or divine *nous*, with the individual's self-consciousness lapsing at death since it is dependent on the bodily state.

It is not surprising that the attitude of the common Greek person remained unaffected by these complex philosophical ideas. True, some Greeks held to a Pythagorean belief in the transmigration of the soul. On this view, the soul becomes defiled either before birth or during earthly life. Such pollution demands that expiation be paid to Persephone, the goddess of the underworld, by successive incarnations and deaths, with intervening periods of reward or punishment, before the purified soul can finally gain release from the cycle of rebirth, "the sorrowful weary wheel." But the evidence of Greek epitaphs suggests that most people shared vague Homeric ideas of the hereafter rather than having a Platonic or Pythagorean outlook. That is, apart from heroes and notorious sinners who had particular destinies suited to their deeds, people survived death simply as bodiless shades in Hades without any personal consciousness or identity. Such shadowy relics or "doubles" of former living persons had a permanent changeless existence in Hades, unaffected by transmigration.

5. *Three reactions to "resurrection"*

Whether they were sophisticated intellectuals or simple artisans, Greeks had one feature in common: resurrection was totally foreign to their worldview. Confronted with a claim of resurrection, or with what seemed to be a case of resurrection, they reacted, it would appear, in one of three ways— straightforward rationalization, outright mockery, or cautious curiosity. These three reactions may now be illustrated in turn.

Apollonius of Tyana was a wandering neo-Pythagorean philosopher of the first century A.D. who had extraordinary powers as a clairvoyant and wonder-worker. In his *Life of Apollonius of Tyana* 4.45 (c. A.D. 217) Philostratus recounts a "marvel" (*thauma*) that Apollonius performed at Rome on a girl who belonged to a consular family. He chanced to meet the doleful funeral procession of this girl, a bride who had been "on the point of being married." Following her bier was the bridegroom who was lamenting his unfulfilled marriage. Apollonius halted the procession with the words, "Put down the bier, for I will stop your tears for this maiden." Instead of delivering a speech, as the crowd had expected, he merely touched the girl and secretly whispered some spell over her, at which she woke up, spoke out loudly, and then returned to her father's house, "just as Alcestis did when recalled to life by Hercules."[6]

The comments of Philostratus on this episode are most revealing. Twice in this paragraph he expresses doubt whether the girl was actually dead: "a girl, in the hour of her marriage, seemed to be dead ... he woke up the maiden from her apparent death." These hints are followed up by an explicit rationalization.

> But whether he detected a spark of life in her, which her attendants had failed to notice—for they say that although the air was moist with rain, the vapor of her breath could be seen—or whether his touch rekindled and restored her

life when it was really extinct, is a mystery that neither I
nor those who chanced to be present could solve.

The second and third possible reactions of Greeks to
"resurrection"—outright mockery, cautious curiosity—are
both illustrated in Luke's account of Paul's speech before the
council of the Areopagus (Ac 17:22–34). Luke notes the two
reactions of the councillors when they heard Paul mention a
"resurrection of the dead" (*anastasis nekrōn*). "Some began
jeering" (WEYMOUTH; "laughed outright," PHILLIPS). "But
others said, 'We will hear you again on this topic'" (Ac
17:32).

The "some" who openly mocked (Ac 17:32a) probably
were the Epicurean philosophers who had earlier scoffed at
Paul as an "intellectual scavenger" who picked up others'
ideas from here and there and passed them off as his own
without understanding them (*spermologos*, Ac 17:18a, a
derogatory term of Athenian slang for an idler who picked up
scraps in the marketplace). Epicurus (341–270 B.C.), the
founder of the Epicurean school, taught that the purpose of
life was the attainment of pleasure during the here and now.
Such pleasure came by acquiring true knowledge about the
universe, by cultivating moral virtue, personal imperturbabil-
ity, and human friendship, and by living in tranquil obscurity.
Natural phenomena were all adequately explicable by mecha-
nistic causes so there was no place for a personal deity who
intervened in the physical world. Since both body and soul
disintegrated into their constituent atoms at death, there was
no life beyond the grave. Little wonder, then, that the
Epicureans laughed derisively when Paul announced that God
had raised Jesus from the dead in evidence of the fact that he
had appointed him to be the executor of divine judgment on
the world of men (Ac 17:31). To a Greek the term *resurrection*
would signify "reanimation" when used of persons, so that
the expression "the resurrection of the dead" (Ac 17:32)
would mean "the resuscitation of corpses," a patent absurdity
to an Epicurean in light of the disintegration of soul and body
at the moment of death.

The "others" who, as a matter of cautious curiosity and traditional courtesy, requested further instruction from Paul at some later date (Ac 17:32b) may well have been the Stoics who imagined that Paul was "a herald of foreign divinities" (Ac 17:18b).[7] These are precisely the reactions we would have expected from Stoics, whose philosophical system accommodated both an afterlife of sorts and a plurality of names for the supreme Power. Zeno (335–263 B.C.), a student of the Cynic philosopher Crates and the father of Stoicism, taught that virtue consisted of living in accordance with nature, and in particular, in conformity with right reason. Reason (*logos*) was the principle governing both the physical universe and the moral world. While Stoicism lacked any formal doctrine of immortality, the soul was thought to survive the death of the body. Local and national gods were accommodated alongside the impersonal and pantheistic Stoic deity by being recognized as symbolic of the different expressions or activities of the one world-principle or spirit that animates all things. In the famous *Hymn to Zeus* composed by Cleanthes (c. 303–232 B.C.), the successor of Zeno, the Stoic divinity is addressed as "you of many names." Having observed, then, that the message of Paul was interpreted by some in a polytheistic sense, Luke hastens to add parenthetically, "this was because he was preaching Jesus [*Iēsous*] and the resurrection [*anastasis*]" (Ac 17:18). Paul's hearers had mistakenly taken "Jesus and the resurrection" to be an allusion to two new deities that Paul sought to introduce at Athens, "the Healer" (*Iēsō*, the Ionic form of the name of the goddess of health and healing, *Iasō*) and his consort "Restoration" (*Anastasis*).[8]

There are probably no lines anywhere in Greek literature that more aptly epitomize the prevailing Greek attitude toward resurrection than those found in the *Eumenides* of Aeschylus (lines 647–48). On the occasion of the founding of the court of the Areopagus in Athens, the god Apollo observes, "Once a man is slain by death and the dust has drunk up his blood, there is no coming back to life [*anastasis*]."

II

Immortality and Resurrection in the Old Testament

It has become customary to discuss the conception of the afterlife in any religion by focusing on two ideas—immortality and resurrection. Sometimes these two terms are used interchangeably, but this is entirely inappropriate. In general terms, immortality relates to the incorruptibility and death-lessness of the postmortem state of the deceased as they continue their existence, while resurrection refers to the raising up of dead bodies or dead persons from the realm of death to renewed life. Our focus in this chapter (and throughout this book) is on resurrection, but brief comments should also be made about immortality in Old Testament thought.

Behind any conception of the afterlife is a particular view about death. Therefore before we examine the Old Testament evidence for belief in immortality or resurrection among Jews of the pre-Christian era, we should sketch the Israelite attitudes toward death.

A. Death

From one viewpoint, death represents the "normal" end of life (Job 5:26), provided a person does not die prematurely or violently or without a surviving heir. Made of dust, man returns to the dust when he dies (Ge 3:19; Ps 90:3). "Like water spilt on the ground that cannot be gathered up again, so we must all die" (2Sa 14:14; cf. Job 7:21; Ps 39:13). But from another standpoint, death is unnatural, being a penalty for sin (Ge 2:17; 3:3–4). It involves the scattering or draining away or withdrawal of a person's vital power (*nepeš*, "soul"; Ge 35:18; 1Ki 19:4).[1] Under ordinary circumstances no one can return to "the land of living" (Job 7:9–10; 10:21; Ps 88:10) to enjoy the blessings of the covenant in the company of God's people. Accordingly, death is to be abhorred for its deprivation (Ps 88:3–12).

Yet death does not bring annihilation, for at death all persons "go down" to Sheol, both the righteous (Ge 37:35) and the ungodly (Nu 16:30). Sheol is located below the earth's surface (Eze 31:15, 17) and is a place of darkness (Job 10:21–22; Ps 143:3), silence (Ps 94:17; 115:17), and forgetfulness (Job 14:21; Ps 88:10–12). Going down to Sheol can be compared to descent into the jaws of an insatiable monster (Isa 5:14; cf. Hab 2:5). In Sheol, elsewhere called "the pit" (Ps 30:3; Eze 31:14–15) or "destruction" (Job 26:6; Pr 15:11; 27:20), people dwell as "shades" (*rĕpā'îm*), faint shadows of their former selves (Isa 14:9–10; 26:14), deprived of light and strength. In the Hebrew mind, what is destroyed by death is all meaningful existence, but not existence as such. The doubts with which the Israelites wrestled were not uncertainties about whether humans beings existed after death, but whether Yahweh's power could release persons from the grip of Sheol. Although there are some hints of the independence of Sheol (Ps 88:5, 10–12, "Is your saving help known in the land of oblivion?" [v. 12b]; Isa 38:18, "Those who go down to the pit cannot hope for your faithfulness"), the view that prevailed was that Sheol, even "lowest Sheol," was still within the scope of Yahweh's sovereign power (Dt 32:22; Ps 139:8; Am 9:2). Yahweh was the living God and ruler of all, so that even the departed were still within God's created universe and therefore were not beyond his reach.

Yet a pressing question remains. Are we to identify Sheol, the place of the dead, with the netherworld or with the grave?

It has become traditional to equate Sheol with the under-world, the subterranean realm of departed spirits. Within this general view, some have concluded that the Old Testament does not distinguish between the destiny of the righteous and the fate of the wicked; all descend to Sheol and remain there, without distinction.[2] Others hold that Sheol was ultimately compartmentalized, the godly being segregated from the ungodly who suffer "destruction" or "corruption" in the "pit."[3] Or again, some have argued that although all persons were viewed as descending to Sheol at death, Sheol was ordained to be the permanent abode only of the ungodly, for the righteous were destined to be resurrected and to enter God's presence (cf. Ps 49:15).[4]

The close association between the grave and Sheol has long been recognized.[5] In some instances "grave" seems an appropriate rendering for $š^e$'$ôl$ ("Sheol") (e.g., Ge 37:35; Isa 14:11; Eze 32:26–27). The KJV uses this translation some thirty-one times (Sheol occurs sixty-five times in the Old Testament). Among modern English versions, the NIV is unique in regularly, although not invariably (e.g., Isa 38:10, "death"), translating Sheol by "grave."[6]

An ingenious combination of these two views is proposed by A. Heidel, who argues that when the wicked are in view, Sheol usually signifies the "netherworld," the subterranean realm of separated souls, although it may exceptionally denote the grave; but when the death of the righteous is mentioned, Sheol always means "grave."[7]

Both of these views have advantages and difficulties. But given the negative biblical descriptions of Sheol and the intimations of immortality and resurrection discussed below, it seems impossible to hold that Sheol was finally regarded as the ultimate abode of the righteous.

B. Immortality

The Hebrew Bible has no distinct term for immortality, but in Proverbs 12:28 we find the coined expression "not-death" (

'al-māweṯ): "On the road of righteousness is [eternal] life; and the treading of her path is [or, brings] immortality" (literally, "not-death").[8] Three Hebrew terms denote unlimited duration of time and in a prepositional phrase they can mean "forever," but only in reference to God does this clearly refer to eternal existence.[9]

On the other hand, when the Psalmist speaks of the "pleasures forever" (NIV, "eternal pleasures") at God's right hand (Ps 16:11) after mentioning "the path that leads to life," or when he declares that God is his portion "forever" (Ps 73:26; cf. 16:11) just after he has affirmed that "you guide me with your instruction, and afterward you will take me to glory" (Ps 73:24), or when he states that in Zion "the Lord has conferred the blessing—life forevermore" (Ps 133:3), individual immortality may well be in view. Indeed, a recent commentator on the Wisdom Literature, M. Dahood, has made the startling proposal that on ten occasions in the Psalms and four times in Proverbs the term ḥayyîm ("life") may be rendered "eternal life,"[10] the positive corollary of immortality. Few scholars have been convinced by all these examples; but as a result of Dahood's research, fewer scholars will now insist that the doctrine of the afterlife emerged within Israel only in the late postexilic period.[11]

Quite apart from the fourteen possible examples in Psalms and Proverbs where Dahood claims ḥayyîm signifies eternal life, the "life" that is promised to those who keep the commandments (e.g., Eze 18:9, 19, 21) seems to refer to prolonged earthly life (Dt 6:2; 11:9) or the immortality of one's name (Isa 56:4–5) or the reproduction of one's life in one's progeny, rather than to the enjoyment of an eternal and heavenly existence.

There is only one place in the Old Testament where the ideas of resurrection and immortality are clearly interrelated—Daniel 12:2–3. The "everlasting life" to which righteous sleepers will awake (v. 2) could refer to the indefinite prolongation of the life of reanimated corpses, but v. 3

suggests otherwise. In describing the destiny of the "wise . . . who turn many to righteousness," the writer says they will shine "like the brightness of the heavens, . . . like the stars forever and ever." "Shining like stars" symbolizes the transformed resurrection life (cf. Mt 13:43), while "forever and ever" points to the permanence and indestructibility of that new bodily life in the messianic kingdom, a kingdom that itself "shall never be destroyed" (Da 2:44; cf. 7:14, 27). This interpretation of the phrase "will awake . . . to everlasting life" in Daniel 12:2 is reflected in the Johannine reference to "the resurrection that leads to (eternal) life" (Jn 5:29).

C. Resurrection

Quite apart from particular texts which may reflect a belief in resurrection from the dead, there are six Old Testament incidents relevant to our discussion. In the Elijah-Elisha sagas, there is a record of the raising of three persons from the dead: the son of the widow of Zarephath (1Ki 17:17–24), the son of the woman of Shunem (2Ki 4:18–37), and the man thrown into Elisha's grave (2Ki 13:20–21). In each case the miracle occurred shortly after death and served merely to prolong earthly life, for we may assume that the three simply resumed their former lives. Such restorations to physical life were therefore unlike an awakening to everlasting life (Da 12:2), but they demonstrated that Yahweh's power extended to Sheol and could revive even the dead.

Two Old Testament figures were spared death by being snatched away from earth to heaven—Enoch (Ge 5:24) and Elijah (2Ki 2:10–11). In both cases the verb *lāqaḥ* ("take") is used and thus becomes a technical term for the assumption or exaltation of a person to the presence of God. In Genesis 5 the refrain "and he died" is conspicuously absent from the reference to Enoch. Clearly, "then he was no more, for God took him" implies that he did not personally pass through death (cf. Heb 11:5). In Elijah's case it was stated that heaven was his destination (2Ki 2:1, 11); we may legitimately infer that the same was true in the case of Enoch. This terse description of Enoch's departure from earth later became the inspiration for a considerable body of Jewish apocalyptic literature which specified the mode of Enoch's translation and the content of the revelations entrusted to him. It was no mere coincidence that Enoch and Elijah were the chosen objects of Yahweh's favor; in both Testaments each one is portrayed as a righteous man of faith who walked with God and pleased him (Enoch: Ge 5:22a, 24a; Heb 11:5; Elijah: 1Ki 18:22, 36–37; Lk 1:17; Jas 5:17–18). In this way there was established the link between holiness of life on earth and splendor of destiny in the hereafter, a link that is fundamental to any doctrine of resurrection.

Taken together, these three instances of restoration to life and two instances of bodily assumption in preexilic Israel helped to pave the way in the minds of the people for the emergence of belief in resurrection. The supremacy of Yahweh over death was clearly established. He is able to save from death, either before or after it occurs.

The final incident that deserves attention is recorded in 1 Samuel 28:3–25. With the daunting Philistines encamped at Shunem, Saul sought guidance from the Lord concerning the advisability of battle, but no response came. So he disguised himself and visited a medium at Endor who, at his request, conjured up the spirit of Samuel and then said to Saul, "I see a spirit [or, godlike being, $^{\prime e}l\bar{o}h\hat{i}m$] emerging from the earth" (v. 13). The "disturbance" felt by Samuel (v. 15) relates to his unease in ascending from Sheol to the world of men. This episode and the general availability of mediums prior to Saul's own purge (v. 3) are, or course, no indication of embryonic resurrection faith but they do establish Israelite belief in one precondition of resurrection—the survival of persons in their individual identity beyond death. Samuel appeared apparently in the same form as he had at the time of death, as "an old man wearing a robe" (v. 14).

We turn now to discuss those Old Testament passages in which scholars have found a nascent or developed belief in resurrection. We shall discuss them in their canonical order and then summarize Old Testament teaching regarding resurrection. It is outside our purpose to investigate the vexed question of the stages by which resurrection faith developed.[12]

1. 1 Samuel 2:6

The Song of Hannah (1Sa 2:1–10) is a prayer celebrating the supreme power of Yahweh in intervening on behalf of the needy and in routing the mighty and the wicked. After mentioning the fruitfulness of the barren (v. 5b), the hymn continues, "Yahweh kills and brings to life (ḥāyâh); he brings down to Sheol and raises up" (v. 6; cf. Dt 32:39). The two statements are in synonymous parallelism, so that Yahweh's infliction of death is described as his bringing down the deceased to the grave, while his bringing to life is his raising him up. It is unlikely that this latter pair of expressions refers to Hannah's giving birth to Samuel, for while the verb ḥāyâh regularly means "bring *back* to life," perhaps only once does it mean "bring to life" in the sense of "give life" (Job 33:4). And we might then have expected the order "birth—death." If, alternatively, Hannah was actually thinking of Yahweh's power in raising up the dead from Sheol, in "restoring to life" (BDB 311c, 3.a),[13] she was simply enunciating a general truth about Yahweh, viz. that his power had been (often) demonstrated in resurrections. Such an interpretation is certainly possible, but what the verse seems to be saying is that Yahweh not only "kills" (= brings death as a penalty; BDB 560b, 2.) but also "preserves alive" (a very common sense of ḥāyâh, BDB 311b, 1.c) or "raises up" from the verge of death. "Just as death . . . is for the Israelite the weakest form of life, so any weakness in life is a form of death."[14] Illness, for example, may be viewed as death and recovery as resurrection (Ps 71:20). On this view Hannah is lauding

Yahweh's ability to rescue those endangered by death (Ps 30:3; Jnh 2:6) rather than revive those overcome by death.

2. Job 19:26-27

In response to Bildad's second speech (Job 18:1-21), Job first describes his humiliation at God's hand (19:1-22) and then looks to the future when he might gain the vindication that is denied him in the present (vv. 23-29). But even the approval of future generations—if a permanent record of his case could be made on tablet or rock (vv. 23-24)—would not begin to alleviate his sense of alienation from God. Relief must come from God himself.

> [25]*I know that my Defender [or, Vindicator, gō'ēl] lives*
> *and that in the end he will stand upon the earth [or, upon my grave, 'al-'āpār].*
> [26]*And after my skin has been destroyed, then [or, yet] in my flesh [or, apart from my flesh, mibbᵉśārî] I shall see God.*
> [27]*I myself shall see him with my own eyes, and not as a stranger [or, I, and not another].*

On the basis of the nature and function of the gō'ēl in the Ugaritic Ras Shamra texts, some believe that the defender is a man. But given Job's own description of God as his witness and advocate (16:19, 21) and the fact that Job is addressing his accusing friends, we are on surer ground to identify God as the one whom Job expects ultimately to champion his cause and publicly vindicate his innocence and integrity. The verb "stand" in v. 25b means "arise [to vindicate]" (BDB 877d, 1.f). Job envisages Yahweh as his future vindicator. The time of the vindication is more likely to be after death than before it, since Job had already renounced the hope of living (17:1, 13-16). Moreover, "in the end" ('aḥᵃrôn, v. 25b) points to the distant rather than the immediate future (but see BDB 31a, b.), and the expression "after my skin has been destroyed" (v. 26a) more naturally refers to Job's death than to the state of his body before death but after his disease has wrought its havoc.

Perhaps the exegetical crux of the passage is the meaning of v. 26b. The preposition *min* in *mibbᵉśārî* may denote separation (so GK 382 § 119w; BDB 578c, 1.b, "probably"), "without (or apart from) my flesh"; or it may indicate the source, "from in my flesh" (similarly most English versions). In the former case, Job anticipated that he would witness his own vindication at the hands of God in a disembodied state, but "with my own eyes" (v. 27) perhaps counts against this. In the latter case, he may have expected to be clothed in his resurrection flesh when he saw God acting as his defender; or else he may be expressing a confident hope in his assured vindication *after* his resurrection, so that it is not the resurrection itself that will be Job's vindication but it will be the means enabling him to witness his vindication. Even if Job is describing a special, divinely revealed privilege to be accorded him alone, such sentiments served to accelerate the formulation of a general doctrine of resurrection.

3. The Psalms

a. Psalm 16:9–11

At the time of writing David is confronted by some unspecified peril ("Preserve me . . . I will not be shaken . . . you will not abandon me to Sheol," vv. 1, 8, 10), perhaps the machinations of a personal enemy or the danger of losing his present happiness, but he entrusts his lot to God, his counselor and protector. The psalm celebrates the temporal and eternal benefits of trust in God and loyalty to him. If vv. 1–4 describe the hallmarks, and vv. 5–8 the present blessings of the believer, vv. 9–11 depict the future blessings.

> ⁹*Therefore my heart is glad and my spirit rejoices; my body also will dwell in safety,*

> [10]*because you will not abandon me [or, my soul] for Sheol to possess, or let your holy one [or, covenant partner] experience the pit [or, decay, cf. LXX diaphthoran].*
> [11]*You will show me the path that leads to life; you will fill me with joy in your presence and with pleasures forever at your right hand.*

Experiencing the benefits outlined in vv. 5–8, David is moved to joy ("Therefore . . . ," v. 9a). Since v. 9b is parallel to v. 9a it must speak of present security, not security in Sheol after death. Nowhere does the Old Testament affirm that the dead dwell in the dust or grave *in safety*. Dwelling in safety refers to divine protection (Ps 4:8). David is assured that God will protect him from imminent danger (v. 9b), as is proved by the fact that (explicative *kî*, "because"; see BDB 473d, 3.c for the usage) he will not leave or abandon his soul to Sheol or let him undergo the corruption that besets those in the grave (v. 10). Instead of falling under the divine wrath and being abandoned to Sheol in premature death (cf. Ps 6:1, 5), David is destined to receive divine direction for his path, a path that issues in eternal life (v. 11a) and eternal joy in the divine presence (v. 11b).

Now it is true that both Peter and Paul find in v. 10 a prophecy of the resurrection of the Messiah (Ac 2:24–31; 13:34–37), but this fact does not preclude the relevance of the verse also to David's own situation. In its original setting, v. 10 provides only an implicit affirmation of belief in resurrection: the whole man ("my body . . . my soul," vv. 9b, 10a) is destined for life, not death. But even if David is reviewing in vv. 9–11 his future prospects primarily on earth, the words seem designedly ambiguous and are applicable, albeit in a secondary sense, to his future prospects in the hereafter. He overlooks the advent of death and its consequences, and affirms the character of the believer's life both in this world and in the next. Life, not death, is his divinely appointed lot. It is immortality rather than resurrection that is in view in the original setting of the psalm, insofar as it refers to David himself.

b. Psalm 17:15

In this psalm David laments the injustice meted out to him by his enemies when he is convinced of his own innocence (cf. 1Sa 23:26; 24:11). God, he clearly recognizes, is his only and final court of appeal. The psalm concludes with a vigorous plea for vindication (vv. 13–15): "Rise up, O Lord, confront them, overthrow them! Rescue me . . . from men of this world whose reward is in this life. . . . As for me, in righteousness I shall see your face; at my resurrection [or, when I awake; $b^e h \bar{a} q \hat{i} \bar{s}$], I shall be satisfied with seeing your form" (cf. Nu 12:8).

"Awakening to see God's form" could refer simply to rising from sleep to a new day in fellowship with God or even (in the context of asylum) to nothing more than waking in safety to greet the divine host in the morning, but both of these interpretations ignore the context. The prayer is addressed to Yahweh (vv. 1, 6, 13), not some divine host, and David is contrasting the lot of his adversaries who have no hope or reward beyond the present world (v. 14a) with his own reward and portion in the world to come. If this is so, resurrection is seen to lead to the beatific vision of God.

c. Psalm 49:15 (MT, 49:16)

Following an appeal for universal attention (vv. 1–2) to the coming words of wisdom and understanding (vv. 3–4), the psalmist introduces his theme—the folly of fearing oppression from materialists and of trusting in earthly riches (vv. 5–6). First he observes that the power of money is not unlimited, for a man cannot buy off God (vv. 7–9) and death is the great leveler (vv. 10–12). Then he contrasts this equality in death with the inequality of destiny that follows death (vv. 13–15). Finally he teaches that knowledge of this coming reversal of destinies in the hereafter gives a proper perspective on wealth in the here and now (vv. 16–20).

In the section relevant to our study (vv. 13–15), the psalmist declares that "those who trust in themselves" (v. 13a) are destined to be led into Sheol by the shepherd Death, there to decay (v. 14), whereas the upright will experience release from Sheol through God's intervention: "But God will redeem my soul from Sheol, for he will take me to himself" (v. 15). The significant "but" (adversative *'ak*) of this verse looks back to vv. 7–8 and to v. 14. Although man is unable to pay the ransom price for the soul (vv. 7–8)—"no payment is ever enough" (v. 8b)—God himself pays the price of redemption which forces Sheol to release its carrion grip on the deceased, and then he takes the person thus ransomed to his presence (vv. 14–15). As in Genesis 5:24; 2 Kings 2:3, 5, 9–10; and Psalm 73:24 the technical term *lāqaḥ* ("take") appears: "he will take me to himself." In comparison with those who have riches but not understanding (v. 20) and "who will never see the light" of life in the presence of God (v. 19b), the upright *will* see this light. What the psalmist seems to envisage is his assumption to heaven immediately after death, but no indication is given of his bodily state before or after the translation.

d. Psalm 73:23–26

As in Psalm 49, so here in Psalm 73, the problem addressed is the prosperity of the wicked—"always at ease, they increase in wealth" (v. 12). Not until the psalmist entered God's sanctuary was he relieved of the oppressive burden of this problem (vv. 16–17). There he gained the knowledge that the wicked will ultimately reap their true desserts (vv. 18–20). A new ingredient in the solution, not found in Psalm 49, was the discovery that true riches consist of personal fellowship with God (vv. 23–26).

> [23]Yet I am continually with you;
>   you hold me by my right hand.
> [24]You guide me with your instruction,
>   and afterward you will take me to glory.
> [25]Whom do I have in heaven except you?
>   Since I have you, I desire nothing else on earth.
> [26]My flesh and my heart may fail,
>   but God is the strength of my heart
>   and my portion forever.

The psalmist does not anticipate that God would grant him various material benefits or human acclaim (cf. v. 25b) such as the wicked enjoyed, but he does know that God will "take" him to enriched fellowship in heaven. Again we find the technical term for "assumption," lāqaḥ. "Afterward" (v. 24b) implies a contrast with present guidance during life (v. 24a); only when the guidance had ceased—with the failing of the flesh and heart at death (v. 26a)—would the assumption occur. The advent of death, however, would in no way diminish the reality of communion with God (v. 23), for he was the psalmist's portion forever (v. 26).

This cursory treatment of the principal passages in the Psalms relevant to our theme has shown that the psalmists' confidence in the face of death, where this comes to expression, is not based on a philosophical assurance of the soul's natural immortality but on a religious conviction of the supremacy of Yahweh over death and of the "unendingness" of the fellowship that the righteous presently enjoy with him. Death can neither frustrate the designs of Yahweh nor separate the believer from fellowship with him.

4. Isaianic passages

a. Isaiah 25:8a

The so-called "Isaiah Apocalypse" (Isa 24:1–27:13) proclaims God's ultimate victory in the overthrow of earthly and

supernatural enemies (e.g., 26:20–27:1): "In that day the
LORD will punish the powers in the heavens above and the
kings on the earth below" (24:21 NIV). Isaiah 25:8a reads "He
will swallow up death for ever and the Lord God will wipe
away the tears from all faces." The passage anticipates the
certain abolition of death, and therefore decay, and with their
removal the eradication of any ground for sorrow and pain.
"The shroud that enfolds all peoples" (v. 7 NIV), the shroud
of suffering and mourning, will be destroyed precisely by the
extermination of death. Paul cites this verse in a resurrection
context (1Co 15:54), but in its original setting the point is not
the eradication of death through the resurrection of the dead
but the removal of grief through the destruction of death.

b. Isaiah 26:19

In Isaiah 26:7–18 we find a prayer of longing for divine
intervention to vindicate the righteous and punish the wicked.
The divine response is resurrection for one group (v. 19) and
judgment for the other (vv. 20–21).

> [19]*Your dead shall live;*
> *my dead bodies [lit. "my corpse," n^{e}bēlātî, here a*
> *collective singular, BDB 615c, 1.a] shall rise.*
> *You who dwell in the dust,*
> *wake up and sing for joy.*
> *For your dew is like morning dew;*
> *the earth shall cast forth her dead.*

Here the speaker calls on the dead to awake and rejoice
because just as the morning dew that comes from God waters
the earth and causes it to produce plant life, so he will send his
life-giving dew (Hos 14:5) to the earth that contains his dead
and so cause them to come to life: "Your dead shall live . . .
the earth shall cast forth her dead." The identity of the
speaker is not immediately obvious. It could be the worshiping community or its representative (the prophet?) or it could
be Yahweh himself. Either way, a general resurrection is not

envisaged. "*My* dead bodies" will refer to the righteous dead, especially martyred Israelites who were persecuted by the "other lords" mentioned in v. 13 and who belong either to the community or to Yahweh. The language employed suggests that the type of resurrection here envisaged is a resuscitation of corpses; at least no reference is made to transformation.[15]

c. Isaiah 53:10b–12

The fourth Servant Song (Isa 52:13–53:12) is a poem of five stanzas, with three verses in each stanza. In the final stanza (53:10–12), which, like the first (52:13–15), depicts the Servant's exaltation, resurrection is clearly presupposed. It is only after he had made his life a guilt offering in death that the Servant would see his offspring (v. 10); it was because he had already poured out his life in death that he would divide the spoils of victory with the strong (v. 12). This postmortem exaltation of the suffering Servant had to involve resurrection if it involved prolonged or immortal life (v. 10). An allusion to his resurrection may be found if, with some commentators (e.g., C. R. North[16]) and modern versions (e.g., JB, NIV), we follow the two Qumran scrolls of Isaiah and the LXX in reading "light" as the object of "he shall see" in v. 11a. This "light" in store for the vindicated Servant could well be resurrection life: "he will see the light [of life]" (NIV). But to the extent that the Servant is a corporate figure—the whole nation or its righteous remnant—there is implied the regeneration or restoration of a group, not the resurrection of an individual.

5. Ezekiel 37:1–14

Not a few church Fathers regarded Ezekiel's vision of a valley strewn with dry human bones bleached by the sun as a clear prophecy of the resurrection (e.g., Tertullian, *On the Resurrection of the Flesh*, 30), and one manuscript of the

LXX (codex Marchalianus) has the note "the revival of the dead" written in its margin, which may reflect the thinking of some diaspora Jews of the pre-Christian era. The question is: Did Ezekiel have in mind the national revival of "dismembered" tribes or the individual resurrection of deceased persons?

The passage is one of the four principal visions in Ezekiel, the others being chapters 1–3 (the prophet's inaugural vision and his call), 8–11 (a vision of temple idolatry), and 40–48 (a vision of the New Temple and its cult). It has two parts—the vision itself (vv. 1–10) and its interpretation (vv. 11–14). The historical occasion of the vision was the despair of the exiles in captivity: "our bones are dried up, our hope is gone, we are cut off" (v. 11b; cf. 33:10). With the fall of Jerusalem it seemed that national hope had been so dried up and national survival so threatened that the exiles felt as good as dead, drained of all signs of vital national life. The vision depicts the restoration of the nation by the symbolism of the resuscitation of the unburied slain who are strewn about on the floor of a valley. "These bones are the whole house of Israel" (v. 11). But "the whole house of Israel" cannot be identified with the Babylonian exiles, so the restoration depicted is not merely the return from exile but also the reunification of Israel and Judah (vv. 15–28).

The vision, then, portrays a coming national revival. But it is not surprising that the imagery used—that of individual persons becoming infused with new life, as at creation (Ge 2:7)—suggested more than this. To have Yahweh ask "Can these bones become alive again?" (v. 3) would as readily suggest corporeal resurrection as political or spiritual renewal. Indeed, in v. 12 (cf. v. 13) the import of the vision is restated specifically using resurrection terminology: "I will open your graves and bring you up from them." The valley-plain, the land of exile, has become a mass of graves, the tombs of the Babylonian captivity; many corpses have become many bones. But that the prophet is still thinking primarily of a revival of national life, not of physical resurrection, is clear from v. 12c, "I will bring you home into the land of Israel." It is commonly held, therefore, that Ezekiel's vision of a corporate resurrection paved the way for a doctrine of personal resurrection. With good reason, however, one may argue that the reverse was the case, that a doctrine of national resurrection rested on an earlier doctrine of individual resurrection. Ezekiel 37 is then understood as a figurative application to national life of the idea of personal resurrection with which the prophet was already acquainted. It is difficult to imagine that Ezekiel would have employed this sustained imagery of resurrection without some prior knowledge of the doctrine.

6. Danielic passages

a. Daniel 12:2–3

Daniel 12:1–4 forms the climax of the section beginning at 11:2 that summarizes those aspects of history from the Persian period down to the reign of Antiochus IV Epiphanes that were of special relevance and interest to Jews. At either 11:36 or 11:40 or 12:1, there is a transition from the time of Antiochus to the End time, for in 12:1–3 there are unambiguous references to unparalleled tribulation, resurrection, and final reward and judgment.

> ²And multitudes—those who sleep in the dusty earth—will awake, some to everlasting life, some to shame and everlasting contempt.

> ³Those who are wise will shine like the brightness of the heavens, and those who have turned many to righteousness like the stars forever and ever.

Almost all scholars are agreed that these verses speak of a future resurrection of the dead. But two burning questions remain. Is a "particular" or a "general" resurrection spoken of? Is the resurrection merely a resuscitation of corpses, or is transformation involved?

To address the first question: as in Job 19:26, so here in Daniel 12:2, the Hebrew preposition *min* opens up two possible interpretations. We may render the verse "Many *of* [partitive *min*] those who sleep in the dust of the earth will awake." These "many" could then be identified with the exceptionally righteous or wicked, either in Israel or in general, or with all Israelites, or with the righteous remnant in Israel (in which case the "others" who awake "to shame" will be the apostates of Da 11:32). In the wake of the persecution under Antiochus IV, resurrection is seen as the means by which recompense would be given to the righteous martyrs (11:33, 35), to the evil persecutors, and perhaps to the notorious renegades. If 12:1 refers to the deliverance of the faithful who are living at the time of the tribulation, vv. 2–3 address the problem of the fate of the faithful dead who perished at the hands of Antiochus Epiphanes. But a resurrection that is here depicted in direct reference to Israelites need not exclude non-Israelites.

If, alternatively, we translate v. 2 "Many, *namely* [explicative *min*; for this usage, see BDB 581b, 3.b.e; GK 382 n. 2] those who sleep in the dust of the earth, will awake," a general resurrection is in view, although there might well be an allusion to Israelites in particular. *Many* is used to emphasize the myriads of participants. It is of interest that in John 5:28–29, a passage that clearly echoes Daniel 12:2 in describing a twofold resurrection, the "many who sleep in the dusty earth" become the "all who are in their graves." We express a tentative preference for this second interpretation, understanding v. 1 not only of oppression under Antiochus IV but also of the period of the Antichrist, for biblical prophecy often looks beyond its primary historical reference to a final fulfillment at the End.

What type of resurrection is here described? Although the body is not mentioned, a bodily resurrection is undoubtedly in view—witness the expressions "sleeping in the dusty earth" and "contempt" (dērā'ôn, "abhorrence," used in Isa 66:24 of rotting corpses). Since we would be unjustified in distinguishing the destiny of the "some" who awake to eternal life (v. 2) from the lot of the wise leaders (v. 3), we may say that the resurrection involves participation in heavenly radiance, assumption of angelic form (stars, angels, and the resurrected righteous are often associated in apocalyptic terminology) and living forever. Such characteristics clearly imply a transformation in the bodily form of the righteous. The unrighteous, on the other hand, are condemned to become everlasting objects of reproach and abhorrence. Their resurrection involves nothing more than reanimation.

In its use of two crucial terms (dust, awake), Daniel 12:2 is reminiscent of Isaiah 26:19, but in three important particulars the passages differ. Whereas for Isaiah the resurrection itself is the vindication of the righteous, in Daniel resurrection is a prerequisite for the receipt of recompense, the means that enable the giving of reward or punishment. The second difference relates to the extent of the resurrection. In the Isaianic text, only the righteous are raised; in the Danielic passage, both the just and the unjust experience resurrection. Thirdly, whereas the resurrection of the righteous seems to imply mere reanimation in Isaiah, it leads to the gaining of immortality in Daniel and therefore involves transformation as well as revival.

b. Daniel 12:13

We need simply note that the heavenly messenger here assures Daniel that he is destined to share the inheritance of the righteous, viz. resurrection, eternal life, and heavenly glory (12:2–3). "But go your way until the end [of your life]. You shall rest [in the grave] and then at the end of the days [i.e., in the messianic age] you will rise [ta'amōd, LXX *anastēsē*; see BDB 764b, 5.b, "of revival after death"] to receive your inheritance."

7. Passages in Hosea

a. Hosea 6:1–3

As in Isaiah 26:19, so here in Hosea 6:1–3, there is uncertainty about the identity of the speaker. Hosea himself may be appealing to the nation for genuine repentance (cf. Hos 5:15) and assuring them of divine healing and reinvigoration if they return to Yahweh, or he may possibly be verbalizing their shallow profession of repentance born of self-interest and their reckless presumption on the divine mercy (cf. Hos 6:4–6). Alternatively, the exiles may be appealing to one another in this "word of exhortation." However that may be, the confidence is expressed that Israel's master physician (Ex 15:26) will heal the wounds he has inflicted by the Exile (v. 1). After a brief period ("after two days . . . on the third day") he will apply his remedy and bring his son Israel up from the grave of the exile (v. 2a) to a place where he affords protection, health (v. 2b), and fruitfulness (v. 3). These three verses illustrate the power of Yahweh to effect a spiritual restoration to life and vigor. Corporeal resurrection is not in view, although some of the prophet's hearers might well have inferred that what Yahweh could perform in the spiritual sphere, he could, *a fortiori*, execute in the physical realm. Spiritual resurrection would count for little if it were permanently terminated by physical death. We conclude that, as in Ezekiel 37:1–14, resurrection terminology ("he will revive us . . . he will raise us up, that we may live. . . ." v. 2) is used in reference to national restoration, and that such usage presupposes a doctrine of personal resurrection.

b. Hosea 13:14

Up to this point in Hosea 13, Yahweh has been remonstrating with Ephraim for his waywardness as an unwise son.

Ephraim was like a mother experiencing the pains of child-birth or like a child about to be born who refused to appear at the opening of the womb at the right time and so endangered life (vv. 12–13). Yahweh continues:

> *¹⁴Shall I ransom them from the power of Sheol?*
> *Shall I redeem them from Death?*
> *Where, O Death, are your plagues?*
> *Where, O Sheol, is your destruction?*
> *I have no mind to repent.*

On this reading of the passage (reflected in the RSV), Yahweh expresses despair over an unrepentant people who refuse to allow him to spare them the pains of Exile. He invites Death and Sheol to come and be the instruments of his judgment on Ephraim; his determination to punish the nation is fixed (cf. vv. 15–16).

But another interpretation is possible. The first two lines may be taken as statements, not questions ("I will ransom . . . I will redeem . . ."; thus RV, NIV), and so contain a divine promise rather than a threat or a statement of negative resolve. Though his people go into captivity, Yahweh will ultimately deliver them from the death of the Exile, so that death will be deprived of its plagues and Sheol of its destruction. Nothing will alter Yahweh's resolve to redeem as well as punish; as Hosea 6:1 puts it, the one who had "torn" in judgment would finally "heal" in mercy. Judgment was inevitable but beyond it lay deliverance.

It is incontestable that the immediate and wider context of v. 14 speaks of coming judgment, not of certain salvation (see Hos. 12:2, 14; 13:3, 7–10, 13, 15–16). Chapter 14 is Hosea's final plea to the nation to repent, and the promises of healing and renewal contained in that chapter relate to the situation after repentance, not the situation after the Exile. Moreover, lines 3 and 4 of v. 14 are certainly more apposite and potent if they relate to preexilic rather than postexilic times.

When Paul combines the second half of this verse with

Isaiah 25:8a in 1 Corinthians 15:54–55, he follows some Greek version unknown to us in reading "Where, O Death, is your *victory*?" (the LXX has "your judgment") and follows the LXX in reading "Where . . . is your sting?" In its context in 1 Corinthians 15 the quotation is a mocking challenge to moribund Death to rally in the midst of its death throes. But in its original context it is hardly possible to see more than an invitation to personified Death and Sheol to use their powers at the direction of Yahweh. The GNB aptly renders the verse: "I will not save this people from the world of the dead or rescue them from the power of death. Bring on your plagues, death! Bring on your destruction, world of the dead! I will no longer have pity for this people." What this invitation proclaims, then, is the supremacy of Yahweh over Death, so much so that Death is treated as a vassal obliged to do his Lord's bidding. While the passage contains no prediction of resurrection or of the death of Death, it demonstrates that death is Yahweh's servant and that resurrection is therefore not impossible.

8. Conclusions

To summarize our findings: belief in a resurrection of persons from the dead finds expression in some eight passages (Job 19:26; Ps 17:15; 49:15; 73:24; Isa 26:19; 53:10–12; Da 12:2; 12:13). Resurrection terminology is borrowed on two notable occasions (Eze 37:1–14; Hos 6:2) to portray a future national and spiritual restoration brought about by a return from exile.

As for the *nature* of the future bodily resurrection, it may involve the mere reanimation of the corpse or at best the receipt of a material body comparable to the present physical body (Job 19:26; Isa 26:19); or it may be a matter of transformation (Da 12:2–3 and perhaps 12:13) or glorification (Ps 73:24) after reanimation, in the case of the righteous. But sometimes no hint is given regarding the future bodily state

(Ps 17:15; 49:15; Isa 53:10–12). In its *function*, resurrection may itself be a personal vindication (Isa 26:19; 53:10–12) or may be a means that will enable the witnessing of one's vindication (Job 19:26–27). It may be a prelude to reward or punishment (Da 12:2; 12:13), an assumption to heaven and enriched fellowship with God (Ps 49:15; 73:24, 26), or a preface to the beatific vision of God (Ps 17:15, and possibly Job 19:26). When we think of the *extent* of the resurrection, sometimes it is portrayed as an exceptional privilege (Job 19:26; Isa 53:10–12), sometimes as a personal experience, typical of the destiny of the righteous (Ps 17:15; 49:15; 73:24; Da 12:13), and at least once as the lot of all God's people (Isa 26:19). On only one occasion is a general resurrection in view (Da 12:2), but it is uncertain whether this passage envisages the resurrection of all the just and unjust or only of the preeminently righteous and wicked. Finally, with regard to the *time* of the resurrection, some passages are silent (Ps 17:15; Isa 26:19; 53:10–12), some place it at the End (Job 19:26; Da 12:2; 12:13), while it is possible that in Psalm 49:15 and 73:24 an assumption to heaven immediately after death is anticipated.

What led to Israel's belief in resurrection? We suggest there were two such impulses: the Israelite doctrine of God and the Israelite experience of God.

Basic to the Old Testament is the affirmation that Yahweh is the living God (Ps 18:46; Jer 23:36; Hos 1:10). This sets him apart from mortal men and lifeless idols. Since he ever lives, death cannot be the supreme reality in the universe. Yahweh's sovereignty over death was evident from the fact that he could rescue persons in danger of dying ("Yahweh preserves alive," Dt 32:39; 1Sa 2:6; cf. Ps 16:10; Jnh 2:6), persons who had already died (1Ki 17:17–24; 2Ki 4:18–37; 13:20–21), and other persons from ever dying (Ge 5:24; 2Ki 2:10–11). Death was Yahweh's obedient servant (Hos 13:14) and was finally to be destroyed (Isa 25:8a). But not only was Yahweh the living God whose power could reach the dead in Sheol. He was also the righteous King whose reign and justice were universal (Ge 18:25; Ps 47:7; 95:3; 103:19) and whose jurisdiction extended to Sheol (Job 26:6; Ps 139:8; Pr 15:11; Am 9:2). Resurrection enabled the just to be rewarded and the wicked to be punished (Da 12:2). Thus God's moral governance of the world would be vindicated.

The second theological instinct lying behind belief in resurrection was the Israelite experience of God. It was clear to Israelite sensibilities that holy men such as Enoch, Elijah, or the suffering Servant who had lived in unbroken fellowship with God during their earthly lives could not have that intimate relationship forever terminated by the advent of death. Enoch and Elijah illustrated the principle that communion with God in life led to fellowship with God after death. It became increasingly evident to the Israelites that fellowship with a covenantal God was a reality that must be as enduring as God was, and therefore was independent of the passage of time and the onset of death, together with the changes they both brought. Indeed, from one viewpoint, living in the divine presence transcended temporal limits so that the person who was in communion with the living God had a never-failing source of joy and lived in a type of timeless present.[17]

III

Immortality and Resurrection in Intertestamental Judaism

By common tradition among Christian scholars, the term *intertestamental* refers to the period roughly between 200 B.C. and A.D. 100. Jewish scholars, of course, would refer to the same period in general terms as that between "the Bible" and the Mishnah.

It has long been customary to deal with the intertestamental Jewish texts relating to the afterlife in two categories— Palestinian Judaism and Diaspora (or Alexandrian or Hellenistic) Judaism. This convenient geographical division tends to suggest the homogeneity and radical distinctiveness of each category. In reality, with respect to eschatological matters there is considerable variety within each of these branches of Judaism and at the same time substantial similarity between them. For example, the motif of a Last Day when God's justice will be vindicated by his punishment of sinners and rewarding of the righteous constantly recurs in all types of texts (with the exception of 4 Maccabees and the Testament of Abraham). Or again, belief in a bodily resurrection is clearly expressed in some texts from the Greek Diaspora, texts that are sometimes thought to speak only of an incorporeal immortality. No longer therefore can anyone legitimately maintain that belief in the resurrection of the dead was a distinctive characteristic of Palestinian Judaism whereas adherence to the immortality of the soul was a hallmark of

Diaspora Judaism. With these necessary qualifications, the time-honored distinction may still be usefully employed.

If we consider Jewish intertestamental literature as a whole, its dominant characteristic is the bewildering variety of its detail concerning the life to come. So diversified are the sentiments expressed—often within a single work—that very few generalizations may legitimately stand. Our treatment here will therefore stress this diversity of view rather than attempting to isolate the elements of uniformity.[1]

The Jewish literature of this period presents three views concerning the fate of the dead. There is the belief that all persons descend into Sheol where existence is unrelieved by any hope of resurrection. There is the doctrine of the resurrection of the body, in the case of martyrs, or the faithful in Israel, or all Israel, or all mankind. And there is the concept of the immortality of the soul or spirit that is gained at death or at the End, with or without a resurrection of the body. Even these three categories are not mutually exclusive. For example, in the Biblical Antiquities of Pseudo-Philo which is usually dated A.D. 70–100, belief in a resurrection of the righteous at the End is found alongside the older doctrine of Sheol as the final abode of all the dead.[2]

A. Immortality

As in chapter II, so here, we shall deal with this topic more briefly than with resurrection. During the period 200 B.C.–A.D. 100 the concept of immortality gained a new prominence in Jewish texts. We may conveniently classify the texts under three headings. Some texts emphasize or refer exclusively to immortality. Other documents simply juxtapose the ideas of resurrection and immortality, without awareness of any need to harmonize the two ideas or at least without any attempt to interrelate them. But some texts do seek to combine the two notions, often through recourse to the notion of an "intermediate state" during which an immortal soul awaits bodily

resurrection in the Consummation. In each of the three
categories, we shall discuss one notable instance, but otherwise the references will be merely listed.[3]

1. Texts emphasizing or referring exclusively to
   immortality
   a. Palestinian Judaism
      (1) Jubilees (late second century B.C.) (23:31)
      (2) Essenes (flourished first century B.C. and
          first century A.D.) (*apud* Josephus)[4]
      (3) Testament (or Assumption) of Moses
          (probably early first century A.D.) (10:7–10)
      (4) Testament of Abraham (? first century A.D.)
          (Recension A. 1:7; 7:8–12; 11:1–12;
          Recension B. 4:9–12; 13:1; 14:7)
   b. Diaspora Judaism
      (1) 4 Maccabees (late first century B.C. or early
          first century A.D.)

In developing the theme of the power of "reason inspired
by piety" to control the passions (1:1, 13–14; 18:2),
4 Maccabees recounts the courage of Eleazar (cf. 2Mc 6:18–
31) and of the seven young men and their mother (cf. 2Mc
7:1–42). In spite of a probable dependence on 2 Maccabees 6–
7 with its insistence on a resurrection of the flesh, the author,
a sophisticated Hellenistic Jew possibly from Alexandria,
deliberately replaces resurrection terminology by references
to immortality (compare 4Mc 10:15 with 2Mc 7:14) as a divine
gift granted to the souls of the obedient at death, especially in
the case of martyrs. Thus we read that "none of the seven
youths turned coward, none shrunk in the face of death, but
all hastened to death by torture, as if running the road to
immortality [*athanasia*]" (14:4–5). The eldest brother "nobly
endured the torment, as if he were being transformed into
incorruption [*aphtharsia*] by the fire" (9:22; cf. 17:12). As for
the mother, she entreated them to die for religion's sake "as
though she were bringing forth her brood of seven sons, for a

second time, into immortality [*athanasia*]" (16:13). The book
ends on this triumphant note: "the sons of Abraham, with
their victorious mother, are ranged in the choir of their
ancestors, having received from God pure and deathless
[*athanatos*] souls" (18:23). Immortality is variously explained
as "a divine inheritance" (18:3), "living to God" (16:25),
"being with God" (9:8), "eternal life" (10:15; 15:3), "a life of
[an indefinitely] long duration" (17:12), "the life of eternal
blessedness" (17:18).

> (2) Wisdom of Solomon (first century B.C.)
>   (2:23–24; 3:1–4; 4:7; 5:5, 15; 6:19)
> (3) Philo (c. 25 B.C.–c. A.D. 50) (*Op. Mund.*
>   135; *Gig.* 14; *Leg. Gaj.* 91; *Spec. Leg.*
>   1.345)

2. Texts in which the ideas of resurrection and
   immortality are juxtaposed without attempted
   harmonization
   a. Palestinian Judaism
      (1) 1 Enoch 91–104 (134–95 B.C.)

In these chapters, which form a self-consistent unit, Enoch
exhorts his children and reviews the future bliss of the
righteous and plight of the wicked. Three passages allude to
resurrection and may reflect the terminology of Daniel 12:2–3.
In 91:10 the righteous are said to arise from the sleep of death
and in 92:3–4 this statement is expanded by a description of
resurrection life as walking in eternal goodness, grace,
uprightness and light (a description which implicitly relates
resurrection to immortality). Then in 100:5 the righteous
"sleep a long sleep" as they await resurrection after the final
judgment (100:4). Yet within this same "Book of Exhorta-
tions" we find the assurance that "the spirits of those who
have died in righteousness . . . shall live and rejoice, and . . .
shall not perish" (103:3–4), although at death their souls
descended in grief into Sheol (102:5). The spirits of the wicked
will be cast into the furnace of fire (98:3) or slain in Sheol

(99:11), a judgment from which their spirits cannot escape (103:7–8).

        (2) Testaments of the Twelve Patriarchs (c. 100 B.C. with a Christian redaction c. A.D. 200) (TSim 6:7; TJud 25:1, 4; TZeb 10:1–2; TAsh 6:5; TBen 10:6–8)
    b. Diaspora Judaism
        (1) Testament of Job (late first century B.C.) (4:9; 39:12–13; 40:3–4; 52:2–9)
  3. Texts in which the ideas of resurrection and immortality are consciously interrelated
    a. Palestinian Judaism
        (1) 1 Enoch 1–36 (early second century B.C.) (22:1–13)
        (2) 1 Enoch 37–71 (= Parables or Similitudes of Enoch) (M. A. Knibb, first century A.D.; J. T. Milik, A.D. 250) (37:4; 40:9; 45:4–5; 51:1–5; 58:3–4; 62:14–16)
        (3) Psalms of Solomon (c. 50 B.C.) (3:11–12; 13:11; 14:4, 10; 15:12–13)
        (4) 4 Ezra 3–14 (= Apocalypse of Ezra) (A.D. 80–100)

Although the fact of resurrection rarely comes to expression in this Apocalypse, it is clear that all persons, the righteous and the unrighteous, will be raised and judged (4:41–43; 7:32, 37; 14:35). There are two ways in which the notions of resurrection and immortality are integrated. First, in the concept of a conscious intermediate state, belief in the continued existence of the soul after death is combined with belief in a future universal resurrection. Immediately after death, when the soul has been separated from the body (7:78), the souls of the righteous are granted seven days in which to view the future punishment of the ungodly and the bliss of their own post-resurrection state before they are committed to "store-chambers" where they await resurrection (7:88–101).

The souls of the wicked, on the other hand, are condemned to the torment of fruitless wandering until the final judgment (7:79–87). Secondly, the state of the righteous after their resurrection is described as deathlessness or incorruptibility: they are destined to receive "spacious liberty . . . with enjoyment and immortality" (7:96); their faces are to shine like the sun or stars, being "henceforth incorruptible" (7:97); "death is abolished . . . corruption is forgotten . . . and in the end the treasures of immortality are revealed" (8:53–54).

    (5) 2 Baruch (= Syriac Apocalypse of Baruch) (c. A.D. 90) (21:22–23; 30:2–4; 51:9)
  b. Diaspora Judaism
    (1) 2 Maccabees (120–100 B.C.) (7:9–11, 14, 36; 14:46)
    (2) Josephus (c. A.D. 37–100) (*War* 2.163; 3.372, 374–75; *Ant.* 18.14)
    (3) 2 Enoch (= Slavonic Enoch) (c. A.D. 1–70) (9:1; 22:8–10; 42:3B; 65:8B, 10)

B. Resurrection

In the following survey we shall look briefly at the works that reproduce the traditional doctrine of Sheol or are silent regarding resurrection, and then we shall summarize the doctrine of the resurrection of the dead as it is portrayed in the intertestamental literature.

Several texts of this period simply perpetuate the view that at death the souls of both the righteous and the wicked descend to Sheol. Sheol is depicted as the realm of death beneath the earth or the cosmic ocean that supports the earth, where all souls remain forever as paralyzed or truncated personalities, spirits without bodies or else spirits with shadowy bodies. For example, in the book of Sirach (= Ecclesiasticus; 190–180 B.C., from Palestinian Judasim) those in Hades are in an unenviable state (Eccus 14:16; 22:11),

cut off from communion with God (17:27–28; cf. Ps 6:5; Isa
38:18–19). There is no natural immortality of the soul (19:19 is
to be omitted with the manuscripts Aleph A B C), only an
immortality of the nation and of a person's name and deeds
(37:26; 44:9–15). There is no mention of resurrection ("May
their bones sprout" [46:12a; 49:10] means only "May the
memory of them flourish"; see 46:11, 12b). And from
Diaspora Judaism there is 1 Baruch (100–50 B.C.): the dead
remain in the grave and are unable to praise the Lord (1Ba
2:17, echoing Ps 115:17).

The other intertestamental writings that are silent regarding
resurrection are, from Palestinian Judaism, Judith (second
century B.C., but Jth 16:17 seems to imply the postmortem
punishment of the wicked), the Martyrdom of Isaiah (second
century or early first century B.C.), Tobit (c. 150–100 B.C.),
1 Maccabees (c. 100–70 B.C.) and Paralipomena Jeremiou
(A.D. 70–130; sometimes called "The Rest of the Words of
Baruch," 3 Baruch, 4 Baruch, or Christian Baruch; chapter 9
that describes the death and resurrection of Jeremiah is a
Christian addition); and from Diaspora Judaism, 1 Esdras in
LXX (= 3 Ezra in Vulgate; 165 B.C.–A.D. 90), the Letter of
Aristeas (c. 130 B.C.), and 3 Maccabees (c. 100 B.C.). It might
well be argued that silence about resurrection does not
amount to a denial of resurrection. But against this should be
set the fact that even where a reference to resurrection or
immortality would have been appropriate or expected, none is
found (e.g., 1Mc 2:62–64, from the final words of Mattathias
to his sons, encouraging their active resistance).

It is clear, then, that there are both Palestinian and Diaspora
texts that betray no acquaintance with any doctrine of
resurrection. Whether this silence signifies a repudiation of
the notion of resurrection and an adherence to the traditional
view of Sheol cannot always be determined. What it does
establish is that the resurrection was not an essential ingredient in the religious thought of all Jews at the beginning of the
Christian era. This is confirmed by the explicit denial of the

resurrection of the dead by the Sadducees, according to the
New Testament (Mk 12:18; Ac 4:1–2; 23:8; cf. 26:8), Josephus
(*Ant.* 18:16; *War* 2.165), and rabbinic traditions (TB Sanh.
90b).

Inscriptions on Jewish tombs shed little further light on
common expectations about life after death. Vague references
to "peace" or "rest," or to God as helper, or even to being
"blessed" or "happy," simply point to belief in the fact of
postmortem survival but give no hint concerning its nature.
Archaeology has as yet uncovered no Palestinian inscription
belonging to the period c. 200 B.C.–A.D. 100 that clearly refers
to a future resurrection. Theories abound regarding the
implication of certain facts (e.g., Jewish refusal to burn their
dead; the custom of sending ossuaries from the Diaspora to
Palestine), but we seem dependent on literary works such as
the following for firm evidence of Jewish belief in the
hereafter.[5]

Most Jewish texts belonging to this period do, however,
refer to a future resurrection from the dead, usually in the
context of a discussion of rewards and punishments in the
afterlife. Generally, "resurrection" involves a reuniting of the
soul that had been resident in Sheol or in some intermediate
abode such as "treasuries" or "chambers," with the body
that had been lying in the grave. In this way the rupture of the
two that had been caused by death was mended and the
individual was restored to personal integrity and therefore to
full personal relations. Only rarely do we find a reference to
the "resurrection" of the soul or spirit (e.g., 1En 103:3–4).

1. The nature of the resurrection body

Two principal views are expressed regarding the nature of
the resurrection body. One stresses the *identity* between the
body buried and the body raised. The resurrection will restore
to their former integrity fractured or dismembered limbs (2Mc
7:10–11) and even the bowels (2Mc 14:46). According to the

Sibylline Oracles 4:176–82, after the whole earth and all of humankind have been destroyed by fire and "reduced to dust and ashes . . . God himself will fashion again men's bones and ashes and will raise up mortals once more as they were previously." The other viewpoint highlights the *transformation* that occurs after resurrection, leading to the possession of a heavenly body.[6] The classic statement of this two-stage process (viz. resuscitation and transformation, separated by judgment) is found in 2 Baruch 49:1–51:10. The dead are raised from the dust without change (the identity motif) (42:8; 50:2) as a prelude to judgment (50:4). Then the physical bodies of the righteous are progressively transformed into spiritual bodies that are fit to inhabit a renewed, incorruptible world (51:1–5). Thus the righteous attain (51:5, 10) or even surpass (51:12) angelic glory. This description of the resurrection state as an angel-like existence is also found in 1 Enoch 104:4, 6 and 2 Enoch 22:10. Elsewhere the transformed resurrection body is called an everlasting garment of glory given by the Lord of spirits (1En 62:15–16; 2En 22:8–10).

2. The scene of resurrection life

As one might expect, if the future kingdom was regarded as earthly the resurrection body was generally depicted as physical, but if the kingdom was heavenly or at least supramundane, the resurrection body was spiritual. The Sibylline Oracles, for example, mentioned above as picturing a "resurrection of the flesh," localize the scene of resurrection life or the site of the eternal messianic kingdom as being on the earth as it is (Sib 3:767–84; 4:187–91). On the other hand, 2 Baruch, 1 Enoch 37–71 (= the Similitudes), and 2 Enoch, cited above as describing a glorified resurrection body, place the coming kingdom on a transformed or newly created earth or in heaven (1En 45:4–5; 2Ba 15:7; 44:15; 2En 65:10), for the authors could not envisage the present world with all its sin and misery as the scene of God's eternal reign.

3. The extent of the resurrection

Who is destined to be raised? What is the extent of the resurrection? The most common view restricts resurrection to the righteous within Israel (e.g., 1En 83–90, esp. 90:32–36; 91–104, esp. 91:10; TZeb 10:1–2; PS 3:12; 9:9; 13:11), especially the patriarchs (TJud 25:1; TBen 10:6) and the martyrs (TJud 25:4). But since Israel as a nation was God's covenant people (1En 60:6) the privilege of resurrection was sometimes extended to all Israel (2Mc 7:32–33, 37; 14:15; 1En 1–36; 37–71, esp. 51:1–5 and 61:4; Apoc. Mos. 13:3, but see 41:1–3; cf. M. Sanh. 10:1[7]), apart from the incurably evil (1En 22:13). Later Judaism too excluded certain Jews such as those who denied the authority of the Torah (TJ Ket. 111b). Finally, in several places a resurrection of all mankind is envisaged (TBen 10:8; 4Ezr 7:32, 37; Sib 4:176–90; LAB 3:10; 2Ba 30:2– 5; 42:8; 49:1–51:10). Those who claim that a universal resurrection is never taught in this period dismiss these passages as Christian interpolations, but such a procedure is totally unwarranted. With the flowering of the concept of religious individualism whose seeds had been firmly planted by Jeremiah and Ezekiel in an earlier era, and with the intensification of the problem of theodicy during the Maccabean period, more attention was given to the question of the final destinies of the righteous and the wicked.

4. The function of the resurrection

Closely related to the extent of the resurrection is the function of the resurrection. If all people are raised, the purpose is to enable individuals to appear before God for judgment (Sib 4:181–84; 2Ba 50:2–4). Resurrection is in this case the means by which rewards and punishments are dispensed (TBen 10:8, "all men shall rise, some to glory and some to shame"; cf. Da 12:2). Alternatively, if the participants in the resurrection are the faithful remnant in Israel or all Israel as a nation, resurrection is viewed in a positive light as the vindication of the righteous who were persecuted for their observance of the Torah (2Mc 7:9, 23, 30, 37), as recompense for injustice or undeserved suffering (TJud 25:4), as the means by which the righteous receive the promised blessings denied them in life (1En 108:11), or as the prelude to the enjoyment of eternal life (2Mc 7:9; TJud 25:1; PS 3:12) and of the divine presence (1En 62:14) in union with the faithful (2Mc 7:29).

In this matter of resurrection from the dead the Jewish intertestamental literature represents a considerable advance on the Old Testament and therefore serves as a bridge between the Old Testament and the New. Without this bridge we are left with an inexplicable gap between the two Testaments, for, whereas resurrection faith is (to change the metaphor) a flickering light in the Old Testament, it becomes, as we shall see, a powerful beam in the New Testament that totally dispels the uncertain gloom of the hereafter. With this bridge we are better able to understand the development of the doctrine of resurrection from its Jewish expressions to its Christian forms.

We shall revert to this overview of ancient Egyptian, Greek, and Jewish views of the hereafter (viz. chapters I–III) when we have examined the corresponding New Testament evidence. It will then be possible (in chapter XVI) to undertake a comparison between the perspectives of New Testament writers and views representative of these other cultures.

IV

"Raisings" in the Gospels (and Acts)

In spite of all their fascinating differences, the four gospels of the New Testament have certain central features in common. Not only do they all deal with the life and teaching of Jesus, but they also move inexorably toward an identical climax, his crucifixion in Jerusalem, and they end with the same triumphant aftermath, his resurrection from the dead. One of the ways in which the gospel writers prepare us for this final scene is to relate instances of "resurrection" that occurred during Jesus' public ministry, when he himself demonstrated his divine power by raising certain individuals from the dead. Three such occasions are recorded—the raising of the widow of Nain's son (recorded in Luke's gospel), the daughter of Jairus (Matthew, Mark, Luke), and Lazarus (John).

A. The Widow of Nain's Son (Luke 7:11–17)

[11]Soon afterward, Jesus went to a town called Nain, and his disciples and a large crowd went along with him. [12]As he approached the town gate, a dead person was being carried out—the only son of his mother, and she was a widow. And a large crowd from the town was with her. [13]When the Lord saw her, his heart went out to her and he said, "Don't cry."

[14]Then he went up and touched the coffin and those carrying it stood still. He said, "Young man, I say to you,

get up!'' [15]The dead man sat up and began to talk, and Jesus gave him back to his mother.

[16]They were all filled with awe and praised God. "A great prophet has appeared among us," they said. "God has come to help his people." [17]This news about Jesus spread throughout Judea and the surrounding country. (NIV)

After describing the birth and childhood of Jesus and the inauguration of his messianic mission, the third Evangelist deals with the Galilean ministry of Jesus (4:14–9:50), concentrating particularly on the deeds of the Messiah. The account of the raising of the widow of Nain's son falls within a section which elucidates the distinctive character of the Messiah's mission (6:12–7:50). By including this incident, Luke shows that death (7:11–17), as well as disease (7:1–10), is subject to the Messiah's power: he not only heals the sick but also raises the dead. His mission involves emancipation from the tyranny of death rather than that of Rome. Also the story forms a necessary introduction to 7:18–35 which discusses the distinctive roles of John the Baptist and Jesus, for one aspect of Jesus' distinctive ministry as the servant of Yahweh was that through him "the dead are restored to life" (7:22; cf. Isa 26:19), which was aptly illustrated by the occurrence at Nain.

1. The circumstances of the miracle (Luke 7:11–13)

Soon after healing the centurion's servant at Capernaum, Jesus traveled to Nain, a small village six miles southwest of Nazareth, accompanied by his disciples and a large crowd. Near the town gate this procession met another procession, a funeral cortège that was just emerging from the town to bury a young man at a burial site outside the city. First came the widowed mother along with other women relatives and friends, then the bier on which the dead man was lying, probably with his face uncovered, and finally male relatives and friends, the hired mourners and musicians, and "a large crowd from the town" (v. 12).[1] Jesus was filled with pity for the mother, recognizing or learning that to a widow's loneliness was now added a mother's grief at the premature death of an only child. After Jesus had told the mother to stop weeping (v. 13) and had moved forward to halt the procession by touching the bier, the noise of movement and of mourning would have subsided.

2. *The performance of the miracle (Luke 7:14)*

Whereas the centurion's servant at Capernaum had been healed at a distance (Lk 7:7, 10), in this case Jesus not only went right up to the bier but actually touched it and thereby became ritually unclean (Nu 19:11, 22). His purpose in touching the bier was not to effect the miracle—that did not happen until the word of command was spoken—but to halt the procession and (probably) indicate to the bearers of the bier that they should set it down. There is no indication that Jesus touched the body or took the dead man's hand (cf. Luke 8:54). It was merely by the spoken word that the miracle occurred: "Young man, I say to you, get up!"

This revival of a dead person is portrayed as effortless. The way is prepared for the display of the potency of "the word of the Lord" by which the heavens were made (Ps 33:6) by the use of "the Lord" in v. 13. Since Luke's account of this miracle at Nain has several clear reminiscences of Elijah's miracle at Zarephath,[2] we should not rule out the possibility that Luke intended a contrast to be drawn between Elijah's expenditure of physical and spiritual effort in performing the miracle and the sublime effortlessness of the new Elijah in performing his. "Then he [Elijah] stretched himself out upon the child three times, and cried to the Lord [three times?], 'O Lord my God, let the breath of life return to this child's body'" (1Ki 17:21). Another remarkable feature of the story is that Jesus' command is addressed to a corpse. It was not a case of prayer addressed to God on behalf of the dead person (as in 1Ki 17:20–22), but just as God "gives life to the dead and commands the things that do not exist as if they did" (Ro 4:17), so too does "the Lord" (v. 13).

3. The outcome of the miracle (Luke 7:15–17)

By noting that the son sat up and began to speak (v. 15a) Luke indicates that he was fully restored to life, for movement and speech are indicators of physical and mental alertness. The cause of death was not specified, but it is clearly implied that the miracle involved restoration to health as well as to life. "Jesus gave him back to his mother" (v. 15b), which alludes to 1 Kings 17:23, must mean that Jesus presented the young man to his mother, alive and well and (presumably) now standing upright.

Verse 16 notes the two effects of the miracle on all the bystanders (including the mother), that is, the sizable crowd of each procession (vv. 11–12) who had by now doubtless intermingled. "Everyone was awe-struck" (TCNT). The term *phobos* ("awe") here denotes not only the people's natural reaction to an event that was unprecedented in their experience but also their recognition that supernatural power had been displayed in the revivification. Their second reaction was to glorify God with the words "A great prophet has appeared among us," and again, "God has come to help his people." Each statement must be understood in the light of the other. The people hailed Jesus not simply as a prophet or even a "great prophet," but as a great prophet by whom God had intervened to bring salvation to his people.

4. The historicity of the miracle

There are several pointers to the authenticity of the miracle. The circumstantial detail is true to fact. In Galilee, as opposed to Judea, women walked in front of the bier.[3] It was therefore natural that Jesus, coming in the opposite direction, should

speak to the mother before approaching the bier (vv. 13–14).
If the whole event was fictitious, it is remarkable that the
Evangelist has located the miracle at Nain, a small, insignificant village that is nowhere else mentioned in the Bible and
that he has made no reference to the postmortem state or
whereabouts of the young man and does not have him speak at
all or divulge secrets gained by his passage to the "other
side." As an account of the instantaneous reanimation of a
corpse, the story is remarkably restrained and unadorned;
sensational detail is conspicuously absent. Such extraordinary
sobriety of diction points to its authenticity. Nor should it be
forgotten that this is only one of four miracles of "raising"
recorded in the Lukan writings.[4] To explain one miracle
naturalistically is not to explain them all.

B. The Daughter of Jairus (Matthew, Mark, Luke)

This is the only miracle of Jesus' raising the dead that is
recorded by all three Synoptic Gospels. Mark's account
(5:21–24, 35–43) is slightly longer than that of Luke (8:40–42,
49–56), while Matthew's report (9:18–19, 23–26) is less than
half the length of Mark's. Another distinctive feature is that in
each Evangelist's narrative the story of the woman with a
hemorrhage is interwoven with the story of Jairus's daughter.[5]

1. Features common to all three Evangelists[6]

From the features common to all the narratives we can
reconstruct the following sequence of events.

> A certain ruler approached Jesus with a request that he
> should come and heal his daughter. Jesus began to follow
> him but was delayed by an incident involving a woman
> suffering from a hemorrhage. On entering the ruler's house
> and hearing the commotion, Jesus rebuked those who were
> now mourning the young girl's death, and said that she was

not dead but sleeping. This prompted their mockery. But
he took the girl's hand and she stood up.

Some of these features are worthy of further comment.

a. *The ruler.* All the Evangelists depict him as a "ruler," but
while Matthew uses only this term (Mt 9:18, 23), Mark
introduces him as "one of the rulers of the synagogue" (Mk
5:22) and Luke as "the ruler of the synagogue" (Lk 8:41). As
such, he was both a member of the synagogue board of
(usually) seven persons (Mark) and the synagogue president
(Mark and Luke), the lay official responsible to the board for
the actual administration of the synagogue, especially its
services and its maintenance. It must therefore be deemed
probable that Jesus was known to this man through his
participation in the synagogue services in Capernaum (Mk
1:21–22, 39). Given the acknowledged dignity of the position
of synagogue president (it was a special privilege to marry his
daughter), it is significant that in his hour of dire need he
sought out Jesus and made his urgent request, assuming the
posture of a desperate suppliant (Mt 9:18).

b. *The commotion.* On entering the crowded house of this
"ruler of the synagogue" Jesus saw the commotion and heard
a cacophony of sounds—the strident weeping and wailing of
the relatives as they beat their breasts over the girl's death,
the antiphonal chanting and hand clapping of the professional
mourners, mingled with the plaintive sound of the flutes (Mk
5:38; Mt 9:23; Lk 8:52). The action of Jesus in evicting all
these noisy mourners (cf. Ac 9:40) was perhaps prompted by
this, that those indulging in disorderly grief or simulated grief
or callous scorn were not suitable witnesses of the quiet and
mysterious act of raising the dead.

c. *Death and sleep.* All three Evangelists record the
enigmatic words of Jesus: "She is not dead but asleep." Both
Matthew and Luke leave us in no doubt that the girl had died
(Mt 9:18; Lk 8:42, 53). In affirming that the girl was
"sleeping," Jesus was not denying the reality of death nor

teaching that all death is sleep but rather was using picturesque, figurative language to indicate that, in this girl's case,
death was like sleep in that it was not permanent and was to
be terminated by an awakening (cf. Jn 11:11–14). In this view,
"she is not dead" is ironic hyperbole and a foil for the main
point that follows. Jesus is saying, in effect, "As far as I am
concerned, this young girl did not die in any final sense but is
temporarily in the sleep of death."

2. The historicity of the miracle

Not a few commentators explain this "raising" as an
instance of healing rather than of revivification, or an example
of extraordinary knowledge rather than of supernatural
power. In reality, it is suggested, the girl was in a deathlike
coma that might well have led to her death but for Christ's
intervention. With skillful medical diagnosis, he recognized
certain signs of life in the girl and raised her up either from a
terminal coma (a miracle of healing) or from a state of
temporarily suspended animation (an example simply of his
superior knowledge). "She is not dead" would then mean
"she is not really dead" or "she is only apparently dead."

Now it is true that in the first century A.D. medical science
was inexact so that there was always the danger of an
erroneous diagnosis of death. But presumably in the present
case many people in addition to the parents had observed the
young girl closely after her death and before she was placed in
some inner room (Mk 5:38–40), especially in view of the fact
that among Jews theological significance was found in the
time, manner and posture of a person's death. What is more,
professional mourners would not be unaccustomed to recognizing—accurately—the signs of death. Moreover, Jairus had
set out to find Jesus and enlist his help when his daughter was
already "at death's door" (Mk 5:23). Before the messengers
were dispatched to find Jairus and inform him of his daughter's death, there must have been a consensus that the young

girl had in fact died. Finally, nowhere else in the Gospels does Jesus give a medical diagnosis—as if he were saying "Her death is only apparent; she is merely in a deep coma." Nor should we dismiss as insignificant the uniform testimony of the three Evangelists, each of whom clearly believed that the girl was dead (Mt 9:18; Mk 5:35; Lk 8:49, 53).[7]

Also, the narratives include a wealth of unexpected and unnecessary circumstantial detail that bespeaks authenticity—details such as Jairus prostrating himself before Jesus (Mk 5:22; Lk 8:41); the pressing throng hindering Jesus' progress to the house of Jairus (Mk 5:24; Lk 8:42); Jesus overhearing (*parakousas*) the message delivered to Jairus by his servants (Mk 5:36); Jesus' repeated directive (*elegen*) to the professional mourners—"Out you go!" (Mt 9:24); the outburst of derision when Jesus said that the young girl was not dead but asleep (Mk 5:40; Mt 9:24; Lk 8:53); Jesus' order that the reanimated girl should be given food (Mk 5:43; Lk 8:55). Moreover the narratives lack the fantastic features that characterize some of the miracle tales of the apocryphal Gospels.

C. Lazarus (John 11:1–44)

It has become customary to describe the first twelve chapters of the fourth gospel as "The Book of Signs" because they contain six (or seven) signs that Jesus performed in demonstration of his glory (Jn 2:11). The raising of Lazarus is the final sign in this book (1:19–12:50), but it also forms a prelude to "The Book of Glory" (13:1–20:31) for the Evangelist presents the Lazarus incident as precipitating the climax of Jewish opposition to Jesus (11:46, 53) and as triggering that sequence of events, beginning with the triumphal entry (12:12–18), that finally led to Jesus' death and to his resurrection, the supreme sign of the whole gospel.

The narrative falls into three parts.

(i) *Setting (11:1–6): the illness of Lazarus*

A message is sent to Jesus in the region beyond Jordan that his friend, Lazarus, the brother of Mary and Martha, is ill in Bethany.

(ii) *Complication (11:7–37): the death of Lazarus*

When his "hour" has come, Jesus proposes to his disciples that they should all go to Judea so that he can wake Lazarus out of his sleep of death. As Jesus approaches Bethany, on the fourth day after Lazarus's death, he is met first by Martha and then by Mary, both of whom wistfully comment, "Lord, if you had been here, my brother would not have died." A sense of anticipation is aroused by Martha's confidence that "even now I know that whatever you ask from God, God will give you," by Jesus' assurance "I am the resurrection and the life," and by his question "Where have you laid him?"

(iii) *Resolution (11:38–44): the revivification of Lazarus*

Jesus orders the stone to be removed from the shaft tomb, prays to God, and addresses Lazarus with the words "Come out!" Lazarus emerges, bound in graveclothes, and Jesus directs him to be released.

1. The miracle as history

In favor of the historical trustworthiness of John's reporting of this story, we may mention the following points. He clearly assumed that an actual reanimation had taken place, for he traced the decision of the authorities to try to encompass the death of Jesus to their receipt of news of Lazarus's reanimation (Jn 11:45–53) and on three subsequent occasions (Jn 12:2, 9, 17) he identifies Lazarus as the person whom Jesus had raised from the dead. Noticeable, too, is the wealth of circumstantial detail (11:6, 12–14, 28, 33, 35, 39, 44), including geographical notes (11:1, 18) and personal references (cf. Lk 10:38–42), and the numerous surprising details that would be improbable in a work of fiction or historical romance (11:16, 20b, 37, 42). There are also surprising silences—about the character and postmortem experience of Lazarus or the reaction of the bystanders—and the actual raising of Lazarus is reported with remarkable simplicity and brevity (11:44).[8]

2. The miracle as theology

For the fourth Evangelist history and theology were not opposites. The reporting of history was a means of stating and illustrating theological truth. Both dialogue and narrative may become didactic history.

Whether they are viewed from the standpoint of content or structure, vv. 25–26 are of central importance in John 11. "I am the resurrection" (v. 25a) is expanded in v. 25b: "the person who believes in me, though he should die, shall come to life [through a resurrection effected by me]." "I am the life" (v. 25a) is developed in v. 26a: "and whoever lives [through that resurrection] as a believer in me, shall never die." Jesus is presented as the pledge and agent of both resurrection and immortality.[9] He raises the dead and gives them life. Now these two characteristics of the Son of God correspond precisely to two that are mentioned in John 5:21– 29. "For as the Father raises the dead and gives them life, so also the Son [raises the dead (cf. 5:25, 28–29) and] gives life to whom he will" (5:21). This earlier passage in the gospel anticipates chapter 11 also in emphasizing that "the dead . . . will live" as a result of hearing the voice of the Son of God (5:25, 28).

John 5, then, presents Jesus as "the resurrection," the one who raises the dead by his command, and as "the life," the one who dispenses life to anyone he chooses. John 11 affords a concrete and dramatic illustration of the truth of these claims. Just as the teaching of John 5:21–29 precedes the summary statement of John 11:25–26, so these latter verses provide an advance interpretation of the event described in John 11:43–44. When Jesus cried out in a loud voice (11:43; cf. 5:25, 28), Lazarus, who had been dead in the tomb (11:17; cf. 5:28) for four days, came out (11:44; cf. 5:29a).

But the raising of Lazarus did more than dramatize and validate the claims of Jesus. It also pictured the destiny of the followers of Jesus. As surely as the dead Lazarus responded to the command of the earthly Jesus and rose from the dead, so whoever believes in Jesus, though he or she die, will hear the voice of the exalted Son of God and come to life. Physical death remains real (11:14, 17, 21, 25, 32, 37, 39, 44) but does not have the final word. Almost certainly, however, the author intends his readers to recognize, along with this similarity, a stark contrast between the reanimation of Lazarus and the resurrection of believers. His was a revivification on the fourth day (John 11:17, 39), leading merely to renewed mortal life. Our next glimpse of Lazarus is of a person sitting at a dinner table (Jn 12:1-2), a potent reminder of the materiality of his restored life. And the subsequent plot to kill him (John 12:10) underlines this renewed mortality. On the other hand, theirs will be a resurrection on the Last Day (Jn 6:39, 40, 44, 54), leading to eternal life (Jn 5:29).

There is also an implicit contrast between the circumstances of the revival of Lazarus and those of Jesus' resurrection. Both died, Lazarus as a result of illness (Jn 11:1-4), Jesus at his own volition (Jn 10:18). In each instance a stone sealed the tomb, but in one case it was removed by natural means (Jn 11:38-41), in the other, by supernatural means (Jn 20:1, by implication). Both were bound in graveclothes when buried, but whereas Lazarus needed others to unbind him when he emerged from the tomb (Jn 11:44), Jesus left his own burial cloths intact in his grave as a sign of his resurrection (Jn 20:5-7). Both rose from the dead, Lazarus with a new lease of physical life (Jn 12:2, 10), Jesus as the possessor of a transformed body (Jn 20:17, 19-20, 26).

D. These Three Miracles of Revivification as Dramatized Theology

The three specific instances of Jesus' raising the dead recorded in the Gospels point to and illustrate theological truths, all of which relate to the person of Jesus.

1. They pointed to the messiahship of Jesus

Because they met with unbelief as well as belief, these miracles were not in themselves "proofs" of Jesus' messiahship, but they were indicators of the presence of the messianic kingdom and so of the Messiah (Mt 11:2, 5; Lk 7:18–19, 22). In the fourth gospel, "signs" that have reference to Jesus (such as the raising of Lazarus) are miraculous occurrences that to the eye of faith point beyond themselves to Jesus' glory (Jn 2:11; 11:40, 45; 12:18) as the messianic Son of God (Jn 20:30–31).

2. They demonstrated the power of Jesus

In each instance there is an emphasis on the "deadness" of the person whom Jesus raises to life,[10] an emphasis that highlights the sheer potency of his spoken word which is always the sole means by which the miracle is performed: "Young man, I say to you, get up!" (Lk 7:14); "Little girl, I say to you, stand up!" (Mk 5:41); "Lazarus, come out!" (Jn 11:43). Also noteworthy is the fact that on each occasion health and strength were regained as well as life restored. Whatever the cause of their death and whether or not bodily decomposition had set in, the subjects returned (so the texts imply) to life as they had known it before their death, illness or injury apart. It was a case of reanimation (breath returned, Lk 8:55) with healing but not transformation; Lazarus did not become a young man, nor did the twelve-year-old daughter of Jairus become a woman. The raisings were instantaneous, and proof of the miracle was afforded by the subject's speaking (Lk 7:15), walking about (Mk 5:42), and eating (Mk 5:43; Lk 8:55).

3. They illustrated the compassion of Jesus

Those who were restored to life are not depicted merely as a man, a young man, and a little girl, but principally as an only brother, an only son, and an only daughter whose deaths aroused Jesus' compassion and prompted his action. This shows his sensitive understanding of the strength of human and family ties and the sorrow of bereavement.[11] Through Jesus, the God of all comfort was comforting the downcast (cf. 2Co 1:3–4; 7:6). The tender concern of Jesus is also seen in the fact that at Nain the miracle was unsolicited, prompted by a providentially timed meeting, and no reference is made to the mother's faith: it was sheer compassion, especially since Jesus contracted ceremonial defilement by touching the bier (Lk 7:14; cf. 8:54). In all three instances, also, Jesus graciously cared for the physical or emotional needs of the person raised (Mk 5:43; Lk 7:15; Jn 11:44).

4. They pictured the conquest of Jesus over death

In our three stories death is seen to be not only real but also universal, striking both child and adult, both male and female, and severing the most cherished of ties, whether parent-child or brother-sister. But equally clearly there is shown the total sovereignty of Jesus over all death, wherever it is found. Moreover this full mastery is demonstrated by his raising one person from a deathbed, another from his funeral bier, and another from the grave. Because he is able to rob death of its prey, death becomes for his followers a "falling asleep" (*koimasthai*, Jn 11:11) or "sleep" (*katheudein*, Mk 5:39), and despair in the face of death is illegitimate (Mt 9:23–24; Lk

8:52; Jn 11:33) although grief is natural (Jn 11:35; cf. 1Th 4:13).

5. They prefigured the resurrection of Jesus and of all people

How are the "raisings" linked to "resurrection"? In the synoptics the link is forged by the ambiguity of the verbs *egeirein* and *anhistanai*, which may mean "get up" from a reclining or lying position, or "arise" from the dead. So when Jesus addresses the young man at Nain (Lk 7:14) and Jairus's daughter (Mk 5:41) with the words "Up you get!" or "Arise!" the Christian reader thinks of the coming resurrection day when the same command will be issued, "Arise!" (cf. Eph 5:14). When, in response to the command of Jesus, it is said that the little girl "got up" (*ēgerthē*, Mt 9:25; *anestē*, Mk 5:42; Lk 8:55), the reader would have recalled that exactly the same forms were traditionally used of the resurrection of Jesus (e.g., Mk 16:6 and 1Th 4:14, respectively) and the same verbs of the resurrection of Christians (e.g., 1Co 15:52 and 1Th 4:16, respectively).

As for John's gospel, the link is effected by means of concept rather than by terminology. Just as Lazarus in his tomb was raised at the command of Jesus and came out (Jn 11:43–44), so all the dead who are in the tombs will hear the voice of the Son of God and come forth (Jn 5:25, 28–29). Also we have already noted the implied contrasts in John 11:38–44 between the raising of Lazarus and the resurrection of Jesus.

Thus far we have examined the three cases in the Gospels of a dead person being restored to life before Jesus himself rose from the dead. But the New Testament also recounts two such instances after he rose, viz. Peter's raising of Tabitha at Joppa, and Paul's raising of Eutychus at Troas. Then there is the Matthean record of the raising of "the saints," either at the death of Jesus or after his resurrection. It will be convenient to discuss these three instances briefly at this point.

E. The Raising of Tabitha (Acts 9:36–42)

Tabitha (Dorcas in Greek) was a disciple who lived at Joppa (modern Jaffa) and was devoted to Christian charity, in particular making garments for destitute widows. Following an illness she died. After she had been washed in accordance with the Jewish rite of "Purification of the Dead," she was placed in an upper room. The fact that she was not anointed and buried, and that an urgent request was sent to Peter to come from Lydda some ten miles away, suggests that Tabitha's friends hoped she would be miraculously restored to life; Peter was not summoned to conduct a funeral service! On his arrival from Lydda, Peter put out all the mourners, knelt and prayed, and then addressed the corpse with the words, "Tabitha, get up!" She opened her eyes, sat up, and Peter helped her to her feet and presented her alive to the local believers, whom he had assembled. News of the miracle spread and many came to faith.

F. The Raising of Eutychus (Acts 20:7–12)

At the end of his seven-day visit to Troas, Paul gathered with the Christians on Sunday evening "to break bread," that is, for a fellowship meal that included a celebration of the Lord's Supper. Among those present was a young man named Eutychus, who was sitting on the ledge of the window (merely an opening in the wall), with the lattice wide open, undoubtedly so that everyone might benefit from any fresh air, for the room was crowded and the smoke of the torches was having a soporific effect as the evening wore on. As Paul continued to talk beyond midnight, Eutychus dropped off to sleep, overbalanced, and fell from the third floor to the courtyard below. Paul immediately went down, threw himself on him, and embraced him, no doubt at the same time praying fervently. To the alarmed spectators he said, "Stop this commotion, for he is [now] alive." Apparently Eutychus was cared for until the service had ended (cf. v. 12), when he was presented alive and well to the whole congregation.

It is not altogether clear whether this was a case of severe concussion followed by artificial resuscitation administered by Paul or an actual raising of Eutychus from death after his fall.

The latter seems more probable for several reasons.

(1) Luke states that Eutychus "was picked up dead" (v. 9); "dead" (*nekros*), not "as dead" (*hōs nekros*; cf. Rev 1:17). Since this whole episode occurs in one of the so-called "we-passages" in Acts (viz. 20:5–21:18), Luke, the author of Acts and a doctor, was an eyewitness of proceedings and was able to verify that Eutychus was indeed dead.

(2) "They brought the boy [to the congregation] alive" (v. 12) seems to be deliberately contrasted with "he was picked up dead" (v. 9).

(3) If Paul thought it was merely a case of concussion, it would have been rash for him to have thrown himself (*epepesen*, v. 10) on the young man, for Eutychus may well have sustained multiple fractures from his fall.

(4) "His life is in him" (v. 10) may as easily mean "his life is *now* in him" (as the result of a miracle) as "his life is *still* in him" (in spite of his fall).

Luke portrays both of these events—the raising of Dorcas and of Eutychus—as historical facts, as cases of straightforward revivification carried out by Peter and Paul. This does not in itself establish the historicity of these two miracles but it does mean that those who contest their rootage in history must account adequately for the rise of the remarkable belief among the early Christians that on two occasions apostles of Jesus actually raised the dead. It seems to accommodate more of the data to suppose that in this matter Luke gives us a transcript of what actually happened, than that he knowingly converted "miracles" of medical insight on the part of Peter and Paul into actual miracles of reanimation, or that he failed to recognize in his source material that what appeared to be cases of revivification were in fact merely instances of the revival of comatose persons or the product of a well-orchestrated conspiracy to pass off Peter and Paul as wonder-workers *par excellence*.

Then, too, the stories contain reflections of eyewitness testimony that support their authenticity. In the Dorcas incident, Luke notes the washing of the corpse in accordance with Jewish custom, yet there is no suggestion of burial (Ac 9:37); Peter's act of putting out of the room all the grieving widows, his kneeling to pray (cf. Ac 7:60), his addressing the corpse (Ac 9:40); the three stages of Dorcas's recovery (Ac 9:40–41). In the Eutychus episode, the narrative mentions the two reasons for Eutychus's drowsiness—smoke from the torches, and Paul's prolonged discourse (Ac 20:7–8); that Eutychus was seated "on (*epi*) the window ledge" (Ac 20:9); the three stages of Eutychus's losing fight to stay awake— dozing off (*katapheromenos*), heavy sleep (*hypnō bathei*), sagging down in sleep (*katenechtheis apo tou hypnou*) (Ac 20:9); Paul's throwing himself on Eutychus (*epepesen autō*, Ac 20:10); Paul's blunt remark, "Stop making such a fuss!" (Rieu) (*mē thorybeisthe*, Ac 20:10).

G. The Raising of "the Saints" (Matthew 27:52–53)

> [52]The tombs broke open and the bodies of many holy people who had died were raised to life. [53]They came out of the tombs, and after Jesus' resurrection they went into the holy city and appeared to many people. (NIV)

The language of this difficult passage is often explained as figurative.

> If the tearing of the temple curtain [Mt 27:51] signals the end of the old age, the resurrection of the dead marks the beginning of the new . . . The saints of the Old Testament

> go into the city of God's promise, the center of salvation,
> the eschatological Jerusalem. At Jesus' death, God fulfills
> his ancient promise made through Ezekiel to the covenant
> people [viz. Eze 37:12, "Behold, I will open your graves,
> and raise you from your graves, O my people; and I will
> bring you home into the land of Israel"].[12]

However, coming as it does between the stark account of
the death (Mt 27:50) and the burial (Mt 27:57–61) of Jesus, the
passage hardly lends itself to a purely symbolic interpretation.
For instance, if "the holy city" is heaven (note that in Mt 4:5
it clearly is Jerusalem), it seems decidedly odd to say that
resurrected saints appeared to many in heaven. What is more,
history and symbolism are not mutually exclusive categories:
a historical event may be symbolic. That is, any isolated
resurrections that occur before the End may prefigure the
general resurrection of the Last Day. While it is true that there
is no mention of these resurrections and appearances elsewhere in the New Testament, the argument from silence is
usually inconclusive, for silence does not in itself prove
ignorance. In the present case the silence of other New
Testament writers about these occurrences may simply reflect
their conviction that these appearances of "many" holy
people to "many" persons (believers or unbelievers, or both?)
were far less momentous and of less apologetic value than the
resurrection appearances of their recently crucified Messiah.[13]

Verses 51–53 form a single sentence in Greek, but present a
significant problem of punctuation and translation. In essence
the question is: Were these "many holy people" raised to life
at the time of Jesus' death (v. 50) or after his resurrection
(v. 53)? The differences between the three punctua-
tion/translation options may be most clearly seen through a
chart (see p. 99).

The difficulty with the first view[14] is the three-day interval
between the opening of the tombs and the raising of the
bodies. The second view[15] is even more awkward, for it
implies that the resurrected saints remained within their tombs

for at least three days (by inclusive reckoning). The least difficult view is the third,[16] for resurrection naturally follows immediately after the opening of tombs and emergence from the tomb naturally follows immediately after resurrection. Yet this view means that the resurrected saints delayed their appearance in Jerusalem until the resurrection of Jesus; perhaps it was only after his resurrection that maximum benefit to the Christian cause could be realized by their appearances, for *then* those appearances could point to the permanent triumph of Christ over death.

	At Jesus' Death		After Jesus' Resurrection	
1	v. 52a	tombs opened	v. 52b	bodies raised
			v. 53	emergence from tombs entering holy city appearing to many
2	v. 52	tombs opened bodies raised	v. 53	emergence from tombs entering holy city appearing to many
3	v. 52	tombs opened bodies raised	v. 53b	entering holy city
	v. 53a	emergence from tombs	v. 53c	appearing to many

Did the "many holy people" (perhaps certain believers of the Old Testament and intertestamental eras) who were raised to life emerge from their tombs in earthly bodies or in bodies suited for heaven? That is, were they merely reanimated, or were they also transformed? Probably the former, for four reasons.

(i) Matthew's silence about the final lot of those resurrected is not surprising if they simply returned to normal physical life. In the five New Testament examples of restoration to life already discussed, there is a comparable silence. On the other hand, if the "holy people" had risen in "spiritual bodies," some allusion to their avoidance of further death and their ascension or translation to heaven might have been expected.

(ii) In 1 Corinthians 15:20, 23 Jesus is described as the

"firstfruits" of the Christian dead, and in Acts 26:23 as "the first to rise from the dead." If the "holy people" rose at Jesus' death (views 2 and 3 on the chart above) in heavenly bodies, *they* would have been the first to rise with immortality.

(iii) Paul indicates that the next group, after Christ, to rise with immortality are "those who belong to Christ," but this full harvest will be gathered in "at his coming" (1Co 15:23)—not before.

(iv) The verb used here to describe the post-resurrection "appearances" of these "holy people" (viz. *emphanizō*, v. 53) is not the verb regularly used to denote such appearances (viz. *horaō*) in the case of Jesus.

We have now discussed all six instances that are recorded in the New Testament in which a person or persons were brought back to life—apart from the resurrection of Christ. Four of these occurred before his resurrection (the widow of Nain's son, Jairus's daughter, Lazarus, the "holy people" of Mt 27), and two after (Dorcas, Eutychus). Three of the raisings were performed by Jesus himself (the widow of Nain's son, Jairus's daughter, Lazarus), the other three by God's power (channeled through Peter in the case of Dorcas and Paul in the case of Eutychus). All six were simply cases of restoration to physical life—what we might call reanimation or revivification or "raisings," pointing forward or backward to *the* Resurrection, that of Jesus, and all anticipating the general resurrection of the Last Day. What distinguishes his resurrection from those six "raisings" is the fact that whereas others were merely given a new lease on physical life, he rose with immortal life, never to die again (Ro 6:9). His was a resurrection to immortality. He was the first to be "raised incorruptible" (1Co 15:52), as the King James Version and the memorable climax of Handel's *Messiah* express the point.

But this is to anticipate one of our discoveries in our next major section, "The Resurrection of Christ," to which we now turn.

The Resurrection of Christ

— V —

Resurrection *from* the Grave: Verifiable History

A. Introduction

No one can contest that the early Christians attached supreme importance to the resurrection of Christ. It was at the heart of their message to the world. Whether they were preaching the Good News in Jerusalem (Ac 4:33) or in Athens (Ac 17:18), its essence was "the resurrection of the Lord Jesus" or "Jesus and the resurrection." Where Paul is identifying the four pillars on which the Christian faith is built, he mentions the death, the burial, the resurrection, and the appearances of Jesus (1Co 15:3–8). The burial proved the reality of the death, and the appearances were evidence of the reality of the Resurrection. Moreover, the Resurrection showed the efficacy of Christ's death, for the first Christians saw the Resurrection as God's dramatic vindication of the Messiah whom Israel had rejected and crucified (Ac 2:36; 3:14–15; 4:10–11). So without the Resurrection the New Testament loses its soul and the Christian faith its central pillar. Without a risen Christ, the Christian message becomes meaningless and the Christian's faith futile: "If Christ has not been raised, our preaching is useless and your faith too is pointless" (1Co 15:14). "A person cannot give himself to a dead man, nor can he expect anything or receive anything from a dead man,"[1] yet the apostolic proclamation called for personal surrender to a man who had died (Ac 10:39, 43;

16:31; 20:21; 25:19) and the Christian claimed to have received eternal life from a man who had died (Jn 10:11, 28). "Jesus Christ, risen from the dead" (2Ti 2:8) is the focal point of the New Testament and of Christianity.

But nowhere does the New Testament suggest that the resurrection of Jesus was merely the resuscitation of his corpse and his return to a normal life as a carpenter or itinerant rabbi. Such a resurrection would not set Jesus apart from a Lazarus, who was raised from the dead only to die once more (see above, chapter IV.C). Certainly the resurrection of Jesus involved his departure from the realm of the dead (Mt 28:7), his coming to life again (Ro 14:9), and his emergence from the tomb in which he had been buried (Jn 20:1–8). But to equate his Resurrection with reanimation is to overlook two other features in the New Testament records.

Not only was Jesus restored to life. He rose to new life in a transformed body whose capacities seemed to outstrip immeasurably a merely physical body. He could appear and disappear at will (Lk 24:31, 36); he could "travel" from one place to another without visible means of locomotion (Lk 24:31, Emmaus; 24:36, Jerusalem); he could pass through solid objects such as the door or walls of a room (Jn 20:19, 26); on occasion there was a mysterious change in his outward appearance which prevented immediate recognition of him (Lk 24:16, 31); he could ascend into the sky (Lk 24:51). Resurrection involves both bodily reanimation and bodily transformation. These are the two aspects of the resurrection of Jesus that are open to ordinary historical inquiry. The historian's task is to assess the truth of this Christian claim that Jesus of Nazareth returned from the dead in a transformed body by a careful evaluation of all the relevant evidence.

But there is a second feature of the New Testament record of the Resurrection that must be taken into account. The early church made the stupendous claim that after being restored to life in a transformed body, Jesus was exalted to the right hand of God (Ac 5:30–31; Heb 1:3). This intimate connection between resurrection and exaltation is nowhere more clearly seen than in Peter's sermon on the day of Pentecost. "God raised this Jesus to life and we are all witnesses of this fact. Being therefore [*oun*] exalted by God's right hand . . . " (Ac 2:32–33). Clearly this belief in the elevation of Christ to the right hand of God is a tenet of faith that is not open to historical investigation.

Raised—transformed—exalted. There are the three ingredients that belong to resurrection in its full-orbed New Testament sense. Strictly speaking "resurrection" refers only to a person's restoration to life after an interval spent in the realm of the dead (see Appendix C.3). But because the life to which Jesus was "restored" was not mere physical life, the motif of transformation must enter into any discussion of his resurrection. Similarly, because Jesus was raised up from the grave to a unique position of honor and power in heaven, his exaltation is inseparable from his resurrection. In its widest sense, then, the resurrection of Jesus was his rising *from* the grave *in* a transformed body *to* glory at God's right hand. These three small prepositions sum up the elements that compose the New Testament view of resurrection: from (reanimation), in (transformation), to (exaltation). Our treatment of the resurrection of Christ in the next three chapters will reflect these distinctions—as does the title of the present book, *From Grave to Glory*. But before we embark on that journey, something more should be said about the Resurrection, history, and faith.

The reason why the Resurrection as reanimation and transformation is open to the probing of the historian is obviously not because it is a natural phenomenon. Equally with the Exaltation, the believer sees the reanimation and transformation of Jesus as the work of God and therefore their cause comes into the area of faith. But whereas no one claimed to have witnessed the installation of Jesus as universal Lord, people did claim to have seen Jesus alive after his death and did allege that he transcended the normal limitations of physical existence. Resurrection may therefore be described as an event that occurred simultaneously within history and beyond history. It is "historical" in that it is open to historical investigation that a person who died was restored to life and that he gained what Paul called a "spiritual body." But it is not "historical" in the sense of being an incident that was observed by witnesses or even an incident that could have been observed by mortal gaze. There were no witnesses of the Resurrection itself, and in his resurrected state Jesus was normally not visible to the human eye (see below, chapter VI.A.1).

It is "transhistorical" not simply because it has implications that lie beyond human history, nor simply because it makes a spiritual appeal to men and claim upon them (cf. Ac 17:30–31), but because it was a transaction between God and Jesus in which the Father raised the Son in a transformed state to his right hand forever. Such a transaction clearly lies outside the scope of historical research; it is an item of faith.[2]

B. Christ's Predictions of His Passion and Resurrection

There are three major passages, common to the three Synoptic Gospels, in which Jesus explicitly predicts his death and resurrection.

(i)   Matthew 16:21–23; Mark 8:31–33; Luke 9:22
(ii) Matthew 17:22–23; Mark 9:30–32; Luke 9:43b–45
(iii) Matthew 20:17–19; Mark 10:32–34; Luke 18:31–34

One of the passages may be cited in full.

> [32b]Again he took the Twelve aside and told them what was going to happen to him. [33]"We are going up to Jerusalem," he said, "and the Son of Man will be betrayed to the chief priests and teachers of the law. They will condemn him to death and will hand him over to the Gentiles, [34]who will

mock him and spit on him, flog him and kill him. Three
days later he will rise." (Mk 10:32b–34 NIV)

It is often suggested that in these prophecies we have a
classic example of "prophecy after the event."[3] That is to say,
after the passion and resurrection of Jesus the early church or
the Evangelists were concerned that these unexpected events
should be interpreted as part of the divine plan for Jesus. They
therefore placed on his lips these predictions of coming
suffering at the hands of men and certain vindication at the
hand of God.

If this were the case, however, one would expect a
reference to Jesus' exaltation, an essential ingredient of the
early church's proclamation about their crucified Messiah (Ac
2:32–33; 5:31; 10:42). Another difficulty with the proposal is
the remarkable absence of any theological interpretation of
the facts mentioned in the "prophecy." That is, if this were a
"prophecy after the event" we might have expected a form
such as: "The Son of Man must suffer many things and be
rejected *according to the Scriptures* (Lk 24:25–27), and be
killed *for our sins* (1Co 15:3), and on the third day God will
raise him *from the dead as the firstfruits* (Lk 24:46; 1Co 6:14;
15:20, 23) and exalt him by his *right hand* as Leader and
Savior (Ac 2:32–33; 5:31)."

Unless one rejects the possibility of genuine prophecy out
of hand, there is no reason to doubt that on more than one
occasion Jesus explicitly predicted his death and his subsequent vindication by resurrection, using slightly different
words each time.

But alongside these three major passages, the Gospels
contain several more general predictions of Jesus' postmortem
vindication, that is, implicit prophecies of resurrection. For
instance, we have the word of Jesus enjoining silence about
the Transfiguration until after the Resurrection (Mk 9:9–10);
the affirmation in the parable of the tenants in the vineyard
that in spite of the murder of the beloved son by the scheming

tenants, he was destined to receive from God the place of preeminence (Mk 12:10–11); the promise that after his resurrection Jesus would go ahead of his disciples into Galilee (Mk 14:28); and the prediction that the Son of Man would be vindicated by his enthronement and parousia, events that imply his deliverance from death (Mk 14:62; cf. 8:38). And in particular we recall that during the Last Supper Jesus looked beyond his impending death (Mk 14:24) to the time when he would drink "the fruit of the vine" afresh in the kingdom of God (Mk 14:25). Whether Jesus was referring to the messianic banquet over which he would preside at the End or to the renewal of fellowship in his Father's presence (cf. Jn 17:5) immediately after his death, he clearly anticipates a return from death. Then again, the fourth Evangelist notes that it was in the Resurrection that Jesus' disciples discovered the key to his enigmatic prediction "Destroy this temple and in three days I will raise it up" (Jn 2:19–22; cf. Mt 26:61; 27:40).

In spite of Jesus' repeated, explicit announcements of his resurrection (cf. Mk 8:32a, "he said this plainly"), his disciples failed to comprehend (Mk 9:10), and they dismissed news of the Resurrection as "sheer nonsense" (*lēros*) and "continued to disbelieve" (*epistoun*) the report of the women (Lk 24:11). Hence the explanation: "They did not understand the saying and were afraid to ask him" (Mk 9:32; similarly Lk 18:34). Peter understood Jesus' statement about his coming suffering sufficiently clearly for him to deliver a pointed rebuke to his master (Mk 8:32–33). But his response, probably reflecting the attitude of all the disciples, focused exclusively on the fact of coming suffering. He overlooked or ignored two crucial parts of Jesus' answer: the divine necessity of his suffering ("the Son of Man must [*dei*] suffer . . . be rejected . . . be killed," Mk 8:31), and the divine necessity of his vindication ("the Son of Man must . . . rise again," Mk 8:31). Presumably no one would ever object to resurrection, especially after undeserved suffering! But the prediction of resurrection was not heard or was simply ignored. If Jesus' references to his resurrection were merely literary creations, "prophecies after the event," how does one account for the statements about the disciples' failure to take seriously a prediction that was given more than once and was free of ambiguity? It is difficult to find an adequate explanation for their origin unless they reflect actual responses to actual prophecies.[4]

C. The Empty Tomb

When we speak of the "empty tomb," we are referring to the Christian claim that on the third day after Jesus had been crucified, his body was no longer to be found in the tomb of Joseph of Arimathea where he had been buried. But the tomb was not totally empty, for the Evangelist John carefully notes the presence, the precise position, and the shape of Jesus' burial linens that were left behind in the tomb (Jn 20:5–8).

1. Evidence for the empty tomb

a. The tradition of the empty tomb is recorded in all four gospels.

It is true that multiple attestation is no proof of truth. A falsehood does not become true because it is repeated four times. But what is significant about the Gospels' tradition concerning the empty tomb is that it reflects three or four *independent* strands of material, viz., Mark (16:1–8), Matthew's special material that is not found in Mark or Luke (commonly designated M) (Mt 28:11–15), John (20:11–18), and probably Luke (24:1–12). When we remember that countless "facts" of ancient history rest on the testimony of a single literary witness, this fourfold literary testimony to the emptiness of the tomb becomes a powerful argument.

Also of relevance is the fact that on some thirty occasions in the New Testament, the phrase "from the dead" is added to the expression "God raised Jesus" or "Jesus rose." Acts 13:29–30 makes it clear that in the case of Jesus' resurrection, "from the dead" means "from the tomb": "They took him [Jesus] down from the tree, and laid him in a tomb. But God raised him from the dead" (see also Ac 2:29–32).

b. The earliest account of the discovery of the empty tomb is extraordinarily restrained and unadorned.

Most scholars agree that Mark was the first of the four gospels to be written and that this earliest gospel originally ended at 16:8.[5] As we read those eight verses (Mk 16:1–8), we find no description of the Resurrection itself, no record of any appearances of Christ, no indication of the excitement of the witnesses at their discovery, and no attempt to introduce theological motifs such as the fulfillment of Old Testament prophecy or the beginning of the new Age. All this argues for the reliability of the empty tomb tradition. If Mark's record were a legendary fabrication, we might have expected the narrative to be adorned with fantastic features befitting an event which, if true, must from any perspective have been the most stupendous occurrence in human history. Legendary features are clearly evident in such later Christian writing about the resurrection as the Gospel of Peter (mid-second century A.D.). With its extraordinary sobriety, Mark's narrative has the "ring of truth."

It is generally agreed that even before Mark's account of the passion and resurrection of Jesus was written, there was in existence a passion narrative, the earliest connected account of any portion of Jesus' life produced in the early church, that ended by recounting the death and burial of Jesus, the discovery of the empty tomb, and some of his appearances (as in 1Co 15:3–5).[6] If this is so, the antiquity of the empty tomb narrative is guaranteed.

c. The earliest Christians could not have continued to proclaim the resurrection of Jesus in the city of Jerusalem or have continued to survive there as a community, unless the tomb had been empty.

It is inconceivable that when the Christians publicly claimed in Jerusalem that "the God of Abraham and of Isaac and of Jacob" had overturned the Jewish rejection of Jesus by raising him from the dead (Ac 2:23–24; 3:13–15; 4:10; 5:30) the Jerusalem Jews would have maintained a conspiracy of silence if they had proof that the tomb was still occupied or could produce witnesses who could account for the disappearance and disposal of the body. The bold and startling claim of the Christians would have collapsed if someone in the audience could retort, "We know where Jesus was buried, and we have checked—the tomb is still intact," or "Here are witnesses who know the whereabouts of Jesus' body." The claim that the tomb was empty was open to what some call "empirical falsification."

P. L. Maier has expressed the point vividly. Jerusalem, he affirms, is the very last place Christianity could have started

> if Jesus' tomb had remained occupied, since anyone producing a dead Jesus would have driven a wooden stake through the heart of an incipient Christianity inflamed by his supposed resurrection. What happened in Jerusalem seven weeks after the first Easter could have taken place only if Jesus' body were somehow missing from Joseph's tomb, for otherwise the Temple establishment, in its imbroglio with the Apostles, would simply have aborted the movement by making a brief trip over to the sepulcher of Joseph of Arimathea and unveiling Exhibit A. They did not do this, because they knew the tomb was empty.[7]

d. In their polemic against the early Christians, the Jews assumed the fact of the empty tomb.

Matthew 28:11–15 recounts a transaction between the guards who had been sent to watch Jesus' tomb (Mt 27:62–66) and the Jewish authorities.

[11]While the women were on their way, some of the guards went into the city and reported to the chief priests everything that had happened. [12]When the chief priests had met with the elders and devised a plan, they gave the soldiers a large sum of money, [13]telling them, "You are to say, 'His disciples came during the night and stole him away while we were asleep.' [14]If this report gets to the governor, we will satisfy him and keep you out of trouble." [15]So the soldiers took the money and did as they were instructed. And this story has been widely circulated among the Jews to this very day. (NIV)

The last sentence indicates that at the time Matthew wrote his gospel many Jews were seeking to counteract Christian assertions about Jesus by claiming that the empty tomb was the result of "body snatching." What this explanation presupposes is the fact that the tomb was indeed empty. Evidently this Jewish counterclaim continued to have currency throughout the second century and beyond, for both Justin Martyr (c. A.D. 155) in his *Dialogue with Trypho* 108 and Tertullian (c. A.D. 200) in his *De Spectaculis* 30 accuse the Jews of their day of charging that Jesus' disciples had stolen his body. We cannot doubt the accuracy of this testimony of Matthew, Justin, and Tertullian, for they are writing as Christians and therefore recording what amounts to "hostile" evidence.

e. The early Christians, as Jews, would have assumed that resurrection shortly after death implied an empty tomb.

To Jews of the first century A.D., any idea of a resurrection shortly after death involved (at least) the emptying of a tomb or grave and the revival of the physical body. The Jewish contemporaries of Jesus knew that Lazarus could not be raised from the dead until first the stone that lay over his burial cave had been removed (Jn 11:38–44). No one could be regarded as resurrected shortly after death while his corpse lay in a tomb. So the early Christian claim that Jesus was alive necessarily implied that his body was no longer entombed. Accordingly, when Paul asserts, on the one hand, that Jesus was "laid in a tomb" (Ac 13:29) or was buried (1Co 15:4a), and on the other, that he had been raised from the dead (Ac 13:30; 1Co 15:4b), he is implying that the sepulcher in which he had been buried was empty.

f. The empty tomb narratives do not use the "third day" motif.

The Resurrection is everywhere linked with the "third day" (e.g., Mt 16:21; 27:63–64; Lk 13:32; 24:7; Jn 2:19; 1Co 15:4) so that the resurrection appearances may be said to have begun on the "third day," whereas the discovery of the empty tomb is always associated with "the first day of the week" (Mt 28:1; Mk 16:2; Lk 24:1; Jn 20:1). If the story of the empty tomb were a late legend, we would expect some use to be made of the "third day" motif, which is found in primitive credal formulas such as 1 Corinthians 15:4, "He was raised on the third day."[8]

g. The first witnesses of the empty tomb are said to have been women.

According to Jewish legal principles (see SB 3:217, 559–60), the testimony of women was in that age generally inadmissible as evidence, yet the Gospels depict women as the first witnesses of the empty tomb (Mt 28:1–10; Mk 16:1–8; Lk 24:1–10; and probably also Jn 20:1–2). Not only so, but they are specifically named, as women well known in the early church—a risky procedure if the account had been fabricated. The Eleven were in Jerusalem at the time (Lk 24:9) and later saw the risen Jesus (Lk 24:33, 36–43), but, according to the records, they did not have the privilege of discovering that the tomb was empty. If the story of the empty tomb were legendary or of late origin we should have expected the

witnesses to be exclusively men and perhaps the first witness
to be an apostle such as Peter.

h. There is no evidence that the tomb of Jesus was venerated.

The Jews of ancient times venerated the burial places of
prophets and other holy persons such as righteous martyrs
(Mt 23:29; Ac 2:29; 1Mc 13:25–30). It is therefore remarkable
that the early Christians gave no particular attention to the
tomb of Jesus, for they regarded their master as no ordinary
prophet or holy man but as the Son of God. Remarkable, that
is, unless his tomb was empty.

Although it is no argument in favor of the empty tomb, it is
significant that an ever-increasing number of professional New
Testament scholars are convinced of the reliability of the
empty tomb tradition.[9] So much so that we would venture the
opinion that of those who have written on the subject the
majority affirm the historicity of the empty tomb.

Here, then, we have a formidable array of arguments that
cumulatively put it "beyond reasonable doubt" that the tomb
of Jesus was discovered to be empty early on a Sunday
morning some thirty-six hours after his burial.[10] But this
conclusion has not gone unchallenged, so we must now
consider the evidence that some regard as jeopardizing this
conclusion.

2. Alleged evidence against the empty tomb

a. Early Christian preachers did not appeal to the testimony of the empty tomb.

To judge from the specimens of early Christian sermons
recorded in Acts, a direct appeal to the fact of the empty tomb
was not a regular feature of early preaching. When Peter says
that "we all are witnesses of this fact" (Ac 2:32b), he is
referring to God's raising of Jesus (Ac 2:32a), not the

emptiness of the tomb (see also Ac 1:22; 10:40–42). Believers and unbelievers alike might testify that the tomb was empty, but only believers could witness to the reality of Christ's resurrection. In any case the point at issue between Christians and Jews was not the fact of the empty tomb (evidently assumed by both sides as being incapable of disproof), but the significance of this fact. However, an *indirect* appeal to the empty tomb is contained in Peter's Pentecost sermon delivered in Jerusalem. His point in noting that David's tomb "is with us to this day" (Ac 2:29) is that anyone who chooses may inspect the traditional site of his burial in the city. The same is true, Peter implies, of the actual tomb of Jesus in the same city. Although Jesus had died in the recent past (some seven weeks earlier), his grave would be found open and empty.

b. In his letters Paul never mentions the empty tomb.

For some, the silence of Paul regarding the empty tomb is conclusive evidence that this tradition is neither reliable nor early.[11] Now it is true that the primitive Christian formula Paul cites in 1 Corinthians 15:3b–5 contains no reference to the empty tomb, but, as K. Lake observes, the apostle was not attempting to convince the Corinthians that Jesus had risen but was reminding them (1Co 15:1) that he had already convinced them.[12] He is citing "official" personal witnesses of the resurrected Jesus, not corroborative testimony about the tomb. We have already observed that when Paul affirms that Jesus was "laid in a tomb" (Ac 13:29) or buried (1Co 15:4a), and that he had been raised from the dead (Ac 13:30; 1Co 15:4b), he must be implying that the tomb in which Jesus had been placed was no longer occupied by him. The mere fact that Paul nowhere mentions the empty tomb is no proof that he was unaware of the tradition. It is hard to believe that when Paul visited Jerusalem to confer with Peter (Gal 1:18) regarding early Christian traditions, there was no discussion of Peter's discovery of the empty tomb (Lk 24:12; Jn 20:3–10). Our ignorance of the extent of Paul's knowledge does not amount to knowledge of the extent of his ignorance.

Both of these considerations are, at best, negative evidence: the Evangelists' lack of appeal to the empty tomb and Paul's silence about it. But silence or relative silence is not to be equated with ignorance. And just as Peter indirectly appealed to the fact of the empty tomb, so Paul implied that the tomb had been vacated. The reason for this relative lack of interest in the empty tomb was that, apart from the appearances of Jesus, the empty tomb was ambiguous testimony that could be explained in various ways. This point will be developed further below.

3. Explanations of the empty tomb

a. Some have argued that Jesus did not actually die but left his tomb after recovering from the effects of crucifixion.

This view, sometimes called the "swoon theory" or the "apparent death theory," enjoyed considerable popularity among eighteenth- and nineteenth-century German rationalists such as C. H. G. Venturini in his *Natürliche Geschichte des grossen Prophet von Nazareth* (1800) and H. E. G. Paulus in his *Das Leben Jesu* (1828), but the theory is now totally discredited.[13] In general terms, it speculates that Jesus swooned on the cross, was taken for dead, but after burial revived in the cool atmosphere of the sepulcher, escaped from the tomb, and "appeared" to his disciples, who were convinced that he had risen from the dead.

The most recent exponent of a similar view is J. D. M. Derrett, who insists that in reference to Jesus' own experience the Greek word *anastasis* means "revival" in a physical sense, not "resurrection" in a theological sense. "The religious belief in Resurrection was forcibly hooked onto a historical *anastasis* of an individual." Distinguishing "brain death" from "clinical death" (i.e. the apparent cessation of breathing and pulse), Derrett maintains that in the coolness of the tomb Jesus revived from the "clinical" death he had experienced on the cross that had been "masked, perhaps, by a self-induced trance." But he survived only briefly before gangrene and high fever led to his collapse and brain death. His disciples probably cremated his body in the Place of Burning in the Kedron Valley where his ashes would have become indistinguishable from the remains of innumerable Passover animals.[14]

Even in this sophisticated modern guise, the theory totally fails to explain the facts.

(1) The uniform testimony of the New Testament is that Jesus actually died and his corpse was placed in a tomb (e.g., Mt 27:50, 57–66; Ac 13:28–29; 1Co 15:3–4; 1Pe 3:18).

(2) There is unambiguous evidence outside the New Testament that testifies to the actual death of Jesus. Both the Jewish historian Josephus (*Antiquities* 18:63–64, written c. A.D. 93) and the Roman historian Tacitus (*Annals* 15:44, written c. A.D. 115) refer to the execution of Jesus on the orders of Pontius Pilate.

(3) Under no circumstances could Jesus have recovered from the Roman scourging (Mk 15:15) and crucifixion (Mk 15:24), not to speak of the lance thrust (Jn 19:34), as quickly as this theory demands. Moreover the purpose of the lance thrust was to ensure that the victim was actually dead. And, on this view, how are we to explain Pilate's careful cross-questioning of the centurion about the relative speed of Jesus' death before he released the corpse for burial (Mk 15:42–45)?

(4) How could a recently crucified man, desperately needing medical attention, have created the impression on his disconsolate followers that he had conquered death and was worthy of worship (Mt 28:16–20; Jn 20:19–29)?

(5) So far from hinting at Jesus' death after his resurrection, the New Testament affirms that he died once (e.g., Heb 9:28;

10:10) and thereafter will never die again (Ro 6:9; Heb 7:16; Rev 1:18).

b. Some have suggested that the women visited the wrong tomb.[15]

It is said that in the dim light of early morning the women visited the wrong tomb but saw a young man who directed them to the right tomb with the words "He is not here. Look! There is the place where they laid him" (Mk 16:6).

But this view demands that the reference to the Resurrection ("He is risen") be arbitrarily omitted from this verse; that Mark's statement (15:47) that "Mary Magdalene and Mary the mother of Joses" had seen where Jesus was buried be discounted; that the word *neaniskos* ("young man") be taken as a reference to a caretaker or gardener, whereas Mark's description of him as "dressed in a white robe" (cf. Rev 6:11; 7:9, 13) and as giving the divine message (Mk 16:6–7) shows that he regarded him as an angel (cf. Mt 28:5; Josephus, *Ant.* 5:277); and that the women and the young man remained silent about the true explanation of the empty tomb.

No more satisfactory are the proposals that Jesus was treated as a common criminal so that his body was buried in a common grave, or that the Jews were responsible for his burial (cf. Ac 13:29, "they took him down from the tree, and laid him in a tomb").[16] In either case, why did the person or persons responsible for the burial not come forward with their eyewitness testimony and accurate information when the Christians were laying claim to a risen Master?

c. The body of Jesus was stolen from the tomb, either (1) by his disciples, or (2) by the Jews, or (3) by Joseph of Arimathea.

(1) This is sometimes called the "conspiracy theory," for it requires that once the disciples had stolen the body of Jesus, they corporately agreed to announce his resurrection. Appar-

ently this was the first explanation of the empty tomb to be propounded by the opponents of the infant church (Mt 28:11–15).

The difficulties confronting this view are insurmountable. How did the disciples manage to elude or overpower the guard of Jewish temple police that had been posted at the tomb precisely to prevent such a robbery (Mt 27:62–66)? Why would anyone stealing the body bother to unwind and then fold or rewind the several yards of linen cloth that encircled the corpse (cf. Jn 20:6–7)? Moreover, it is difficult enough to believe that dispirited disciples who were oblivious of Jesus' predictions of his resurrection (Mk 8:31–32; Lk 24:6–8, 11) would fix on the desperate plan of stealing the body, of vowing never to divulge the truth, and of proclaiming his resurrection. But it stretches credulity beyond the limit to believe that men were willing to suffer and die for what they knew to be a gigantic hoax and that the truth never slipped out, even to other followers of Jesus. Instead of a physical miracle—the resurrection of Jesus from the tomb—we are asked to accept a psychological miracle.

(2), (3)   If certain Jews or Joseph of Arimathea as a member of the Sanhedrin (Mk 15:43) stole the body, they would have created the very rumors they were anxious to prevent (cf. Mt 27:62–64) and would have been able to refute the Christian assertion that Jesus was alive by producing his corpse or at least the person who carried out the theft. If, on the other hand, Joseph acted as a secret disciple (cf. Jn 19:38) and transferred the body from a temporary to a permanent grave after the sabbath, why did he choose to do this legitimate task in the darkness and why did he not inform the disciples?

d. The empty tomb tradition is legendary.

The most modern explanation of the empty tomb tradition is that it was an apologetic legend created by the church at a comparatively late stage to substantiate its claim that there were witnesses of the risen Jesus. It was also an effort to express in material terms an originally spiritual understanding of Christ's resurrection as God's victory through the cross of Christ.[17]

We should note, however, that neither Acts nor the Epistles contain any hint that in their earliest preaching Christians proclaimed the Resurrection as a spiritual victory without relating it to the bodily resurrection of Jesus. On the contrary, to judge by our sources, the Resurrection was proclaimed as victory precisely because death was thereby forced to release its grip on the body of Jesus (Ac 2:24–32; 13:34–37; cf. Rev 1:17–18). In addition, if the empty tomb tradition was a fabrication for apologetic purposes, it is curious that so many apparent discrepancies between the four records were left "undoctored," and that the reactions of the disciples to the discovery of the empty tomb were portrayed as fear (Mt 28:5, 8), trembling astonishment (Mk 16:8), perplexity (Lk 24:4), and mocking disbelief (Lk 24:11). Also this view leaves us with the problem of the disposal of Jesus' body. If in fact his enemies placed him in a common grave (a suggestion some make on the basis of John 19:31 and Ac 13:29[18]) and the place where he was buried was forgotten, how are we to account for the burial tradition, found in all four gospels, that associates Joseph of Arimathea with the entombing of Jesus, or for the Jewish silence about the facts of the case when the Christians publicly claimed that the "God of Abraham, Isaac, and Jacob" had contradicted the Jewish rejection of Jesus by raising him from the dead (Ac 2:23–24; 3:13–15)?

e. The tomb of Jesus was empty because of an "act of God."

Thus far we have set out eight reasons for believing that the tomb of Jesus was discovered to be empty (1.a–h). In addition we have shown that the objections to the historicity of the empty tomb are unfounded (2.a–b) and that none of the natural explanations of the fact is adequate (3.a–d). This leaves the supernatural hypothesis—that it was as a result of divine intervention that the tomb became empty.

What was the nature of that divine intervention, that "act of God"? Without any further evidence, we might have hypothesized that it was simply the miraculous removal of the corpse from the tomb, perhaps by dematerialization. But other evidence does in fact exist—the claim of many followers of Jesus that they had seen him alive after his death and burial. It is this combination of "empty tomb" and "appearances" that prompts the natural inference that the way in which God acted on the body of Jesus in the tomb was to raise him to life. But this is to anticipate our discussion in the next chapter. Before we leave the present topic, we should address the question, "Was (or is) the empty tomb a basis for faith in the risen Christ?"

The reason why early Christian evangelists apparently made no direct appeal to the witness of the empty tomb is also the reason why the empty tomb was not the primary basis for faith. In itself the empty tomb is ambiguous testimony, capable of several competing interpretations. The discovery that the tomb was empty did not invariably lead to the belief that Jesus had risen. On the contrary, the discovery gave rise to trembling astonishment (Mk 16:8a), perplexity (Lk 24:3–4), doubt (Lk 24:12), or awe (Mk 16:8b), while the report of the empty tomb was greeted with amazement (Lk 24:22–24) or downright skepticism (Lk 24:11). So far from prompting an immediate awareness that Jesus had risen, the empty tomb aroused the fear that his body had been stolen by enemies or removed for some other reason (Jn 20:11, 13, 15). Without some authoritative explanation of the emptiness of the tomb, an empty tomb merely proves that the tomb is empty. If a corpse were to go missing from a mortuary, the empty mortuary would be in itself no evidence of resurrection. There may be a simpler, more natural explanation! Not being in itself a conclusive proof of resurrection, the empty tomb needed someone to give a definitive explanation if its true import were to be known. This is precisely the role of the "interpreting angel" in the empty tomb narrative: "He has risen, he is not here" (Mk 16:6). If the empty tomb were the product of a divine action, it also needed a divinely given interpretation, for even a divine action may be ambiguous as long as it remains uninterpreted by the divine actor. One may cite the parallel cases of the birth or the death of Jesus. His birth is recognized as the incarnation of the Logos (Jn 1:14), his death is seen as a redemptive sacrifice (Ro 3:24–25), only through divine revelation.

Even if in itself the empty tomb was not the source of faith, when interpreted by God it was believed to be sufficient ground to induce faith. For example, if Mark's gospel originally ended at verse 8, the only testimony to the Resurrection would be the empty tomb as authoritatively explained by the angel. For Luke (24:22–27) and John (20:3–9) it was a knowledge of scriptural predictions of the Messiah's resurrection—a knowledge of what we might call God's prior interpretation of the empty tomb—that saved the empty tomb from ambiguity and made it a possible basis of faith. In a sense, what Christian evangelists first proclaimed was God's own explanation of the empty tomb, namely, that he had raised Jesus from the dead, who therefore had been spared the corruption of the grave (e.g., Ac 2:24–32; 13:34–37). This is not to deny that *in the event* the appearances of the risen Jesus were the decisive witness to the Resurrection. But it is to affirm that the empty tomb, once interpreted by the angel or once seen in the light of messianic prophecies, became a potential proof of the Resurrection. But because the first disciples were "too slow of wit, too dull of heart to believe" (Lk 24:25 KNOX), there is in fact no recorded instance of faith's being born through the interpreted empty tomb. The nearest example is in John 20:8 where the "other disciple" believed in the risen Jesus on the basis of the removal of the stone, the empty tomb (in this case without any angelic interpretation), and in particular the position of the grave-clothes (Jn 20:6–7).

Up to this point we have seen that the empty tomb is in itself an *ambiguous* sign but that, with an authoritative interpretation supplied, it may be a stimulus to faith. From another viewpoint the empty tomb was an *indispensable* sign. If the body of Jesus had remained in the tomb, no amount of persuasion would have convinced Jews that the person alleged to have risen from the dead was identical with the person recently laid in the grave. Like the removal of the stone, the emptiness of the tomb was a prerequisite for faith in a risen Lord. In Jewish eyes, had the stone not been removed, the tomb would not have been empty. Had the tomb not been empty, no resurrection was possible. Finally, the empty tomb is a *valuable* sign, since it prevents a docetic view of the Resurrection. The Resurrection was not simply an occurrence in the spiritual world, for the empty tomb stands at the intersection of the spiritual and the material and shows that these two categories are reconcilable.

What, then, are we to make of the celebrated dictum of H. Grass that "we do not believe in the empty grave but in the risen Lord"?[19] We should observe, first of all, that although "believing" generally has a personal object in New Testament usage, propositions may also be believed. The most notable instance of this is the stated purpose of the fourth gospel: "These things have been recorded so that you may believe that [*hina pisteusēte hoti*] Jesus is the Messiah, the Son of God, and so that believing [this? in him?] you may have life in his name" (Jn 20:31). Here "believe that" means "be convinced that." There need be no opposition, therefore, between being convinced that the tomb was empty and entrusting oneself to the risen Lord. Indeed, belief in the person may today directly result from conviction of the fact.

We conclude that although the empty tomb in itself does not afford conclusive evidence of the resurrection of Jesus, it is not irrelevant in the Christian tradition, for, when interpreted, it may serve as the ground for faith in Christ. In addition, it is the presupposition of belief in Jesus' resurrection, a guarantee of the continuity between the earthly Jesus and the risen Lord, and a protection against a spiritualized view of resurrection.

D. Evidence from Archaeology?

It may appear strange to raise the possibility that archaeology could have any relevance to the empty tomb. After all, we do not have a notarized copy of an affidavit sworn by the gardener (cf. Jn 20:15) of the garden-cemetery outside Jerusalem's walls to the effect that he found the tomb of the Nazarene to be mysteriously empty early on the Sunday morning. But there are two archaeological items that deserve consideration.

1. The Nazareth Decree

Part of the Froehner collection in the Cabinet des Médailles in Paris is a slab of white marble, which, the antiquarian Froehner noted, was "sent from Nazareth in 1878." Its significance was unrecognized until 1930, when Franz Cumont published an article (in French) entitled "An imperial rescript concerning tomb violation."[20] The text of the inscription was probably originally composed in Latin but it appears on the slab in what might be called literal "translation Greek."

> Decree of Caesar.
>
> It is my pleasure that sepulchres and tombs, which have been erected as solemn memorials of ancestors or children or relatives, shall remain undisturbed in perpetuity. If it be shown that anyone has either destroyed them or otherwise thrown out the bodies which have been buried there or removed them with malicious intent to another place, thus committing a crime against those buried there, or removed the headstones or other stones, I command that against

such person the same sentence be passed in respect of solemn memorials of men as is laid down in respect of the gods. Much rather must one pay respect to those who are buried. Let no one disturb them on any account. Otherwise it is my will that capital sentence be passed upon such person for the crime of tomb-spoliation.[21]

Although the inscription was "sent from Nazareth" and was presumably acquired there, we cannot be sure that it was erected and subsequently found at Nazareth in Galilee. But it seems a fair inference. Nor can it be finally determined whether in origin the inscription was an imperial rescript, that is, a formal response by the emperor to a question raised by the procurator of Judea or the legate of Syria, or an imperial edict or decree, produced on the emperor's initiative. With more confidence we may date the inscription A.D. 44–50. The skilled eye of the epigraphist informs us that the style of the lettering on the stone belongs to the first half of the first century A.D. But Galilee was not incorporated into the Roman province of Judea until the death of Herod Agrippa I in A.D. 44, so it is unlikely that any edict of the emperor would be set up in or near Nazareth before that date. On this view, the Caesar of the inscription is Claudius, who ruled A.D. 41–54.

There are several points of special interest in the inscription, whose sole purpose was to prescribe the death penalty for tomb violation.

a. It deals with two issues: the destruction of tombs, including the removal of headstones; and the removal of corpses from tombs. Tombs were to "remain undisturbed in perpetuity," and it was absolutely forbidden for anyone to disturb those who were buried.

b. The death penalty for tomb spoliation seems an exceedingly harsh punishment. It was not until the early third century that the desecration of burial became a criminal offense in the Roman Empire.

c. It is remarkable that this rescript or edict is associated with Nazareth in Galilee, the hometown of Jesus.

So the question naturally arises: What prompted an emperor in Rome to give his personal attention to an isolated problem of tomb breaking and body snatching in Galilee (or perhaps more generally in Palestine), and to depart from Roman legal tradition by instituting the death penalty for violation of sepulture?

If the inscription was a rescript of the emperor addressed to a local Roman official, we would have to assume that either the procurator of Judea or the legate of Syria (whose jurisdiction included Judea) had written to the emperor as the ultimate authority, requesting instructions about the procedure to be followed in dealing with a particular case of tomb robbery. But why did Claudius lay down such a severe penalty for only one segment of the empire—significantly the part to which Jesus had belonged?

Whether the inscription was a rescript or was simply an edict emanating from Claudius himself, we must seek to explain his motives for formulating such a decree. We gain a clue from an event that occurred in A.D. 49. Frustrated by the constant rioting among Jews in Rome, Claudius expelled all Jews from the capital (Ac 18:2; Suetonius, *Claudius* 25). Suetonius, the biographer of Claudius, adds that these riots occurred "at the instigation of Chrestus" (= Christ). Although Suetonius wrongly assumed that Jesus was alive in Rome at the time, it is probable that this unrest was fomented by the messianic claims of Jewish Christians in Rome. As a result of the spread of Christianity to Rome, or perhaps in connection with this edict of expulsion, Claudius had made some enquiries about the origin of the Christian movement. Such enquiry would be totally in keeping with what we know of Claudius, the scholar-emperor who authored some thirty-seven books (all lost). He was renowned for his antiquarian interests, and, being eager to carry forward the religious reforms of Augustus, he took an interest in religious issues and problems throughout the Mediterranean. Moreover, Claudius was a close friend of Herod Agrippa I, who had an intimate knowledge of Christian origins and a virulent hatred of Christians (Ac 12:1–5). We may assume that in the course of his enquiry Claudius heard the Jewish claim that the sect of the Nazarenes, which was causing such disturbance in the synagogues of Rome, had been generated by a case of "body snatching," when the disciples of Jesus of Nazareth had broken into his tomb, stolen his body, and then pronounced him to be alive. In this way Claudius may have associated tomb violation with the rise of seditious religious movements. This would have led him to formulate the drastic edict and direct that it be promulgated throughout Galilee or Palestine, or at least in places closely associated with Jesus, such as Nazareth.

We conclude that the Nazareth Decree testifies to the wide circulation and influence of the Jewish explanation of the alleged resurrection of Jesus that Matthew records: "His disciples came during the night and stole him away" (Mt 28:13). But such an explanation—and Claudius's action that was based on it—presupposes the fact of the empty tomb. Both the friends and the adversaries of Jesus agreed that his tomb was empty!

2. The Shroud of Turin

A 14'3" x 3'7" strip of handloomed linen cloth, bearing a double image, front and back, of a crucified male Caucasian about 5'11" tall and weighing about 178 pounds. Is it the actual burial shroud of the crucified Jesus—or the world's most spectacular hoax?

Since 1578 the Cathedral of St. John the Baptist in Turin, Italy, has housed this most famous relic of Christendom. To celebrate the 400th anniversary of the Shroud's arrival in Turin, there was a rare, six-week public display of the relic in Turin's Cathedral, when over 3.3 million people viewed the priceless treasure. As soon as the exhibition closed on October 8, 1978, a team of forty scientists from Europe and the U.S. began to conduct a comprehensive battery of tests on the Shroud for 120 continuous hours, the five days during which they had been permitted to make their investigations. They represented various scientific disciplines, such as chemistry, physics, computer technology, aerodynamics, infrared thermography, biophysics, and forensic pathology.

One unofficial report of the findings of this Shroud of Turin Research Project (STURP) is found in *Verdict on the Shroud* by K. E. Stevenson and G. R. Habermas. The book's subtitle, *Evidence for the Death and Resurrection of Jesus Christ*, reflects the basic conclusions of the two authors, viz. that the Shroud is an authentic burial cloth of a first-century Jew, that this Jew was probably none other than Jesus, and that Jesus actually rose from the dead (ibid. 111–29, 155–59, 176–79). In an article appearing the same year,[22] Habermas summarized three new arguments for the historicity of the Resurrection which he believed were afforded by the Shroud. First, whereas other burial shrouds have only blood and decomposition stains, this Shroud has a double image (front and back) apparently caused by a burst of light or heat radiation from the dead body. Second, since there is no evidence of decomposition on the Shroud, the body must not have remained in the cloth "for more than a very few days." Third, the blood clots on the Shroud are intact and the dried borders of the blood stains are not disrupted, showing that the body was not removed or unwrapped.[23] Habermas concludes that the Shroud's evidence for the Resurrection is so strong that "if Jesus was not buried in this garment, then we might have a problem, for it would seem that someone else would have appeared to have risen from the dead."[24]

But all this was prior to 1988.[25] During that year the crucial test that would finally determine the age of the Shroud—the carbon 14 test—was carried out. Previously the Shroud's custodian, Anastasio Cardinal Ballestrero, had denied permission for this test because it required the removal of handkerchief-sized samples from the Shroud. But recent improvements in testing techniques reduced the size of the samples needed to postage stamp dimensions and the Cardinal gave his permission. *Time* magazine reported the testing procedures as follows.

> Testing was done simultaneously at the University of Arizona, Britain's Oxford University and Switzerland's Federal Institute of Technology in Zurich. Each laboratory received four unmarked samples: a shroud cutting and three control pieces, one of which dated from the 1st century. The samples were chemically cleaned, burned to produce carbon dioxide, catalytically converted into graphite and then tested for carbon 14 isotopes to fix the date by calculating the amount of radioactive decay. Only London's British Museum, which coordinated the testing, knew which samples were which.[26]

Once the data from the three institutions had been correlated and averaged, the startling result emerged. There is a 95 percent probability that the Shroud is to be dated between A.D. 1260 and 1380 and virtual certainty that it does not predate 1200. These findings have been acknowledged and accepted by Cardinal Ballestrero and Pope John Paul II.

What are we to conclude from all this? Three points emerge.

a. If the carbon 14 tests were reliable—and there is no reason to question this—the Shroud of Turin was not the burial cloth of Jesus and therefore has no relevance to the question of the empty tomb or the Resurrection. True, there are some who contend that the question of the authenticity of the Shroud is inconsequential, because in any case the image of the Shroud encapsulates the gospel of a crucified Christ. But that is precisely the difficulty: the image remains that of a man scourged and crucified, not risen and glorified.

b. Yet the Shroud remains a genuine archaeological relic of special interest, because, whatever its origin, it affords an accurate and dramatic visual *impression* of the gruesome and repulsive nature of a Roman scourging and crucifixion.

c. The image on the Shroud continues to be a scientific enigma, for it is said to be superficial, three-dimensional, and non-directional,[27] and the technique for producing such an image has not yet been duplicated even by modern technology.[28]

VI

Resurrection *in* a Transformed Body: Verifiable History

In the last chapter we reviewed the reasons for regarding Christ's emergence from the grave not only as verifiable history but also as verified history. But did he emerge with a body that was in every way identical with the body that was buried? Can his post-resurrection appearances be verified by the historian?

A. The Resurrection Appearances of Jesus

In this section we shall first summarize the information given to us in the New Testament about the resurrection appearances of Jesus and then inquire whether we can regard those appearances as historical.

To judge from the examples of preaching found in the book of Acts, the early Christian evangelists rarely referred to the empty tomb of Jesus but regularly appealed to his appearances after his resurrection when they were proclaiming the risen Jesus. For instance,

> God raised him from the dead, and for many days he appeared to those who came up with him from Galilee to Jerusalem. They are now witnesses concerning him to the Jewish people. (Ac 13:30–31)

This is supported by Paul's summary of early Christian belief and preaching in 1 Corinthians 15:3b–5. In these verses a fourfold "that" (*hoti*) introduces four verbs which form the pillars of early Christian preaching:

(1) ". . . that Christ died for our sins according to the Scriptures, and

(2) that he was buried, and

(3) that he was raised on the third day according to the Scriptures, and

(4) that he appeared to Cephas, then to the twelve."[1]

Here we have the essence of the Gospel—the death, the burial, the resurrection, and the appearances of Jesus. Paul's emphasis falls on the first and third elements (cf. Ac 17:2–3; 2Co 5:15; 1Th 4:14), with the second and fourth being confirmatory. That is, the burial of Jesus verified the fact of his death, while his appearances confirmed the reality of his resurrection.

1. The nature of the appearances

In the first place, the resurrection narratives leave no room for doubt that all the appearances were personal, physical appearances of the Jesus of Nazareth whom his disciples had known before his death. The risen Jesus was precisely the same person as Jesus of Nazareth, with identity of personal characteristics in areas such as memory, disposition, attitudes, diction, and habits. The angelic declaration was "You seek Jesus of Nazareth who was crucified. He has risen" (Mk 16:6). Jesus' resurrection body was not a fresh creation of God, a "creation out of nothing." Jesus was recognized by his followers when he appeared to them after his resurrection because of such features as his tone of voice (Jn 20:16), his bodily movements (Lk 24:30–31, 35), and the marks of the crucifixion (Lk 24:39–40; Jn 20:27). Those to whom Jesus appeared were said to "see" him or to "recognize" him (e.g., Mt 28:7, 17; Lk 24:31; Jn 20:14, 18, 20, 29), where the normal verbs denoting visual recognition are used. When he appeared he was not only seen but also heard (Lk 24:25–27; Jn 21:15–18; Ac 1:3) and touched (Mt 28:9). To assure the disciples of his reality he even took food (Lk 24:38–43).

Another way of expressing this point would be to say that the resurrection appearances are never depicted as psychological visions. There is no New Testament instance of an "appearance" of Jesus at night or in a dream or during sleep. Had New Testament writers wished to express the idea that Jesus always or occasionally "appeared" to various disciples in a manner resembling a person's appearance in a dream, the most suitable verb would have been *phainomai* ("appear, show oneself") which in fact occurs only in the secondary text Mark 16:9. When Jesus communicated to Paul at night in a vision (Ac 18:9; 23:11), he is not said to "appear." Nor is the term *vision* (*horama* or *optasia*) found in the gospel records of Jesus' appearances, in spite of the fact that *horama* can mean simply "what is seen" (Mt 17:9). Although Paul can describe his seeing the risen Lord outside the city of Damascus (Ac 22:6–15) as a heavenly "vision" (*optasia*, Ac 26:19), he clearly distinguishes it from his subsequent "visions" or ecstatic raptures (*optasiai*) that were given by the Lord (2 Cor. 12:1) but did not involve "seeing" the Lord, at least not in the same way (e.g., Ac 22:17–21).

Secondly, the initiative in the resurrection appearances always rested with Jesus. He appeared to whom he chose, when he chose. This is clear from the three main verbs used by New Testament writers to denote the appearances of the risen Lord.

a. *phaneroō*, "reveal," as in John 21:1, "Jesus revealed himself";

b. *optanomai*, "appear" (Ac 1:3b);

c. *horaō*, in its aorist passive form *ōphthē*, "he appeared," as in 1 Corinthians 15:5–8 (four times). In Acts we find the composite expressions "he presented himself alive" (Ac 1:3a) and ("God . . . permitted him) to become visible" (Ac 10:40).

Thirdly, Jesus appeared only to believers or to those

destined to become believers because of his appearance to them. Never did Jesus appear to the general public. Peter frankly acknowledges this in his sermon in the house of Cornelius. "God raised Him up on the third day, and granted that He should become visible, not to all the people, but to witnesses who were chosen beforehand by God" (NASB).

The only two unbelievers to receive a resurrection appearance were James, the brother of Jesus (Mk 6:3; Jn 7:5), and Saul of Tarsus. Both were brought to faith through the encounter (Ac 1:14–15; 1Co 15:7, for James; Ac 9:1–19; 1Co 15:8, for Paul). There is no evidence that the soldiers guarding Jesus' tomb even overheard the angel's message to the women, far less were witnesses when Jesus met the women (Mt 28:1–10). Since verses 2–4 of Matthew 28 are parenthetical,[2] this means that the guards had fled from the tomb before the women arrived. And, significantly, none of the other three Gospels mentions the guards when recounting the women's arrival at the tomb. Only in the apocryphal gospels do unbelievers become witnesses of the risen Jesus—and remain unbelievers.[3]

2. The purpose and result of the appearances

If the disciples had not been foolish and spiritually sluggish (Lk 24:25) they would have believed the angelic interpretation of the empty tomb and seen the resurrection of Jesus as the fulfillment of prophecy. Apart from the beloved disciple (Jn 20:8) and possibly Joanna and the women from Galilee (Lk 24:22–23), the empty tomb, even when divinely interpreted, failed to bring the disciples to faith. The appearances, therefore, were in part accommodations to human faithlessness. For the majority of the disciples, only "seeing" led to "believing." It was not the divinely given interpretation of the empty tomb but personal encounters with the risen Jesus that produced belief in his resurrection. The case of Thomas was typical. Rejecting the testimony of the angels and of his fellow disciples, he declared his refusal to believe unless he saw and touched (Jn 20:25). When he saw, he believed (Jn 20:28–29). For the earliest disciples, belief was ideally not dependent on sight, but historically it was. For subsequent generations of disciples, believing could not be dependent on seeing (Jn 20:29b), but only on the testimony of eyewitnesses. So we may speak of the ideal primacy of the empty tomb as a generator of resurrection faith but of the historical primacy of the resurrection appearances.

But even a resurrection appearance was no guarantee of immediate belief. Sometimes it prompted fear and uncertainty (Lk 24:37–38) or doubt (Mt 28:17b), at least temporarily. But more often it resulted in faith (Jn 20:16, 25, 28; 21:7), joy (Lk 24:50–52; Jn 20:20), and worship (Mt 28:9, 17a; Jn 20:28).

3. The locality of the appearances

Two localities are involved—Galilee, and Jerusalem or its environs. The location is not always given, but in these cases some of the appearances may tentatively be equated with localized appearances (e.g., 1Co 15:7b = Lk 24:50–52, in Jerusalem) while others clearly occurred in or near the city of Jerusalem. However, the appearance to the 500 or so (1Co 15:6) and the appearance to James (1Co 15:7a) cannot be tied with certainty to any particular locality.

The New Testament seems to record some eleven separate appearances:

(1) to Mary Magdalene (Jn 20:11–18)—Jerusalem (J)
(2) to Mary the mother of James, and Salome (Mt 28:9–10) (J)
(3) to the two travelers on the road to Emmaus (Lk 24:13–32) (near J)
(4) to Peter (Lk 24:34; 1Co 15:5) (J)
(5) to the Eleven (and others), Thomas being absent (Lk 24:33, 36–43; Jn 20:19–23; 1Co 15:5) (J)

(6)   to the Eleven (Jn 20:26–29) (J)
(7)   to seven of the disciples (Jn 21:1–22)—Galilee (G)
(8)   to the Eleven (Mt 28:16–20) (G)
(9)   to more than 500 brethren (1Co 15:6; Lk 24:44–49) (probably J)
(10) to James (1Co 15:7a) (location uncertain)
(11) to the Eleven (Lk 24:50–52; Ac 1:6–11; 1Co 15:7b) (J).[4]

The New Testament also records three appearances of Jesus after his ascension into heaven: to Stephen (Ac 7:55–56), to Paul (Ac 9:3–7, 17, 27; 22:6–10, 14–15; 26:12–18), and to John (Rev. 1:12–18). In these instances the person who saw Jesus looked *upward* into heaven, not *outward*, as had been the case before the Ascension.

4. The historicity of the appearances

So far we have simply summarized what the New Testament tells us about the resurrection appearances of Jesus. But did they really occur, or were they in fact simply the product of the fertile imagination of excitable women or expectant disciples?

There are at least five reasons for believing that the appearances were historical.

a. According to the records, Jesus' appearances after his resurrection were extraordinarily varied, and this points to their authenticity.

We are not confronted in the resurrection narratives with a single appearance of Jesus to one individual or to a group, nor with a single distant sighting of him by one person or by many. The records point to multiple appearances—to individuals,[5] to small groups ranging in size from two to eleven persons,[6] and to at least one larger group.[7] The Christians claimed that he appeared to both men[8] and women[9]; that he appeared outside his tomb[10] and on a mountain,[11] in the city[12] and in the country,[13] by the lake[14] and in an upper room[15]; that he appeared for brief periods[16] or for longer periods[17]; that he appeared in the morning,[18] the afternoon[19] and the evening[20]; and that he engaged in a variety of activities during his appearances, such as teaching,[21] walking and talking,[22] preparing breakfast,[23] and taking food.[24]

b. The tradition of the appearances goes back to within two or three years of the events.

We have seen that 1 Corinthians 15:3b–5 contains a tradition about the death, burial, resurrection, and appearances of Jesus.[25] In verses 1–3a Paul distinguishes three "moments" in the transmission of this tradition: "I would *remind* you, brothers, of the terms in which I *preached* the gospel to you . . . for I delivered to you as of primary importance what I also had *received*. . . ." There was the time of writing when he was resident at Ephesus (c. A.D. 55), the time of his first visit to Corinth (c. A.D. 50–52), and the time when he himself had received the tradition. This latter was probably at Damascus after his conversion (c. A.D. 33), for Luke records that Paul "immediately proclaimed Jesus" (Ac 9:20) and "preached boldly in the name of Jesus" (Ac 9:27). It is difficult to imagine how Paul could have attempted to prove that Jesus was the Messiah (Ac 9:22) without knowing the rudiments of the gospel as outlined in 1 Corinthians 15:3b–5. The latest date when Paul could have received the tradition would have been c. A.D. 35, when he went up to Jerusalem from Damascus on his first post-conversion visit to the holy city (Ac 9:23–26; Gal 1:17–19) and engaged in house evangelism (Ac 9:28–29). Paul spent fifteen days with Peter and during this time he must have made certain that the gospel he was proclaiming was identical with that of the Jerusalem apostles (cf. 1Co 15:11).

If the death and resurrection of Jesus took place in A.D. 30 and Paul became aware of the tradition of the appearances to Peter and the "Twelve" (1Co 15:5) immediately after his conversion in A.D. 33, we may assume that knowledge of these appearances and others began to circulate as soon as they occurred, just as the gospel narratives themselves assert (Jn 20:18, 25).

This is significant because it demonstrates that the tradition was generated by the events themselves, for insufficient time had passed for legends to be born. The only way to account for the rise of this early, uniform tradition is to postulate actual appearances lying behind the tradition.

c. We have eyewitness testimony that Jesus was seen alive after his resurrection.

It is true that the apostle Paul is the only New Testament writer who, using the first person, says, "He appeared to me (also)" (1Co 15:8) or asks, "Have I not seen Jesus our Lord?" (1Co 9:1). But we have numerous records of the claims of various Christians that they personally saw Jesus after his resurrection, spoke with him, and ate with him.

It would be difficult to overestimate the importance of this testimony. In 1 Corinthians 15:6 Paul refers to some 500 witnesses, most of whom were still alive at the time of writing, viz. c. A.D. 55, some twenty-five years after the Resurrection. This continuous presence of eyewitnesses in the church for two or more decades after the Resurrection served to guarantee the accuracy of the traditions as they became crystallized and widely disseminated, and also had the effect of checking any tendency to create or embellish traditions. Hearing a denial of the Resurrection or some fanciful story about what Jesus did after he had risen, an eyewitness could easily refute it with the simple assertion "I know; I was there!"

In this regard, the situation of first-century eyewitnesses of the risen Jesus was not unlike that of twentieth-century survivors of the Holocaust. In 1981 a four-day gathering was held in Jerusalem of Jewish survivors of the Nazi concentration camps. About 6000 people from some twenty-three countries joined 3000 Israelis and about 800 children of survivors in "a celebration of life." Interviewed on TV, Mr. Ernest Michel, the chairman of the organizing committee and himself a survivor of the Auschwitz and Buchenwald concentration camps, attacked those who suggested that the Holocaust never took place.[26] "These hands have carried off [for burial] more corpses than I care to remember. And some say that the Holocaust never happened! We know; we were there!" What twentieth-century Jewish eyewitnesses say with grief, first-century Jewish eyewitnesses said with joy: "We know; we were there!"

d. The records indicate that Jesus appeared first to certain women.

If the sequence of appearances given above (A.3) is correct, Jesus appeared first of all to Mary Magdalene (Jn 20:11–18) and then to Mary, the mother of James, and Salome (Mt 28:9–10). Neither of these appearances is mentioned in Paul's list in 1 Corinthians 15:5–8. It was not his purpose to list all the appearances, only those of special relevance to the Corinthians. And he creates a structural balance of three individuals (Cephas = Peter, James, himself) and three groups (the Twelve, the 500, "all the apostles"). Another reason for Paul's "omission" of any reference to the women may be the fact that among the Jews of that day the testimony of women was not admissible as legal evidence except in a very few particular situations (SB 3:217, 559–60).[27] If all the traditions of Jesus' appearances were merely fabrications, a litany of lies, the privilege of being the first to see the risen Jesus would never have been given to women. So the very existence of this tradition regarding the women confirms its reliability.

e. Alternative explanations of the appearances fail to explain all of the facts and are psychologically improbable.

If the appearances were *subjective visions*,[28] we should have expected the disciples to be in a psychological condition that was conducive to hallucinations. But so far from being full of expectancy and absorbed in meditative prayer, the disciples who earlier had misunderstood Jesus' prophecies regarding his resurrection, had gathered behind locked doors for fear of the Jews (Jn 20:19). They had gloomy faces (*skythrōpoi*, Lk 24:17; cf. Jn 20:11) because the crucifixion had shattered their fondest messianic hopes (Lk 24:19–21). What is more, they greeted the first news of the Resurrection as "utter nonsense" (*lēros*, Lk 24:11). Alternatively, if the hallucinations were induced by physical conditioning such as prolonged lack of food and sleep, how are we to explain the continuation of the visions for forty days (Ac 1:3)? When a person has a visual hallucination, he or she perceives patterns of light or objects that are not recognizable by any other persons present. It is an individual, private occurrence. But the Gospels record "appearances" to groups at different times and in various places—two on the road to Emmaus in the afternoon, seven beside the sea of Galilee in the morning, ten in a house in the evening. And, with regard to Jesus' appearance to over 500 people on a single occasion, we may ask whether simultaneous, identical hallucinations are psychologically feasible. Moreover, hallucinations may account for sight, but not for sound. In the resurrection narratives the words of the risen Jesus figure prominently. He is both seen and heard. And why the initial difficulty in recognizing Jesus on at least three occasions (Lk 24:13–31; Jn 20:14–15; 21:4)? Why the abrupt halt to the visions after forty days?

Recognizing the weaknesses of the subjective vision hypothesis, some propose that God induced *objective visions* of Jesus in the consciousness of Jesus' disciples to convince them that his resurrection was a spiritual reality.[29] Advocates of this hypothesis often proceed on the assumption that the empty tomb traditions are legendary. But God can scarcely be acquitted of duplicity in initiating such "telegrams from heaven" (as they have been called) if there was no correspondence between what was "seen" (viz. Jesus in some recognizable and therefore bodily form) and what was actually true (viz. his body was decaying in some grave in Jerusalem or else had been disposed of by burning). Also, the disciples' ability to recognize Jesus, be it an immediate or a delayed recognition, is evidence not only that the same person who died had risen but also that he had risen with the same body, albeit in a transformed state. Nor does this view comport with the auditory and kinetic aspects of the appearances. It seems that Jesus never remained silent or motionless when he appeared but engaged in actions such as walking, talking, teaching, preparing food, and eating. Finally, if the appearances are explained as being "veridical hallucinations" that were telepathically induced,[30] it becomes difficult to account for the persistence of the conviction that Jesus was alive, once the psychic phenomena had ceased and the generation of eyewitnesses had passed away.

B. The Resurrection Body of Jesus

Nowhere does the New Testament give us a description of the physical features of Jesus of Nazareth. The writers are preoccupied with his character, his action, and his teaching. Nor does the situation change in the resurrection narratives, even though Jesus is alive from the dead in an immortal bodily form.

If we analyze the Gospels and Acts with regard to the nature of Christ's resurrection body, we discover two distinct sets of information, one stressing the material nature of his body, the other suggesting its nonmaterial character.

1. The materialistic statements

Mt 28:9   "They [probably Mary the mother of James, and Salome] came up to him, clasped his feet, and worshiped him."

Lk 24:15   "Jesus himself overtook them and began to walk along with them."

Lk 24:39   "Look at my hands and my feet and you will see that it is I myself. Touch me and understand, because a ghost does not have flesh and bones, as you see I have."

Lk 24:43   "He took it [a piece of broiled fish] and ate it before their eyes."

Lk 24:50–51   "He led them out to the vicinity of Bethany, lifted up his hands, and gave them a blessing. And as he was in the act of blessing them, he departed from them and was taken up into heaven."

Jn 20:20   "He showed them his hands and side."

Jn 20:27   "Then he said to Thomas, 'Put your finger here and look at my hands. Reach out your hand and place it in my side.'"

Ac 1:4   "And while he was eating with them . . ."

Ac 10:41   ". . . to us . . . who ate and drank with him after he rose from the dead."

In addition to these specific verses, there is the general testimony of the Evangelists that Jesus engaged in the normal human activities of walking (e.g., Mt 28:18; Lk 24:15, 28, 50) and talking (e.g., Mt 28:9–10, 18–20; Lk 24:17, 25–27). We have already noted that he was recognized by his followers when he appeared to them after his resurrection because of such individual features as his tone of voice, his bodily movements, and the marks of the crucifixion. When he appeared, Jesus stood on *terra firma*, was not suspended in the air; his body was solid, not ephemeral, and tangible, not immaterial.

2. The nonmaterialistic statements

Lk 24:31	"He disappeared from their sight."
Lk 24:36	"While they were still reporting this, Jesus himself stood among them."
Lk 24:44	"This was the meaning of my words which I spoke to you while I was still with you."
Jn 20:19	"Although the doors were locked for fear of the Jews, Jesus came and stood among them."
Jn 20:26	"Although the doors were locked, Jesus came and stood among them."
Ac 1:3	". . . appearing to them at intervals over the course of forty days."
Ac 10:40–41a	"God raised him up on the third day, and permitted him to become visible, not to all the people, but to us . . ."

Also of relevance here is the verbal form *ōphthē*. In the Greek of Plato's day it generally meant "he was seen," but in New Testament times it gained an intransitive sense, "he appeared," "he became visible."[31] On nine occasions the word describes an appearance of the risen Christ.[32] Although the same word is used of the appearance of God (Ac 7:2), of angels (Lk 1:11; 22:43; Ac 7:30, 35), of Moses and Elijah (Mt 17:3; Mk 9:4; Lk 9:31), and of Moses (Ac 7:26), no instance is a precise parallel, for Jesus appeared in bodily form, at his own initiative, and for the purpose of revealing himself and his will.

Neither of these two sets of data should be overlooked. But some writers have done so, declaring either that Jesus' resurrection body was a normal physical body of flesh and blood or that the Resurrection enabled him to return to his pre-incarnate state as a purely spiritual being. Although both of these solutions must be rejected, we should not imagine that any solution that accommodates both sets of data is necessarily "correct" and authoritative. We are here gently probing a mystery, for Jesus was the first person to rise immortal in a spiritual body.

There are three main solutions.

(i)   Jesus' resurrection body was basically "material," or "fleshly" but either was capable of temporary demate-rialization or had nonmaterial properties.[33]

(ii) In his resurrected state Jesus possessed a "spiritual body" which could be expressed in an immaterial or a material mode.[34]

(iii) His body was in the process of transition from the material to the spiritual during the forty days of appearances.[35]

Each of these hypotheses does justice to the diverse data of the New Testament, so that no one of them should be dismissed as unorthodox.

On the second view, which the present writer espouses, the resurrection of Jesus was not his transformation into an immaterial body but his acquisition of a "spiritual body" which could materialize or dematerialize at will. When, on occasion, Jesus chose to appear to various persons in material form, this was just as really the "spiritual body" of Jesus as when he was not visible or tangible. In each instance it was his body and was "spiritual," so that he was not guilty of deception when he affirmed "See my hands and my feet, that it is I myself" (Lk 24:39). As opposed to angels who by nature are disembodied spirits (Heb. 1:14) yet can materialize (Heb. 1:7), the risen Jesus is a permanently embodied Spirit who, during the forty days, occasionally became visible to human eyes and palpable to human touch. After the forty days, when his appearances on earth were ended, Jesus assumed the sole mode of being visible to the inhabitants of heaven but having a nonfleshly body. Diagramatically, we might express it thus.

Resurrection body of Jesus during the forty days from an earthly perspective

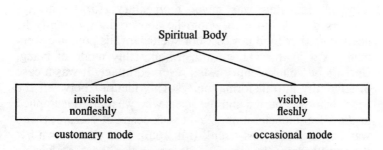

Resurrection body of Jesus after the forty days from a heavenly perspective

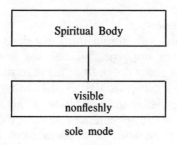

Several related questions clamor for an answer. What was the relation between Christ's bodily state before the Resurrection and his mode of existence after the Resurrection? A review of the properties of his resurrection body makes it clear that a radical transformation had occurred. In his risen state he transcended the normal laws of physical existence. He was no longer bound by material or spatial limitations. He could pass through a sealed tomb (this is implied by Mt 28:2, 6) and through closed doors (Jn 20:19, 26). He was "transported" without physical movement (e.g., "Jesus stood among them," Lk 24:36; Jn 20:19, 26) so that generally there was no spatial approach or withdrawal (but see Lk 24:15). He appeared and he disappeared in an instant (Lk 24:31, 36)—although his stay was never momentary, for he always conversed with those to whom he appeared. Apparently he needed neither food nor rest nor shelter for his personal well-being. Yet in this change into a nonearthly mode of being, Christ's personal identity was preserved intact. It was a case of "identity-in-transformation."[36] This identity between the Jesus who was buried and the Jesus who was raised is implied in the angelic declaration, "You seek Jesus of Nazareth who was crucified. He has risen" (Mk 16:6). It is also shown by: the empty tomb; the marks of the crucifixion that were visible at least on two occasions when he appeared (Lk 24:39–40 = Jn 20:20; Jn 20:27); a familiar set of actions in "the breaking of the bread" (Lk 24:30–31, 35); and a familiar tone of voice (Jn 20:16).

Our second question is this. If Jesus was not normally visible to human eyes during the forty days, where was he when he was not appearing? Later we shall see that the enthronement of Jesus dates from his resurrection (Mt 28:18; Ac 2:32–33 and see below, VIII.B.3) and that the subsequent Ascension is the visible dramatization of this invisible reality. If this is so, all of the appearances lie on the other side of the exaltation of Jesus, and he appears from heaven, as the triumphant plenipotentiary of God. It was the Resurrection, not the Ascension, that marked the terminus of Christ's sojourn on earth—else his resurrection would have been a mere resumption of earthly existence. We do not need, therefore, to surmise the whereabouts of Jesus between his various appearances.

If the resurrection body of Jesus no more required food to sustain its strength than it needed rest to regain strength, why did Jesus take food during some of his appearances (Lk 24:41–43; Ac 10:41; cf. Lk 24:40; Jn 21:12–13)? It is an established principle of learning that the new can be appreciated and understood only by means of, and in relation to, the old. As the possessor of a spiritual body which had remarkably different properties from any "body" the disciples already knew, Jesus faced the challenge of proving his reality and introducing his disciples to a phenomenon beyond their experience and imagination. Not surprisingly, when Jesus suddenly appeared among the disciples (Lk 24:36 = Jn 20:19), they at first imagined he was a bodiless spirit who had returned from the unseen world and assumed a visible form as a ghost (Lk 24:37). To calm their fears and assure them of his identity, he invited them to look at the scars from his crucifixion and thus know "that it is I myself," to handle him and so understand that he was no bodiless spirit (Lk 24:39). Then, because they were "still disbelieving for sheer joy and were lost in wonder," he asked for something to eat (Lk 24:41), not to satisfy his hunger or meet his physical needs, but to reassure them of his reality. Luke emphasizes the evidential purpose of Jesus' action by noting that he ate "before their eyes," "in front of them" (*enōpion autōn*, Lk 24:43).

Finally, why did the risen Jesus sometimes invite certain disciples to touch him, or permit their doing so, yet at other times prohibit it? Perhaps the answer lies in the particular need of the disciple. The Ten, who thought the risen Lord was a ghost or some incorporeal being (Lk 24:37–40), and Thomas, who deemed the Resurrection to be impossible (Jn 20:24–27), were invited to handle Jesus. He permitted Mary and Salome to clasp his feet as an expression of their worship (Mt 28:9). But to Mary Magdalene, who imagined that Jesus had already ascended to his Father and who wished to perpetuate her former relationship with him, Jesus firmly says, "Stop clinging to me! (*mē mou haptou*), for I have not yet ascended to the Father" (Jn 20:17). Her spiritual relationship with him was not to be compromised by preoccupation with externals.

We conclude that the theory of a resuscitation and transformation of the crucified body of Jesus more adequately accommodates the data of the appearances than does any alternative explanation. But like the empty tomb, the appearances do not conclusively "prove" that Jesus rose from the dead. The fact of the Resurrection remains an inference— although a necessary one—from the fact of the appearances. Yet these appearances afford more direct evidence of the Resurrection than does the empty tomb, since resurrection is only one of several possible interpretations of the empty tomb, whereas only one inference may be drawn from the appearances. So although the appearances no more compelled faith than did the discovery of the empty tomb, they did induce faith more readily.

C. The Credibility of the Records

A detailed assessment of the historical reliability of the four gospels is not possible here, so our remarks will of necessity be general and restricted to the resurrection stories. But mention should be made of C. L. Blomberg's convincing defense of the Gospels' trustworthiness entitled *The Historical Reliability of the Gospels*,[37] which itself is a popularization and extension of a massive six-volume series entitled *Gospel Perspectives*, produced at Tyndale House, Cambridge (U.K.).[38]

All four resurrection narratives have a self-authenticating character. The reader cannot help being impressed by the extraordinary sobriety of the four gospel writers as they relate what from any perspective, must, if true, have been the most stupendous event ever to occur in human history. The most notable characteristics of Mark's narrative (16:1–8)[39] are its remarkable restraint and indirectness. There is no explanation of how or why the stone was removed. It is only implied, not explicitly stated, that the tomb was empty (v. 6b). The supernatural character of the messenger (v. 5) is not directly affirmed (cf. Mt 28:2, 5; Lk 24:4), although it is clearly hinted at in the description of the "young man" as dressed in white, in the revelatory content of the message (v. 6), and in the response of the women (agitation and awe, vv. 5–6). There is no description of the Resurrection itself. It was not witnessed by human beings and is not announced until verse 6. As it stands, the record contains no resurrection appearance of Jesus, although one is implied in verse 7. The bold, blunt announcement "he has [just] risen, he is not here" (v. 6) gives no precise details of the time or means of Jesus' resurrection or of his present location.

Although John's account of the discovery of the empty tomb, like Mark's, is remarkably restrained and unadorned, it pulsates with a vitality unmatched by any other New Testament resurrection narrative. Among the verbs that depict the action in these ten verses (Jn 20:1–10) there are eight "historic presents," nine aorists, and two imperfects. The result is a racy style that suitably reflects the trembling excitement of eager expectation and then momentous discovery. Verses 3 and 4 illustrate the point: "So Peter left the house with the other disciple and they set off for the tomb. And they broke into a run, the two of them, side by side, but that other disciple outstripped Peter and was the first to arrive at the tomb."

If the Gospels were legendary fabrications, we may rest assured that at least one of the Evangelists would not have missed the opportunity of depicting the actual resurrection and of adorning the narrative with fantastic features befitting the scene. We now know, in fact, of some celebrated early Christian attempts to rectify these "omissions." In "The Testament of Hezekiah" (= The Ascension of Isaiah 2:13b–4:18) that may be dated about A.D. 100, we read the prophecy:

> the angel of the Holy Spirit and Michael, the chief of the holy angels, will open his [Jesus'] grave on the third day, and that the Beloved [= Jesus], sitting on their shoulders,

will come forth and send out his twelve disciples, and that they will teach to all the nations and every tongue the resurrection of the Beloved (3:16–18a).[40]

In the fragmentary Gospel of Peter (mid-second century A.D.) we read:

Now in the night in which the Lord's day dawned, when the soldiers, two by two in every watch, were keeping guard, there rang out a loud voice in heaven, and they saw the heavens opened and two men come down from there in a great brightness and draw nigh to the sepulchre. That stone which had been laid against the entrance to the sepulchre started of itself to roll and gave way to the side, and the sepulchre was opened, and both the young men entered in. When now those soldiers saw this, they awakened the centurion and the elders—for they also were there to assist at the watch. And whilst they were relating what they had seen, they saw again three men come out from the sepulchre, and two of them sustaining the other, and a cross following them, and the heads of the two reaching to heaven, but that of him who was led of them by the hand overpassing the heavens. And they heard a voice out of the heavens crying, "Thou hast preached to them that sleep," and from the cross there was heard the answer, "Yea" (35–42).[41]

Another notable account of the actual resurrection of Jesus is found in the reading of the Old Latin codex Bobiensis (dating from the fourth or fifth century A.D.) at the beginning of Mark 16:4:

But suddenly at the third hour of the day there was darkness over the whole circle of the earth, and angels descended from the heavens, and as he (the Lord) was rising (reading *surgente eo*) in the glory of the living God, at the same time they ascended with him; and immediately it was light.[42]

Then there is the London Text (K²) of the Coptic work "The Book of the Resurrection of Jesus Christ, by Bartholomew the Apostle" that may date from the sixth or seventh century A.D., in which Death engages in a dialogue with the corpse of Jesus on the "second day" (the Saturday). On being asked "Who are you?" Jesus removes the napkin from his face and laughs at Death, who then flees away along with his sons. After this has happened again, Jesus rises in the chariot of the cherubim.[43]

In the light of these four examples, the silence of the gospels regarding the actual rising of Jesus and the absence of fantastic features are eloquent testimony to the veracity of the gospel records and therefore to the Resurrection. It would indeed have been four sophisticated and extraordinary fabricators who suppressed their literary instinct to describe the Resurrection itself and to depict the disciples as reacting enthusiastically to the news of the empty tomb and the appearances of Jesus, all purely in the interests of verisimilitude! If the stories were fabricated, we should have expected the number of miracles performed by Jesus to have increased markedly once he gained "all authority in heaven and on earth" (cf. Mt 28:18), but in fact only one miracle is recorded as having occurred during a resurrection appearance (viz. Jn 21:6). Another hint of the Gospels' "ring of truth" we have already mentioned—the prominent place accorded to women in the resurrection narratives. Three women were the first witnesses of the empty tomb. In addition, of these three, Mary (the mother of James and Jesus) and Salome were granted the first angelic appearance and announcement, and Mary Magdalene the first appearance of Jesus. Given the fact that according to Jewish principles women were legally unqualified to serve as witnesses except in rare situations, it seems incredible that a fabricator would create an apologetic embarrassment by granting the primacy to women in these three important matters.

D. Other Evidence for the Resurrection as Verifiable History

Here we shall discuss evidence of a more general nature that affords powerful support to the testimony of the New Testament itself about the Resurrection.

Only the Resurrection adequately explains *the existence and survival of the church*. Any movement's "papers of association" must be taken seriously in seeking to trace its rise. The early Christians traced the origin of their movement to one event, and only one—the resurrection of Christ. That explanation should stand until historical investigation shows it to be inadequate. But it is the other possible explanations that prove inadequate. Neither in Greek philosophy nor in Jewish theology can we find the stimulus for Easter faith. Gentile philosophers scorned the notion of resurrection, while there was no precedent in Jewish thought for a permanent resurrection from the dead before the Last Day. The doubt of the disciples in the face of the announced Resurrection (Lk 24:11) and the persistent skepticism of Thomas (Jn 20:25) lead us to dismiss the contention that the disciples were gullible fantasizers whose hopes created a resurrected Master. It was not the church that mothered the Resurrection; it was the Resurrection that mothered the church. As to the survival of the church, would so improbable a conviction as belief in the resurrection of a crucified Messiah have enabled the church to remain distinct from its parent Judaism unless that belief corresponded to reality?[44]

We should also note *the transformation of the disciples*. Some potent cause must be found to explain the radical conversion of Jesus' disciples from frightened cowards who fled in panic when Jesus was arrested (Mk 14:50) to courageous witnesses who could not be silenced by the Jewish Sanhedrin (Ac 5:17–41). First Corinthians 15:5 suggests the cause: "he appeared to the Twelve." The famous Cambridge classical scholar, T. R. Glover, once remarked:

> Great results have great causes. We have to find, some-
> where or other, between the crucifixion and the first
> preaching of the disciples in Jerusalem, something that
> entirely changed the character of that group of men. . . .
> The evidence for the Resurrection is not so much what we
> read in the Gospels as what we find in the rest of the New
> Testament—the new life of the disciples.[45]

And how else shall we adequately account for the dramatic
about-face of Saul of Tarsus, at one moment a ruthless
exterminator of Christians (Ac 26:11), but at the next a
champion of the messiahship of Jesus and an indefatigable
pioneer missionary (Ac 9:1–30), unless it be that the risen
Jesus appeared to him (1Co 15:8)?

Some momentous occurrence is needed to explain *the early
Christian change from the Sabbath to Sunday as the principal
day of worship.* Particularly during the "intertestamental
period" (c. 200 B.C.–A.D. 100) there were three characteristics
of the Jews that marked them out as distinctive from other
nations—the practice of circumcision, the observance of
dietary laws, and preeminently, the keeping of the Sabbath.
The intensity of Jewish commitment to the Sabbath may be
illustrated by two facts. The twenty-four hours from 6:00 P.M.
Thursday to 6:00 P.M. Friday was called "the Day of
Preparation" (Lk 23:54; Jn 19:31, 42; cf. Jubilees 2:29), that
is, the day when tasks (including essential tasks such as
cooking) were performed in advance of the Sabbath, so that
cessation from labor might be strictly observed on the holy
day. Secondly, a myriad of regulations grew up around the
Sabbath and formed a "hedge" around the fourth command-
ment, protecting people from any possible infringement of this
law. At a later period the Jewish Talmud specified some
thirty-nine types of work that were not permissible on the
Sabbath. Although Jesus disapproved of the numerous man-
made regulations that had become attached to Sabbath
keeping (e.g., Mk 2:23–3:6), he regularly attended the synagogue on the Sabbath (e.g., Mk 1:21; Lk 4:16).

With the Jewish reverence for the Sabbath and with the
example of Jesus, it would have been perfectly natural for the
early Christians, as loyal Jews who were zealous for the law of
Moses (Ac 21:20), to have formalized the Sabbath as the day
of Christian worship. But the reverse was in fact the case.
Although at first the Christians in Jerusalem met daily in the
temple for worship (Ac 2:46; 5:42) and observed the Sabbath,
"the first day of the week" gained special significance at an
early date (Jn 20:19, 26). To judge from Acts 20, by c. A.D. 57
Sunday had become, at least in Asia Minor, the regular day
for Christians to gather to celebrate the Lord's Supper (Ac
20:7).[46] Early in the second century A.D., Ignatius of Antioch
noted that "those who followed ancient customs [= the Jews]
have come to a new hope, no longer celebrating the Sabbath
but observing the Lord's Day, the day on which our life
sprang up through Christ" (*To the Magnesians* 9:1; similarly
Epistle of Barnabas 15:9), and Pliny, the Roman governor of
Pontus-Bithynia, informed the emperor Trajan that the Christians met "on a certain fixed day [= Sunday] before
daybreak" (*Epistles* X. 96–97), the latter phrase clearly
alluding to the hour of Christ's resurrection. That is, the
"momentous occurrence" that triggered the change in the
Christians' day of meeting was nothing other than the
Resurrection. Sunday was termed "the Lord's Day" (Rev.
1:10) because it was the day when the Lord Jesus rose and the
day when Christians gathered to worship the Lord. So
dramatic was the change, so powerful was the Resurrection,
that Paul, the ardent Pharisee who had been thoroughly
trained in every point of Jewish ancestral law (Ac 22:3), could
link the weekly Sabbath with annual festivals and monthly
new moons as all being "merely a shadow of what was to
come" (Col 2:16–17).

Finally, we should not overlook *the testimony of Christian
believers*. Historically speaking, this has probably induced
more conversions to Christ and Christianity than all other
evidences of the Resurrection combined, for here the Resur-

rection is imprinted for all to see on the living tablets of human lives. Christians claim that Jesus lives because he produces and sustains beneficial change in the whole fabric of their lives—thinking, feeling, willing, and acting.

Our assessment of the relevant historical evidence, both within and outside the New Testament, has led us to the firm conclusion that Jesus appeared to certain persons after his death in a recognizable, material, but transformed bodily form.

VII

Objections to the Resurrection as Verifiable History

Before we go on to discuss the aspect of the Resurrection that is not based on evidence that can be examined by the historian, we should pause to consider briefly some of the main objections that have been raised against the belief that Jesus rose from the dead in a transformed body.

A. Philosophical Objections

1. "No events are absolutely verifiable." Some have asserted that because the historian can never reach absolute certainty about any event, Christian belief in the Resurrection must remain correspondingly insecure if it rests on the results of historical research.[1]

It is true that historians aim at establishing probabilities, not certainties. If we demanded irrefutable proof for every event before we believed it, we would necessarily become thorough-going historical skeptics, believing nothing about the past. But why should we impose an exceptional standard in the case of evidence for the Resurrection, insisting that only conclusively demonstrable evidence merits complete faith? Faith in the risen Jesus cannot be pronounced either insecure or illegitimate merely because the historical basis for the Resurrection cannot be proved with certainty. Provided that basis can be shown to be secure, resting on a high degree of probability, the faith is valid. But if the basis can be shown to be inadequate, the faith is useless. Paul affirms this principle in 1 Corinthians 15:17, "If Christ has not been raised, your faith is futile." So then, faith and history are interrelated. Faith in a risen Jesus, however generated, derives its validity from the fact that Jesus rose from the dead. Although the historian cannot conclusively establish that fact, he can adduce persuasive evidences that show this to be by far the most plausible interpretation of all the relevant data, well able to sustain the full weight of total faith.

2. "Miraculous occurrences should be ruled out as impossible on *a priori* grounds." In other words, because the notion of resurrection flies in the face of natural law and historical observation, the resurrection of Jesus could not have occurred. "An historical fact which involves a resurrection from the dead is utterly inconceivable."[2]

No one will contest that the Resurrection was an exception to an observed regularity in the natural sphere: that persons who die do not return to life. However, the exclusion of the possibility of resurrection on an *a priori* basis, before the historical data are examined, is an arbitrary procedure that assumes that science has conclusively defined all natural laws. Surely it is more scientific to examine the available historical evidence and then determine what is or is not within the bounds of possibility rather than to decide in advance that a resurrection could not have occurred and therefore conclude that Christ's resurrection did not occur. Ideally, all science and historiography is inductive, first ascertaining all the relevant facts and then drawing conclusions. What proves to be exceptional cannot be labeled unreal or nonhistorical. There is a sense in which every historical event is unique in that the combination of circumstances that produced the event at a particular time in a particular form will never be repeated. The Resurrection, however, is "uniquely unique," since human history affords no analogy or precedent for a dead person's acquisition of immortal life. Yet even this fact does not automatically make the Resurrection nonhistorical.[3]

B. Historical Objections

1. "The proven theological tendency of the Gospels points to their historical unreliability." In this view the Resurrection is called into question as a historical event on the ground that the documents which describe it are tendentious, having a theological orientation that sits loose to history.

Few will want to deny that the resurrection narratives, like the Gospels as a whole, are "confessional history" or "kerygmatic history." They reflect the church in its worship and preaching. They were not written to satisfy the curiosity of the detached historian but to induce or strengthen faith in Christ. This theological purpose need not, however, prejudice the historical reliability of the narratives. History as "uninterpreted fact" or history without presuppositions or purposes is now recognized to be a myth. When we isolate an apologetic interest in the Matthean resurrection narratives or a eucharistic emphasis in Luke or a confessional interest in John, we are not calling into question the accuracy of what they record; we are demonstrating that fact, interpretation, and literary purpose are inseparably interwoven in all writing of history.

2. "The discrepancies between the resurrection narratives in the four gospels establish the non-historicity of the Resurrection itself."[4] W. Marxsen, for example, arrived at the verdict "that the stories contradict one another, that they cannot be harmonized and that they therefore cannot be historical."[5] Since this is the most commonly voiced objection, it merits more detailed consideration.

That there are, at first sight, numerous inconsistencies between the four gospels at this point will be obvious to anyone who has examined the texts. We may try to account for the variations by pointing to the fragmentary nature of local traditions or the editorial activity of each Evangelist as he molded inherited traditions to serve his particular theological purpose. But merely to account for the presence of the differences is not to rebut the charge that they are so substantial and so numerous that harmonization is impossible. Some minimize the differences and call them insignificant. Some emphasize the differences but claim that from the perspective of faith the alleged facts of Easter, be they harmonious or inconsistent, are in the last resort matters of indifference. Others point to the differences as indirect evidence of historicity. The very difficulty of harmonizing the accounts points, it is said, to the absence of the collusion between the Evangelists that would have been needed if a lie were to be substantiated. It also indicates the reliability of the accounts, since fabricated stories would tend to be harmonized before publication.

How are we to deal with these apparent discrepancies? Two points should be made. The first is that the presence of discrepancies in circumstantial detail is no proof that the central fact is unhistorical. Even if there are contradictions between the resurrection narratives, the bodily resurrection of Jesus from the grave is not thereby disproved. We may illustrate our point thus. It is well known that the Greek historian Polybius (iii. 50–56) and the Roman historian Livy (xxi. 31–37) disagree in the description of the route of Hannibal as he crossed the Alps into Italy during the second Punic war. Commenting on Livy xxi. 31.9, W. W. Capes observes that

> from this point onwards it is hopeless to reconcile the accounts of the march in Polybius and Livy, who while agreeing in much of the description, especially in the details which admit of rhetorical treatment, yet widely diverge in local data. The former traces the route almost certainly over the little St. Bernard, the latter probably over Mont Genèvre.[6]

In discussing this vexing problem, some commentators have claimed that one account or the other is in error since the two narratives are irreconcilable; others have been content to let the apparent inconsistency stand, recognizing the relatively fragmentary nature of the data; while others have resorted to conjectural emendation in an effort to eradicate the differences. But no modern writer (to my knowledge) has doubted the reality of Hannibal's passage over the Alps with soldiers, horses, and elephants on the basis of the difficulty of reconciling Polybius with Livy.

Or take another example from ancient history. Among the writers who record the circumstances of the Great Fire of Rome of A.D. 64, there is disagreement about the precise whereabouts of Nero when he "fiddled" while Rome burned. Tacitus places him on the stage of his private theater, Suetonius locates the exhibition in the tower of Maecenas, whereas Dio Cassius says it took place on the palace roof.[7] Yet, for all these irreconcilable differences, no historian of the principate of Nero doubts that he played the lyre and sang while the city was ablaze.

Our second point is this. A harmonization of the resurrection narratives is not impossible, at least in principle. There is at present a strong antipathy among New Testament scholars to the procedure of harmonization, although it is a recognized literary tool, employed by all historians, whether they are recording and interpreting events or tracing the history of ideas.[8] Harmonization operates on two fundamental literary principles: (i) the assumption of "innocence"; (ii) the complexity of "truth."

(i)   Any two accounts of the same incident or phenomenon written by independent authors or even by the same author on different occasions are bound to exhibit some differences; indeed, the presence of apparent or actual discrepancies is *a priori* evidence of noncollusion. Given these probable differences, it is appropriate and fair to give a writer who purports to be truthful the benefit of the doubt and to begin by assuming his accuracy or consistency rather than to assume that he is "guilty until proven innocent" and thereby arbitrarily to impugn his veracity or self-consistency before the data are examined.

(ii) Where two or more accounts of the same incident or phenomenon seem to differ or actually do differ in matters of detail or substance, the truth is as likely to be found in both accounts as in one, for "truth" in the realm of history as in the realm of thought is more often complex than simple.

Of course, forced harmonization is to be rejected.[9] Better to acknowledge differences between writers' purposes or to appeal to paucity of data or to create a historical or theological "suspense account" of unresolved problems than to propound a highly improbable harmonization. With regard to the resurrection narratives, the fact that no two efforts at harmonization will totally agree is a testimony, not to the impropriety of the task or the blatantly contradictory nature of the evidence, but merely to the paucity of the data and the evident lack of collusion between the witnesses. Having made these introductory remarks, we may set down a tentative harmony of the resurrection narratives,[10] hoping that it may validate our basic point that a harmonization of the records is not an impossibility.[11]

(1) After the actual resurrection had taken place, but before dawn, an earthquake occurred, an angel rolled away the stone from the entrance of the tomb, and the guards trembled and fled (Mt 28:2–4).

(2) As Sunday morning was dawning, Mary Magdalene, Mary the mother of James and Joses, and Salome approached the tomb, intending to anoint Jesus with the perfumed oil brought by other women who evidently set

out later (see #7). To their amazement they found the stone rolled away (Mt 28:1; Mk 16:1–4; Jn 20:1).

(3) One or more of the women entered the tomb and announced that the body was not there (an inference from Jn 20:2, where Mary Magdalene does not simply say, "The stone has been taken away").

(4) Mary Magdalene immediately returned to tell Peter and John that the body had been removed (Jn 20:2).

(5) Mary (the mother of James) and Salome saw an angel (= "a young man" in Mark) inside the tomb who announced the Resurrection and directed the women to tell the disciples that Jesus would meet them in Galilee (Mt 28:5–7; Mk 16:5–7).

(6) These two women returned to the city without greeting anyone on the way, for their holy awe rendered them temporarily speechless (Mt 28:8; Mk 16:8).

(7) Certain women from Galilee, along with Joanna (cf. Lk 8:3), arrived at the tomb, carrying perfumed oil to anoint the body of Jesus. They met two "men" (= "angels"; cf. Lk 24:4, 23) and then returned to report the angels' message of the resurrection "to the Eleven and to all the rest" (Lk 24:1–9, 22–23) who had evidently now gathered together (cf. Mt 26:56).[12]

(8) Meanwhile, informed by Mary Magdalene, Peter and John (and others? Lk 24:24) ran to the tomb (without meeting Mary and Salome), observed the graveclothes, and returned home (Jn 20:3–10; and Lk 24:12, if this is the true text).

(9)   Mary Magdalene followed Peter and John to the tomb,
        saw two angels inside, and then met Jesus (Jn 20:11–17;
        cf. Mk 16:9).

(10)   Mary Magdalene returned to inform the disciples that
        Jesus had risen (Jn 20:18; cf. Mk 16:10–11).

(11)   Mary (the mother of James) and Salome met Jesus and
        were directed to tell his brethren to go to Galilee (Mt
        28:9–10).

(12)   The disciples had now had reports concerning the
        empty tomb or the Resurrection from three sources
        (viz. Mary Magdalene; Joanna and the women from
        Galilee; Mary [and Salome]), but they refused to believe
        these reports (Lk 24:10–11; cf. Mk 16:11).

(13)   During the afternoon Jesus appeared to two disciples on
        the way to Emmaus. They then returned to Jerusalem to
        report the appearance to the Eleven and others (Lk
        24:13–35; cf. Mk 16:12–13).

(14)   Jesus appeared to Peter (Lk 24:34; 1Co 15:5).

(15)   That evening Jesus appeared to the Eleven and others
        (Lk 24:33), Thomas being absent (Lk 24:36–43; Jn
        20:19–23; 1Co 15:5; cf. Mk 16:14).

(16)   One week later Jesus appeared to the Eleven, Thomas
        being present (Jn 20:26–29).

(17)   Seven disciples had an encounter with Jesus by the Sea
        of Tiberias in Galilee (Jn 21:1–22).

(18)   The Eleven met Jesus on a mountain in Galilee (Mt
        28:16–20; cf. Mk 16:15–18).

(19)   Jesus appeared to more than five hundred brethren (1Co 15:6; Lk 24:44–49).

(20)   He appeared to James (1Co 15:7).

(21)   Immediately before his ascension, Jesus appeared to the Eleven near Bethany (Lk 24:50–52; Ac 1:6–11; 1Co 15:7; cf. Mk 16:19–20).

If someone objects that this makes the day of the resurrection (#1–15) incredibly complicated, we should note that the day's events began about 5:30 A.M. and continued until dark, and that, given the stupendous nature of the occurrence, it is no surprise that there was a flurry of excited activity.

Although the various objections to the Resurrection must be faced with all seriousness, they are insufficiently strong to overthrow the "firm conclusion" already arrived at—that Jesus rose from the dead and appeared to various persons in bodily form.

VIII

Resurrection *to* Glory at God's Right Hand: Item of Faith

Thus far in our discussion we have been employing all the techniques normally used by the historian or the lawyer in evaluating evidence. In this chapter we move out of the domain of historically verifiable evidence into the realm of faith. Our focus of interest has changed from the question "Was the tomb empty?" to "Who emptied the tomb?" From "Did Jesus rise from the dead and appear to certain individuals?" to "What did his Resurrection signify?" As in the last three chapters, the information supplied by the New Testament is foundational, but here that information will be subjected to theological reflection, not historical evaluation. When the New Testament writers claim or imply that God vindicated and exalted Jesus by raising him up from the dead to a position of honor in heaven, all that the historian can do is to investigate whether that claim was made, not whether it is true. If we accept the truth of the claim, it will be because it is an article of faith taught in Scripture, not because impartial historical investigation has demonstrated its probable truth.

A. The Resurrection as God's Vindication of Christ

It has always been typical of God that he vindicates his people. "He will make your vindication shine like the dawn, the justice of your cause like the sun at noonday" (Ps 37:6; cf. 135:14). This is particularly true for those who are obedient to his will and those who are oppressed. "The Lord GOD has opened my ears, and I have not been rebellious, I have not turned back. . . . He who vindicates me is near" (Isa 50:5, 8a). "The LORD works vindication and justice for all the oppressed" (Ps 103:6; cf. Isa 62:1–2 RSV). It comes as no surprise, then, to discover that the early church viewed the Resurrection as God's vindication of his obedient and oppressed Son.

1. The Resurrection vindicated the messiahship of Jesus

In the estimation of any Jew of the first century A.D. who knew the Law, the crucifixion of Jesus amounted to far more than the Roman infliction of the death penalty on a fellow Jew. Their Scriptures taught them that any man "hanged on a tree" was the object of a divine curse (Dt 21:22–23).[1] A crucified Messiah was a contradiction in terms and therefore a stumbling block (1Co 1:23). Little wonder that the early church soon confronted the Jewish taunt "Jesus is cursed" (1Co 12:3) and that later Jewry referred to Jesus as "the hanged one"! For there to be any reversal of this verdict, the initiative must come from the One who pronounced the curse, God himself. It was precisely he who had raised Jesus from the dead, so claimed Peter on the Day of Pentecost (Ac 2:23–24). The verdict, "Jesus is cursed," had once seemed inevitable and proper in the light of the Law. But now, in the light of the Resurrection, this verdict was seen to be ultimately false (cf. Gal 3:13). In its place stood the final, divine verdict, "Jesus is Lord and Messiah" (cf. Ac 2:36). Through the Resurrection the stone rejected by human builders had become the cornerstone of God's spiritual house (Ac 4:10–11; cf. 1Pe 2:4–7).

Throughout his public ministry Jesus had discouraged the open declaration of his messiahship (e.g., Mk 8:29–30) lest his messianic purpose of suffering for sin should be thwarted by the common people who held vigorously nationalistic and militaristic views of the Messiah (cf. PS 17:21–25; John 6:15). Yet he acknowledged his messiahship when confessed by others (Mt 16:16–17), and sometimes dramatized his claim to be Messiah by acted parables such as the feeding of the five thousand, the triumphal entry into Jerusalem, or the cleansing of the temple, parables that were transparent to the spiritually sensitive but opaque to those who were spiritually obtuse. For those with eyes to see, Jesus had received divine accreditation by his "mighty works, wonders and signs" (Ac 2:22). But such accreditation was canceled in the eyes of even responsive Jews when Jesus was crucified, for this was proof that he had been rejected by God. But the Resurrection was the great divine reversal. The same One who had once declared "a hanged man is accursed" (Dt 21:23) now declared "this hanged man is accepted" (cf. Ac 3:14–15). He whom man rejected, God accepted and installed as his Messiah, no longer Messiah-elect or simply Messiah by right, but Messiah in reality. Since the God-appointed messianic destiny remained unfulfilled until Jesus had suffered, it was only after and because of his suffering that he could be acknowledged as Messiah in reality.[2] At his trial before the Sanhedrin, the high priest asked Jesus, "Are you the Messiah, the Son of the Blessed?" In reply Jesus spoke of a time when his hearers would witness his "sitting at the right hand of Power, and coming with the clouds of heaven" (Mk 14:62). There may be an allusion here to the vindication of Jesus' messiahship in certain imminent events, notably his resurrection (note "you will see the Son of Man sitting . . ."). But such a reference certainly does not exhaust the meaning of the saying, for the order of the phrases places the "coming" after the "sitting," so that the primary allusion must be to the Parousia of the Son of Man as universal judge, a "coming" that will finally vindicate Jesus before men.

2. The Resurrection vindicated and confirmed the sonship of Jesus

During his ministry Jesus laid claim to an intimate and unique relation to God (e.g., Mt 11:27). He summed it up in the term "Abba" ("dear Father") by which he addressed or referred to God, and in the title "Son" or "Son of God" by which he sometimes referred to himself (e.g., Mk 12:6; 13:32) or others sometimes referred to him (e.g., Mt 16:16; 27:54). What Jesus had always been, although in hidden form, the Resurrection openly declared him to be, namely, the Son of God. Paul describes the gospel of God as being "about his Son, Jesus Christ our Lord: with regard to his physical descent, he was born of David's line; he was designated Son of God with power by the Spirit of holiness as a result of the resurrection of the dead" (Ro 1:3–4). In these two verses the apostle is defining the two successive stages of Christ's "career." His earthly existence had its beginning in his descent from David, whereas his open installation as Son of God came about at the time of, and because of his resurrection from the dead (*ex anastaseōs nekrōn*).[3] It was not the sonship of Christ but his sonship "with power" that was inaugurated by the Resurrection, for elsewhere Paul teaches that Jesus was God's Son before the Resurrection occurred (e.g., Ro 8:3, 32; Gal 4:4). Through the Resurrection what previously had been a secret reserved for the few (e.g., Mk 9:2, 7, 9) became an open secret clear for all to see. For the enemies of Jesus who ridiculed his claim to sonship (Mt 27:43; Jn 10:33–36), the Resurrection was a powerful vindication of that sonship. For his friends, it was a potent corroboration.

3. The Resurrection vindicated the work of Jesus

Without the Resurrection, an ominous question mark is left hovering over the cross. Did Christ's self-offering meet with God's approval? After all, his intent to suffer and his actual suffering had scandalized even his own disciples (Mk 8:31–33; 14:50). The certification of Christ's messiahship through the Resurrection implies that the divinely appointed task he performed as Messiah was also fully approved (cf. Ac 5:31). He would not have been installed as Messiah unless his messianic mission of redemptive suffering (Lk 9:22; 24:46) had been successfully accomplished. So then, if the death of Christ was God's "No" to man's sin, the resurrection of Christ was God's "Yes" to Christ's righteousness. Or, as J. A. Schep expresses it, "The resurrection is God's 'Amen' to Jesus' loud cry: 'It is finished.'"[4] Instead of being an occasion of shame, the cross became, in the light of the Resurrection, an object of boasting (Gal 6:14) and an evidence of divine love (Ro 5:8).

First Timothy 3:16 also deals with the vindicative and probative character of the Resurrection. The verse is part of an early confessional hymn that celebrates the triumph of Christ. The first two lines, which closely parallel the two antithetical clauses in Romans 1:3–4, express the humiliation-exaltation theme: "He was manifested in human form; he was vindicated in spirit." How was Jesus vindicated in the spiritual realm or by the Spirit (*en pneumati*)? Presumably by his resurrection to immortal life, which proved that his obedience to God had been complete, his messianic claims had been warranted, and his suffering for sin had been effective. Like the voice from heaven that Jesus heard at his baptism (Mk 1:11) and transfiguration (Mk 9:7), the Resurrection was a divine word of approval and vindication.

4. The Resurrection of Jesus vindicated his followers and his Father

Jesus described his disciples as those who had continued with him in his trials (Lk 22:28), and they characterized themselves as those who had left everything to follow him (Mk 10:28). Just as the Resurrection justified Jesus' trust in

God (Lk 24:46; Heb 5:7), so also it justified the disciples' belief in Jesus and their loyalty to him in the midst of his trials. One reason for the gladness the disciples felt when they saw the risen Lord for themselves (Jn 20:20) was doubtless their relief that their decision to follow him had been justified. God himself was also vindicated when he raised Jesus, because the mission on which he had sent his Son was seen to be accomplished (Ro 8:3) and because his "trustworthy promises made to David" and later reaffirmed through the prophets were thus fulfilled (Ac 13:34; cf. 15:16).

B. The Resurrection as God's Exaltation of Christ

In the previous section we have seen that the Resurrection was more than a particular instance of the operation of some general moral law according to which self-surrender in the service of others is always ultimately vindicated. It was the supreme example of divine power counteracting the machinations of men and reversing a human verdict. As the great reversal the Resurrection vindicated the person and mission of Jesus. But the Resurrection was more than the Father's rescue of his Son from death and misrepresentation. It amounted to more than his restoration to life and his reinstatement in dignity after the indignity of death by crucifixion. It was a necessary prelude to his exaltation. Christians of all generations have been convinced that the once-crucified Jesus not only lives but also reigns. It has always been a tenet of Christian belief that once he had achieved our redemption, Jesus came to occupy a unique position of dignity and authority in heaven where he reigns over and sustains the whole created universe, animate and inanimate, and especially his church, until the day when he will act as judge of all the living and all the dead.

1. The terminology of Exaltation

There are three verbs that often express this exaltation of Jesus. In a literal sense, *hypsoō* ("raise high") is used to describe the action of Moses lifting up the bronze serpent on a pole for all to see (Jn 3:14; cf. Nu 21:9). When used figuratively of the elevation of Jesus, it denotes his being placed in a position of highest honor and supreme power (Ac 2:33; 5:31; Php 2:9, where we find the compound form *hyperhypsoō*, "raise to the loftiest height" or "exalt more highly"). In the fourth gospel the literal and figurative uses are blended to great effect. The crucifixion is seen as simultaneously man's act of lifting Jesus up on a cross to die and God's act of lifting Jesus up to a place of supreme glory and lordship (Jn 3:14; 8:28; 12:32, 34). The hour of death was the hour of glorification (Jn 17:1). The second verb is *kathizō* which may mean either "cause to sit down," "seat" (Eph 1:20) or "sit down" (Heb 1:3; 8:1; 10:12; 12:2). Thirdly, there is *kathēmai*, "sit" (Col 3:1) or "sit down" (Ac 2:34; Heb 1:13). Clearly, then, the exaltation of Jesus is closely associated with his "sitting down," his session.

2. The Session of Christ

It was the language and symbolism of Psalm 110:1 that shaped the thought of the early Christians as they reflected on the exaltation of Jesus. This psalm has the distinction of being the part of the Old Testament most frequently quoted or alluded to by New Testament writers.[5] Psalm 110:1 (109:1, LXX) reads: "The Lord says to my Lord: [i] 'Sit [*kathou*] at my right hand [ii] until I make your enemies your footstool.' "

Each part (i, ii) is applied to Jesus in the New Testament. First, there is the past act of "sitting down." After his death and resurrection Jesus "sat down" (Heb 1:3) or God "caused him to sit down" (Eph 1:20). In the second place, there is the present state of sitting. The imperative "sit!" (Heb 1:13) envisages Christ's session as a continuous state, while the phrase "until I make your enemies your footstool" implies that Christ remains seated (at least) until all enemies of his reign are reduced to submission. Accordingly he is said to be "sitting" (Col 3:1) or simply "to be" (1Pe 3:22) at God's right hand, a position of honor and power. These two temporal aspects of the session of Christ—"he sat down," "he is sitting"—demand further attention.

a. The Session as a past event

The fact of "sitting down" points to the completion of a task. When Christ "sat down" the words "mission accomplished" were written over his earthly career. As the author of Hebrews expresses it: "After he had offered for sins a single sacrifice of permanent efficacy, he sat down at the right hand of God" (Heb 10:12; cf. 1:3). Where he sat down is as important as the fact that he sat down. To be at someone's right hand is to be in the position of special honor and privilege (1Ki 2:19). In the case of Christ this meant sharing God's throne (Rev 3:21) or occupying the second throne alluded to in Daniel 7:9 and Mark 14:62 (cf. Heb 1:8). Although believers are destined to share Christ's rule (Mt 19:28; 2Ti 2:12), they are nowhere said to share God's throne or to sit at God's right hand. Session at the right hand of God is the privilege of Christ alone. When Paul speaks of Christians' spiritual identification with Christ, he can say "God has enthroned us with him (Jesus) in the heavens" (Eph 2:6), but significantly he does not add "at his right hand," a phrase which is applied to Christ in a comparable statement in Ephesians 1:20. Christ's exalted status cannot be shared. Angels stand or fall down in worship (1Ki 22:19; Rev 4:10) in God's presence; the exalted Son sits.

In the fourth gospel Christ's return to heaven is described as a resumption of his glory in his Father's presence (Jn 17:5, 11). But from another point of view, on his return "home"

Jesus was accorded a hero's welcome. His glory was increased as a result of the accomplishment of his mission. In the Christological hymn found in Philippians 2:5–11 Paul observes that the outcome of the suffering of Christ in obedience to his Father was his exaltation by the gracious act of God (v. 9). We could render the expression *auton hyper-hypsōsen* (v. 9) either "he raised him to the highest station" or "he raised him to a higher station." In either case, the new title *kyrios*, "Lord" (v. 11), indicates that in his exalted state Jesus has a new rank involving the exercise of universal lordship. What he refused to seize by asserting his rights, he was graciously given at the Father's initiative. The gain was in official, not essential, glory. Jesus did not become divine through exaltation. But with his receipt of the name and function of Lord he became, in human estimation, "equal to God" (cf. v. 6). Equally with the Father, he came to be recognized and worshiped as the all-powerful creator and redeemer. The heavenly glory he had enjoyed in the Father's presence before his incarnation had been restored—and augmented. Jesus is now "crowned with (fresh) glory and honor because he suffered death" (Heb 2:9). At his exaltation he not only reentered glory but entered into new glory (Lk 24:26; 1Pe 1:21), the glory befitting the obedient suffering servant of Yahweh after he had poured out his soul to death (Isa 53:12).

b. The Session as a present state

The other tense of Christ's session relates to his present state of "sitting." More is involved in this than the celebration of his triumph. The New Testament affords no ground for thinking that the session of Christ is a period of inactivity during which Jesus passively waits for the End to arrive. There is ceaseless work, but without exertion and without failure. The principal feature of Christ's present ministry is *the exercise of his universal rule*, for when Jesus was exalted he

entered into his kingdom (cf. 1Co 15:24; Col 1:13). To sit at
God's right hand is to acquire unlimited power as well as
unparalleled honor. Philippians 2:10–11 indicates that this
dominion extends to angels ("those in heaven"; cf. Heb 1:13;
1Pe 1:22), human beings ("those on earth"; cf. Ro 14:9; Rev
1:5) and demons or the dead ("those under the earth"; cf. Ro
14:9). But this threefold division of the universe may stand for
the whole created order or for the angelic powers that were
commonly thought to rule over the three regions of the
universe. However that may be, the whole hierarchy of
authorities and powers, including death (Rev 1:18), is subject
to the risen and exalted Lord (Eph 1:20–21; Col 2:10; 1Pe
3:22). While not yet universally recognized, Christ's lordship
over the cosmos is presently celebrated within the church as
believers applaud his supremacy and acknowledge his headship (Eph 1:20–22).

Here we are faced with a paradox. Christ has been exalted
to cosmic lordship, yet opposition to his reign flourishes. For
Christ, "sitting" at God's right hand involves neither rest
from work nor relief from opposition. As Paul says: "He must
continue to exercise his rule until he has put all enemies under
his feet" (1Co 15:25). In the phrase "until I make your
enemies your footstool," Psalm 110 hints at some delay before
the reign will be consummated (cf. Heb 2:8; 10:13). The
enthronement of Christ will be followed by warfare, but not
interminable warfare, for ultimately the enemies of the newly
inaugurated reign will all be crushed. Paul's discussion of this
point indicates that God's progressive subjugation of Christ's
enemies occurs between his exaltation and his second advent
(1Co 15:24–28). The time at which the supremacy of Christ
will become universally acknowledged would seem to be the
time of judgment, when Christ displays his lordship by acting
as judge of the living and the dead (Ac 10:40–42; 17:31).

Another aspect of the exalted Christ's present work is *his
creatorial role*. In the physical realm he sustains the whole
created order by his powerful word (Heb 1:3), affording the

physical universe its principle of coherence (Col 1:17). In the spiritual sphere he is completing the building of his church (Mt 16:18; Ac 2:47) by saving those who call on his name (Ro 10:13; 1Co 1:2).

Finally there is his mediatorial function. As the exalted redeemer or high priest he intercedes for his people in the presence of God (Ro 8:34; Heb 7:25). This intercession of Christ would seem to be neither a vocal petitioning of God nor simply the personal presence of Jesus in the throne room of heaven (cf. Heb 9:24). It is real, effective, yet nonverbal prayer, comparable to the immediate communion between the Spirit and God that does not depend on spoken words (Ro 8:26–27). Involved in his intercession is Christ's advocacy of the cause of the repentant sinner (1Jn 2:1). But as well as "ascending mediation," there is "descending mediation" as Christ brings divine gifts to humankind, giving sympathetic support to those in temptation or other special need (Heb 2:18; 4:15) and answering the prayers of believers (Ac 1:24; 7:59–60; 2Co 12:8).

3. Resurrection and Exaltation

We have seen that the exaltation of Jesus was God's act of raising Jesus on high by granting him that position of unparalleled honor and universal authority which is summed up in the name "Lord." This is simply another way of saying that it was God's act of "causing Jesus to sit down" at his right hand (= the "session" of Christ, viewed as a past act).

Among New Testament writers John is distinctive in regarding the death of Jesus as the first stage of his exaltation or glorification. He uses the ambiguous verb "lift up" (*hypsoō*) to denote simultaneously the death of Jesus by being lifted up on a cross and his consequent elevation to glory (Jn 3:14; 8:28; 12:32, 34). But we cannot equate Exaltation simply with the Crucifixion: an ascent into heaven directly from the cross would be a resurrection of the spirit that would make the

Resurrection, if not the Ascension, redundant. But John knows of an empty tomb (Jn 20:4–9) and of an Ascension (Jn 20:17). So this being lifted up through crucifixion was the beginning, not the consummation, of Jesus' exaltation. John seems to envisage Crucifixion—Resurrection—Ascension as the three consecutive moments in a single, indivisible process: the return of the Son to his Father and to his former glory.

All New Testament writers who refer to both the resurrection and the exaltation of Jesus closely associate the two.[6] For instance, Paul speaks of God's mighty power "which he exercised in the case of Christ when he raised him from the dead and enthroned him at his right hand in the heavenly realms" (Eph 1:20; cf. 2:6). And Peter describes God as the One "who raised him from the dead and glorified him" (1Pe 1:21). Also it is clear that the Exaltation took place before the Ascension. It is the risen Jesus, not yet ascended, who says, "All authority in heaven and on earth has been given to me" (Mt 28:18)[7] and "Was it not necessary for the Messiah to undergo these sufferings and then enter into his glory?" (Lk 24:26). That is, consistently throughout the New Testament, the exaltation of Christ is linked with the Resurrection rather than the Ascension.[8]

Then how may we more precisely define the relation between Resurrection and Exaltation? The terms are not synonyms. Both *resurrect* and *exalt* may mean "raise up," but the emphasis in the word *resurrection* is on a raising up *from death*; in the word *exaltation* the emphasis is on a raising up to *an elevated status*. However, the two ideas are inseparably and intimately related. When the sons of the women of Shunem and Zarephath were raised or when Lazarus was raised, there was resurrection without exaltation, and in the case of Enoch's and Elijah's translation into heaven, there was exaltation without resurrection. But in the case of Jesus, resurrection implies exaltation and exaltation implies resurrection. "The risen Christ is at the same time the

Exalted One, and the Exalted One is always also the Risen One."[9] Consider the following passages:

(i) Luke 24:26, 46	Was it not necessary for the Christ to suffer these things and then enter his glory? . . . He told them, "This is what is written: the Christ will suffer and rise from the dead on the third day."
(ii) Acts 2:32–33	It was this Jesus whom God raised up to life, and of that fact we are all witnesses. Being therefore (*oun*) exalted by the right hand of God . . .[10]
(iii) Acts 3:13, 15	The God of Abraham, Isaac, and Jacob, the God of our fathers, glorified his servant Jesus . . . You killed the author of life, but God raised him from the dead.
(iv) Romans 8:34	What judge will condemn us? Will Christ Jesus who died, and more than that, was raised to life, who indeed is at the right hand of God, and is actually pleading our cause?
(v) Colossians 3:1	Since, then, you have been raised with Christ, seek the realm above where Christ is, seated at the right hand of God.

Also, the fact of Jesus' resurrection is presupposed in cases where only his exaltation is mentioned (e.g., Heb 1:3; Php 2:9), for, unlike Enoch and Elijah who ascended into heaven without dying, Jesus had actually died. In addition, his resurrection has its corollary in his exaltation, for whenever the New Testament describes the present state of Christ he is portrayed not merely as risen from the dead but as an enthroned monarch in heaven.

We propose that the Resurrection was the means of Jesus' exaltation; it was a case of Exaltation through Resurrection. Moreover, Exaltation was the outcome of Resurrection. Jesus became Lord through the Resurrection (Ac 2:24–36; Ro 14:9). From one viewpoint, then, the Resurrection may be seen as God's Exaltation of Christ to heavenly glory.

C. The Resurrection and the Ascension

If the enthronement of Jesus occurred at the time of his resurrection, what was the significance of his ascension after forty days?[11]

1. New Testament references to the ascension

We owe to Luke the only two New Testament descriptions of the Ascension itself. The Evangelist brings his gospel to a climax (Lk 24:50–53) with a brief scene set in the neighborhood of Bethany depicting the departure of Jesus from his disciples while he was blessing them. They responded with joyful worship before returning to Jerusalem where they continually praised God in the temple. Acts 1:6–11 is a more detailed account of the same event, associating Jesus' departure with the coming of the Spirit (vv. 8–9; cf. vv. 4–5) and linking the Ascension with the Parousia (v. 11).

These two Lukan passages have certain important features in common. The Ascension is not seen merely as an ascent "into the sky" (*eis ton ouranon*, Ac 1:10, 11 [first occurrence]) although it involved that, but also as an assumption into heaven itself (*eis ton ouranon*, Luke 24:51b; Ac 1:11 [second and third occurrences]). A second similarity is that the Jesus who rose from the dead is the Jesus who ascends. The ascended Lord is none other than the risen Christ.

Thirdly, both passages hint at the slow departure of Jesus—witness the imperfect *anephereto* in the midst of aorists ("he was [slowly] taken up," Luke 24:51) and the expression "they were gazing intently into the sky while He was departing" (Ac 1:10 NASB). This marks off this disappearance from his previous sudden withdrawals (e.g., Luke 24:31, "he vanished from their sight") and suggests its unique significance. A fourth common point is this: the Ascension meant the separation of Jesus from his disciples. "He parted from them" (Lk 24:51). "A cloud took him up, out of their sight" (Ac 1:9). So it was that the Ascension marked the beginning of the church era, whether in worship (Lk 24:52–53) or in mission (Ac 1:6–8). Finally, since the verbs denoting the actual ascent are in the passive voice, the Ascension is portrayed as a divinely appointed act. The cloud is a divine vehicle (Ac 1:9) as well as a symbol of the divine presence (Ex 16:10; 40:34; Dt 1:33).

Neither Matthew nor Mark contains any allusion to the Ascension. But scattered throughout the fourth gospel are references to a future "going away" or ascent or "going to the Father" (e.g., Jn 6:62; 14:12; 16:7) that incorporates the coming death, resurrection, and ascension of Jesus. John uses the word pair "descend-ascend" (*katabainō-anabainō*) to denote the Son of Man's coming from heaven to earth (Jn 3:13) and his return to heaven from earth (Jn 6:62; 20:17). Along with the Crucifixion and Resurrection, the Ascension forms part of the progressive glorification of Christ, according to John.

Outside the Gospels and Acts, specific references to the Ascension are rare. There is Ephesians 4:8–10 ("he ascended," three times), 1 Timothy 3:16 ("he was taken up in glory"), and 1 Peter 3:22 ("he has gone into heaven"). With its references to the entrance of Christ into the heavenly sanctuary (Heb 4:14; 6:19–20; 9:12, 24), Hebrews contains more direct allusions to the Ascension than any other epistle. But we should also observe that the Ascension is implied wherever the exaltation of Christ is mentioned (e.g., Mk 14:62; Ro 8:34; Col 3:1; Heb 1:3; Rev 5:13–14) or his future descent or second advent is predicted (e.g., 1Th 1:10; 4:15–16; Php 3:20; Rev 1:7).

2. The significance of the ascension

a. Christ's visible ascent into the sky forty days after the Resurrection (Ac 1:3) dramatized for the benefit of his disciples his earlier invisible ascent to God's right hand at the time of his resurrection. The Ascension was a vivid acted parable: Jesus was "lifted up" (Ac 1:9) in full view of his disciples to dramatize the fact that already he had been "lifted up" by God to cosmic preeminence (Php 2:9–11).

b. The Ascension indicated that Christ's resurrection appearances on earth had come to an end. At his ascension he departed slowly, whereas previously his withdrawals had been sudden (Lk 24:31). From now on he was permanently resident in heaven, so that when Stephen and Paul saw the risen Jesus after his ascension they looked upward, not outward (Stephen, Ac 7:55–56; Paul, Ac 9:3–5; 22:6–8; 26:13–15, 19). Also the setting of John's vision of the glorified Christ was clearly in heaven (Rev 1:12–18).

c. The Ascension marked the beginning of the church era, when people would come to believe in Jesus without seeing him visibly (Jn 16:10, 16; 1Pe 1:8). No longer would faith be based on sight; it must now rely exclusively on the testimony of eyewitnesses (Jn 20:25, 29).

d. Christ's ascension was a natural and necessary consequence of his resurrection. If, at his resurrection, Jesus gained a spiritual body whose natural habitat was heaven (cf. 1Co 15:44, 48–49; Php 3:20–21), it would have been strange had he continued to appear on earth intermittently. A heavenly body demands a heavenly home. A permanent return to the spiritual realm was a natural climax of his reentry into that realm through resurrection, especially when that realm was his Father's home.

e. Christ's departure to heaven was a prerequisite for the coming of the Spirit. "Unless I go away, the Paraclete will not come to you" (Jn 16:7). The descent of the Spirit must follow the ascent of Christ. If we ask why the Spirit was not sent as soon as Jesus was exalted immediately after his resurrection, two suggestions may be made: the disciples needed personal preparation for the event (note the injunctions to stay in Jerusalem and wait—Lk 24:49; Ac 1:4); and such timing would have excluded the possibility of resurrection appearances, for the Spirit mediates the presence of the *absent* Lord. The earliest time at which the Spirit could be "poured out on all mankind" was when Jesus had terminated his resurrection appearances through the Ascension.

f. The Ascension points to the ultimate assumption of believers into heaven, for when Christ ascended he took into heaven the humanity he had assumed at the moment of the Incarnation. Human nature is to be redeemed, not destroyed; it is to be exalted from earth to heaven. Like the Resurrection, the Ascension is an essential ingredient in the Christian hope. As Christ was raised, so too will Christians be raised. As Christ ascended into heaven, so too will believers be taken up to their heavenly home (1Th 4:16–17).

A comment might be added here on the relationship between Christ's resurrection, his exaltation, and his ascension. In early Christian teaching, as reflected in the New Testament, no sharp distinction was drawn between the three, although each was regarded as a separate occurrence. This trio (or, in John, the Crucifixion, Resurrection, and Ascension) represents three movements of a single process or three scenes in a one-act drama, that is, the enthronement of the crucified Christ at the Father's right hand as Lord of the universe. If we may relate the three movements chronologically, the sequence will be: Resurrection—Exaltation—Ascension. The Ascension visually dramatized the unseen reality of Christ's exaltation to and by God's right hand which occurred through the Resurrection. Each movement is so intimately related to the others that any one of the three may subsume the other two, as so often happens in the New Testament.

D. Conclusion

When God raised Jesus from the dead, he not only reanimated and transformed his physical body. He vindicated the person of Jesus as his Messiah and Son, and the work of Jesus as a suffering Redeemer. He also exalted him to a position of unparalleled honor and glory as Lord of the universe and Lord of the church. The Resurrection was God's means of vindicating and exalting Jesus. If the Exaltation was Christ's invisible ascent to God's right hand at the Resurrection, the Ascension was his visible ascent into heaven at the end of the forty days, dramatizing his earlier invisible exaltation and marking the end of his resurrection appearances.

All these truths are items of faith, and are not open to historical probing or scientific investigation. Earlier we indicated that it is quite properly within the domain of the historian to examine the evidence for the Christian claim that Jesus rose from the dead in a transformed body. But once we assert that it was *God* who brought about that revival and transformation, the issue is no longer in the historian's domain. We are then not dealing with verifiable history but with faith assertions, which are no less true but all the more true for being the product of divine revelation rather than the probable or assured result of man's historical or scientific inquiry.

We end this discussion of the resurrection of Jesus with the conclusion that while his exaltation to God's right hand is an item of faith whose factual reality cannot be investigated, there are compelling historical evidences[12] that encourage and validate the belief that Jesus rose from the dead in a transformed bodily state some thirty-six hours after his death and burial.

Resurrection after Christ

— IX —

The Resurrection of Believers (1)

Any view of resurrection cannot be properly considered apart from the concept of death. Paul expressed the point succinctly. "What you sow does not come to life unless it dies" (1Co 15:36). There can be no resurrection without a prior death; the two concepts are correlatives. Some attention should therefore be paid to the New Testament view of death. What range of meaning attaches to the terms *die, dead,* and *death*?

A. Death

Physical death includes the gradual weakening of bodily powers (2Co 4:12, 16) but generally refers to the irreversible cessation of bodily functions (Lk 7:12, 15; Php 1:21; Heb 9:27). It is therefore a process as well as an event. *Spiritual death* refers to man's natural alienation from God and hostility to God that is evident in sin (Jn 5:24; Ro 7:9; Eph 2:1–3). The "*second death*" denotes the permanent separation from God that befalls those who have already experienced physical death and whose state of spiritual deadness was not reversed during their lifetime through regeneration, with the result that their names are "not found written in the book of life" (Rev 20:14–15). Those who have come to spiritual life through being raised with Christ (Ro 6:13; Eph 2:5–6) are called on to regard themselves as *dead to sin* and alive to God (Ro 6:11), that is, as unresponsive to the appeal and power of sin but alert and responsive to the voice of God. Then occasionally death is regarded either as a material realm (Rev 1:18; 20:13) or as a person (1Co 15:26; Rev 20:14).

Something more should be said about the nature of physical death for the Christian. The Christian view of death is nothing if it is not realistic. Death is seen as *destruction*. When a person dies, his tent dwelling becomes permanently dismantled; his earthly house is totally demolished (2Co 5:1, where the verb *katalyo* means "dismantle" or "demolish"). The deprivative character of death is also evident later in this same passage, where Paul expresses his preference "to depart from this body and take up residence with the Lord" (2Co 5:8). Death means *departure* from mortal embodiment (so also Php 1:23, where the verb *analyō* is used, which may denote breaking up camp or weighing anchor) or departure from this world (2Ti 4:6, *analysis*; 2Pe 1:15, *exodos*, a word used of Jesus' death in Lk 9:31), or the putting off or doffing of a tent (2Pe 1:14, *apothesis*).

But there is also a positive aspect to this departure, for while death robs the Christian of the security of the familiar, it brings him or her to the promised land of Christ's immediate presence. A departure implies a destination as well as an evacuation, a "to" as well as a "from." Death does not leave believers homeless but simply brings a change in the location of their residence. Absent from their bodily home on earth, they are at home "with [*pros*] the Lord" (2Co 5:8) or "with [*syn*] Christ" (Php 1:23). In itself, this preposition *with* signifies nothing more than a passive, spatial juxtaposition. But when it is used to define the relationship between two living persons previously "spatially" separated, it denotes an active, mutual fellowship qualitatively superior to that experienced during the period of separation (2Co 5:6–7). That is, if death removes the Christian from one form of embodiment, the physical, it augments another, since to the "in Christ" embodiment which remains intact through death is added a personal "with Christ" dimension. Membership in the body of Christ and personal union with Christ persist at and after death, as is shown by the phrase *hoi nekroi en Christō* (1Th 4:16) which means not "the dead who died in Christ" but "the dead who are in Christ." Since, then, the dead remain "in Christ," "being *with* Christ" (Php 1:23), which is never used of the earthly experience of Christians, is not linked in a time sequence to "being *in* Christ" (2Co 5:17), as though Christians were "in Christ" only during life but "with Christ" after death. The difference between "the dead in Christ" and Christians who are still living is not in their status ("being in Christ") but in the quality of their fellowship with Christ and the degree of their proximity to Christ ("being with Christ").

While the New Testament writers see death as the end of life on earth, it means the enrichment, not the negation, of life itself. Death may terminate the pilgrimage of faith, but it inaugurates the vision of Christ. For Christians it suffices to know that the destruction caused by death leaves untouched their incorporation in Christ and that the departure that occurs at death leads immediately to an arrival in the presence of the Lord.

In Paul's letters we are confronted by the intriguing fact that the resurrection of believers is presented as a two-stage event. From one viewpoint it has yet to take place; from another, it has already occurred. It is both a future hope and an accomplished fact. Alongside the statement "God raised the Lord and will also raise us up" (1Co 6:14), there stands "God . . . raised us up with him [Christ]" (Eph 2:4, 6). We may therefore speak of two stages by which the Christian's resurrection is realized or of two tenses of Christian resurrection. There is a past, spiritual, or "inward" resurrection and a future, bodily, or "outward" resurrection.[1]

B. The Past, Spiritual Resurrection

Resurrection is not simply a bodily reanimation and transformation *after* physical death. It is also, according to Paul, a moral or spiritual renewal *before* physical death. What is involved in this spiritual resurrection and when did it take place?

For Paul, life "in Christ" involved the Christian's participation in the four principal experiences of Christ as they were outlined in the earliest apostolic preaching (1Co 15:3–5). Christ died, and believers died or were crucified with him (Ro 6:5–6; Gal 2:19; Col 2:20). He was buried, and they were buried with him (Ro 6:4; Col 2:12). He was raised, and they were raised with him (Eph 2:6; Col 2:12; 3:1). He appeared (*ōphthē*), and they will appear (*phanerōthēsesthe*) with him (Col 3:4; cf. Ro 8:18–19). At this point we focus on the idea of resurrection with Christ, an idea that finds its clearest expression in Ephesians and Colossians.[2]

In the phrase "God raised us up with him" (= Christ) (Eph 2:6), the primary reference is not to the resurrection of Christ but to the spiritual transformation of believers, who share Christ's resurrection triumph. Certainly the death previously referred to (in Eph 2:1, 5a) is not the death of Christ, but the spiritual deadness of individuals because of their "trespasses and sins," and believers were made alive and raised up precisely at the time they were dead (Eph 2:5a). Therefore the resurrection, like the deadness, refers to that of believers. But while the apostle did not say "God raised up Jesus, and us with him," there is a clear allusion in Ephesians 2:5–6 to the historic event of Christ's resurrection and an explicit association between believers' spiritual resurrection and Christ's bodily resurrection.

The parallel passage in Colossians 2:12 and 3:1 employs the passive voice ("you were raised," *synēgerthēte*), with the divine agency clearly implied (cf. 2:13), while 2:12b adds the significant qualification "through your faith in the effective power of God, who raised him [Christ] from the dead." Faith does not create the fact of Christ's resurrection, but it is the means by which individuals appropriate the new spiritual life made available by Christ's resurrection. This emphasis on

personal appropriation by faith is reminiscent of an earlier
Pauline statement in which the Roman Christians are enjoined
to *consider themselves* "alive to God" (Ro 6:11). The other
important feature of Colossians 2:12 is that here baptism is
mentioned as the time of resurrection: "You were buried with
him in baptism, in which (*en hō*) you were also raised with
him."[3] In Colossians 3:1 the fact of this historic identification
of Christians with the resurrected Christ by faith forms the
basis of Paul's appeal that the Colossians should follow
spiritual pursuits. "If you were raised with Christ, seek the
realm above."

On the issue of the time of believers' spiritual resurrection,
we must distinguish four stages: the resurrection of Christ
itself; the corporate identification of Christians with their
representative Head; the individual identification of Christians
with their risen Lord; the consequent state of resurrection life.
We may suggest that corporately believers were actually
raised with Christ, in the divine estimation, when Christ the
representative Man was raised, but that only at their regeneration when they are personally united with the risen Christ
does the truth of resurrection with Christ become a reality of
individual experience. That is, in regeneration what was
actually achieved by Christ is applied personally. Thereafter
believers "live to God," under his control and for his honor,
as they share the power of Christ's resurrection life. Believers
rose when Christ rose only in the sense that the one Christ
represented the many in his redemptive acts or in the sense
that his resurrection is the pledge of the bodily resurrection of
Christians and the ground of their spiritual resurrection.

C. The Future, Bodily Resurrection

The classic passage dealing with this theme is 1 Corinthians
15. This chapter falls into two clear parts: verses 1–34 treating
the *that* of resurrection (*hoti*, "that," vv. 4, 12), and verses
35–58 the *how* of the resurrection (*pōs*, "how," v. 35). Paul

first enunciates the *premise* he shares with his opponents: the resurrection of Christ (vv. 1–11), and then proceeds to draw a *conclusion from this premise*: that the dead in Christ will rise (vv. 12–32). In this latter section, he shows the outcome of denying this conclusion, viz. the denial of the premise (vv. 12–19), and specifies the outcome of accepting this conclusion, viz. the function of Christ in the Last Days (vv. 20–28). Then follow two *ad hominem* arguments supporting this conclusion (baptism for the dead [v. 29]; apostolic peril and labor [vv. 30–32]), before a warning to avoid bad company and conduct (vv. 33–34). Part two of the chapter (vv. 35–58) spells out two difficulties with this conclusion. First, there is *the nature of the resurrection body* (vv. 35–50). The question posed in verse 35a ("How are the dead raised?") is answered in verses 36–41, which discuss the conceivability of resurrection, the possibility of a resurrection body. This leads to Paul's reply to the question of verse 35b ("With what kind of body do they come?"), in which he expounds the manner of resurrection, the properties of the resurrection body (vv. 42–50). Secondly, there is *the destiny of Christians alive at the second advent* (vv. 51–57). Having categorically asserted that "What you sow is brought to life only if it dies" (v. 36) Paul needs to explain how those who do not die become prepared to enter the kingdom. His answer is that their transformation will be analogous to the resurrection-transformation experienced by the dead. The chapter ends with a call to unflagging and enthusiastic devotion to the Lord's work (v. 58).

But why does Paul expound the doctrine of the resurrection at all and at such length? An influential sector of the Corinthian church evidently rejected the notion of resurrection (1Co 15:12). There is, however, no scholarly unanimity concerning the precise nature of their denial. This vocal minority may have asserted that (1) the concept of resurrection is superfluous, since the soul perishes with the body; or (2) resurrection is impossible, since only the soul survives death and is immortal; or (3) the resurrection is past, since at their baptism Christians were spiritually raised with Christ to "walk in newness of life" (cf. Ro 6:4). Whatever the exact views of Paul's opponents at Corinth, evidently two aspects of resurrection were being denied—its futurity and its bodily nature.

1. The nature of the resurrection body

a. Paul's argument in 1 Corinthians 15:35–50

We may now move to a more detailed examination of 1 Corinthians 15:35–50, where Paul discusses this topic. A paraphrase may help to explain the movement of Paul's thought, which is not immediately obvious. In verse 35, using the rhetorical style of the diatribe, Paul offers two objections to the doctrine of resurrection.

> First of all, someone will doubtless object, "How can it possibly be that dead men are raised? (v. 35a) . . . Does not death mark the end of life?" Not at all, you foolish fellow! The analogy of the seed that is sown, the seed that "dies," shows that death is a prerequisite for life (v. 36) and is a means of effecting change because what the farmer sows is, of course, not the matured plant but simply a leafless grain of some cereal or other (v. 37). It is man's function, then, merely to sow the seed so that it can "die" in the ground, but it remains God's sole prerogative to bring about the change and give this sown seed its appropriate plant body in accordance with what he willed at creation (v. 38a). Different seeds have different types of "bodies" (v. 38b), for even now, quite apart from the change to be brought by resurrection, not every kind of "flesh" is the same. There is, for example, one kind for men, another for animals, another for birds, and yet another for fish (v. 39). What is more, there are bodies suitable for heavenly existence (such as stars), just as there are bodies adapted for life on earth (such as the

persons, animals, birds, and fish just mentioned) (v. 40a). And the beauty or luster of heavenly bodies is different from the beauty or luster of earthly bodies (v. 40b). Even among the heavenly bodies there are differing degrees of brightness: the sun has a splendor all its own, as does the moon and the stars. Why, even stars differ from one another in brightness! (v. 41). That is, within nature there is plentiful evidence of somatic variation provided by God. No one, therefore, should dismiss the possibility of more than one type of human body! A resurrection body is not an impossibility!

My questioner's second objection is sure to be this: "With what kind of body—since the earthly body decomposes—are we to imagine that the dead will reappear?" (v. 35b). The remarkable difference between bodies in the natural order (vv. 38b–41) well illustrates the difference between the two types of body involved in the resurrection of the dead (v. 42a). The sowing of one's life on earth, ending in death, is marked by perishability and decay, while the raising up to new life will be marked by imperishability and immortality (v. 42b); the sowing by disability and lack of glory, the raising up by beauty and luster; the sowing by weakness and powerlessness, the raising up by vitality and power (v. 43). A physical or "soulish" body, that is, a body animated and controlled by the *psychē* ("soul") is sown, and a spiritual body, a body animated and controlled by the *pneuma* ("spirit") will be raised up (v. 44a). So great is the evidence of somatic variety in nature that if there is a physical body for man on earth, we can reasonably assume that God will provide a spiritual body for him in heaven (v. 44b). This, indeed, is the significance of the scriptural text: "The first man Adam became a soul who had life and a physical body," whereas the last Adam through resurrection became a spirit who gives life and has a spiritual body (v. 45). (Note, at this point, that it was not the spiritual body that came first, but the physical—followed by the spiritual) (v. 46). Adam, the first man, came out of the ground, being a man made of dust. Christ, the second Man, now enjoys heavenly, resurrection life and will come from heaven (v. 47). But these two personages are representative prototypes, so that what each of them was, others of his race became or will become. So then, corresponding to the man made of dust who had a physical body are all those who also were made of dust and have physical bodies, and corresponding to the Man who comes from heaven and has a spiritual body are all those who are of heaven and will have spiritual bodies (v. 48). To restate the point and apply it to ourselves: just as we have borne in our physical bodies the image of the man who was made of dust and whose body was physical, so we are destined to bear in our spiritual bodies the image of the Man who comes from heaven and whose body is spiritual (v. 49). What I mean, brothers and sisters, is this. Unless we experience bodily transformation and acquire the spiritual body that God will provide because of our union with Christ, the head of the new humanity, we cannot, as frail mortals, ever inherit God's kingdom, nor can what is perishable inherit what is imperishable (v. 50).

From this paraphrase of the section of 1 Corinthians 15 that deals with the nature of the resurrection body, it will be evident that after establishing the *possibility* of a form of human embodiment different from the present physical body (vv. 36–41), Paul proceeds to infer (under divine inspiration) the *existence* of this new, spiritual body. He draws this inference by appealing to: (1) the evidence of somatic variety within the universe (v. 44b); (2) the corroborative testimony (*houtōs kai*) of the scriptural statement about the *first* Adam, who had a physical body, which implies a last (or second) Adam who had or gained a spiritual body (v. 45); and (3) the self-evident truth that creatures of "flesh and blood" cannot hope to inherit the eternal kingdom of God in their perishable, physical bodies (v. 50). But, although he does not explicitly say so, undoubtedly Paul found in his own conversion encounter with the risen Christ the conclusive evidence of the existence of the spiritual body. At that time he "saw" Jesus (Ac 9:27; 1Co 9:1). Moreover, he knew of many other witnesses (1Co 15:5–7) who could confirm the fact that the resurrected Christ now possessed a spiritual body. And the representative headship of Christ as the second Adam (1Co 15:45, 47) meant that others too, would ultimately gain spiritual embodiment (1Co 15:48–49).

b. The characteristics of the resurrection body

No New Testament writer broaches the subject of the anatomical or physiological constitution of the spiritual body. Details of its anatomy or physiology were of no more consequence to Paul and the early Christians than was the geography of heaven. But the picture we are given of the resurrection body involves at least eight features.

(1) *Of divine origin* (1Co 15:38; 2Co 5:1–2)

The phrase "God gives it a body" (1Co 15:38) applies primarily to the "bare kernel" that is sown in the ground (v. 37), but, given the wider context of the whole chapter, it must also be applicable to human beings whose life and death are comparable to sowing. Divine agency in supplying the resurrection body is also implied by the passive voice in verse 36, "What you sow *is* not *brought to life* [*zōopoieitai*, cf. v. 22] unless it dies." Like the germination of the seed, the resurrection of the body demands divine intervention. Human beings may sow, but only God can give the increase. And the diverse types of "bodies" in the universe (vv. 39–41) illustrate God's ability and willingness to provide humans with bodily organisms different from their earthly bodies and suitable for their residence in heaven. When Paul conceives of the resurrection body as a "building" or "habitation," he

traces its origin to God as its architect and builder ("from God
... from heaven," 2Co 5:1-2).

(2) *Spiritual* (1Co 15:44; 2Co 5:1)

How is the adjective *spiritual* (*pneumatikos*, 1Co 15:44) to
be defined? Some give it a *substantial* or material sense,
"composed of spirit," as though "spirit" were some ethereal,
heavenly substance. R. Kabisch, who holds this view, claims
that "in the Pauline view of the universe there is nothing
immaterial."[4] "Spirit" would be the substance and "body"
the form of the resurrection body.[5] However, because Greek
adjectives ending in *-ikos* carry a *functional* or *ethical* meaning
(MH 378), it is preferable to understand *pneumatikos* in the
sense "animated and guided by the spirit [*pneuma*]," with the
spirit as the organizing or governing principle. This "spirit"
could be the Spirit of God but more probably is the human
spirit as revitalized by the divine Spirit. In the resurrection
state the believer will have a body enlivened by and responsive to his or her redeemed spirit, which in turn will be
completely amenable to the power and guidance of God's
Spirit.

Moreover, the resurrection body is a house "not constructed by [human] hands" (*acheiropoiētos*). To judge by the other
two New Testament uses of this adjective (Mk 14:58; Col
2:11), it signifies that the resurrection body is a *spiritual* or
supernatural building, one "erected" purely by divine agency
and belonging to the new creation (cf. Heb 9:11). Just as the
earthly body of the Christian is a temple of the Holy Spirit
(1Co 6:19), so his heavenly body will be a spiritual temple
constructed "without hands" (cf. Da 2:34, 45, LXX). Another
element in Paul's description is found in the threefold
antithesis of verses 42b-43. The "sowing" of man's life on
earth, terminating in his death and burial, or in other words,
the physical body, is characterized by perishability, dishonor,
and weakness. The reaping of the harvest of the resurrection,
or in other words, the spiritual body, is characterized by
imperishability, glory, and power.

(3) *Imperishable* (1Co 15:42; 2Co 5:1)

Because it is constantly renewed by the Spirit, the spiritual body is *imperishable* (1Co 15:42, 50, 52–54). Humans will no longer be characterized by physical decay (*phthora*, "perishability"). The Christian's "building from God" is "eternal," that is, permanently durable (*aiōnios*, 2Co 5:1). This adjective *eternal* derives its precise significance from its implied contrast with *earthly* and *tent* on the one hand, and *dismantle* on the other: "We know that if our earthly tent dwelling is dismantled, we have a building from God, eternal . . ." (2Co 5:1). Compared with the earthly and therefore transient character of the physical body, the spiritual body is permanently durable, transcending all the effects of time. Compared with earthly corporeality with its irreversible tendency to decay which finally issues in death, the heavenly embodiment is *indestructible*, incapable of deterioration or dissolution and therefore not susceptible to disease or accident.

(4) *Glorious* (1Co 15:43)

Paul's contrast here is between "glory" and "indignity." In the resurrection, man's existence will no more be marked by physical indignity (*atimia*, "dishonor"), what Paul elsewhere calls the condition of "lowliness" (Php 3:21). The animal aspects of human life, the indignities associated with man's physical constitution, will never again be present. The believer will have a "glorious body," comparable to Christ's (Php 3:21), a body completely suffused with the Spirit and radiant like the sun (Mt 13:43; cf. Ps 104:2; Da 12:3).

(5) *Powerful* (1Co 15:43)

Just as physical weakness and limitation (*astheneia*) are the hallmarks of finite mortals, so spiritual power and expansiveness will characterize the resurrection body, because it will be permanently energized by the Spirit. Gone forever will be the dependence of childhood, the distressing infirmity associated with illness and old age, and the frustration of physical limitation felt even by the healthy.

By this threefold contrast in 1 Corinthians 15:42–43 Paul is teaching that with a transformed body that is invariably under the sway of the creator Spirit, the believer will have permanent invigoration, unsurpassed beauty, and endless energy.

(6) *Heavenly* (1Co 15:40, 47–49; 2Co 5:1, where "in heaven" = "heavenly")

As Paul develops his contrast in 1 Corinthians 15:45–49 between the first man, Adam, and the second Man, Christ, he emphasizes that these two archetypal representatives share the characteristics of their places of origin. Formed from the dust of the ground, Adam and his physical descendants are earthlings, liable to sin, decay, and death. Coming from heaven at his second advent, the risen Christ bears a heavenly image that is sinless, incorruptible, and immortal, an image to be shared by his spiritual descendants. Heaven is the natural habitat of the resurrection body, its normal sphere of operation. And this "heaven" is not simply a condition but also, although secondarily, a place.

(7) *Angel-like* (Mt 22:30; Mk 12:25; Lk 20:36)

In his controversy with the Sadducees regarding the resurrection, Jesus affirmed that those who are raised "neither marry, nor are given in marriage but are as angels in heaven" (Mk 12:25; Mt 22:30). This contrast suggests that the resurrection body will be *without sexual passions or procreative powers* (cf. 1En 15:4, 6–7), not that the resurrected righteous will be sexless (since sexual identity is an essential part of personality, and personality is retained in the resurrection). In the Lukan account of Jesus' reply, the angel-like nature of the resurrection state is related to *deathlessness*: the resurrected dead do not marry "for they cannot die any more, because they are equal to angels" (Lk 20:36).

(8) *Adaptable*

If the resurrection body is perfectly suited to life in heaven, it follows that were a resurrected person to appear on earth, some alteration of bodily form would be needed. From the resurrection appearances of Jesus we may deduce that although the spiritual body is normally imperceptible to the physical senses, it has the ability to become visible and tangible to earthlings (see above chapter VI.A, B). The resurrection body may assume either an immaterial or a material mode.

The question remains: What does the term *body* (*sōma*) signify in the expression "spiritual body"? There are two main positions. One view identifies the "body" with the physical or fleshly body with its five senses and various vital organs. From this viewpoint the spiritual body is "a physical body renovated by the Spirit of Christ and therefore suited to heavenly immortality,"[6] or a body of flesh "qualified by the Spirit, who dwells in it with all his fullness and through whom it is a center of heavenly, imperishable life, an inexhaustible source of heavenly energies."[7] One potential difficulty with this interpretation is that if the spiritual body is simply a body of flesh totally under the control of the Spirit, Jesus had a spiritual body before his resurrection.

According to the second view, the "body" is "an organ for self-manifestation"[8] or a vehicle for self-expression. So then the spiritual body is "a mode of personal expression that is final and fitting,"[9] or the organ of the resurrected person's communication with God and the heavenly world. Paul seems to support this second view in 1 Corinthians 15, where he dramatically contrasts two distinct forms of embodiment, the physical or natural and the spiritual, and concludes that "flesh and blood cannot inherit the kingdom of God" (1Co 15:50).[10]

2. The relation between the physical body and the spiritual body

The seed analogy Paul employs in 1 Corinthians 15 suggests that there is some relation between the Christian's successive forms of embodiment. Outwardly the full-grown plant may appear unconnected with the seed buried in the ground, but in reality there has been unbroken continuity between the two.

While the analogy may highlight not so much the identity as the difference between what is sown and what is raised, it nevertheless suggests both continuity (1Co 15:36) and discontinuity (1Co 15:37–38), that is, *identity with difference*. Each of these aspects merits consideration.

a. Identity

Consider the following statements. "I am the *same* person you met seven years ago." "This is the *same* watch which my grandfather owned." In the latter case the "sameness" amounts to a material identity, but in the former case something other than identity of cellular particles is meant, for biochemists inform us that during a seven-year cycle the molecular composition of our bodies is completely changed. Even during our present life the continuity between the body now possessed and the body possessed seven years ago resides in personality, not materiality. In spite of the permanent mutation of the material particles comprising our physical bodies, our personal identity is retained.

> My body certainly does not consist of the same atoms that composed it when I was six months old; nor is it recognisably similar in appearance, except in certain very general respects. It may perhaps be said that this is purely a verbal question; it all depends on what you mean by "same." If by "same" you mean "composed of the numerically identical particles," then I have not the same body that I had forty years, or even half an hour, ago. But I have the same body if you define sameness in terms of continuity of spatial extension and of association with a continuous mental life, a continuity which it is no doubt difficult to specify precisely, owing to its complexity, but which is perfectly familiar to all of us. In fact, it will be said, we all know what I mean if I say that I have the same body now that I had in childhood; and I do not mean that it consists of the same material particles.[11]

In a similar way, we suggest, the link between the Christian's successive forms of embodiment—the physical, then the spiritual—lies in the same identifiable *ego*. Just as there is a historical continuity—an identity—between our present body and the body we had at birth, so there will be a historical continuity—an identity of identifiable personal characteristics—between the present body and the resurrection body.[12] One essential ingredient of the Christian view of the hereafter is the preservation of individuality. So far from involving a mystical absorption of individual personalities into the one Person, or a pantheistic absorption of the many into the One, the Christian hope entails the retention—intact—of personhood. "God will raise up *us*" (1Co 6:14). Those who are to bear the image of the heavenly man will not be personally different from those who bore the image of the man made of dust (1Co 15:49). From the fact that resurrected persons will all bear the one image of Christ (Ro 8:29) we may not infer that they are, so to speak, "mass produced," lacking any semblance of individuality. The subject of the successive forms of corporeality is the same distinctive personality, the same "self," albeit transformed by the Spirit of life at the resurrection.

But is not God able to gather together, sort out, and reassemble the scattered particles of decomposed or incinerated corpses, so that the resurrection body will have the same molecular structure as the body that was laid in the grave or cremated? Indeed he is. And, of course, such a miracle, though awe-inspiring, would be less amazing than God's original creation of matter "out of nothing." But even if God were to follow this procedure on the morning of the resurrection, the material identity would still not be complete or absolute, for in the course of natural processes there has been an ongoing movement of the same material particles from one living organism to another, so that the reconstruction of persons as they were at the time of their death would necessarily involve the fresh creation of at least some material particles. And what of persons who were deformed through-out life or who were fatally injured in an accident? Will they rise with their deformities or their injuries? And will children be eternally assigned to childhood?

All these considerations make it inevitable that we reject the notion that resurrection involves the regaining of exactly the same material particles of which our physical bodies were composed at the time of death. The majority of Christian scholars, both ancient and modern, concur in rejecting this notion.[13]

But if complete material continuity between the two bodies cannot be claimed, what is the extent of that continuity? On this question there has never been unanimity in the church. Some affirm that everything that is necessary for the integrity of human nature will be retained, including all physical organs and senses.[14] Others believe that the substratum of the resurrection body will be formed by some of the decomposed matter of the earthly body.[15] Some claim there will be a "physical connection" even if the resurrection body has none of the material particles that belonged to the physical body.[16] Others are convinced that Paul taught an "essential continuity and identity," although the "how" remains God's secret.[17] And not a few assert that there is only a personal, not a material, continuity between the two forms of embodiment.[18]

b. Difference

In stressing the dissimilarity between the present body and the future body, Paul uses two basic formulas: the physical body may be said to be *transformed into* the spiritual body or to be *replaced by* the spiritual body. That is, there are two distinct but complementary ways of describing the resurrec-tion change—metamorphosis and exchange. In one case, the element of continuity between the two types of bodily existence is stressed: "this perishable body must put on imperishability" (1Co 15:53). In the other, the principle of discontinuity is emphasized: "a physical body is sown, a spiritual body is raised" (1Co 15:44).

In 1 Corinthians 15 the "exchange" motif is present (v. 44) alongside the dominant "transformation" motif (vv. 36–37, 51–54). But it is in 2 Corinthians 5 that the complementary nature of the two ideas is most clearly seen. In verses 1 and 8 Paul refers to a destruction (*katalysis*) and a departure (*ekdēmia*). He alludes to the replacement of the earthly house by the God-given dwelling (v. 1) and of one place of residence by another (v. 8). From this viewpoint the new body is qualitatively and numerically distinct from the old body. But balanced against this "exchange" principle is the motif of change evident in the dual concepts of "super-investiture" (*ependysis*, vv. 2, 4) and ingestion (*kataposis*, v. 4). Paul longed to put on his heavenly habitation over his earthly tent-dwelling (vv. 2, 4) so that his mortal body might be swallowed up by life (v. 4). It is unnecessary to regard this "putting on over" and this "swallowing up" as privileges reserved for Christians destined to live to see the Parousia. All believers, both those who survive until the Advent and those who experience a pre-Parousia death, will undergo a "super-investiture" whose aim and outcome is the swallowing up of mortality by immortal life. While both concepts allude to the transformation of the physical body into the spiritual, "swallowing up" views the change negatively from the side of the physical body, while "putting on over" views it positively from the side of the spiritual body.

But Paul was not alone in recognizing that a transformation was essential before what was perishable could inherit the imperishable (1Co 15:50). This is precisely the point Jesus made against the Sadducees. In their effort to confound Jesus by a *reductio ad absurdum* regarding the woman who had married seven times, the Sadducees showed that they were laboring under a misconception about the resurrection state. They thought it amounted simply to the indefinite extension of present relationships, the resumption of earthly life in a new locality. What they failed to reckon with, said Jesus, was the effects of God's power. "Is not this precisely why you are wrong—that you fail to understand either the tenor of the Scriptures or the power of God to effect a resurrection transformation in accord with his covenantal promises so that the dead become like angels?" (Mk 12:24). The point of Jesus' answer is not that in the resurrection there will be the abrogation of existing earthly husband-wife relationships or that the resurrection state obliterates any distinction between male and female and introduces a sexless society. It is that the resurrection state is radically different from the earthly state because of the intervention of God's power. Resurrection involves transformation into a new mode of being, one comparable to the angelic, in which preoccupation with God and with doing his will becomes the focus of existence. This is a mode of being in which neither sexual desire (Mk 12:25) nor death (Lk 20:35–36) has any place. Consequently the Sadducees' question ("In the resurrection whose wife will she be[come]?") was irrelevant. No determination of the woman's marital status would be needed, for resurrection brought transformation into a deathless state in which sexual relations were impossible.

It is clear that in relating the future to the present, New Testament writers maintain the dual emphasis of continuity and discontinuity. There has been a tendency for interpreters of the New Testament evidence so to stress the differences between the here and the hereafter that justice has not been done to the delicate balance or creative tension of the New Testament, and the elements of continuity have been minimized.

One element of continuity is seen in the fact that the event of resurrection involves the acceleration and climax of the process of transformation. That the Christian life is marked ideally by a progressive approximation to the image of Christ is a common Pauline sentiment (e.g., Col 3:10), but nowhere is this present process more clearly related to its future climax than in 2 Corinthians 4:16–5:4. First Paul delineates two concurrent processes which he knew operated in his life. On the one hand, there was a steady irreversible process of physical deterioration (2Co 4:16a) which would terminate in the dismantling of his tent, the destruction of his physical body (2Co 5:1a). On the other hand, matching this progressive weakening of his physical powers there was the daily renewal of his spiritual powers (2Co 4:16b), a process which would be climaxed by the final swallowing up of mortality by divine life (2Co 5:4), the acquisition of a resurrection body (2Co 5:1b). In spite of this ongoing process of spiritual rejuvenation, the believer's present "lowly body" can never, here on earth, totally resemble Christ's "glorious body" (Php 3:21). As the climax of the process of renewal begun on earth, resurrection must therefore imply the acceleration of the process of "Christification." For Paul the spiritual body was not simply the state of his "inner man" at the time of his death. It was not a case merely of the appearance at death of an already formed but concealed spiritual body, but of the acceleration and completion of a process by which the spiritual body was already being formed inwardly. This is not to imply that bodily resurrection is progressive, but it is to assert that Paul regarded resurrection not as a *creatio ex nihilo*, a sudden divine operation unrelated to the past, but as the fulfillment of spiritual processes begun at regeneration. That Paul could regard the spiritual body as a future gift given by God (2Co 5:1) did not prevent his viewing it as being created by God within man (cf. 2Co 3:18). From one point of view it will come by outward investiture; from another point of view it will come by inward transformation. As the result of the final convulsion of resurrection, the butterfly of the spiritual body will emerge from the chrysalis of the "inward man." Paul does not explicitly say that his inward man (2Co 4:16), his whole person reconstituted by God as a new creation in Christ (2Co 5:17–18), was the embryo of his spiritual body or bore its undeveloped image, but the natural transition of his thought from 2 Corinthians 4:16 to 2 Corinthians 5:1–4 shows that this sentiment would have been congenial to him. As the inner man is continually renewed and progressively transformed into the image of Christ (2Co 3:18), as he becomes more and more responsive to the Spirit of God, at the same time the spiritual body is being progressively formed within the believer. Yet only with a dramatic acceleration of the process through resurrection will this act of divine creation be brought to completion.

3. The time of the bodily resurrection

a. At the second advent of Christ

According to 1 Thessalonians 4:15–16 the dead in Christ will rise at "the coming of the Lord," "at the sound of God's trumpet" on the Last Day. It is similar to 1 Corinthians 15, where the resurrection is placed "at his [Christ's] coming" (vv. 22–23), "at the last trumpet call" (v. 52).

If, then, believers do not receive their spiritual bodies until Christ's parousia, what is their locality and state between death and resurrection? There are basically two representations in the New Testament regarding the whereabouts of the Christian dead (irrespective of the question of the time of their resurrection). From the viewpoint of the living who witnessed the burial of the dead and saw them disappear from view, they are resting in the grave (Jn 5:28–29; 1Th 4:16–17; cf. Ac 13:36), or are resident in Hades (Ac 2:27, 31), the invisible realm in the heart of the earth (Mt 12:40) in which all the dead are temporary residents. From the viewpoint of a faith that sees the invisible, they are in proximity to God in heaven, whether this be expressed as table-fellowship with Abraham (Lk 16:23); as inhabiting resting places in the Father's house (Jn 14:2) or eternal abodes (Lk 16:9); as fellowship with Christ in paradise (Lk 23:43) or heaven (Jn 12:26; 2Co 5:8; Php 1:23);

or, in the case of martyrs, as waiting under the heavenly altar (Rev 6:9).

The expression "the intermediate state" is not found in Scripture, but in Christian theology it traditionally refers either to the condition of all mankind between death and resurrection or to the period of time that elapses (from an earthly viewpoint) between the death of the individual and the consummation of history. This condition or period is called "intermediate" because it lies between two fixed points, death and resurrection, and because it is temporary, ultimately being eclipsed by the "final state" of humankind.

As to the intermediate state of the Christian dead on this view (resurrection at the Advent), two positions have been taken.

(1) Throughout church history some Christians have held that the believer's disembodied spirit or "inner man" is in a state of sleep in Christ's presence, secure in the Spirit's possession and awaiting the resurrection of the body (psychopannychism, the doctrine of "soul sleep").[19] There are several objections to this view.

(a) The verb *koimasthai*, used by Paul nine times, always in reference to the death of Christians, generally means "fall asleep."[20] Only in reference to physical sleep need the verb mean "be asleep." Christians who die "fall asleep," in that they cease to have any active relation to the present world. If this common euphemism for the act of dying has any further implications, it is that a resurrection "awakening" is certain, not that the intermediate state is one of unconsciousness or suspended animation. (b) Immediately after death the Christian is "with" the Lord (*meta*, Lk 23:43; *pros*, 2Co 5:8; *syn*, Php 1:23), which refers to active interpersonal communion, not impassive spatial juxtaposition. (c) Paul prefers (2Co 5:8) or desires (Php 1:23) to depart and be in Christ's presence. He would hardly have viewed unconscious rest with Christ in heaven as "far better" than conscious communion with Christ on earth. (d) Luke 16:19–31 suggests that in the intermediate state there is (at least) awareness of circumstance (vv. 23–24), memory of the past (vv. 27–28), and rational thought (v. 30; cf. Rev 6:9–11).

(2) The traditional view regarding departed believers is that they await the second advent of Christ and the resurrection of the body as incorporeal spirits. Only at the Parousia is the integrity of the personality reconstituted, with the reunion of a preserved soul and a transformed body. So it is that J. N. Sevenster distinguishes between a preliminary "being with Christ" (Php 1:23) in a disembodied state immediately after death, and the ultimate "being with the Lord" (1Th 4:17) in an embodied state after the return of Christ.[21]

b. At the death of each believer

Many hold that death is the moment when believers acquire their heavenly embodiment, so that the intermediate state is not an interval of incorporeal existence but a period of fellowship between resurrected disciple and risen Lord in anticipation of the corporate consummation of the church.

Those who hold this view find this change of perspective in 2 Corinthians 5:1–10, claiming that Paul there views death as the time when the spiritual body will be received. They argue that the present tense "we have" (*echomen*) in verse 1 ("we have a building from God") cannot refer to a present possession, because it indicates what would become true if, and only if, or when and only when, Paul's tent dwelling was destroyed. Referring then, to a future acquisition of the resurrection body, this present tense suggests that between the destruction of the earthly house and the provision of the spiritual house there would be no interval of homelessness. "When our earthly tent dwelling is taken down, we [immediately] become possessors of a building from God" (2Co 5:1). Then by using "put on over" in 2 Corinthians 5:2, 4, Paul further underlines the immediate succession between the two forms of embodiment. Since the "putting on" presupposed no "putting off," it was more accurately a "putting on over." Moreover, just as in verses 1–4 the "residence" metaphor of verses 6 and 8 is implicit, so in verses 6 and 8 the "clothing" motif of verses 2–4 is implicit. Therefore it is probable that the reference in verse 8 to "taking up residence with the Lord," so far from implying disembodiment, conceals a reference to investiture with the spiritual body. And such an investiture must occur at death, for verse 6 implies that as soon as residence in physical embodiment ceases, so also does absence from the Lord. The "departure" of verse 8a, then, is not followed by temporary or permanent homelessness, but by the immediate assumption of a new form of residence (the spiritual body) in a new location ("in the presence of the Lord").[22] According to this position, the Parousia marks the open display of the glorious, resurrected state of the sons of God (Ro 8:19; Col 3:4), while the resurrection, as a future event, involves the assembling together of deceased and living Christians in union with Christ and their subsequent corporate completeness as the glorified body of Christ.

Various objections may be leveled against this view: that this is a possible but not a necessary understanding of 2 Corinthians 5:1–10; that this passage is prefaced by "we know" (v. 1) which suggests that traditional teaching will follow; that to place the resurrection of the body at death is to rob the Parousia of its temporal significance, and remove the tension between the "already" and the "not yet" which characterizes the entire period between the two advents of Christ; that non-Pauline parallels to the idea of transformation at death seem to be lacking. But the principal difficulty relates to the apparent contradiction between 2 Corinthians 5 and Paul's earlier letters (viz. 1Th 4 and 1Co 15) concerning the time of the receipt of the spiritual body. Several different attempts have been made to reconcile the two views (viz. resurrection at the Parousia, resurrection at death), of which four deserve mention.

(1) Paul held to the rabbinic conception of the Age to Come as both an eternal reality and a future event, and therefore could have simultaneously entertained the ideas of resurrection at death and resurrection at the Parousia without any sense of contradiction.[23]

(2) The "house not made by human hands" received at death is "a temporary phase of the eternal body of the deceased, just as the physical body is a temporary phase of the eternal body of the survivors" (until the Parousia).[24]

(3) Paul could regard death as the moment of investiture with the glorified body because the departed Christian is not *aware* of any interval between death and the Parousia. The dead are not within time or space as we experience these entities, so that the expression "intermediate state" is an accommodation of language on the part of earthbound human beings.[25]

(4) Second Corinthians 5, written from the perspective of the individual Christian, envisages transformation at death, while 1 Corinthians 15, expressing the corporate hope of the church, places the resurrection at the second advent.[26]

We may usefully conclude this discussion of the time of the bodily resurrection with some general remarks about the intermediate state.

Why is the New Testament relatively silent about this subject? Undoubtedly because the writers were more concerned with the nature of the eternal state (e.g., Rev 21:1–22:5) and with the character of a person's life on earth as determinative of final destiny (Lk 16:27–30) and reward (2Co 5:10) than with the transitory interval between death and the consummation. Their main attention was focused on the ultimate, not the penultimate, stage of the divine plan. Whether this interim state be one of embodiment or disembodiment,[27] the ultimate destiny of the Christian is not freedom from all corporeality but the receipt of a superior form of embodiment that will perfectly mediate consciousness of the presence of the Lord. Irrespective of the question of the precise anthropological state of the believer in the interim period after death, he or she has one fundamental assurance that makes all other matters pale into insignificance: "Whether we live or whether we die, we belong to the Lord" (Ro 14:8), secure in his possession (Lk 23:46; Ac 7:59) and assured of sharing his destiny (Ro 8:17).

What does the metaphor of "falling asleep" or "sleep" signify? The state of the Christian dead is one of unconsciousness or sleep only in the sense that they are no longer active in, and therefore conscious of, the earthly world of time and space. But they are conscious of their heavenly or spiritual environment, in that they "live spiritually, as God does" (1Pe 4:6) and "live for God's glory" (Lk 20:38) "in the presence of Christ" (Php 1:23), evidently having the ability (at least) to recall the past and to think rationally. The postmortem state of the Christian is not marked by "the sleep of the soul" but by conscious, enriched fellowship with Christ, this being the distinctively Christian description of the intermediate state.[28]

What "part" of a person survives death? This question is relevant only if the intermediate state is a time of disembodiment. If individuals assume their final state at death by receiving a heavenly body, the issue of what "part" of a person lives beyond death becomes irrelevant and the question may be restated "What is the element of continuity between the physical body and the spiritual body?" (an issue already considered). While the New Testament can represent departed believers as spirits (Ac 7:59; 1Co 5:5; Heb 12:23) or souls (Rev 6:9; 20:4), the reference is not to a "part" of a person that has been unaffected by death but to a person in his or her total postmortem existence in the presence of God, a person as now belonging exclusively to the spiritual realm. The New Testament is unconcerned to identify one "part" of the person that survives death to the exclusion of other "parts." The interchangeability of the terms *spirit* and *soul* to designate the departed Christian well illustrates the point.

One notable attempt to answer our question should be mentioned. In the second part ("Christian Hopes and Expectations") of his book *The Christian in the Theology of St. Paul*,[29] L. Cerfaux traces the successive principal emphases in the apostle's eschatological thought. Second Corinthians 5 and Philippians 1 are not concerned with the Parousia or resurrection but with the state of Christians between death and the Parousia—a pressing and personal issue for Paul (191–92, 200, 234) once his pre-parousia decease seemed "possible, if not certain" (191). Far from being extemporized, his view of the intermediate state evolved during a lengthy period of time, assuming a definite shape in 2 Corinthians 4:7–5:10 under the stimulation of his "contact with Greek circles" (201). But this freshly formed doctrine found more succinct expression in Philippians 1:19–26, where Paul's earlier agitation about disembodiment, hesitancy of tone, and dependence on Hellenistic terminology are no longer apparent (190–99). In these two passages Paul views death as the "inner man's" departure to the Lord and the intermediate state as the survival (until the resurrection of the body at the Parousia) of an immortal Christian "self" deprived of embodiment but in conscious fellowship with Christ. This "self" that is independent of the body is an intellectual soul, an "ego" in relationship with Christ, an "inward man" (193–94, 202). So it is that Paul redefines, in distinctively Christian terms, insights concerning the nature of death and the character of the soul which he borrowed from the Greek philosophers, especially Socrates and Plato (193, 197 n. 3, 198, 202). By this doctrine of the survival and beatitude of the personal "self" of the Christian during an interim period of temporary disembodiment, Paul effected a compromise between Judaism and Hellenism. He "freed himself in part from the shackles of Jewish anthropology" (155) that precluded the possibility of an incorporeal survival in a heightened form of existence (197 n. 3, 198, 206, 549), at the same time avoiding any suggestion that the soul was naturally immortal (202 n. 1) or that the spiritual was incompatible with the physical (181–82, 201–2).

This view, which Cerfaux expounds carefully and persuasively, accords with the general tenor of the New Testament, even if (of necessity) it goes beyond the New Testament texts.

D. The Interrelationship of Spiritual and Bodily Resurrection

How are these two tenses of resurrection related? On occasion Paul speaks as though a bodily resurrection were the only type of resurrection (e.g., in 1Co 15), yet at other times (as in Colossians and Ephesians) it would appear at first glance that he believed only in a spiritual resurrection. Only rarely does he relate the two types of resurrection. In Romans 6 Paul can without embarrassment juxtapose references to a future union with Christ in a resurrection like his (v. 5) or to a future life with Christ (v. 8) and statements about being presently alive to God through union with the risen Christ (v. 11) after crucifixion and death with him (vv. 6, 8). From Romans 8:10–11 it becomes evident that bodily resurrection looks back to and presupposes spiritual resurrection. Paul argues from the new spiritual life enjoyed by believers as a result of acquiring righteousness (v. 10) to the new bodily life they will receive as a result of Christ's indwelling Spirit (v. 11). The only other passage where the two elements are related is Philippians 3:10–11. Paul's knowledge of "the power of Christ's resurrection" in his present moral renewal and patient endurance of suffering (v. 10) would qualify him (by God's grace) for personal participation in the future resurrection from the dead (v. 11). When the apostle says,

". . . if *possibly* I may attain to the resurrection from the dead," he is not expressing uncertainty about his own salvation but of his self-distrust, modesty of hope, and total dependence on divine grace. He is certainly not suggesting that it is possible to experience an "inward" resurrection (v. 10) and yet be denied the "outward" resurrection (v. 11).

The nearest parallel to this Pauline teaching is in John 5:24–25, 29. A bodily resurrection that leads to immortality (v. 29) is the corollary or climax of an earlier spiritual resurrection, that is, "passing from (spiritual) death to (spiritual) life" (v. 24), or "living" as a result of heeding the voice of God's Son (v. 25). But the parallel is not precise, for the earlier spiritual change is not called a resurrection, and there is no notion of being raised with Christ.

We may systematize the relationship by proposing that spiritual resurrection not only precedes but also guarantees bodily resurrection. Because believers presently enjoy new spiritual life, they will also inherit new bodily life. Each implies the other. To elevate spiritual resurrection and deny bodily resurrection, as (apparently) did Hymenaeus and Philetus (2Ti 2:17–18) and a Corinthian minority (1Co 15:12), is to deviate from the truth (2Ti 2:18). On a subjective level, the greater the awareness of spiritual resurrection with Christ, the more intense the longing for the complementary bodily resurrection.

In Paul the resurrection of believers is a two-stage event—a resurrection with Christ, and a resurrection to become like Christ. The tension created by viewing resurrection as both past occurrence and future event corresponds to the "already—not yet" tension that characterizes all New Testament teaching about the End. The Age to Come and the kingdom of God have dawned with the first advent of Jesus, but they have yet to be consummated by his second advent. But our discussion of the past resurrection with Christ revealed that this event led to a present sharing of the resurrection life of Christ. In the interval between the two resurrections, the Christian is (from a spiritual standpoint) in a resurrected state, knowing in ever-increasing measure "the power of Christ's resurrection." It is, therefore, not inappropriate to designate the Christian's resurrection as epochal (since each resurrection begins a distinctive era) and as a state as well as a dual event. Rather than following A. Feuillet who delineates a triple resurrection—baptismal, moral or daily, bodily[30]—we propose that it is preferable to speak of two episodes of resurrection, each leading to a resurrection state (see further below, Appendix, C.4).

X

The Resurrection of Believers (2)

A. Believers' Resurrection and Christ's Resurrection

One assumption that underlies New Testament teaching about Christ and his people is the integral relation between his resurrection and their past and future resurrection. Each implies the other. Yet Christ's resurrection preceded both the spiritual and the bodily resurrection of believers. How, then, does the New Testament relate them?

1. Spiritual resurrection

The intimate connection between the resurrection of Christ and the spiritual resurrection of believers is evident from the simple fact that they are said to have been raised "with Christ" (Col 3:1) or "with him" (Eph 2:6; Col 2:12). This prepositional phrase indicates not only an identification or solidarity in destiny between Christians and Christ but also that the resurrection of Christians to new life is grounded in Christ's resurrection. Without a risen Christ who rose supreme over "all rule and authority and power and dominion" (Eph 1:20–21), believers could never experience, before their death, a resurrection life of victory over all powers of evil (Eph 2:1–6; Col 3:1, 5–8).

The closeness of the nexus is well illustrated by the fact that just as Christ rose once for all, so believers rise to new spiritual life once for all. It would have been easy for Paul to say, "Since Christ was (once) raised, you too are (continually) to rise." As it is, he says to the Colossians in effect, "Since you were raised with Christ at the time of your (one) baptism (Col 2:12), act as resurrected persons" (cf. Col 3:1). To the single resurrection of Christ there corresponds the single raising of believers, reflected in a single baptism. Although there is a perpetual dying to sin (Ro 6:11–12), there is no repeated rising with Christ, only a continuous walking "in the new sphere of Life" (Ro 6:4 MOFFATT). Another similarity is that references to both Christ's resurrection and the spiritual resurrection of Christians are invariably in the past tense. Christ will never rise again, for he will never die again (Ro 6:9–10). So, too, although believers will experience a future bodily resurrection after a future physical death, they will not experience a second spiritual resurrection, for they will never suffer a second spiritual death.

Following the resurrection event is a resurrection state. After noting that God "made us alive together with" (*synezōopoiēsen*, aorist) Christ, Paul adds the parenthesis, "by grace you are now in a state of salvation" (*este sesōsmenoi*, perfect) (Eph 2:5). In this state, too, there is an integral association with Christ. It is "in [union with the risen] Christ Jesus" that Christians are alive to God, that is, are in enjoyment of resurrection life (Ro 6:11). There is not merely parallelism between the life Christ "lives to God" after his resurrection (vv. 9–10) and the life believers live as those "dead to sin and alive to God" (v. 11) after they have been "brought from death to life" (v. 13). The present life of believers is based on the life and power of Christ (Ro 5:10) which stem from his resurrection (Php 3:10). They rise to new life (Col 3:1–4a) just as, and because, he rose to new life (Ro 6:10). The resurrection life that follows crucifixion with Christ is sustained by the indwelling, risen Christ (Gal 2:20a).

To summarize: just as the event of spiritual resurrection is founded exclusively on the resurrection of Christ, so the

ensuing state of spiritual resurrection is totally dependent on
the risen life of Christ.

2. Bodily resurrection

As we compare the resurrection of Jesus with the future,
bodily resurrection of believers, we discover, not surprisingly,
many similarities. But not to be overlooked are several
important differences.

a. Similarities

These fall into two broad groups—similarities with respect
to the event of resurrection in general, and similarities
involving the characteristics of the resurrection body or the
resurrection state.

(1) With regard to resurrection in general

(a) *its cause*

The apostle Paul makes it clear that Christ's resurrection
and the resurrection of believers have a single cause—the
creative power of God. The God whom Paul characterizes as
the one who "gives life to the dead" (Ro 4:17) or "raises the
dead" (2Co 1:9) will display his life-giving power and his
concern for the body in raising dead believers just as he raised
the Lord Jesus (1Co 6:14; 2Co 4:14). It is the same God who
raised Christ from the dead who will endow believers' mortal
bodies with resurrection life (Ro 8:11).

(b) *its nature*

	Christ	Believers
reanimation	Mk 16:6; Ro 8:11; 14:9	Jn 5:28–29; Rev 20:4
transformation	Lk 24:31; Ac 1:3	1Co 15:42–43, 51–54

| exaltation | Ac 1:9–11; 2:32–33; 5:30–31 | 1Th 4:17; 2Ti 2:12 |

(c) *its results*

	Christ	Believers
immortality	Ro 6:9; Rev 1:18	1Co 15:42, 52–54
possession of a glorified body	Php 3:21	1Co 15:42–44, 49; Php 3:21
residence in heaven	Ac 3:20–21; Eph 1:20; 1Th 4:16	2Co 5:8; 1Th 4:17; Php 1:23

(2) With regard to the resurrection body

Characteristic	Christ	Believers
(a) spiritual	1Co 15:45	1Co 15:44
(b) from God	Ro 8:11	1Co 15:38; 2Co 5:1–2
(c) imperishable	Ro 6:9	1Co 15:42, 50, 52–54; 2Co 5:1
(d) glorious	2Co 4:6; Php 3:21a	1Co 15:43a; Php 3:21
(e) powerful	Php 3:10, 21b	1Co 15:43b
(f) heavenly	1Co 15:49; 1Th 4:16	1Co 15:40, 47–49; 2Co 5:1

From this comparison we may conclude that Paul's abbreviated answer to his own question, "With what kind of body do they come?" (1Co 15:35b) would have been, "With a body like Christ's!"[1] Indeed, when he actually comes to answer this question in 1 Corinthians 15:42–50, he probably has the Adam-Christ antithesis in mind from the outset, so that not only in verses 44b and 45 but also in verses 42–43 he is contrasting the bodily state of Adam before any resurrection with Christ's state after resurrection. As a living being and a man of dust, Adam gave the physical body its characteristics of perishability, dishonor, and weakness. As a life-giving spirit and the Man from heaven, Christ gave the spiritual body its characteristics of imperishability, glory, and power. In Paul's view, then, Christ now is what redeemed human beings will be. The glorified Christ is the firstfruits of perfected humanity.

b. Differences

Basic similarities between Christ's resurrection and ours do not exclude significant differences. Christ was raised "on the third day" (1Co 15:4), while his people experience resurrection on the Last Day. In the case of Christ, resurrection on the third day preserved him from decaying in the grave (Ac 2:27–31; 13:34–37), whereas the bodies of believers who die before the second advent are not spared dissolution. Again, although believers first acquire immortality through their resurrection (1Co 15:53–54), the raising of Christ meant that he regained the immortality that he surrendered when he became "obedient to death" (Php 2:8; Rev 1:18). Only of Christ can it be said that through his resurrection he "became a life-giving spirit" (1Co 15:45), was vindicated as the suffering Son of Man (Mk 8:31; Lk 24:26, 46), and conquered death (Ac 2:24–28; Ro 6:9; Rev 1:18). Only of Christ is it true that resurrection was his public installation as Son of God (Ro 1:4), as universal Lord (Ac 2:32–36; Ro 14:9; Eph 1:20–21), and as judge of the living and the dead (Ac 10:40–42; 17:31). It is clear, therefore, that in certain areas relating to the person and work of Jesus, his resurrection was unique and distinctive.

c. The resurrected Christ as "firstfruits"

These twin ideas of similarity and difference are implied in the term "firstfruits" (aparchē) by which Paul picturesquely sums up the relationship between the resurrection of Christ and the resurrection of Christians. "Christ has been raised from the dead, the firstfruits of those who have fallen asleep" (1Co 15:20).

In the Old Testament the firstfruits were the initial part of the annual production of grain, wine, oil, and sheared wool that was offered to God to acknowledge his ownership of all the produce of the field and flocks and to thank him for his generous provision.[2] It seems natural for Paul to have thought of Christ as the "firstfruits," because the day of Christ's resurrection—Nisan 16—was the day (viz. the second day of Passover week) on which the first ripe sheaf of the harvest was offered to the Lord (Lev 23:10–11, 15), and Paul may have been writing this letter shortly after Passover (see 1Co 5:7–8; cf. 16:8). We suggest that, as used by Paul in 1 Corinthians 15:20, 23, the metaphor of firstfruits establishes two basic points—that the resurrection of Christ and the resurrection of his people are essentially one, and yet they may be distinguished with regard to time and significance. These two points will now be developed.

The firstfruits are related to the harvest as the part is to the whole (compare the use of *aparchē* in Ro 11:16). As the first part of the harvest, the firstfruits were representative of the whole harvest. That is, the total harvest was representatively and potentially present in the firstfruits. So it is that the whole, of which the resurrection of Christ is the first part, is the resurrection of "those who belong to Christ" (1Co 15:23). The resurrection of all believers is the necessary aftermath of the resurrection of Christ since the two are intrinsically connected, belonging as they do to a single harvest. "As is the man of heaven, so will be those who are of heaven . . . we shall bear the image of the man of heaven" (1Co 15:48–49).

It is helpful to view resurrection in its bodily aspect either as a single continuum, marked at one end by the resurrection of Christ and at the other end by the resurrection of believers, or as a single unit with the resurrection of believers proleptically or ideally involved in the resurrection of Christ. Such a view is nowhere explicitly expressed in the New Testament but there are several clear hints of it. From Acts 4:1–2 we learn that the Sadducean authorities were incensed that untutored Galileans such as Peter and John should be teaching in the temple courts "and proclaiming Jesus as an instance of resurrection from the dead" (MOFFATT). Then in Romans 1:4 Paul asserts that "as a result of the resurrection of the dead" (*ex anastaseōs nekrōn*) Jesus Christ was decisively declared to be the Son of God. In the phrase cited, Paul must be alluding primarily to Christ's own resurrection from the dead, but the generalized nature of the expression ("of the dead") suggests that Paul viewed the resurrection of all believers as ideally achieved in the resurrection of Christ. Finally, there is 1 Corinthians 15:21, "Since by a man came death, by a man came also the resurrection of the dead." Admittedly translators are obliged to supply the verbs in this verse, but the parallelism of the two parts points to the appropriateness of supplying past tenses (as in KJV, RV, RSV, NASB, NEB). The resurrection of the dead began with the resurrection of Christ. Resurrection is not simply a future possibility but a present reality.

This essential unity between the firstfruits and the harvest is basic to the whole argument of 1 Corinthians 15. To affirm Christ's resurrection is to affirm the resurrection of his people (1Co 15:12, 20, 23). To deny their resurrection is to deny his (1Co 15:13, 15–16). Each implies or is involved in the other. Paul cannot envisage the firstfruits without the full harvest, nor can he contemplate the full harvest without the firstfruits.

But the two resurrections remain distinguishable. The term "*first*fruits" itself implies priority in time. Firstfruits were gathered before the remainder of the harvest was ripe. Jesus' resurrection inaugurated "the last days" (Ac 2:16–17, 32–33) which would be terminated by the resurrection of the righteous (1Co 15:23–24). Paul specifies two "ranks" or "orders" (*tagmata*) that are related by succession: "Each in his own rank: Christ the firstfruits, then [*epeita*, next in sequential order], at his coming, those who belong to Christ"

(1Co 15:23). This priority of Christ in resurrection to death-lessness is a recurrent New Testament theme. As "the first to rise from the dead" (Ac 26:23; cf. Ro 6:9), Jesus inaugurated the new creation (2Co 5:17). He became the "forerunner" who has entered the inner shrine of heaven, God's immediate presence, as a guarantee of the subsequent admission of his people (Heb 6:19–20; cf. 12:2).

Conceptually, as well as temporally, the two resurrections may be distinguished. Although the part may represent the whole, it cannot be equated with it. The firstfruits are not the whole of the harvest but its anticipation. It is at this point that another New Testament metaphor becomes relevant. The seer of Revelation describes Jesus Christ as "the firstborn of the dead [*ho prōtotokos tōn nekrōn*] and the ruler of kings on earth" (Rev 1:5). It is possible to interpret "firstborn" here, as in Colossioans 1:18 ("He is the beginning [*archē*], the firstborn from the dead," *prōtotokos ek tōn nekrōn*), solely of chronological precedence, i.e. Christ was the first person ever to rise from the dead with immortal life. But if this were the case, we might have expected the simple term *first* (*prōtos*) to be used, as it is in the same connection in Acts 26:23 cited above. As *prōtotokos* in relation to the dead, Jesus is not only first in time but also superior in status. To him belongs a personal precedence as well as a temporal priority. This interpretation is supported by the earlier use of *prōtotokos* in Colossians 1:15 ("His is the primacy over all created things," NEB) and the probability that Revelation 1:5 alludes to Psalm 89:27, "I will also appoint him my firstborn [*prōtotokon*, Ps 88:28 LXX], the most exalted of the kings of the earth" (NIV). And it is perhaps relevant to observe here that in both Hebrew and Greek the word for "firstfruits" is etymologically related to the idea of headship and supremacy (in Hebrew, *rē'šît* and *rō'š*, respectively; in Greek, *aparchē* and *archē*).

d. Christ's resurrection as pledge and pattern of believers' resurrection

One important question remains to be raised. If the resurrections of Christ and believers are intimately connected while being clearly distinguishable, can Christ's resurrection be termed the cause of believers' resurrection?

There are three personal causes of the resurrection-transformation of the righteous mentioned in the New Testament: God (e.g., Jn 5:21; Ac 26:8; 1Co 6:14), Christ (Jn 5:21, 25; 6:39–40, 44, 54; Php 3:20–21), and the Spirit (Ro 8:11; and perhaps Gal 6:8). The ostensibly impersonal causes include the power of God (Mk 12:24; 1Co 6:14), the glory of the Father (Ro 6:4), and the vision of Christ (1Jn 3:2). Perhaps the most satisfactory way to accommodate all these data is to distinguish between God the Father, acting powerfully, as the ultimate cause of resurrection, Christ and the Spirit as proximate causes, and the vision of Christ as an indirect cause.

If, then, the category of cause-effect is inapplicable to the relation between Christ's resurrection and that of believers, what is their precise interrelationship? Nowhere is the word *pledge* (*arrhabōn*) used of the resurrected Christ, as it is of the Spirit indwelling the believer (2Co 1:22; 5:5), but this expression aptly summarizes the relationship in question. The risen Lord or his rising from the dead is the guarantee of the bodily resurrection of all his followers. One indication of this is the prepositional phrase "with Jesus" (*syn 'Iēsou*) found in two Pauline passages. The apostle claimed that he declared the good news with confidence because he knew that the God who raised the Lord Jesus would raise him as well "with Jesus" (2Co 4:14). Then in 1 Thessalonians 4:14 he asserts that through the power of Jesus (*dia tou 'Iēsou*) God would bring (= raise) "with him" those who had fallen asleep. Obviously the phrase "with Jesus" cannot mean that Jesus will undergo a second resurrection. Probably we should paraphrase it: "as pledged by the resurrection of Jesus," or "by virtue of association with the risen Jesus." In addition, the very notion of firstfruits hints at a divine pledge that as Christ rose, so too will his people rise. As surely as the harvest follows the firstfruits, the resurrection of the members of the body will follow the resurrection of the Head. At least this is how the fifth-century Antiochene commentator Theodoret understood 1 Corinthians 15:20: "In the resurrection of our Savior we have a guarantee [*echenguon*] of our resurrection" (*Comm.*, ad loc.).

Another term that suitably expresses the relation of Christ to his people is "pattern" or "prototype." Sometimes the destiny of Christians is defined as conformity to the image of the glorified Christ (Ro 8:29; 2Co 3:18; Col 3:10) or the bearing of the image of the Man who will come "from heaven" at his second advent (1Co 15:49). Here Christ's resurrection and resurrected state are clearly being adduced as the exemplar of the Christian's resurrection and immortality. "Corresponding to the heavenly Man are the heavenly men" (1Co 15:48b). As is the risen Christ, so will be those who belong to him. His resurrection, and what it involved by way of bodily transformation, are paradigmatic. Just as those who have Adam as their head share his nature and likeness, so those who acknowledge Christ as their Head will share his nature and likeness (1Co 15:48).

Just as Christ has a spiritual body, so his "descendants" will have spiritual bodies. Through a radical transformation, bodies that at present bear all the marks of frailty and mortality will become resplendent bodies bearing the impress of Christ's likeness (Php 3:20–21; cf. 1Jn 3:2, "we shall be like him"). His transformation through resurrection is the model and pattern for the metamorphosis of believers through their resurrection. "By his power God *both* raised [*ēgeiren*] the Lord *and* [*kai. . .kai*] will raise up [*exegerei*] us" (1Co 6:14). One other passage that points to this paradigmatic function of Christ's resurrection is 2 Corinthians 5:1, which contrasts physical with spiritual embodiment. "We know that if our earthly tent dwelling is *destroyed*, we have a *building* that God supplies, *not made by human hands*, but eternal and heavenly." This description of the future resurrection body of believers is strongly reminiscent of the dominical saying about the temple preserved in Mark 14:58, "I will *destroy* this temple that is made by human hands, and in three days I will *build* another, *not made by human hands*." This is a saying that the fourth gospel relates primarily to the resurrection body of Jesus (Jn 2:21–22).

To summarize: the resurrection of Christ is similar to the bodily resurrection of believers in four main respects: in cause, nature, results, and characteristics of the heavenly body. Both are effected by direct divine action; both involve reanimation, transformation, and exaltation and form part of a single Easter harvest; both result in a resurrection life in heaven that is immortal and is expressed through a spiritual body that is provided by God, a body that is imperishable, glorious, and powerful. On the other hand, these two resurrections differ with regard to the time and nature of the occurrence and its theological significance. In particular, the resurrection of Christ was the first and most important part of a series, forming both the pledge and the pattern of the bodily resurrection of believers.

B. The Role of the Holy Spirit in Believers' Resurrection

New Testament teaching about the Spirit's relation to resurrection is virtually restricted to Paul's epistles, and even there it is only in and after 2 Corinthians that the relation becomes a special interest. A study of the relevant passages enables us to identify four functions of the Spirit with regard to the resurrection of believers.

1. The Spirit is the pledge of a future resurrection transformation

In three Pauline passages (2Co 1:22; 5:5; Eph 1:14) the Spirit is called the *arrhabōn* that God has given to believers. This technical term had two basic meanings in Greek commercial usage. It was a first installment of a purchase, a *down payment* or deposit, that required further payments but gave a legal claim to the goods in question. Sometimes this partial payment was a sizable portion of the total, but on other occasions it was merely a token deposit. In its other sense, *arrhabōn* denoted a *pledge* or guarantee that differed in kind from the actual payment but rendered it obligatory. Many commentators prefer the former meaning, pointing to a parallel thought in Romans 8:23 where Paul speaks of "the firstfruits [*aparchē*] of the Spirit." But because this phrase may simply refer to "the firstfruits *brought* by the Spirit" (that is, the spirit of sonship to be consummated in adoptive sonship, Ro 8:14–16, 23), we need not insist on the meaning "down payment" for *arrhabōn*. Significantly, in modern Greek one word for "engagement ring" is *arrhabōn*, a pledge of lifelong love and fidelity. Although some modern translations prefer to retain both senses (e.g., MOFFATT, "pledge and instalment"; NIV, "a deposit, guaranteeing what is to come"), we may follow those versions that render the term by "pledge" or "guarantee" (WEYMOUTH, GOODSPEED, TCNT, RSV, NASB, NEB).

Clearly not all the commercial nuances of the word may be pressed. Salvation is not a process of reciprocal bargaining ratified by a contractually binding agreement. Rather, it is the result of the grace of God, who bestows his Spirit on believers as an unsolicited gift. We may also be sure that Paul did not regard the Spirit as a returnable pledge (cf. Ge 38:17–20) or as a mere advance sample and therefore an inferior part of the Christian's inheritance.

A comparison of 2 Corinthians 1:22 and 5:5 shows that for

Paul "sealing" denoted God's giving of the Spirit as a pledge. But the crucial question remains: as a pledge of what? Paul states, "Now God himself has prepared us for this very purpose and has given us the pledge of the Spirit" (2Co 5:5). The "purpose" referred to is the receipt and possession of the spiritual body which verses 1–4 have described in various ways: as the acquisition of a building from God (v. 1), as investiture with a heavenly dwelling (v. 2), and as the swallowing up of the mortal body (v. 4). Confirmation of this comes from Ephesians 1:13–14 where "the promised Holy Spirit" is described as "the pledge of our inheritance until the day God finally redeems his own possession." God's gift of the Spirit is therefore not only the fulfillment of promise (Gal 3:14; Eph 1:13) but also the promise of fulfillment (2Co 5:5; Eph 1:14). It remains to note that the Spirit who is the pledge of the Christian's inheritance also inspires a longing for that inheritance (Ro 8:23; 2Co 5:2, 4–5).

2. The Spirit is the means God will use to effect a future resurrection transformation

It is somewhat surprising that the New Testament nowhere explicitly states that God raised Jesus from the dead *through the Holy Spirit*. There are strong hints of this, as when the resurrection of Christ is credited to God's power (1Co 6:14; cf. 2Co 13:4) or "the working of his mighty strength" (Eph 1:19–20). But Romans 8:10–11 does explicitly trace the resurrection of believers to the operation of the indwelling Spirit.

"If Christ is in you, although your bodies are indeed dead [= subject to death] because of your sin, the Spirit is life [-giving] because of your righteousness. So, if the Spirit of him who raised Jesus from the dead dwells within you, he who raised Christ from the dead shall impart life to your mortal bodies as well, through his Spirit who dwells within you." There are some who interpret this "impartation of life" as the daily spiritual renewal of believers effected by the Spirit or as the transformation of Christians living at the Parousia. However, it is more natural to view it as including the transformation of the dead as well as of the living, because verses 10 and 11 both contrast life with physical death or mortality. The movement of thought as we pass from verse 10 to verse 11 is from the mortality of the present body to the immortality of the transformed body.[3]

This future energizing role of the Spirit is also mentioned in Galatians 6:8. If people "sow to their own flesh," if they live their life as though the sensible world and their own natural desires were the sole realities in the universe, from that same "flesh" they will reap a harvest of decay and death in keeping with their sowing. However, those who "sow to the spirit," who devote time and energy to the enrichment of the human spirit, the sphere in which the Spirit of God operates (Ro 8:16), especially by being receptive of spiritual teaching and supportive of spiritual teachers (Gal 6:6), will in due season (Gal 6:9) reap a final harvest of eternal life from that same Spirit. It would be arbitrary to distinguish between the Spirit's role in imparting eternal life (Gal 6:8) and his role in effecting a resurrection transformation (Ro 8:11). In each case he is the "life-giving" Spirit (Ro 8:2, 10; 2Co 3:6) operating on those who are dead or are destined to die.

3. The Spirit sustains resurrection life

When Paul observes that the Spirit "imparts life" (2Co 3:6) or he describes him as "life" (Ro 8:10) or the Spirit "of life" (Ro 8:2), the point is single: one characteristic, perhaps the principal characteristic of the Spirit, is that he perpetually imparts the physical and spiritual life of which he is the source. This being so, he must constantly sustain the spiritual life gained by the believer at regeneration and the new bodily life gained by the believer through resurrection.

We have seen that the outcome of "resurrection with

Christ" is sharing his risen life. This life is mediated by the Spirit (Ro 7:6, "the new life brought by the Spirit"). "Those who belong to Christ Jesus have crucified the flesh" (Gal 5:24), have been raised with Christ, and consequently "live by the Spirit" (Gal 5:25). In Titus 3:5 two distinct operations are described as the means of salvation: the washing that effects regeneration, "the water of rebirth" (NEB); the renewal (*anakainōsis*) effected by the Spirit. The rebirth is single and instantaneous. The renewal is continuous and progressive (Ro 12:2, the only other place in the New Testament where *anakainōsis* is used; 2Co 4:16b). Only the Spirit's constant infusion of spiritual life into the believer sustains the new resurrection life received at "rebirth" when the believer was raised with Christ. This renewal of the mind (Ro 12:2; Eph 4:23) by the Spirit corresponds to the strengthening or renewal of the "inner person" by the Spirit (2Co 4:16; Eph 3:16).

What evidence is there that the Spirit will sustain the bodily resurrection life of the believer? We lack any direct statements, but this conclusion seems a fair inference from several pieces of evidence. First, when Paul uses the epithet *spiritual* of the resurrection body he is not defining its material composition but its organizing or regulative principle. It is a body dependent on and controlled by the Spirit of God, a body that receives its supernatural life from the Spirit and is perfectly submissive or responsive to the Spirit. Secondly, perhaps the symbol of the springs or river of "living water" in the Apocalypse (7:17; 21:6; 22:1, 17) indicates the Spirit's permanent role as the giver of spiritual life, since in the fourth gospel water is symbolic of the Spirit (Jn 4:14; 7:38–39). Quite apart from this possibility, there is no reason to believe that the Spirit's function as life-giver will suddenly end when the Age to Come arrives in its fullness. There will be no life that is independent of the Spirit of God in the hereafter any more than there is in the present age. Thirdly, since Paul believed that the resurrection body of Christ was, in general, the paradigm for that of believers (Php 3:21), we may assume that what was true of Christ's resurrection state will be true of the Christian's. Paul notes that although Christ was crucified because of his "weakness," in obeying God and not showing retaliation, he now lives in a resurrection life sustained "by God's power" (2Co 13:4). But "power" for Paul was sometimes virtually synonymous with the Spirit (see, e.g., 1Co 2:4-5 and 1Co 6:14 compared with Ro 8:11). If the Spirit sustains the risen Christ, he will also sustain the future resurrection life of the believer.

4. The Spirit is the link between the pre- and post-resurrection states of the believer

In all the New Testament, the initial stage of spiritual life is never confused or identified with its perfection in the future. "Sowing to the spirit" is quite distinct from "reaping eternal life" (Gal 6:8). There is a Then which is different from the Now. The Age to Come has dawned but has not yet been consummated; Christians still live in "the present evil age" (Gal 1:4). For them the link between the Now and the Then is pneumatological rather than anthropological. That is, it resides in the possession and activity of the Spirit, not in the persistence of a naturally immortal soul.

In the present age or in the overlap of the ages, believers are being progressively transformed into the image of Christ as they gaze on and then reflect the glory of the Lord. This whole process is the work of the Spirit (2Co 3:18; cf. Eph 3:16). Then in the resurrection transformation that God produces in believers in the Age to Come, again through the agency of the Spirit (Ro 8:11), the "good work" of producing conformity to Christ is brought to completion (Ro 8:29; Gal 4:19; Php 1:6; 3:21). Then no longer will it be said that "the body is dead because of sin" (Ro 8:10), for this heavenly body will be pulsating with the Spirit's life. It is inconceivable that once the goal of the Spirit's work—molding people into the image of Christ—is achieved he would suddenly abandon them to their own resources. It should occasion no surprise that the Spirit is the element of continuity between Now and Then. Since he is characterized as the "life-giving Spirit" (Ro 8:2, 10; 2Co 3:6), we should not expect that death would terminate or reverse his work. Death can no more eclipse the operation of the Spirit and remove the Christian from his beneficent influence than it can separate the Christian from the love of God (Ro 8:38–39).

On two occasions the role of the Spirit in both ages is alluded to in a single passage. When we read that "God himself has *prepared* us for this very destiny" (viz. the experience of a resurrection transformation, 2 Co 5:4b, 5a), the "preparation" could be God's giving of his Spirit as a pledge (2Co 5:5b) or could be the daily inward renewal that is produced by the Spirit (2Co 3:18; 4:16). Either way, as the Spirit powerfully strengthens the inner being of the Christian (Eph 3:16) and thus forms the nucleus of the spiritual body, God is in fact preparing him or her for the climactic transformation that will mark the end of the process of renewal. To paraphrase 2 Corinthians 5:5: "Now the One who has prepared us for resurrection transformation by renewing us daily through his Spirit is none other than God himself, who has pledged himself to effect this final transformation by giving us the Spirit, his agent of resurrection." Then there is Romans 8:23. After observing that the whole created universe, up to the present time, had been groaning with the pangs of childbirth, Paul continues, "And not creation only; although we ourselves already have the firstfruits of the Spirit's gifts—the spirit of sonship [Ro 8:14–16] that induces the cry 'Abba'—we too groan inwardly because we eagerly await that redemption of our bodies [through the Spirit, Ro 8:11] which will consummate our adoption as sons." The same Spirit who at present creates an awareness of sonship will at the End seal that sonship by resurrecting the sons and daughters of God.

XI

The "General Resurrection"

Few will doubt that the early Christians believed that Jesus had risen from the dead and that therefore his people would also be resurrected. But what is to be the destiny of unbelievers? Will they too share in Christ's resurrection?

A. Universal Judgment and the Resurrection

As in English, so in Greek, the verb *judge* (*krinō*) and the noun *judgment* (*krisis, krima*) have two basic senses, one neutral, one negative. They can refer to the examination of evidence by a competent authority resulting in the passing of a verdict, or to the passing of a negative verdict and the exacting of the penalty announced in that verdict. For example, when all the dead stand before the great white throne and are "judged" (Rev 20:11–13), this judgment is a judicial investigation that may lead to either a positive or a negative verdict. But if it is determined that a person's name is not written in the book of life and that person is consigned to the lake of fire (Rev 20:14–15), this "judgment" is a verdict of condemnation.

For this reason the New Testament can assert that all persons without exception, both the living and the dead, will be "judged" on the Last Day (e.g., Ac 10:42; Ro 2:12–16).[1] No one will escape notice and avoid the impartial divine assessment. Sometimes God is said to be the judge (e.g., Ro

2:3, 5; 1Pe 1:17), sometimes Christ (e.g., Jn 5:22, 27; 2Ti 4:1, 8). At other times Christ's people (1Co 6:2–3; Rev 20:4) or his angels (Mk 8:38; 2Th 1:7) are associated with him in his exercise of judgment. Because God judges humankind through his Son (Ac 10:42; 17:31; Ro 2:16) so that Christ's judgment is also God's judgment, there is no need to distinguish between the judgment seat of God (Ro 14:10), the judgment seat of Christ (2Co 5:10), and the great white throne (Rev 20:11), as though three separate judgments were indicated. Consequently the Old Testament Day of Yahweh becomes the "Day of the Lord [Jesus]" (1Co 5:5; 1Th 5:2). There will be two bases of judgment: a person's relationship to Christ (e.g., Mt 10:32–33; Jn 3:36) and works performed during one's lifetime (e.g., Ro 2:6; 1Pe 1:17). In the case of the righteous, these deeds are the outcome of faith (1Th 1:3) and will determine reward or its forfeiture (1Co 4:5; 2Co 5:10; Rev 11:18). In the case of the unrighteous, these deeds will seal their doom (Rev 11:18; 20:12–13, 15) because they have refused to obey the gospel (2Th 1:8).

But does a universal judgment imply a universal resurrection? It all depends what is meant by "resurrection" (see the Appendix: "Terms Denoting Resurrection in the New Testament"). Usually the term refers to the receipt by believers of a resurrection body and therefore immortality. On no interpretation of the evidence could it be said that Paul believed that all persons, believers and unbelievers, would receive a "spiritual body." There could not be a resurrection of the wicked to eternal life since a bodily organism suited for the redeemed human spirit now fully under the control of the Holy Spirit would be totally unsuitable for a person whose disposition had always been to reject Jesus Christ and thus grieve that Holy Spirit. The resurrection places the person who already possesses the Spirit completely and permanently under his sway. On this understanding of "resurrection," universality of judgment obviously cannot presuppose universality of resurrection.

But there is another, special sense of resurrection, referring to the resuscitation of dead persons and their appearance before God in some undisclosed bodily form that permits continuity of personal identity. Examples of this usage include: John 5:29, "the resurrection [*anastasis*] of life . . . the resurrection [*anastasis*] of judgment"; Acts 24:15, "a resurrection [*anastasis*] including both the righteous and the unrighteous"; and Revelation 20:4–5, "The rest of the dead did not come to life again [*ezēsan*] until the thousand years were over." It is of significance that the same two Greek terms (*anastasis*, *zaō*) may denote restoration to life in the present age: "Women had their dead restored to them by resurrection" (*anastasis*, Heb 11:35). "My daughter has just died; but come and lay your hand on her, and she will be restored to life" (*zēsetai*, Mt 9:18). Now if resurrection is viewed merely as reanimation, it is fair to conclude that the judgment of all implies the resurrection of all. But if New Testament writers do not regularly speak of a "resurrection of judgment," it is because "resurrection" is not normally a neutral term signifying reanimation, a mere "coming to life again" after death, but a positive concept denoting the receipt of permanent spiritual embodiment comparable to Christ's and implying the enjoyment of eternal life.

John 5:28–29 declares quite unequivocally that "all who are in their tombs" will respond to the voice of the Son of Man and will emerge, "those who have done good, to the resurrection of life, and those who have practiced evil, to the resurrection of judgment." The genitives "of life" and "of judgment" mean "that leads to [or, results in] life," "that leads to [or, results in] judgment" (BDF § 166). These two resurrections that together constitute the "general resurrection" may now be discussed in greater detail.

B. The Resurrection that Leads to Life

It is the uniform testimony of the New Testament that the "resurrection of life" is conditional. People become heirs of eternal life and candidates for a resurrection that issues in immortality only through a saving relationship with Christ. Rather than being the inalienable right of every human being, a resurrection to immortality and reward is everywhere depicted as a privilege reserved for the righteous. For instance, John 5:29 distinguishes "those who have done good" from "those who have practiced evil" and reserves "the resurrection that leads to life" for the former group. Or again, it is only the righteous who enter eternal life (Mt 25:46), only the person who believes in Jesus who will never die (Jn 11:25–26), only "those who belong to Christ" who will be "raised immortal" (1Co 15:23, 52).[2] Lest there be misunderstanding of this use of the terms *immortal* and *immortality*, we should note here that in chapter XIV.B below we shall show that in the New Testament these two terms, as applied to human beings, do not refer merely to the eternal existence of all persons beyond death (as in common usage), true though that is, but to the eternal freedom from decay and death that results from directly sharing in God's life. All persons exist forever, but not all will share the divine life and so be immune from all decay and any form of death.

This resurrection to eternal life is also a resurrection to reward. Of believers Paul writes, "We must all appear before Christ's tribunal so that each may receive due recompense for deeds performed through the body, whether they be good or bad" (2Co 5:10). What Christ will scrutinize is not simply character and motives (1Co 4:5) or even action regarded in its totality as reflective of character (this would require *to agathon* and *to phaulon*), but specific actions, "deeds, whether good [*agathon*] or bad [*phaulon*]." The purpose of this "judgment" by Christ is not to decide the Christian's destiny (that is settled), but to assess his or her works and determine the appropriate reward. No longer trusting in "deeds [*erga*, plural] of the law" as the basis of justification (Ro 3:28), the Christian is nevertheless committed to "action [*ergon*, singular] stemming from faith" (1Th 1:3). So far from undermining the doctrine of justification by grace through faith or from being a relic of Jewish belief unassimilated to the rest of Paul's teaching, the doctrine of judgment by works ensures that the justified sinner lives with a sense of moral earnestness and personal accountability. Nor are the notions of recompense and reward incompatible. Reward may be recompense for good; the "suffering of loss" (1Co 3:15), that is, the forfeiture of reward or privilege, may be the requital for evil. Whatever else may be involved in the Christian's reward, the principal element in it is God's commendation (1Co 4:5; cf. Ro 2:10; 2Co 5:9) expressed in such words as "Well done, good and faithful servant" (cf. Mt 25:21, 23), commendation which may be given or may be withheld and which will be given in varying measure (1Co 3:8; 4:5; cf. Lk 19:12–19).

How does the New Testament depict this "life" to which all believers are raised? We can conveniently summarize the essential ingredients of New Testament teaching about the believer's final state in six adjectives.

(1) *Embodied.* Conscious existence in a bodiless state is possible (God exists as pure spirit), but in both Jewish and Christian thought *true* existence for human beings or a *full* life either on earth or beyond the grave is inconceivable apart from embodiment. Bodily resurrection is the prerequisite for the resumption of true life after the intervention of death. The Christian's goal is not freedom from embodiment but a new form of embodiment, the "spiritual body" (1Co 15:44), a body animated and guided by the redeemed human spirit and revitalized by the divine Spirit.

(2) *Localized.* We have seen that heaven is the natural habitat of the resurrection body, its normal sphere of operation. Although heaven is a condition, that of knowing and serving God, it is also and always a place, the locality where God's presence is most perfectly expressed and felt. P. Badham rightly insists that the concept of a resurrected body and the notion of a nonspatial heaven are irreconcilable. In reality the options are a resurrected body in a place or an

immortal soul existing without location, for "a body is spatial
and a soul is nonspatial."[3]

Scripture makes it clear that the destinies of humans and the
material universe are interlocked. As at the Fall, so in the
Rebirth (Mt 19:28; cf. Ac 3:21), what affects one affects the
other. Creation will be set free from its frustrating imperfection and slavery to decay (Ro 8:18–25; Php 3:20–21) in the
same way that man will be set free from sin and mortality. The
"new heavens and new earth in which righteousness has its
permanent home" (2Pe 3:13) correspond to man's new
resurrection body.

(3) *Personal*. The Christian doctrine of resurrection is a
safeguard against an impersonal view of immortality. Although the link between the physical body and the spiritual
body is not in identical material particles, there is real
continuity beweeen the two in that the same "person" finds
expression in two successive but different types of body.
When the physical body is transformed into or replaced by the
spiritual body, personal identity is preserved. "God will raise
us up" (1Co 6:14). Belief in God's power to restore dead
persons to life and to impress them with the image of Christ
without in any way compromising their individuality leaves no
room for a pantheistic immortality in which the Many are
absorbed into the One, or a generational immortality in which
a person survives solely in his or her posterity. From first to
last God treats us as distinctive individuals.

(4) *Active*. There is a sense in which the dead permanently
"rest from their labors" (Rev 14:13), but relief from toil does
not amount to perpetual inactivity. The final state of believers
will be one of joyful activity as they "follow the Lamb
wherever he goes" (Rev 14:4; cf. 7:17). "Forever and ever"
they will share in Christ's universal reign (Rev 3:21; 5:10;
20:6; 22:5). Free from the taint of sin and from the frustration
of spiritual powerlessness, they will worship and serve God
and the Lamb enthusiastically and acceptably (Rev 7:9–11;
19:9; 22:3–4).[4]

(5) *Corporate*. The life of the Age to Come is not marked by an exclusively individual enjoyment of the vision of God so that myriads of individuals live in fellowship with God but in isolation from other worshipers. Unmediated interpersonal communion between the individual believer and his or her Lord there certainly will be, but this will occur only in the corporate context of the city of God, the capital of the consummated kingdom or new commonwealth and the center of the new heaven and earth. In the classic description of this city (Rev 21:1–22:5; cf. Heb 11:10, 16; 12:22–24), attention is focused not only on its superlative beauty and its inviolate holiness but also on its inhabitants among whom God will dwell in a perfect society.

(6) *Permanent*. "We know that if our earthly tent dwelling is dismantled, we have a permanent heavenly building provided by God and not constructed by human hands" (2Co 5:1). "They shall reign forever and ever" (Rev 22:5). Just as the resurrection body will be permanently durable, not susceptible to decay or dissolution (1Co 15:42, 53–54), so too believers' corporate and individual life with God will be unending. When the son of the widow of Nain and Lazarus were restored to life, they resumed physical lives that were identical with their former lives and therefore not free from ultimate death. But when believers are resurrected from the dead, they will assume an immortality which guarantees the permanency of their resurrection state. Resurrected believers, like the risen Christ (Ro 6:9; 2Co 13:4), "will never die again" because they "live by the power of God." Once a person experiences a resurrection transformation, he or she will know perennial rejuvenation and so be equipped for the worship and service of God "forever and ever."

C. The Resurrection that Leads to Condemnation

1. New Testament references or allusions

The doctrine of a resurrection of the wicked that leads to their punishment is explicitly taught in only two places in the New Testament. One is John 5:29: "Those who have practiced evil" will emerge from their tombs "to the resurrection of judgment," that is, the resurrection that leads to, or results in, a verdict of condemnation. The other passage is Acts 24:15 which forms part of Luke's summary of Paul's defense before Felix (Acts 24:10–21). Paul speaks of his hope in God "that there will certainly be a resurrection including both [*te kai*; BDF § 444(2)] the righteous and the unrighteous." In addition, such a resurrection is clearly implied in Matthew 5:29–30; 10:28; Revelation 20:5, 11–15; and may possibly be inferred from Matthew 12:41–42; 25:31–46; Luke 14:14; 20:35.[5]

2. The nature of the condemnation

In the apocalyptic vision of the separation of the sheep and the goats (Mt 25:31–46) we have a clear—albeit profoundly disturbing—picture of the nature of divine punishment. First there is *deprivation*. To the unrighteous the King-Judge says, "Depart from me, you cursed!" (v. 41; cf. Mt 7:23; Lk 13:25–27). Banishment from the divine presence is the essence of divine punishment. Just as the essence of heaven is fellowship with God, so the essence of hell is exclusion from that fellowship. Contemplation of the enormity and finality of this deprivation causes the mental anguish and spiritual torment often associated with "the outer darkness" or "the deepest darkness" (*to skotos to exōteron*) in New Testament representations (Mt 8:12; 22:13; Lk 13:28). Then there is *retribution*. "Depart from me . . . into the eternal fire (v. 41) . . . And they will go away into eternal punishment" (*eis kolasin aiōnion*, v. 46). Whereas the righteous inherit the kingdom "prepared for *you* from the foundation of the world" (v. 34), the unrighteous are consigned to the eternal fire "prepared for *the devil* and his angels" (v. 41). This shows that eternal election to salvation does not imply eternal election to perdition. However, the permanent rejection of light and truth as embodied in Christ does lead to retributive punishment. "For those who do not obey the truth . . . there will be wrath and fury" (Ro 2:8). "How much more severely do you think a person will deserve to be punished who has trampled the Son of God underfoot . . . ?" (Heb 10:29). These two motifs of deprivation and retribution, frightening in their implications, are associated and perhaps identified in 2 Thessalonians 1:8–9 where the retribution (*ekdikēsis*) inflicted on "those who refuse to know God and on those who refuse to obey the gospel of our Lord Jesus" (v. 8) is described as "the punishment of eternal ruin and exclusion from the presence of the Lord" (v. 9).

But on what ground or grounds is such dire punishment inflicted? In the Matthean apocalyptic vision the unrighteous are declared to be "cursed" because of their rejection of Jesus in their rejection of his messengers and the message about him that they bring (Mt 25:40, 45; cf. 10:40, 42). Expressed in Johannine idiom, the reason for being rejected by God is failure to believe that Jesus is Messiah (Jn 8:24) and so have one's name inscribed in the Lamb's Book of Life (Rev 20:15; 21:27); or in Pauline diction, failure to obey the truth contained in the gospel of the Lord Jesus (Ro 2:8; 2Th 1:8). Alongside this failure to do good—that is, to welcome Jesus and his representatives—as a ground for being pronounced anathema to God, there is the active practice of evil (Mt 7:23; Lk 13:27; Jn 5:29; Ro 2:9; Rev 21:8, 27). All this corresponds precisely to the two bases of judgment mentioned above (under A.), namely, a person's relationship to Christ, and works performed during one's lifetime.

As they await resurrection and final judgment, the unrighteous are already in a state of unalleviated spiritual anguish and

torment in Hades (Lk 16:23–25, 28; 2Pe 2:9). Although the
parable of the rich man and Lazarus (Lk 16:19–31) was told to
illustrate the danger of wealth (Lk 6:24) and the necessity of
repentance (Lk 16:28–30), not to satisfy our natural curiosity
about a human being's anthropological condition after death,
it is not illegitimate to deduce from the setting of the story the
basic characteristics of the postmortem state of both believers
and unbelievers.[6] Both groups are conscious of surroundings:
Lazarus is in Abraham's bosom and comforted (vv. 22–23,
25); the rich man is in Hades and tormented (vv. 23–25, 28).
There is memory of the past: the rich man is instructed to
"remember" earlier circumstances (v. 25), and he can recall
his family and their attitude to "Moses and the prophets" (vv.
27–30). Moreover the whole dialogue with Abraham suggests
that the departed have not only retained their capacity to
reason (v. 30) but also gained an acuteness of perception (vv.
27–28). So far from being a probationary period during which
dross is purged from the character of the believer and a further
opportunity for repentance is afforded to the unbeliever, the
intermediate state is marked by a "parting of the ways" after
a preliminary divine judgment at death that anticipates the
final judgment at the End (Heb 9:27). Since divine judgment is
based on an evaluation solely of one's life on earth (Ro 2:6;
2Co 5:10; 1Pe 1:17), the intermediate state affords the
unbeliever no second chance to repent and embrace the
gospel.

3. The duration of the condemnation

Is this deprivation and retribution a temporary penalty or a
permanent state? In answering this question the crucial issue
is the meaning of the Greek adjective *aiōnios*. With a future
reference the term is used forty-three times with "life" and
seven times in regard to punishment. Five different Greek
nouns are involved in this latter category: fire (*pyr*, Mt 18:8;
25:41; Jude 7); sin (*hamartēma*, Mk 3:29); judgment (*krima*,

Heb 6:2); destruction (*olethros*, 2Th 1:9); and punishment (*kolasis*, Mt 25:46). The use of *aiōnios* in Philemon 15 ("that you might get him back *permanently*") shows that the word need not mean "eternal," but on the other hand its application to God (Ro 16:26) or his Spirit (Heb 9:14) indicates that it can mean "eternal."

Derived from the noun *aiōn*, "age," "eternity," the adjective *aiōnios* has two corresponding senses: (1) "lasting for a [particular] age," "age-long," "aeonial"; (2) "eternal," when used of the future Age that was universally considered to be of infinite duration. It is sometimes claimed that the adjective is fundamentally qualitative in meaning ("having the characteristics of the age" in question) and that the quantitative or temporal sense is secondary. Such a thesis would be difficult to sustain either from secular Greek literature or from the Septuagint, where temporal considerations predominate (see the article on *aiōn* by H. Sasse in *TDNT* 1:197–209). It is of significance that there is a threefold temporal classification of the New Testament meanings of *aiōnios* in BAGD (28): "without beginning" (Ro 16:25; 2Ti 1:9; Tit 1:2); "without beginning or end" (Ro 16:26; Heb 9:14); "without end" (e.g., Lk 16:9; 2Pe 1:11; Rev 14:6; and all other New Testament references).

When we confront a passage such as Matthew 25:46 where the one adjective *aiōnios* is used with both "life" and "punishment," it seems arbitrary to render *aiōnios* by "aeonial" when used with "punishment" and by "eternal" in conjunction with "life," as though the punishment referred to simply belonged to the Age to Come and so would occur *in* eternity rather than lasting *throughout* eternity. If the life that is described as *aiōnios* is without end, so too will be the punishment that is described in the same way. The life and the punishment are identical in duration. So then, the loss involved in permanent banishment from God is not only inestimable (it is "ruin," *olethros*); it is irreversible (it is "eternal ruin" or "eternal destruction," *olethros aiōnios*, 2Th

1:9). The guilty have no recourse to a higher court which might quash the previous finding, for God is the supreme authority whose verdict is final. Hints are lacking in the New Testament of any possible reversal of the lot of the unrepentant. What is more, neither the Old Testament nor the New Testament entertains the possibility of the total extinction of persons.[7] The New Testament contains sufficient warnings of the dire, eternal consequences of rejecting Christ to leave us in no doubt that the early church rejected both universalism and annihilationism.

If several strands of the New Testament teach or imply a resurrection of the unrighteous that results in their permanent deprivation and eternal retribution, the total number of such references is small in comparison with the many references to the resurrection of the righteous to eternal life and immortality. The New Testament stresses the benefits that accrue from believing rather than the deprivation that results from refusal to believe. In their teaching about life after death New Testament authors focus their attention not on the fate of the unbeliever but on the destiny of the believer, and not on the penultimate "intermediate state" of the righteous dead but on the final destiny of resurrected saints: permanent residence in God's immediate presence, worshiping and serving him and the Lamb forever, in spiritual bodies perfectly adapted to the ecology of heaven and totally responsive to the dictates of the Spirit.

XII

Resurrection and Creation

Any discussion of the Last Things faces two dangers: an impersonal eschatology in which events are preeminent and people irrelevant; or an overly personal eschatology in which people are preeminent and "things" irrelevant. In one case the centrality of Christ and his church is overlooked and questions of divine timetabling come to the fore. In the other case, the destiny of the whole material universe is ignored and attention is concentrated on the individual's spiritual encounter with Christ after death. Since resurrection has to do with the raising of individual persons and the perfecting of the body of Christ, there is a real danger that a discussion of the Consummation should ignore or play down the importance of questions relating to the destiny of the whole material order.

Certainly the New Testament is not guilty of any such theological imbalance, for there are three well-known passages where the destinies of man and nature are explicitly interrelated.

A. Romans 8:18–25

Throughout this paragraph, "creation" (*ktisis*) probably refers to the irrational universe, that is, nonhuman nature. Paul describes the plight of creation in two phrases. "Not of its own accord" but by the will of God and because of humanity's sin (Ge 3:17), creation was *subjected to frustration*

(v. 20). Having lost its God-ordained destiny because sinful humanity could not properly fulfill its role of exercising dominion as God's representative on earth, creation became subject to frustrating emptiness, tantalizing imperfection, and disappointment that God's original purpose for creation remained unfulfilled. In addition, creation became characterized by a *bondage to decay* (v. 21). In place of the divinely intended freedom there came an inhibiting slavery to transitoriness, decay, and death. As a consequence the whole created universe now groans in unison (*systenazei*) and in unison travails with the pangs of childbirth (*synōdinei*) (v. 22). Yet there is hope (v. 20b), for creation is destined to be released from its frustrating bondage to decay (v. 21a) and to acquire the liberty that will accompany the revelation of the glory of God's children (v. 21b; cf. v. 19). This hope produces in creation not only the groaning and travailing (v. 22) but also an eager expectation comparable to that of the crowds in the arena who strain forward with outstretched heads as they await (*apokaradokia*) the approach of the chariots or the runners (v. 19). The reason for creation's eager longing is clear: its destiny is inextricably bound up with human destiny (vv. 19b, 21b). Just as nature was involved with humanity in the Fall, so it will share humanity's destiny in gaining release from corruption. Like humanity (v. 23), creation groans (v. 22). Like humanity (vv. 23, 25b), creation waits eagerly for a reversal of present frustration through the intervention of God (vv. 19–20). Like humanity, which shares the corruption and mortality of the material world (v. 23), creation will be redeemed by being emancipated from its slavery to decay (v. 21). But their situations also differ, for only humans are capable of conscious groaning, only humans can articulate this longing for freedom, and only redeemed humans are already a new creation (2Co 5:17).

B. Philippians 3:20-21

This pair of verses contains a remarkable juxtaposition of present and future motifs. "The commonwealth in which we hold citizenship is in heaven, and from there we await a Deliverer, the Lord Jesus Christ, who will transform our lowly bodies by giving them the character of his glorious body, as he effectively exercises the power that enables him also to make the universe subject to himself." What Christians await, Paul is saying, is not so much an event, remarkable as that will be, as a Person, the true emperor from the true capital, who will arrive as a mighty potentate to consummate his work of deliverance. Two acts will complete his work of salvation—the transformation of man (v. 21a) and the subjection of the universe (v. 21b). In an instance of *a fortiori* reasoning, Paul argues from Christ's effective exercise of power in reducing everything to subjection to his ability to effect the transformation of his redeemed creatures. Whereas in Romans 8 the movement of thought is from humanity to nature, here in Philippians 3 the thought moves from nature to humanity. But it is not simply that if Christ is able to perform the apparently greater work on nature, he must also be capable of performing the smaller work on humankind. The lesser work is actually an aspect of the greater. In other words, Christ's transformation of humanity into his own image (cf. Ro 8:29) is an integral part of his subjection of the entire universe to his own person. Transformation is an aspect of subjugation. On other grounds, too, we may suggest that the material creation will be subjugated by means of its transformation (see the discussion below under D.)

C. 1 Corinthians 15:20-28

Here the relation between the resurrection of humanity and the restoration of the universe is not so pronounced, but it is none the less apparent. Verses 20-23 specify two stages in the resurrection: first Christ, then his people. This ushers in the consummation of world history, when the sovereign Christ surrenders his perfected kingdom and himself to his Father (vv. 24–28). During Christ's reign by divine decree from the time of his resurrection until the Parousia, he progressively "puts under his feet" all enemies of his kingdom (v. 25), reducing them to helplessness (*katargein*, v. 24). Although the primary reference is to the sentient world rather than to the material universe, Paul affirms that when Psalm 8:6 (God "has put everything under his feet," originally referring to the dominion of man over the animal world, Ps 8:6a, 7–8) is finally fulfilled in the experience of the representative second Man, Jesus Christ, no part of the universe will remain outside his sovereignty or in rebellion against his lordship; only God himself is not subject to Christ (v. 27). The result of all this will be Paradise Regained, a return to the pristine state of the entire material order where God is "all in all," universally supreme (cf. v. 28).

At first sight it would appear that the relation between resurrection (vv. 20–23) and recreation (vv. 24–28) is purely temporal. That is, after the resurrection of Christ's people (v. 23), the Consummation dawns ("then comes the End" v. 24a). Yet the resurrection is a "bringing to life" (v. 22) and so marks the conquest of death (vv. 26, 54–55), one of the enemies of Christ's kingdom (vv. 25–26). So the resurrection of believers is not merely a necessary prelude to the perfecting of the kingdom but is also a crucial stage in its coming to perfection.[1]

D. New Creation or Renewed Creation?

From these three passages it is clear that redemption embraces the nonhuman cosmos as well as the human realm of creation. But what relation do the "new heavens and new earth" (Isa 65:17; 2Pe 3:13; Rev 21:1) bear to the old heavens and earth? Will the universe attain its God-appointed destiny by being transformed or by being replaced?

The issue generated a lively debate among seventeenth–century Lutheran theologians. Scriptural testimony is equivocal. Some texts suggest that the old will be annihilated and the new will come as a result of a fresh creation. Second Peter 3, for example, speaks of the dissolution or "passing away" of the heavens, the dissolution or melting of the elements (= heavenly bodies, vv. 10, 12), and the "burning up" of the earth along with its works (= buildings? v. 10). Only after this cosmic conflagration and disintegration can there be "new heavens and a new earth in which righteousness has its permanent home" (*katoikei*, v. 13). Other passages point to a recreation or reconstitution of the universe through renewal. Jesus promised his disciples that they would share his role as judge "when the universe is born anew" (*en tē palingenesiā*, literally, "in the rebirth," Mt 19:28). That is, the universe will "again [*palin*] come to be [*ginesthai*]" what it once was. Presumably this conversion to its original state is through its renovation. (Note that in the only other New Testament use of *palingenesia*, the term appears in conjunction with *anakainōsis*, "renewal," Tit 3:5). The recreation of the individual (Tit 3:5) prefigures the repristination of the universe (Mt 19:28). It is probable that the word *apokatastasis* ("establishment," "restoration") in Acts 3:21 alludes to such a "restoration" of the material world to its primeval purity and perfection, for Peter is referring to the fulfillment of all prophetic promises and in particular to the "establishment" of God's kingdom on earth. In the space of six sentences in the Apocalypse we find both the approaches that have been mentioned above. "Then I saw a new heaven and a new earth—the first heaven and the first earth had vanished. . . . And he who sat on the throne said, 'Look! I am making everything new' " (Rev 21:1, 5).

Noting that fire may be an agent of purification as well as of destruction, some scholars have sought to reconcile the two approaches by proposing that it is not a matter of *total* annihilation but of recreation by means of the judgment of purification. We have seen from Romans 8 that creation's destiny is release from decay, not annihilation. Creation stands under God's promise as well as under his judgment. But a choice between the two approaches or an effort to reconcile them is perhaps not necessary. There is an interesting correspondence between the ambivalent Pauline understanding of the way in which the spiritual body is related to the physical body and the ambiguous New Testament teaching concerning the relation between the present universe and the "new heavens and new earth." In each case two seemingly contradictory categories are used: change and exchange, transmutation and replacement. But the categories are not really mutually exclusive.[2] They are alternative and complementary ways of explaining events that are without parallel and beyond human knowledge, for in both cases there are elements of similarity (hence the "transformation" motif) as well as elements of dissimilarity (hence the "exchange" motif).

E. Conclusions

1. Humans are one with creation. As well as representing our individuality, our body (*sōma*) points to our oneness with creation. Accordingly, the destiny of the individual is interlocked with the destiny of the whole created universe and cannot be considered apart from it without seriously undermining the testimony of the New Testament. The emancipation of creation must be involved in our emancipation, for, given our oneness with creation, the redemption of simply that small segment of creation which is humanity is inconceivable. As at the Fall, so in the Restoration, what affects one affects the other. The entire material universe will share the destiny of Christ's people—harmony with the divine will through recreation—

just as it shared in the consequences of human sin. So it is that the "new heavens and new earth" (cf. 2Pe 3:13) correspond to humanity's new, resurrection body.

2. Since there is this indissoluble unity between humanity and nature in the future as in the past, there can be no dualism between spirit and matter. No New Testament writer envisages the salvation of the soul or spirit with the visible material world abandoned to oblivion. The liberty to be enjoyed by the children of God (Ro 8:21) does not consist of the emancipation of the soul from the body conceived of as a material prison house. It consists of the body's liberation from the rule of the flesh through a transformation into Christ's image (Ro 8:23, 29).

3. The New Testament contains several hints that at the consummation the universe will be restored to its pristine state (notably Mt 19:28, and possibly Ac 3:21). Creation's acute disappointment at fallen humanity's failure to rule as God had intended will be reversed. Creation's longing to regain its original integrity will be fulfilled when it is subjected to Christ (Php 3:21) instead of to futility and frustration (Ro 8:20). Just as the resurrection of humanity will restore it to its original openness and responsiveness to the Spirit of God, so the rebirth of nature will restore it to its original harmony and liberty (Ro 8:21). God will be "all in all" (1Co 15:28), and the whole material order will perfectly serve spiritual purposes. Consequently both resurrection and renovation are to be seen as the climax of the divine work of salvation.

4. The object of Christian expectation is primarily a Person rather than an event or a series of events (Php 3:20). Eschatology focuses on the Last One rather than the last things. Whereas the Apocalypse gives the title *Omega* to the Son (Rev 1:17; 2:8; 22:13) as well as to the Father (Rev

1:8; 21:6), Paul would seem (at least in 1Co 15:24, 28) to reserve such a title for the Father, Christ being the Penultimate One.

5. That there is to be a new universe is clear. As the seer of the Apocalypse expresses it, after the resurrection and judgment (Rev 20:11–15) the stage is set for the final act in the cosmic drama, the bringing in of "a new heaven and a new earth," with the holy city, new Jerusalem, which has descended to the new earth, as the seat of God's dwelling among his redeemed people (Rev 21:1–4). But precisely how God will bring in the new heaven and earth is not clear, whether after subjugation or after annihilation, whether by transformation or by replacement. The precise character of redeemed humanity's future state is presently hidden (1Jn 3:2); so too is the exact nature of the new or renewed universe.

——*XIII*——

The Transformation of the Living

Statisticians inform us that the world's population is growing at the rate of over 90 million persons each year and that by the year 2,000 there will be about 6.2 billion people living on our planet. The Christian faith, too, continues to grow, even if, sadly, this growth is not yet keeping pace with the population explosion.

Given these two indisputable facts—massive world population growth and the numerical growth of Christianity—it is probable that at the return of Christ there will be a far greater number of Christians still alive on earth than the sum total of departed believers of all past generations. What will be the destiny of this majority when Christ returns? How can they be raised from the dead if they have not died?

In our analysis of 1 Corinthians 15 (see above, chapter IX.C) we saw that in verses 51–57 Paul is discussing this very issue—the destiny of Christians alive at the second advent. In verse 36 he had made an apparently absolute statement: "What you sow is brought to life only if it dies." But if death is a prerequisite for resurrection, how will they fare who never die? Paul recognized this important exception to his "rule," and addresses this issue after he has answered (in vv. 36–50) the twofold question he posed in verse 35. "Listen, I am telling you a mystery: not all of us are to fall asleep, but *we shall all be changed* [v. 51]—in a flash, in the twinkling of an eye at the final trumpet blast. For the trumpet will sound, the dead will be raised immortal and *we shall be changed*" (v. 52). In verse 52 "the dead" and "we" are clearly contrasted, the "we" therefore referring to Christians who are destined to be alive at the second advent (cf. 1Th 4:15). This then indicates that the "we" in the parallel phrase in verse 51 also refers to those alive at the time of the Parousia, that is, the second advent of Christ. To paraphrase Paul's explanation in verse 51, "I am telling you about an aspect of God's purpose that has been communicated to me by special revelation. I expect that we who are now alive shall not all fall asleep; but the mystery revealed to me is that all of us who survive until the Parousia will be changed." On this view, the essence of the "mystery" (v. 51a) is that those Christians who do not, by a pre-Parousia death, qualify for the transformation that is the prerequisite for the inheritance of the kingdom (v. 50), nevertheless will all without exception undergo the required transformation at the Parousia.

Even if the transformation of the dead is not in view in verse 51, it is certainly implied by verse 52 when this verse is compared with verse 42. "The dead will be raised imperishable [*aphthartoi*]" presupposes a transformation, since "what is sown is perishable [*en phthorā*]." We may therefore safely conclude that Paul envisaged no exceptions to his maxim "the perishable does not inherit the imperishable" (v. 50b). Both the dead and the living must undergo a divinely instituted change before the kingdom of God can be inherited. So Paul's answer to the "problem" posed by Christians who do not die before Christ returns is this: the transformation of the living will be analogous to the resurrection transformation of the dead.

Nowhere, however, does the apostle define the precise nature of the transformation. Certainly the change is sufficiently radical to ensure that, although earthly life and embodiment may be characterized by perishability and comparative dishonor and weakness, heavenly life and embodiment will be marked by imperishability, glory, and power (vv.

42–43). It is sufficiently dramatic to make certain that "the image of the man of dust" will be totally eclipsed by "the image of the man of heaven" (v. 49), that the physical or natural body will give place to the spiritual body (v. 44). The use of the words *glory* (*doxa*) and *image* (*eikōn*) in reference to the heavenly body shows that the transformation involves inner being as well as external form, for in New Testament usage each of these terms denotes inward reality coming to visible expression.

Both the living and the dead, then, are "transformed." But are both "raised"? Verse 52 clearly contrasts the two groups, "the dead will be raised . . . and we [who remain until the coming of the Lord, 1Th 4:15] shall be changed," and reserves the experience of "resurrection" for the dead. This would lead us to conclude that although both the living and the dead are transformed, only the dead are raised—a conclusion that finds support from several other considerations.

To begin with, the very term "resurrection" implies prior death (see the Appendix, C.2), for only someone who has entered the realm of the dead can be restored to life. Death is a prerequisite for resurrection. The point becomes clearer still when the qualification "from the dead" or "of the dead" is added to the word *resurrection* (e.g., Ac 4:2; 1Co 15:42) or spiritual resurrection is said to reverse spiritual death (e.g., Eph 2:1, 5–6). Another relevant consideration is the use of verbs that denote resurrection or transformation. The verb *change* (*allassō*) is applied to the living (1Co 15:51–52), the verb *transform* (*metaschēmatizō*) to the dead and the living (Php 3:21), and the verb *make alive* (*zōopoieō*) to the dead and the living (Ro 8:11; 1Co 15:22 and possibly Jn 5:21b) as well as to the dead only (Jn 5:21a; Ro 4:17; 1Pe 3:18; cf. 1Co 15:36). But there is no clear instance where *raise* (*egeirō*) or *rise* (*anhistēmi*) is used with exclusive reference to those destined to be alive at the Parousia. Finally, the fact that resurrection involves transformation and that the living are transformed is no proof that the living are raised, for where resurrection involves transformation it also implies resuscitation. Our conclusion may therefore stand: both the living and the dead are to be transformed, the latter by resurrection.[1]

So justice is not done to the Pauline data by claiming that at the Parousia living Christians as well as deceased believers are "raised." Both groups are transformed, but only the dead are raised. The dictum "the resurrection of the dead and the transformation of the living" is sometimes taken to be an apt summary of Paul's teaching on this point. If we infer from this dictum that the dead are not transformed, we are distorting the truth. If we deduce that the living are not raised, we are preserving the truth. For both the living and the dead the outcome of the change they experience is identical—possession of the spiritual body and acquisition of immortality.

XIV

Resurrection, Immortality, and Eternal Life

It is a curious fact that few theological issues are as potentially explosive as the doctrines of resurrection and immortality. In the preface to his book *Immortality of the Soul or Resurrection of the Dead?* O. Cullmann confesses, "No other publication of mine has provoked such enthusiasm or such violent hostility."[1] What accounts for this curious fact?

Some who are convinced by arguments for the immortality of the soul have a strong antipathy to the biblical idea of resurrection because they imagine that resurrection means nothing more than reanimation: decomposed corpses are to be revived or scattered fragments are to be reassembled, the resurrection body having the same atomic structure as the body that was laid in the grave or was cremated. Or they find themselves repelled by the prospect of permanent embodiment.

On the other hand, many discern a threat to their faith in any talk of immortality. The term symbolizes for them the differences between Greek philosophy and biblical revelation: whereas Plato argued for immortality, Paul preached resurrection. To try to accommodate the notion of immortality within Christian theology is, they affirm, to invite disaster, for belief in immortality is incompatible with belief in bodily resurrection.

To a large extent the heat generated by the discussion of these issues arises from a misunderstanding of the New

Testament data. We have already alluded to two assumptions that are commonly held, but are in fact erroneous, that according to the New Testament resurrection amounts to nothing more than a return to life, and that Paul never spoke of immortality.

There can be little doubt that in this resurrection-immortality debate, immortality has generally been the loser, witness Cullmann's decisive answer to the question he posed in the title of his book. Few contest that the word *resurrection* has a legitimate place in any theological system built on the New Testament. Some may debate whether the most appropriate qualifying phrase to add to the term is "of the flesh," "of the dead," "of the body," or "of the person," but most agree that the term itself may not be jettisoned without losing an essential ingredient of Christian doctrine. The case is altogether different, however, with the word "immortality." The fundamental cause of the ambivalent Christian attitude toward immortality is that Western Christianity has naturalized the Platonic rather than the Pauline sense of the word, so that immortality is generally taken to mean the endless survival of a substantial soul. Yet most people recognize that in the occasional New Testament use of the term and its cognates a different sense is conveyed. Given this basic ambiguity in the current Christian use of the word, some have suggested that it is best avoided, preferring, for example, the term *resurrection*[2] or the expression "eternal life."[3] But to the present writer it seems unfortunate to allow the dominant contemporary use of a term to dictate acceptable Christian terminology. We acknowledge that the words *raise, rise,* and *resurrection* are much more commonly found in the New Testament than *immortal* or *immortality*. The very presence of these latter terms, however, should guarantee them a permanent place in the vocabulary of those whose view of the future is shaped by biblical teaching.[4]

A. Resurrection in the New Testament

In the Appendix we have examined in some detail the various nouns and verbs that denote resurrection and have made some general observations on their New Testament usage. Three of those observations are relevant to our present discussion.

1. We may distinguish five types of resurrection in New Testament usage:
   a. the past bodily resurrection of isolated individuals to physical life (e.g., Mk 5:41–42; Heb 11:35);
   b. the past bodily resurrection of Christ to immortality (e.g., Ro 6:9);
   c. the past spiritual resurrection of believers with Christ (e.g., Col 2:12);
   d. the future bodily resurrection of believers to immortality (e.g., Jn 5:29a; 1Co 15:52);
   e. the future personal resurrection of unbelievers to judgment (Jn 5:29b; Ac 24:15).

2. Resurrection should not be regarded as both an event and a process, for the present tense of verbs that denote the act of raising or rising is never found in the New Testament. Rather, it is an event leading to a state.

3. Although resurrection may occasionally denote mere restoration to life, in its distinctively Christian sense it also implies transformation and exaltation. In its full theological import, therefore, resurrection signifies the raising of persons from the dead to new and permanent life in the presence of God. Such a definition applies to the resurrection of Christ and to the spiritual and bodily resurrection of believers.

B. Immortality in the New Testament

1. Terminology

The noun *athanasia*, "deathlessness" (three uses), denotes the immunity from death enjoyed by God (1Ti 6:16) and by resurrected believers (1Co 15:53–54). The noun *aphtharsia*, "incorruptibility," "imperishability" (seven uses), signifies the immunity from decay that characterizes the divine state (Eph 6:24) and the resurrection state (1Co 15:42, 50, 53–54). It was "brought to light" by Christ as indicated in the gospel (2Ti 1:10) and is a divine gift granted to the righteous (Ro 2:7). Finally, the adjective *aphthartos*, "imperishable" (seven uses), describes the quality of the divine nature (Ro 1:23; 1Ti 1:17; 1Pe 1:23), the gentle and quiet disposition of the Christian woman (1Pe 3:4), and the Christian's reward (1Co 9:25) or inheritance (1Pe 3:4), and the future state of resurrected believers (1Co 15:52).

2. Observations on the use of these terms

a. Of the seventeen New Testament uses of the three terms, five apply directly or indirectly to God (Ro 1:23; Eph 6:24; 1Ti 1:17; 6:16; 1Pe 1:23) while the remaining twelve apply directly or indirectly to humankind and always (except for 1Pe 3:4) relate to its future destiny, not its present state.

b. The terms are never used in conjunction with the word *soul* (*psychē*) but all three are associated with the spiritual body (seven times, all in 1Co 15).

c. Never do we find the verb *athanatizō*, "I make immortal," "I immortalize," (and in the passive voice) "I am or become immortal," although in passages such as Romans 8:11 and especially 2 Corinthians 5:4 the verb might have proved suitable. Perhaps the New Testament writers avoided the term because it might easily be misunderstood as implying that immortality was procurable apart from resurrection.

d. All of the ten uses of the two nouns are Pauline.

e. Just as *aphtharsia* has the dual sense of "incorruption," meaning nondecay, and "incorruptibility," meaning the quality of being incapable of decay, so *athanasia* has the double meaning of "deathlessness," the state of being free from the principle of death, and "immortality," the quality of being incapable of dying. The person who has *aphtharsia* and *athanasia* is at any given moment free from decay and death and always will remain so. Moreover the terms are complementary. Every person who is immune from debilitating decay will therefore also be immune from death. And every person free from the inward working of the death principle must also be free of its expression in decay. When the terms are used as synonyms, each will signify immunity both from decay and from bodily or spiritual death.

f. Although the three terms are formed with "alpha privative," a negative prefix in Greek comparable to the English *in-* or *un-*, each takes on positive overtones relating to "(eternal) life." For example, just as God is "never-dying" (Ro 1:23; 1Ti 1:17; 6:16) because he is "ever-living" (Jer 10:10; Jn 5:26), so believers are destined to become free from decay and death because they will participate fully and immediately in the eternal divine life (2Pe 1:4).

g. Immortality may therefore be defined as the immunity from decay and death that results from having (in the case of God) or sharing (in the case of humanity) the eternal divine life.

3. The immortality of God

In 1 Timothy 6:16 we find an unequivocal assertion of the uniqueness of God's immortality. He is "the blessed and only

Sovereign . . . who alone has immortality" (*aphtharsia*). What constitutes God's immortality and how is it unique?

Behind each explicit negative definition of God's character lies some implicit positive affirmation. For instance, when we say that God is invisible we are not merely saying that he is not perceivable by human gaze or human enquiry but also implying that he is perceivable and knowable from his self-revelation. God is immaterial in that he is not composed of physical or measurable matter *and* in that he has a spiritual existence. What, then, is Scripture implicitly affirming when it denies God's propensity to decay and death? We propose two things: his incessant life and action and his inviolable holiness of character.

Immortality in God is not some passive inherent protection from the advent of death, nor simply the guarantee that traces of mortality will never appear in his character or conduct. It is the assurance that his incessant activity will never be terminated. He perpetually "gives life to all things" (1Ti 6:13), a statement that occurs, significantly, in the same Greek sentence as "who alone has immortality." He has in himself a constant supply of creative energy (Jn 5:26) that will never be depleted, far less exhausted. "He is the living God and the everlasting King" (Jer 10:10), the "living God" who acts in the physical realm (Ac 14:15–17) and the spiritual realm (1Ti 4:10), and the "everlasting King" who is seated on his throne and lives forever and ever (Rev 4:9–10; cf. Ps 90:2; 102:27; Rev 1:8; 10:6). The notion of immortality is inextricably tied to the ideas of life and eternality. Immortality implies that life and activity are constantly present as well as that inactivity and death are permanently absent.

The second positive truth implied by the scriptural affirmation of God's "nonmortality" is his holiness. One of the principal ways the Greeks distinguished men and gods was by reference to death. People are mortal (*hoi thnētoi*), the gods are immortal (*hoi athanatoi*; see, e.g., Plutarch, *Mor.* 960B). At the root of all other differences between them was this matter of subjection to or immunity from death. In a Christian context such a distinction remains (Ro 1:23) but with an important difference. Humans are mortal as sinners (Ro 5:12), God is immortal as the holy One (he "alone has immortality and dwells in unapproachable light," 1Ti 6:16). It is because of sin rather than simply because of mortality that "flesh and blood" cannot inherit the kingdom of God (cf. 1Co 15:50). Death is inexorably linked with sin, so where there is sin there is death. The complementary truth, however, is that where there is no sin, there is no death. Immortality is a concomitant or corollary of holiness.

The distinctiveness or uniqueness of God's immortality is to be located neither in his bodilessness nor in his spirituality nor simply in his being the only person inherently free from any propensity to deterioration which might lead to death, but rather in his being inherently deathless *as the eternal source of life*. Because the Father has intrinsic life (Ps 36:9; Jn 5:26; 6:57), corruption and death must be extrinsic to him. Immortality is an attribute of self-existence. On the other hand, decay and mortality are a characteristic of all created, dependent life (Ro 1:23; 8:20–22). Only the Creator and Sustainer of life is inherently immortal. Even in the consummation, when believers will become sharers of the divine nature (2Pe 1:4), this distinction between Creator and created will not be obliterated. God will remain the fount of all life and therefore also the source of immunity from decay and death.

4. The immortality of humanity

If, then, only God is inherently immortal, it follows that any immortality that may be ascribed to humankind is gained as a gracious gift of the divine will (cf. Ro 2:7; 6:23). That is, the corollary of the fact that only God is essentially immortal is the truth that man can be only derivatively immortal. His immortality is not essential or intrinsic, but derived or extrinsic.

But were human beings created immortal? In few places is it more important to have precise definitions of terms than in discussing this question. If *immortal* signified "with a soul that persists after bodily dissolution" or "without the seeds of decay and death," many would be willing to answer with an unequivocal "Yes!" But define *immortal* as "immune from decay and death as a result of sharing the divine life" and fewer would be content with an unqualified answer.

(1) Some believe that human beings were created "immortal" but forfeited that immortality through disobedience to God. But there seems to be a logical difficulty in the idea of losing immortality. However defined, immortality implies the permanence and irreversibility of the immortal state. It is hardly satisfactory to affirm that if Adam had proved obedient in his probation he would have gained "permanent immortality."[5] There cannot be degrees of immortality, nor can it be a momentary or temporary state.

(2) Others allege that human beings were created mortal yet were "immortable" (that is, able not to die)[6] in that they had the possibility of gaining immortality through obedience to God.[7]

(3) Still others affirm that human beings were created neither immortal (see Ge 3:22–24) nor mortal (see Ge 2:17) but with the possibility of becoming either, depending on their obedience or disobedience to God. They were created for immortality rather than with immortality. Potentially immortal by nature, human beings actually become immortal through grace. To use the classical distinctions, human beings were not created unable to die (*non posse mori*) but able not to die (*posse non mori*), although after the Fall they were unable not to die (*non posse non mori*).[8] Of the three views mentioned above, this last view seems best to cohere with Paul's insistence on the futurity of immortality.[9]

Our second issue is this: Who is to inherit this immortality? Is it the prerogative of all humanity or a privilege reserved for the righteous?

Romans 2:7–8 delineates two distinct categories of persons who will appear before God on the day of judgment. "To those who seek for glory, honor, and immortality by perseverance in well-doing, he will give eternal life; but for self-seeking people who resist the truth and yield to wickedness, there will be wrath and fury." It is a necessary implication of this distinction that just as those who pursue immortality will not experience wrath, so those who fail to obey the truth will be denied eternal life (which here subsumes immortality, as the parallelism shows).

In 1 Corinthians 15 the dead who are raised are depicted variously—as "those who have fallen asleep in Christ" (v. 18), "we who are in Christ" (v. 19), "those who belong to Christ" (v. 23), and "those who are of heaven" (v. 48), in each case the stress being upon relationship to "the Man from heaven." Even those who find some references to the general resurrection in the chapter agree that verses 51–54 must refer only to those in Christ, for the transformation alluded to in verses 51–52 denotes a conformity to the image of Christ, a destiny reserved for those on whom God fixed his affectionate regard (Ro 8:29). Investiture with imperishability and immortality (vv. 53–54) is therefore denied to those who are "separated from Christ" (Eph 2:12).

Immortality includes sharing the life of God. But this is a destiny belonging only to persons who have escaped the moral decay that is in the world because of lustful passions (2Pe 1:4), and it is inconceivable that any who are doomed to suffer the punishment of eternal exclusion from the presence of the Lord (2Th 1:9) should simultaneously enjoy the blessings of his immediate presence and life.

Finally we may ask, When is this gift of immortality received by the righteous? Second Timothy 1:10 indicates that life and immortality were "brought to light" by Christ Jesus "through the Good News" of his death and resurrection. It is not that Easter brought universal immortality, but it did inaugurate an era marked by the promise of eternal life and immortality. Only with the appearing of Christ did the idea of immortality emerge from Old Testament shadows into the full light of New Testament day. But the availability of immortality is not the same as its possession. Or appeal might be made to 1 Peter 1:23: "You have been born anew as a result of immortal not mortal sowing." That is, spiritual regeneration is the work of an immortal divine sower whose progeny is therefore also immortal. A similar meaning results from the alternative translation—"You have been born anew through imperishable not perishable seed." Just as human seed engenders mortal life so the divine seed of the word of God generates immortal life. But that a person becomes immortal because of and immediately after regeneration is at best an inference from this passage.[10]

According to L. Cerfaux, 2 Corinthians 4:7–5:10 and Philippians 1:19–26 are not primarily concerned with the Parousia or resurrection but with the state of Christians between death and the Parousia. Under the stimulation of his contact with Greek thought, Paul here develops a view of the intermediate state in which the personal Christian "self" acquires immortality at death, and, deprived of embodiment but in conscious fellowship with Christ, awaits the resurrection of the body at the Parousia. This "self" that becomes immortal at death Cerfaux elsewhere describes as the "inward man," the "self" independent of the body, the intellectual soul as a subsisting subject, and the "ego" in relationship with Christ.[11]

But 1 Corinthians 15 seems unambiguously to place the receipt of immortality at the resurrection, for it juxtaposes resurrection and immortality in the phrases "what is raised is immortal" (v. 42) and "the dead will be raised immortal" (v. 52). This latter verse does not mean "the dead will be raised and thus will be seen to be already immortal," but "the dead will be raised and thus become immortal." And, as we shall see below (XIII.D), it is the uniform testimony of the New Testament that a resurrection transformation is regarded as the only way to gain immortality. Of course it is possible that Paul would have linked immortality with regeneration, affirming that the seed of immortality is implanted by regeneration with the full flower appearing only after resurrection, or that the immortality gained potentially at the moment a person comes to be in Christ (cf. 1Co 15:22; 2Co 5:17) becomes an actual possession in the resurrection of the dead. But on the evidence of 1 Corinthians 15, it seems more probable that Paul simply portrays immortality as a divine gift gained through bodily resurrection. That is, immortality is a gift reserved for the afterlife. So far from already possessing immortality or from deserving it, Christians are described as those who "seek" it (Ro 2:7).[12]

Two important consequences follow from all this.

a. The concept of the *natural* "immortality of the soul" does not accord with the tenor of New Testament teaching.[13]

(1) God alone inherently possesses immortality (1Ti 6:15–16).

(2) Immortality is never predicated of the "soul" in the New Testament; "this mortal body" is destined to "put on" immortality (1Co 15:53–54). It is not by birth, but by grace, and through resurrection, that immortality is gained.

(3) The New Testament depicts immortality as a future gift (1Co 15:53–54).

(4) The Christian *summum bonum* is not equated with emancipation from corporeality but with the receipt of a spiritual body as a perfected instrument for the knowledge, worship, and service of God (Ro 8:23; 1Co 15:43–54; Php 3:20–21). What the Christian eagerly anticipates is his heavenly habitation, not incorporeal bliss (2Co 5:2–4).

(5) If a naturally immortal soul enjoys a self-sustaining subsistence before and after death, any sense of its dependence on God is eclipsed; the need for a relationship to Christ is removed; death comes to be regarded as either illusory or beneficial; corporeality is likely to be seen as an impediment; the afterlife tends to become the prolongation of the present life, a perpetuation of the status quo; and divine judgment is rendered inconsequential.

Under Plato's influence the Christian church has always affirmed the "immortality of the soul" in the sense that the soul of every person, by divine fiat, will survive death and exist forever.[14] For example, the Westminster Confession (XXXII.1) speaks of the souls of persons as having "an immortal subsistence." Although the concept behind these phrases is biblical, that is, that individual human beings do not cease to exist at or after death, there is no biblical precedent for attaching the terms *immortal* or *immortality* to the word *soul*. According to the New Testament, what is immortal is the resurrected believer.

b. Immortality, in its New Testament sense, is conditional. Only "those who belong to Christ" are destined to share God's immortality. "Conditional immortality" of this variety is quite different, of course, from the traditional or popular meaning of that expression. As commonly understood, "conditional immortality" is the view that only the righteous will live forever, the unrighteous being consigned to annihilation, either at death or after suffering divine punishment for a period. Paul, however, teaches that immortality is conditional, but only in the sense that there is no eternal life apart from Christ. This does *not* imply that existence beyond death, is conditional or that unbelievers will be annihilated. Because, in New Testament usage, immortality has positive content, being more than mere survival beyond death, its opposite is not nonexistence, but the "second death" (Rev 20:6, 14) which involves exclusion from God's presence (2Th 1:9).[15] Forfeiture of immortality means the deprivation of eternal blessedness but not the destruction of personal existence. All human beings survive beyond death, but not all will become immortal in the Pauline sense.

C. Eternal Life in the New Testament

For the Jew of the first century, eternal life was not a blessing of the "present age" but a boon reserved for "the Age to Come," the age of the resurrection (Da 12:2; PS 3:16; 1En 40:9; 58:3). The life of this future Age differs from the present age in its quality and also its indefinite or infinite duration. This outlook is preserved in the synoptic gospels (e.g., Mt 19:19; 25:46), notably in Mark 10:30 where Jesus promises to his faithful followers "eternal life in the Age to Come." This suggests that in the synoptics, as in contemporary Jewish thought, eternal life was regarded as the life of the Age to Come (= the Rabbinic *ḥayyê 'ôlām habbā'*; on which see *SB* 4:799–976), the life belonging to the future era and to God. This is not to say that the synoptics know only of "life" as earthly existence and physical well-being (e.g., Mt 6:25) and know nothing of present spiritual life. There are hints of (eternal) life as a present possession in the saying "Follow me, and leave the dead to bury their own dead" (disciples of Jesus are the "living") (Mt 8:22), and in the parable of the prodigal son where the father says to the elder son, "Your brother was dead, and is alive" (Lk 15:32).

What is implicit in synoptic teaching becomes explicit in the Johannine writings. Although the synoptic understanding of eternal life as a future blessing is also reflected in the fourth gospel (e.g., Jn 4:14; 5:29; 6:27), the distinctive feature of John when compared with the synoptics or with Rabbinic Judaism is the present dimension of eternal life (e.g., Jn 3:36; 5:24; 6:47; 17:3; 1Jn 2:24–25; 5:11–13). It is not that the Age to Come has actually become the present age but that its future blessings may be enjoyed in advance here and now. While a temporal dualism of "Now-Then" remains in the fourth gospel (witness the juxtaposition of the two aspects in 5:21–29; 6:40, 54), it is modified by the belief that the Then may be at least partially anticipated in the Now, for in its essence eternal life is knowing God and Christ (Jn 17:3). With regard to Paul, we have already discovered that he envisaged immortality as a future acquisition. All of his references to *eternal* life (viz. Ro 2:7; 5:21; 6:22–23; Gal 6:8; 1Ti 1:16; 6:12; Tit 1:2; 3:7; cf. 1Ti 4:8) seem to fall into this same category. It is a future phenomenon, as also in Acts 13:46, 48; Jude 21, which are the only New Testament uses of the expression "eternal life" outside the synoptic gospels, the Johannine writings, and Paul's letters.

Now that we have discussed the New Testament use of these three concepts—resurrection, immortality, eternal life—we are ready to compare each pair briefly.

D. Resurrection and Immortality

The New Testament does not present these two terms as either antithetical or synonymous. They are distinguishable yet intimately related. At this point we should note again, in the light of our earlier discussion of the resurrection of the unjust and of the relation between the resurrection of the dead and the transformation of the living, that it is necessary for the sake of precision to speak not simply of "resurrection" but of "a resurrection transformation." This is a category that embraces only Christians, but not simply Christians who will experience death before resurrection but also those who will be transformed without dying.

1. As inseparable ideas

a. A resurrection transformation is the sole means of acquiring immortality; there can be no immortality without a prior resurrection transformation (Lk 20:35–36; Ac 13:34–35; Ro 6:9; 1Co 15:42, 52–54).

b. Immortality is the inevitable outcome of a resurrection transformation; there can be no resurrection transformation without subsequent immortality (Lk 20:36b; Jn 11:25–26; Ro 6:9; 1Co 15:53–54; Rev 1:18; 20:6).

Although *conceptually* resurrection and immortality may be related by succession (as is implied in the preceding use of the words *means* and *outcome*), in *reality* the moment of final transformation is also the moment when immortality is attained, for the resurrection transformation itself involves an endowment with immortality, the putting on of the garment of immortality (1Co 15:53–54), or the swallowing up of mortality by eternal life (2Co 5:4).[16]

From a Christian perspective, then, the two doctrines stand or fall together. It is a case of resurrection to immortality or immortality through resurrection. To deny resurrection is to deny immortality, since the embodiment involved in a resurrection transformation is, from a Christian outlook, necessary for the enjoyment of the meaningful existence implied by immortality. On the other hand, to deny immortality is to deny resurrection, since the permanent supply of the divine life pledged by immortality is necessary to sustain the resurrection life of transformed persons.

2. As complementary ideas

a. (1) The Christian doctrine of resurrection prevents an impersonal interpretation of immortality. Belief in God's power to restore dead persons to life and impress them with the image of the "man from heaven" without compromising their individuality leaves no room for a mere immortality of influence by which a person lives on in the abstract ideals for which he or she stood, or a simple generational immortality by which a person lives on in his or her posterity, or a pantheistic immortality in which the individual is reabsorbed into the universal divine life.

(2) The Christian doctrine of resurrection forestalls an individualistic understanding of immortality. Resurrection is a corporate experience of "those who belong to Christ" (1Co 15:23), leading to their corporate dwelling with the Lord (1Th 4:17).

(3) The Christian doctrine of resurrection excludes the view that sees immortality as a disembodied or purely spiritual existence. The Christian's desire and destiny is not for release from embodiment but for the redemption of the body through resurrection (Ro 8:23), not for the divestiture of the physical body but for investiture with the spiritual body (2Co 5:2–4).

b. (1) The Christian doctrine of immortality prevents resurrection from being regarded simply as a single, isolated event. Directly resulting from the event of resurrection is the state of immortality, namely, immediate and permanent participation in the eternal divine life that leads to incorruptibility and deathlessness.

(2) The Christian doctrine of immortality precludes any equation of resurrection with the mere restoration of the dead to transient physical life. Immortality guarantees the permanency of the resurrection state. Jesus is not only the Resurrection but also the Life.

(3) The Christian doctrine of immortality forestalls the idea that resurrection life may languish from lack of sustenance. Immortality involves entrance upon a state of freedom from decay and death that is

permanent because it has the constant invigoration of God's endless power.

E. Immortality and Eternal Life

1. Similarities

a. Both expressions may depict in general terms "the final state of blessedness" (as in Ro 2:7) or "the heavenly mode of existence" (as in 1Co 15:52–54; Gal 6:8).

b. Both are gracious gifts of God unrelated to merit (Ac 11:18; 13:48; Ro 6:23; 1Co 15:52–54, 57) but related to the fulfillment of certain conditions: eternal life is the prospect for those who show repentance and faith (Ac 11:18; 13:48; 1Ti 1:16; 1Jn 5:13), who display steady perseverance in well-doing (Ro 2:7), who sow to the spirit (Gal 6:8); immortality is reserved for "those who belong to Christ" (1Co 15:23, 42, 52–54).

c. Both are inseparably related to resurrection transformation (compare Ro 6:22–23 with 8:11, 23, for eternal life; 1Co 15:35–57, for immortality), and therefore relate to whole persons.

2. Differences

a. With regard to form, one is a positive expression, relating to life; the other negative, relating to death. Correspondingly, eternal life refers primarily to quality (*zōē*, "life," denotes life that is really life, life in union with the divine life) and secondarily to quantity (*aiōnios*, "eternal," of unlimited or infinite duration). Immortality on the other hand, refers primarily to quantity (*athanasia*, "undyingness," the destiny of being eternally free from any death) and secondarily to quality (participation in the fullness of divine life).

b. From the perspective of John, who never uses the terms *immortal* or *immortality*,[17] eternal life is a present reality as well as a future experience, whereas for Paul both immortality and eternal life seem to lie in the future. This distinction may perhaps best be explained by observing that in John eternal life (or life) signifies (negatively) an immunity from spiritual death (Jn 5:24) but not from physical death (Jn 11:25), whereas immortality and eternal life in Paul involve immunity from spiritual *and* physical death.

c. As for the precise relation between Johannine eternal life which has future and present aspects, and Pauline immortality which has a negative side (immunity from death) and a positive side (participation in the divine life), we may propose that eternal life is the positive aspect of immortality, and that immortality is the future aspect of eternal life.

F. Resurrection and Eternal Life

1. Similarities

a. Both are initiated by divine action (Jn 6:54; 1Co 6:14, for resurrection; Jn 10:28; Ro 6:23; Tit 1:2, for eternal life).
b. Both are outcomes of present processes—resurrection, the outcome of a life of sanctification (Ro 6:22); eternal life, the outcome of "sowing to the spirit" (Gal 6:8).
c. Both have present and future aspects. Resurrection to new life occurs both in the present (Ro 6:4, 11, 13) and in the future (Jn 5:21; Ro 6:5, 8). For John, eternal life is both a present reality (Jn 3:36) and a future blessing (Jn 6:27).
d. In reference to believers, each implies the other. Everyone who is raised to immortality has eternal life

(Jn 11:25–26), and everyone who has eternal life has been raised to life (Jn 5:24) and will be raised bodily at the Last Day (Jn 6:40).

e. Both are intimately related to immortality (Lk 20:35–36 and 1Co 15:42, 52 for resurrection; Jn 6:54, 58 and Ro 2:7 for eternal life).

2. Differences

a. Resurrection will be the climax of the present experience of eternal life (Jn 6:40, 54). Eternal life is the future outcome of resurrection (Jn 5:29, "the resurrection resulting in [eternal] life").

b. Resurrection as reanimation—transformation—exaltation is a threefold event leading to the state of immortality. Eternal life as the knowledge of God and Christ (Jn 17:3) is a state that presupposes the event of passing from death to life (Jn 5:24).

c. Resurrection, unlike eternal life, is particularly concerned with the bodily aspect of the life to come (1Co 15:35–54).

d. The New Testament speaks of the resurrection of Christ, not of his gaining or regaining immortality or eternal life. His resurrection, not his immortality or his eternal life, is the paradigm for the transformation of believers.

e. Unbelievers will be "raised" in the sense of being restored to life, but they will not be given "eternal life" in the sense of sharing God's life forever.

XV

Resurrection Formulas: Credal and Biblical

In this brief chapter we shall consider the question, "What is the best way for the church to express in credal terms its belief in the resurrection"? Ought we to be content with the simple affirmation, "I believe in the resurrection"? What guidance is afforded by church tradition or biblical terminology or theological discussion?

To begin with, we need to make clear that we are considering here the future resurrection of humankind, not the past resurrection of Christ. Christian creeds regularly distinguish between the two, affirming Christ's resurrection from the dead when speaking of his earthly career, but reserving any reference to the resurrection of humankind until matters relating to the End are considered. In the Nicene Creed, for instance, Christians acknowledge that the one Lord Jesus Christ "rose again on the third day according to the Scriptures" but conclude the confession with "We look for a resurrection of the dead, and the life of the Age to Come."

A. Credal Formulations

1. The resurrection of the flesh

This was the standard credal formulation in the Eastern churches until A.D. 381 and in the West until the Reformation. To a large extent it owed its dominance and popularity to the succession of influential theologians who championed the phrase—Athenagoras, Tertullian, Methodius, Augustine, Gregory the Great, Thomas Aquinas, to name but a few.

To what does the word *flesh* refer in this phrase? English speakers naturally associate *flesh* with the soft tissue that covers the bones. We tend to think of Shylock and his "pound of flesh" in Shakespeare's *The Merchant of Venice*. There are two words for "flesh" in Greek. *Kreas* refers to an animal's "carcass," or, more often, to the flesh or "meat" that is found on an animal's bones. This term is never found in conjunction with *anastasis*, "resurrection," for the simple reason that *anastasis kreōs/kreōn* would mean "the hanging up of meat," as in an abattoir or butcher's shop! The other word is *sarx*. In classical Greek it normally denoted the external, tangible covering of the human or animal frame (as in "pound of flesh"). By synecdoche (part for the whole), *sarx* also meant "body" or "person." But, as J. T. Darragh has shown, in the Greek Old Testament (the Septuagint) the term acquired a wider set of meanings since it represented five distinct meanings of the Hebrew word *bāśār*: (i) "flesh," of animals used as food; (ii) the "flesh" of living human beings; (iii) "flesh" denoting any living creature, including human beings; (iv) "flesh" signifying a blood relationship or blood relatives; (v) "flesh" as the whole person, body and soul; humanity in its entirety, with emphasis on its frailty and mortality.[1] When the early church's theologians, who were steeped in the Septuagint, chose the word *sarx* in the credal formula *sarkos anastasis* ("resurrection of the flesh"), they had in mind either meaning (ii), with "flesh" standing for "the fleshly body" (by synecdoche),[2] or, more probably, meaning (v), the whole person, body and soul,[3] or all humanity, the whole human race.[4]

2. The resurrection of the dead

The First Council of Constantinople was an assembly of over 180 Greek bishops who met in A.D. 381 at the end of the Arian controversy to rally the Eastern church around the Nicene faith. The main achievement of this second of the so-called ecumenical or general councils was the repudiation of Apollinarianism, the erroneous teaching that in the person of Christ the divine Logos ("Word") replaced the human spirit, so that Jesus lacked complete manhood. With respect to the creed, the Council set aside the traditional but nonbiblical phrase, "the resurrection of the flesh," in favor of the biblical expression, "the resurrection of the dead." This change was doubtless also motivated by their desire to remove a possible source of misunderstanding, for, as we have seen, to the secular Greek ear *sarx* ("flesh") meant, first and foremost, the soft tissue that covers the bones of man and beast.

Of all existing creeds, the Constantinopolitan Creed of 381 "is the only one for which ecumenicity, or universal accept-ance, can be plausibly claimed. Unlike the purely Western Apostles' Creed, it was admitted as authoritative in East and West alike from 451 onwards."[5] In this creed the expression "the dead" refers to all deceased persons, the righteous and the unrighteous alike, so that the allusion is to the "general resurrection."

3. The resurrection of the body

It was not until 1552 that this formulation was admitted into the Apostles' Creed as used in Matins and Evensong in the Church of England. In the Baptismal Service, however, and in the Office for the Visitation of the Sick, the phrase "of the flesh" was retained.[6] "The resurrection of the body" has become a common credal formula in Protestant churches.

In this expression, "body" is in all probability simply synonymous with one or another meaning of "flesh," signify-ing either the physical body or humanity in its totality, body and soul. It has never been understood as referring to the church as the body of Christ.

B. Biblical Expressions

1. The resurrection of the dead

The New Testament uses this phrase not only in reference to all the deceased (as in Ac 17:32; 24:21; Heb 6:2), but also in reference to the resurrection of the righteous alone (Mt 22:31; Ac 23:6; 26:23; 1Co 15:12, 13, 21, 42) and once with respect to Jesus (Ro 1:4).

2. The resurrection from the dead

In the four New Testament uses of this variant construction, used only of believers (Lk 20:35; Ac 4:2; Php 3:11; 1Pe 1:3), "the dead" stands for "the realm inhabited by the dead," or, less probably, refers to "death" itself. See the Appendix.

Other formulations have been suggested, such as "the resurrection of the person,"[7] "the resurrection of man,"[8] or "resurrection in the body,"[9] but they do not improve on the expressions already discussed and lack the advantage of credal or biblical authority.

If one must choose between the four major options discussed above, a preference may be expressed for "the resurrection of the dead."

(1) This formulation, and this alone, has both biblical and credal precedent.

(2) Better than any other phrase, this expression accommodates the two main views that have been held by Christians through the centuries regarding the relation between the physical body and the resurrection body of believers—continuity of both person and "substance"; continuity of person but discontinuity of "matter."[10]

(3) This formula juxtaposes virtual opposites (raising to life; dead), and so draws attention to God's victory over death by means of resurrection.

(4) The qualification "of the dead," being personal in reference and plural in form (unlike the other formulas), highlights the communal and interpersonal nature of the resurrection state.

XVI

The Distinctives of the Christian View of Resurrection

When we attempt any comparison of Egyptian or Greek or Jewish thought about the life to come with the Christian viewpoint, we are always in danger of misrepresenting one view or the other through trafficking in broad generalizations. We could, of course, avoid such a danger by making a detailed comparison, for example, between the concept of resurrection and immortality in Paul's Corinthian letters and that reflected in *The Book of the Dead* or Plato's *Phaedo* or the Davidic Psalms. But that would be to assume that these particular books represent the essence or the high point of each religion or culture and to ignore the diversity and development of thought within each tradition. Perhaps we may strike a balance in our effort to sketch some of the broad differences between Christianity and these other religions and cultures with regard to resurrection and the future life, if we take the *Pyramid Texts*, the *Coffin Texts*, and *The Book of the Dead* as representative of Egyptian thought (see above, chapter I.A), Plato as reflecting the zenith of Greek thought, the Old Testament as the crown of Judaism, and the New Testament as normative for Christianity.

A. Egyptian and Christian Thought Contrasted

1. Whereas Osiris was revived after death by his wife's magical power and became king of the netherworld, Christ

was raised from death by his Father's glorious power (Ac 2:24; Ro 6:4) and became Lord of both the dead *and* the living (Ro 14:9; cf. 2Ti 4:1).

2. In his revived state Osiris is always portrayed in picture or statue as a mummified god, whereas the risen Jesus appeared to his disciples as their triumphant Lord and God (Mt 28:18; Jn 20:28; Rev 1:12–18).

3. Whereas in Egyptian religion the mystical assimilation of the deceased with Osiris was achieved by magical formulas, the living Christian's identification with Christ in his death and resurrection (Ro 6:3–5; Col 2:20; 3:1) comes through faith in God's action (Eph 2:4–6; Col 2:12–13).

4. For the Egyptians a morally upright life followed by a proper burial with the necessary magical mortuary rites guaranteed a pleasant afterlife, but for Christians it is faith and good works during one's earthly life that gain God's commendation after death or at the return of Christ (Mt 25:34; Jn 8:24; 1Co 4:5; 2Co 5:10; Gal 5:6; Jas 2:14–26).

5. In Egypt the criterion of judgment was conformity to Truth or Justice; for the Christian it is a personal relationship of trust in Christ (Mt 7:22–23; 10:32–33; Jn 3:36; Ro 5:9; 2Th 1:8–9), evidenced by good works (Ro 2:6; 1Pe 1:17; Rev 20:12–13).

6. Whereas the Egyptians regarded the future life as dependent on the mummified preservation of the earthly body so as to enable the spiritual counterpart or spirit-body to enjoy an other-worldly continuation of the pleasures and pursuits of this life, the New Testament depicts the hereafter as radically different from earthly life in that the redeemed will have bodies adapted to the ecology of heaven (1Co 15:42–44; 2Co 5:1; Php 3:21) and will

worship and serve God forever (Rev 5:11–13; 7:15; 22:3–5) in new heavens and a new earth (2Pe 3:13).

7. For the Egyptian, "resurrection" amounted to a kind of revivification of his personality (*ba*) in collaboration with his personal genius or *ka*, by virtue of his mummified body, and the ability of the "soul" (*ba*) to assume any shape it chose as it left the tomb each morning for its wanderings. For the Christian, on the other hand, resurrection is a rising up from death in a spiritual body to immortality and glory (Ro 2:7; 8:18, 23; 1Co 15:43–44; Php 3:11, 21).

8. In the view of the ancient Egyptians, the persons who were "true of voice" or justified in the judgment hall of Osiris were admitted to dwell among the stars or with the sun-god Ra in the Fields of the Blessed, with the honored and well-equipped tomb as one's "eternal house" to revisit for nourishment from the offerings presented there. Christians see the location of the righteous as being eternally "with Christ" and with all believers of all ages in the city of God, the capital of the consummated kingdom of God (Mt 26:29; Lk 23:43; Php 1:23; 1Th 4:17; Rev 21:2–4, 10; 22:3–5).

B. Greek and Christian Thought Contrasted

We have seen the considerable variety among the Greeks in their view of the hereafter (chapter I.B). But an outlook shared by them all was their rejection of "resurrection," however this term be defined. True, a few writers (such as Euripides and Plato) acknowledge the possibility that the gods could raise the dead,[1] but even in these exceptional cases resurrection merely means reanimation of the physical body through the return of the soul from Hades (e.g., Plato, *Symposium* 179 C). Many educated Greeks, however, aspired to immortality, convinced by the persuasive reasoning of that unrepeatable succession of philosophers—Socrates, Plato, and Aristotle.

Because Platonic arguments for the immortality of the rational soul have exercised a wider influence on Western thought than has Pythagorean teaching on the transmigration of the soul, we may be forgiven for focusing on immortality as the dominant feature of Greek thought about the Beyond and on Plato as its chief exponent. On the Christian side, once the focus is on immortality, we have no option but to turn to Paul, since all of the ten uses of the two New Testament terms for "immortality" (*aphtharsia, athanasia*) are Pauline. So a comparison of "Greek" and "Christian" thought about the life to come easily turns into a comparison between the Platonic and Pauline views of immortality.[2]

1. For Plato immortality was an inherent characteristic of the rational "part" or function of the human soul because of its affinity with the invisible, eternal realm of the Ideas or Forms and because of its participation in the Form of life, but Paul portrays immortality as a natural property of God, and of God alone (1Ti 6:16).

2. In Platonic thought the individual person could lay claim to being immortal as a consequence of having a soul. The immortality of his rational soul was an inherent and present possession, although only the true and unwavering philosopher could be said to be presently enjoying on earth the benefits of godlikeness and immortality, already dwelling in the Islands of the Blest. In contrast, Paul depicts immortality as a future acquisition. Whenever the terms *athanasia* and *aphtharsia* are applied directly and personally to human beings (Ro 2:7; 1Co 15:42, 50, 52–54), the reference is always to a state that commences after death.

3. For Plato the soul could not reenter its true abode in the world of Forms until death released it from corporeality, whereas Paul taught that the destiny of the Christian is bodily immortality, with the spiritual body (1Co 15:44) being the organ of resurrection life. For one, a person is an incarcerated soul; for the other, a person is and will remain a body-spirit unity.

4. It follows from Plato's repudiation of the body both in the here and in the hereafter that although he can juxtapose the concepts of the immortality and the reincarnation of the individual soul, there is no room for the notion of the resurrection of dead persons. For Paul, however, there is no incompatibility between the ideas of immortality and resurrection. Immortality is gained through a resurrection transformation (Ac 13:34; Ro 6:9; 1Co 15:42, 51–54).

5 Whereas Plato saw immortality as the natural property of all human souls, Paul regards it as a conditional as well as a future possession. It is death or a propensity to death, not immortality, that mankind inherits from Adam (Ro 5:12; 1Co 15:22), and it is "those who belong to Christ," not all who are in Adam, who at Christ's coming will be made alive by a resurrection transformation that issues in immortality (1Co 15:22–23, 42, 52–54). Immortality is not a gift bequeathed to all by the First Adam but an inheritance won for the righteous by the Second Adam. Possession of immortality is dependent on one's relationship to the Second Adam, not the First Adam.

6. In the case of Plato, the ultimate ground for the assurance of immortality was belief in the soul's "divinity," in its affinity with transcendent Being. For Paul, the basis of confidence that Christians will inherit immortality is the gracious will of God, who has already given us his Spirit as a pledge of a resurrection transformation that will result in

immortality (2Co 5:4–5) and has promised immortality to those who seek it by perseverance in well-doing (Ro 2:7).

C. Jewish and Christian Thought Contrasted

As noted above, in this comparison we shall take the Old Testament to represent Jewish thought, and the New Testament Christian thought.

1. Although there are several clear references to resurrection in the Old Testament, this concept never occupies the central place that it does in the New Testament, where the advent—death—resurrection of Jesus marks the fulfillment of the divine promises spoken by the prophets (Mk 1:15; Lk 24:25–26; Ac 2:22–28; 13:26–35), the end of the present age (1Co 10:11; Heb. 9:26; 1Pe 1:20), and the dawning of the Age to Come, the age of the Spirit (Ac 2:17, 32–33). The earliest Christian message, first proclaimed in Jerusalem, was basically "Jesus and the resurrection" (Ac 4:2, 33; 17:18; Ro 10:9).

2. The Jews always placed resurrection at the end of human history, never within human history. The isolated examples of resurrection reported in the Old Testament amounted to reanimation, followed by restoration to a normal physical life on earth until death occurred a second time. A resurrection to eternal life and glory could not occur until God had ushered in the Age to Come. Martha's response to Jesus regarding Lazarus expresses the Jewish view perfectly: "I know that he will rise again in the resurrection on the Last Day" (Jn 11:24; cf. Lk 14:14). But from a Christian viewpoint, the resurrection of the dead began with the resurrection of Christ (Ro 1:4; 1Co 15:21 RSV), so that he is portrayed as the firstfruits of the full harvest yet to come (1Co 15:20, 23). Resurrection is a

present reality already operative within history, not merely a future hope to be realized at the end of history.

3. Whereas the Jews always conceived of resurrection in corporate terms, speaking only of the resurrection of the group (whether the faithful remnant within Israel, the whole nation, or humankind as a whole), the early Christians claimed that a single individual, Jesus the Messiah, had risen from the grave, never to die again (Ac 13:34; Ro 6:9; Rev 1:18).

4. In the Old Testament, participation in the resurrection to everlasting life depended on a faith relationship to Yahweh during life, whereas in the New Testament resurrection to immortality is reserved for "those who belong to the Christ" (1Co 15:23 TCNT), Yahweh's Messiah.

5. The Old Testament lacks a developed view of immortality. Only in Daniel 12:2 is it affirmed that resurrection issues in immortality. But this precise association of ideas becomes common in the New Testament (Lk 20:35–36; Jn 11:25–26; Ac 13:34–35; Ro 6:9; 1Co 15:42, 52–54; Rev 1:18; 20:6).

XVII

Conclusion

Jesus Christ is the center of human history. This is reflected in the Gregorian calendar that is used throughout the world for civil purposes. History is reckoned as being either *anno domini* (A.D.), "in the year of the Lord," or Before Christ (B.C.).

Jesus Christ was also the center of early Christian preaching. The essence of the good news proclaimed by the first Christians was "Jesus and the resurrection" (Ac 17:18) or "the resurrection of the Lord Jesus" (Ac 4:33) or "Jesus Christ, risen from the dead" (2Ti 2:8). Central in the preaching about Jesus was the announcement of his resurrection.

We have endeavored to reflect these facts in the structure of this book: "Resurrection Before Christ," "The Resurrection of Christ," and "Resurrection After Christ." So it is fitting in these concluding observations that we return to the heart of the matter, "Jesus Christ, risen from the dead," and consider first of all, three timeless truths about the risen Jesus, and then three appropriate responses to the risen Jesus.

A. Timeless Truths About the Risen Jesus

1. Jesus is alive forever

There is a quaint Italian proverb which says *Traduttori, traditori*, "translators are traitors." That is, no translator can ever do full justice to the text he or she is translating, for no two languages fully correspond in such matters as grammar, word order, word meaning, and idiom; and where the translator does less than justice, he or she is, inevitably, a traitor to the original author and his text. A most notable example of the truth of this proverb is found in the way English translations are forced to translate the term *egēgertai*, which occurs no fewer than seven times in 1 Corinthians 15:1–20 in reference to Christ's resurrection and only twice elsewhere in the New Testament (Mt 11:11; Mk 6:14). In form, it is the perfect passive of the verb *egeirō*, "raise." Most versions render it "[Christ] has been raised." This is an entirely proper translation into English, except that it fails to do full justice to the Greek perfect tense, which implies a past fact ("he rose" or "he was raised," *ēgerthē*) but focuses our attention on the present and permanent results of that past fact, that "he is risen." The problem in English is compounded by the very first use of this form in 1 Corinthians 15, where Paul adds "on the third day" (v. 4). We cannot say in English "he has been raised on the third day" or "he is risen on the third day," only "he rose on the third day" or "he was raised on the third day." If we are to bring out the sense of the Greek tense here, we must indulge in a paraphrase, "he was raised on the third day—and is alive today."

Paul was as convinced as anyone of the past fact of Christ's rising from the dead. But he recognized equally clearly that this stupendous historical event has permanent consequences. Jesus died, but he is no longer on the cross. He was buried, but he is no longer in the grave. He is alive—and will always remain so. As Paul expresses it elsewhere, "We know that Christ, once raised from the dead, will never die again" (Ro 6:9).

If Jesus is alive forever, we may justifiably ask "Where is he now?" and "What is he doing?" To these questions the New Testament gives unambiguous answers. He holds a position of unparalleled honor and power in God's immediate presence and serves as the Leader of the new people of God and as the Savior of all who look to him for salvation from sin. He is building his church, sympathetically supporting those in temptation or need, advocating the cause of the repentant sinner, interceding on behalf of his people, and enlightening the conscience of all. And in addition to these "spiritual" activities, he continues to sustain the physical universe by his authoritative word. All his activity on earth is carried out by his Spirit, his Other Self, who makes the presence and power of Jesus real in the experience of believers. But Jesus has promised a personal return visit to earth, this time not to deal with human sin but to gather together all his followers to celebrate and share in his universal reign. Even as we eagerly await his return and seek to carry out his purposes on earth, we enjoy his constant companionship, for his final promise before his departure to heaven was "Remember, I am with you constantly, until the close of the age" (Mt 28:20).[1]

2. Jesus is conqueror of death

The natural human reaction to death is twofold. There is fear before the unknown and anger when confronted with the inevitable. "What will happen to me when I cross into the Great Unknown?" "Why should all human beings without exception have to suffer the indignity of being deprived of life?"

The fear of death is universal. It is not simply the by-product of the instinct of self-preservation. It is also born of uncertainty about the time and manner of our death and about the pain possibly involved in the process of dying. But above all this recoil from death stems from the natural intuition of human beings that we are accountable to some Being after death for our conduct during life. "People are destined to die but once, and afterwards comes judgment" (Heb 9:27).

The notion of anger in the face of death finds classic expression in a poem by Dylan Thomas. It is an incantatory protest against death, written as he observed his father's fading strength while battling with a terminal illness.

Do not go gentle into that good night,
Old age should burn and rave at close of day;
Rage, rage against the dying of the light.

Wherever the New Testament speaks of the risen Jesus, he is depicted not only as someone who is alive forever but also as the triumphant victor over death and the grave. In Revelation 1:17–18 we read of John's reaction to the vision of the resurrected Christ—he fell into a deathlike swoon. But Jesus reassures John with the words, "Stop being fearful! I am the First and the Last, and the Living One—for I was dead but now I am alive forever and ever, and I own the keys that unlock the prison of death and the grave." Not only did the ever-living One surrender his immortality and die; he rose in a deathless state and with supreme authority over the whole realm of the dead. He burst out of the prison of death, carrying the keys of the prison with him! This truth that the risen and exalted Christ has permanent dominion over death is the positive complement of Romans 6:9, "death no longer has dominion over him."

Celebration of Christ's deathlessness and his victory over death has always been part of Christian worship.

Death cannot keep his prey,
Jesus, my Savior!
He tore the bars away,
Jesus, my Lord!

Up from the grave He arose,
With a mighty triumph o'er His foes;
He arose a Victor from the dark domain,
And He lives forever with His saints to reign!
He arose! He arose!
Hallelujah! Christ arose!

Or again,

> Lo! Jesus meets us, risen from the tomb;
> Lovingly He greets us, scatters fear and gloom;
> Let the Church with gladness hymns of triumph sing,
> For her Lord now liveth; death hath lost its sting.
>
> *Thine be the glory, risen, conquering Son,*
> *Endless is the victory Thou o'er death hast won.*

All this has revolutionized the Christian's attitude toward death. Instead of feeling anger or "rage" (as Dylan Thomas advocated), the believer feels deep sorrow when confronted by "the dying of the light" of life. It was at the tomb of Lazarus that Jesus "burst into tears" (*edakrysen*, Jn 11:35). It was as he contemplated his own imminent death that Jesus prayed "with earnest cries and tears" (Heb 5:7; cf. Lk 22:44). Jesus is the pattern for believers. Yet any kind of despairing grief is inconsistent with Christian hope (1Th 4:13).

And what of fear in the face of death? The Christian attitude toward dying seems to be ambivalent. Since death deprives us of physical embodiment and corporateness, removing us totally and finally from the securities of earthly existence, and since physical death is the result of sin (Ro 5:12; 6:23), Christians should never eagerly anticipate or embrace the experience. On the other hand, in that death's sting was drawn by Christ's triumph over the grave (1Co 15:55–57) so that death now brings enriched communion with Christ (Php 1:23), the arrival of death is not to be dreaded. That is, for the believer death is neither to be welcomed nor to be feared.

3. Jesus is judge of all persons

The climax of Paul's address before the Court of the Areopagus in Athens was reached when he affirmed that "God has fixed a day on which he will judge the world with justice in the person of a man whom he has appointed for this task. He has given everyone assurance of this fact by raising him from the dead" (Ac 17:31). Here we see the unmistakable link between Jesus' resurrection and his role as judge. Paul saw the Resurrection as God's pledge that Jesus is the future judge of the world. What is meant by "the world" is clear from Paul's last letter, where he describes Jesus as the one "who is to judge the living and the dead," that is, all humankind, whether they be alive or dead at his appearing (2Ti 4:1). On that Day no person will be able to avoid an appearance before Christ and no secrets will remain undisclosed (Ro 2:16; 1Co 4:5). There will be no jury or jury deliberation, for God himself will be the Judge, acting directly through his Son alone (Ac 10:42). The verdict will be fair and impartial (Ro 2:5, 11), and no appeal to a higher court will be possible, for this is the Supreme Court *par excellence*.

How should this affect our conduct? In his Areopagus speech Paul is explicit on this point. "God now commands everyone everywhere to repent, *because* [*kathoti*] he has fixed a day on which he will judge the world . . ." (Ac 17:30–31). A complete change of attitude and behavior with respect to God and sin is the inevitable response when we are overtaken by a sense of our future accountability to God for every aspect of our lives. But what of those who have already "repented"? Here, too, Paul supplies the answer. "We make it our constant aim to please him [Christ], for we must all appear before Christ's tribunal so that each person may receive due recompense for deeds performed while in the body, whether these deeds be judged good or bad" (2Co 5:10). That is, because of our future accountability to Christ we make it our present goal in life to please him in every respect.

B. Appropriate Responses to the Risen Jesus

1. Reverential awe

Most students of the New Testament believe that Mark's gospel was the first to be published and that it originally ended at 16:8. Whether or not that be so, this verse ends with the simple words, "for they were filled with awe" (*ephobounto gar*).

Mark's account of the discovery of the empty tomb (Mk 16:1–8) focuses attention on *the reaction of the women*. Verses 1–3 underline the women's state of unpreparedness for what follows and so heighten the dramatic effect of the *dénouement*. They were returning to the tomb to anoint the head of Jesus with aromatic oil (v. 1) so that decomposition might be temporarily arrested or at least the foul odors caused by decomposition might be reduced. Obviously they were not expecting Jesus to rise from the dead in the near future. Verse 3 reads as a vivid eyewitness detail. For all their careful preparation the women had overlooked the one obvious problem—the removal of the stone from the entrance to the tomb. Following their nervous anxiety at this embarrassing oversight (note the imperfect tense, *elegon*, "they repeatedly said," v. 3), they were overtaken by surprise and alarm (grave robbers?) to discover the stone already rolled back (v. 4). This turned to amazement (vv. 5, 6a) as they were confronted by a heavenly visitor. When he proclaimed that Jesus was risen and would appear in Galilee (vv. 6–7), they trembled and were utterly bewildered (v. 8a). At verse 8 a psychological crescendo has been reached. An agitated awe (v. 5) has given place to a reverential awe (v. 8b). This final response of deferential fear marked their total reaction to the whole series of events, rather than merely to the angelic announcement (vv. 6–7). Theirs was no cringing fear of discovery and reprisal by the Roman or Jewish authorities, but a holy awe in the face of direct divine intervention displayed in the resurrection of Jesus and the removal of the stone (vv. 4–6) and direct divine revelation given in the angelic announcement (vv. 6–7). Throughout Mark's gospel the experience of awe was a typical human reaction to the presence of Jesus or the display of his power or authority.[2] It cannot therefore be deemed inappropriate for Mark to conclude his gospel with a reference to the only suitable human response to the stupendous fact of the resurrection of Jesus— "holy awe overpowered them."

We have not been privileged to be among the contemporaries of Jesus or to see Jesus alive from the dead. Yet the reaction of the women should be ours too, for the fact of his rising is no less stupendous for our being denied these privileges.

As we reflect on the "mystery" of this resurrection to immortality, our sense of awe deepens still further. No mortal eyes actually saw the Resurrection: certain people saw the risen Christ, but no one saw Christ rise. The Resurrection was a sacred and private transaction between the Father and his Son whom he dearly loves. Like the incarnation of Jesus in the womb of Mary, the resurrection of Jesus from the tomb of Joseph took place in the deep silence of God. There was angelic singing at the birth of Jesus (Lk 2:13) and seismic convulsions at the death of Jesus (Mt 27:51), but silence surrounded his conception and his resurrection. Here is profound mystery that evokes awe.

2. Humble worship

But it is not enough simply to be overwhelmed with awe at the fact and mystery of the Resurrection. We must progress from reverential awe before the fact of Jesus' resurrection to humble worship of the Jesus who rose.

We have seen that Mark's narrative emphasized the amazement and awe of the women who visited the tomb. This emphasis is no less prominent in Matthew (28:5, 8, 10), but he introduces two additional notes—joy and worship. The women "departed quickly from the tomb, in awe and great joy" (Mt 28:8). As they hurried off to break the news to Jesus' disciples, "suddenly Jesus was there in their path" (Mt 28:9 NEB). Reassured by his warm greeting, "they came up to him, clasped his feet, and knelt before him in worship" (Mt 28:9).

Their awe at the empty tomb and the angelic message, "He has risen" (Mt 28:6), was complemented by their worship of the risen Lord. And in the final episode of his gospel Matthew records that when the eleven disciples had gathered on the Galilean mountain where Jesus had arranged to meet them, although some of them seem to have failed to recognize Jesus at a distance, the majority worshiped him as soon as they saw him (28:16–17).[3] In a similar way, Luke concludes the third gospel with the remarkable scene of the disciples worshiping Jesus as he was being carried up into heaven and after he had disappeared from their view (Lk 24:52).

3. Simple belief

Even when we have been awestruck by the fact that a Person has returned from the grave in an immortal body and have felt compelled to bow before him in worship, we may still remain outside the kingdom of God—until we take a final step of faith. From hearts filled with awe and worship must come the simple affirmation of faith, first addressed to the risen Jesus by Thomas, "My Lord and my God!" (Jn 20:28).

It is difficult to overestimate the importance of the Thomas story (Jn 20:24–29) both in John 20 and in the whole gospel. It stands as the last of the four resurrection stories in the chapter, immediately before a statement of the purpose of this gospel (vv. 30–31). The reader is expectant. It was the second time that the disciples had met behind locked doors "in the house," the second time that Jesus "came and stood among them" and pronounced the blessing "Peace be with you." If Jesus had commissioned his disciples and granted them the Spirit at his first appearance, what would mark the second? The author answers: Thomas recognizes the deity of the risen Jesus (v. 28), and Jesus delivers the last and greatest beatitude (v. 29).

Thomas's cry "My Lord and my God!" (v. 28) is an exclamation specifically directed to Jesus, as its subject and recipient. "Thomas answered him." We know that this confession of faith was not an extravagant acclamation because of two facts. First, the Evangelist records no rebuke of Jesus to Thomas for his worship.[4] Thomas was not guilty of worshiping the creature over the Creator. Indeed, Jesus' word to Thomas—"You have believed" (v. 29a)—implies the acceptance of his confession. Second, John has endorsed Thomas's confession by making it his final and climactic affirmation about Christ. The author found in Thomas's cry a convenient means by which he might bring into sharp focus at the end of his gospel the ultimate implications of his portrait of Jesus. As "Lord" in the physical and spiritual realms, Jesus shared his Father's authority, functions, and rights (cf. Jn 5:17–18, 21–23, 26). As "God," he was one with the Father in his being (Jn 1:1, 18; 10:30). "My Lord and my God!" In these words we have the final pinnacle of the Gospel. Just as Israel honored Yahweh as "the Lord our God" (Ps 99:8) and Christians honor the Father as "our Lord and God" (Rev 4:11), so now all people are to "honor the Son, even as they honor the Father" (Jn 5:23).

The episode ends with the last and perhaps the greatest beatitude of Jesus, a blessing pronounced on those who believe without "seeing." "Then Jesus told Thomas, 'Because you have seen me, you have believed in me. Blessed are those who believe without ever seeing me!'" (Jn 20:29).

When Jesus, risen from the grave and exalted to glory, meets us, he comes to us as One who is alive forever, the Conqueror of death, and the Judge of all. He evokes our reverential awe; he prompts our humble worship; he invites our simple belief. If we respond with a wholehearted and lifelong commitment of ourselves to him, we in turn shall follow him from grave to glory.

──── ENDNOTES TO PART 1 ────

I: The Afterlife and Resurrection in Egypt and Greece

[1] I am indebted to Dr. Gleason L. Archer, Jr., for his detailed and helpful comments on this section. For further reading on Egyptian eschatology, see C. Andrews, *Egyptian Mummies* (Cambridge, Mass.: HUP, 1984); E. A. T. W. Budge, *Osiris and the Egyptian Resurrection*, 2 vols. (London: Warner/New York: Putnam's, 1911); S. G. F. Brandon, *The Judgment of the Dead* (London: Weidenfeld and Nicolson, 1967), 6–48; cf. his briefer treatment "Life after Death -IV. The After-Life in Ancient Egyptian Faith and Practice," *Expository Times* 76 (1965): 217–20; A. H. Gardiner, *The Attitude of the Ancient Egyptians to Death and the Dead* (Cambridge: CUP, 1935); G. Wagner, *Pauline Baptism and the Pagan Mysteries* (ETr. by J. P. Smith) (London: Oliver & Boyd, 1967), 89–98, 114–35, 260–62 (on Osirian legends and rituals).

[2] Full treatments of this theme are found in E. Rohde, *Psyche. The Cult of Souls and Belief in Immortality among the Greeks*, 8th ed. (London: Kegan, 1925); A. S. Pringle-Pattison, *The Idea of Immortality* (Oxford: Clarendon, 1922), 19–71; C. H. Moore, *Ancient Beliefs in the Immortality of the Soul* (London: Harrap, 1931), 3–36. The analysis that follows is indebted to these discussions.

[3] On immortality in Plato, see R. L. Patterson, *Plato on Immortality* (University Park, Pa.: Pennsylvania State University, 1965); R. S. Bluck, *Plato's Phaedo* (New York: Bobbs-Merrill, 1955), especially 18–33, 56–57, 62–64, 73–74, 117–19. Plato had not always entertained belief in the immortality of

the soul, for neither in the *Apology* nor in the earliest portion of the *Republic* (viz. 3.368–5.460C) does he abandon the Socratic view that death brings the unconsciousness of dreamless sleep or a migration of the soul to a realm not unlike the Homeric Hades (see Rohde, *Psyche* [n. 2 above], 477–78 n. 8).

[4]F. Copleston, *A History of Philosophy, Volume 1. Greece and Rome*, 2d ed. (New York: Newman, 1947), 209–10.

[5]Rohde, *Psyche* (n. 2 above), 472. See also his important footnote (486–87 n. 73) where he justifies his conclusion. For a contrary view, see G. M. A. Grube, *Plato's Thought* (London: Methuen, 1935), 147–49, who stresses the relation between Plato's developing view of the nature of the soul and his arguments for immortality, but asserts that "from first to last the aim of the Platonic philosopher is to live on the universal plane, to *lose himself* more and more in the contemplation of truth, so that the perfect psyche would, it seems, lose itself completely in the universal mind, the world-psyche. Hence it remains individual only in so far as it is imperfect, and personal immortality is not something to aim at, but something to outgrow."

[6]For a detailed comparison between this "wonder" and the Lukan account (Lk 7:11–17) of the raising of the widow of Nain's son by Jesus, see M. J. Harris, "'The Dead are Restored to Life': Miracles of Revivification in the Gospels," in *Gospel Perspectives. Volume 6. The Miracles of Jesus*, ed. D. Wenham and C. Blomberg (Sheffield: JSOT, 1986), 301–3, where it is concluded that "the differences between the accounts are so numerous and substantial . . . that any theory of their interdependence or their dependence on a common tradition may be discounted" (303).

[7]This interpretation of Ac 17:18, 32 assumes (1) that the Epicurean philosophers mentioned in v. 18 are the "some" (*tines*, second occurrence) of v. 18a who said "What is this fellow trying to say with his scraps of learning?" *and* the "some (*hoi men*) of v. 32a who mocked Paul after his speech; and (2) that the Stoic philosophers also mentioned at the beginning of v. 18 are the "others" (*hoi de*) of v. 18b who commented "He seems to be a preacher of

foreign deities" *and* the "others" (*hoi de*) of v. 32b who offered him a further audience at another time. The just-ification for this suggestion is the remarkable consonance between what is known of Epicureanism and Stoicism and the two differing reactions Luke records both in v. 18 and v. 32, and the fact that Paul alludes to certain tenets of their thought in vv. 25 and 28 (on which see F. F. Bruce, *The Acts of the Apostles. The Greek Text*, 2d ed. [London: Tyndale, 1952], 336, 338–39).

8Cf. F. F. Bruce, *The Book of the Acts* (Grand Rapids: Eerd-mans, 1988), 331 and n. 35.

II: Immortality and Resurrection in the Old Testament

1See A. R. Johnson, *The Vitality of the Individual in the Thought of Ancient Israel*, 2d ed. (Cardiff: University of Wales, 1964), 87–88.

2E.g., T. H. Gaster, "Dead, Abode of the," *The Interpreter's Dictionary of the Bible*, ed. G. A. Buttrick et al., 4 vols. (Nashville: Abingdon, 1962), 1:787–88. For Gaster, the only clear reference to resurrection in the Old Testament is found in Daniel 12:1–2 (dated by Gaster as 168 B.C.), a passage which "does not represent a natural development of previous Hebrew thinking, but is simply a clever exploita-tion of popular 'pagan' notions, designed, on the one hand, to reassure the devout, and, on the other, to hoist the infidels with the petard of their own apostatic beliefs" ("Resurrection," ibid. 4:39–40). For a discussion of this passage, see below 6.a.

3E.g., BDB 2b–c, under *'ăḇaddôn*; 983 a–b, under *šᵉ'ôl*; 1001 c–d, under *šaḥaṯ*. See n. 13.

4E.g., D. Alexander, "The Old Testament view of life after death," *Themelios* 11 (1986): 41–46, especially 45. I owe my references in n. 3 to this article.

5See N. J. Tromp, *Primitive Conceptions of Death and the Nether World in the Old Testament* (Rome: Pontifical Bibli-cal Institute, 1969), 129–40, 212.

6See R. L. Harris, "Why Hebrew *Shᵉ'ôl* was translated 'Grave'" in *The NIV The Making of a Contemporary*

Translation, ed. K. L. Barker (Grand Rapids: Zondervan, 1986), 58–71. Cf. his earlier article, "The Meaning of the Word Sheol as Shown by Parallels in Poetic Texts," *Journal of the Evangelical Theological Society* 4 (1961): 129–35.

7*The Gilgamesh Epic and Old Testament Parallels*, 2d ed. (Chicago: University of Chicago, 1949), 173–91. Apparently the KJV also reflects this distinction, for it translates "Sheol" by "hell" (= the netherworld) thirty-one times, and "the grave" thirty-one times (and "the pit" = the netherworld, three times).

8The expression here rendered "immortality" is '*l-mwt*, vocalized as '*al-māwet*, "not-death" (following both GK, 479 § 152 g and BDB, 677 under *nātîb*). On this view, the two clauses of this verse stand in synonymous parallelism, so that immortality may here be interpreted not only as deathlessness ("nondeath"), but also as "[eternal] life." Life and immortality would then constitute the hope that the righteous person entertains in the face of death (Pr 14:32; cf. 15:24)—and that Christ brought to light through his incarnation, death, and resurrection (2Ti 1:10). However, most modern translations find antithetical parallelism in Proverbs 12:28, following the Septuagint (*eis thanaton*) in reading '*el-māwet*, "to death," in the second line: "Life lies along the path of virtue, the way of the vicious leads to death" (JB).

9The three Hebrew terms are *nēṣaḥ*, "everlastingness," "perpetuity"; '*ôlām*, "long duration" (in reference to the remote past or future), pl. "eternity"; '*ad*, "perpetuity." With the preposition *l*-each may mean "forever." Used of the divine existence or attributes, the word *forever* refers to eternality (e.g., *lāneṣaḥ*, Ps 9:7; *l*-'*ôlām*, Ex 3:15; *lā*'*ad*, Ps 111:3), but in reference to human life or relations it denotes continuous existence, or indefinite duration, "as long as life lasts" (e.g., *lāneṣaḥ*, 2Sa 2:26, of the sword's destructive power; *l*-'*ôlām*, Ex 21:6, of slavery in perpetuity; *lā*'*ad*, Pr 29:14, of the permanence of a dynasty). It was customary court etiquette to greet a king with the words "Let the king live forever" (Ne 2:3; cf. 1Ki 1:31; Da 2:4). We must not imagine, therefore, that "forever[more]" is synonymous with "throughout eternity." Each occurrence of the phrase should be interpreted by its context. In Genesis 3:22–23 God dismisses Adam from the Garden of Eden lest he should also eat of the "tree of life . . . and live forever." But this "eternal life" was not direct participation in the unending divine life, but rather a permanent continuation of man's earthly and corporeal existence. Again, the assurance that death will be swallowed up "forever" in the messianic kingdom (Isa 25:8) should not be read as an implicit affirmation of individual immortality in the future age, for in a comparable passage elsewhere in Isaiah (65:17–22), the days of Yahweh's people in that future era are likened to the days of a tree (v. 22), and the person who dies a hundred years old is considered a child (v. 20).

[10]*Psalms. III* (101–150) (New York: Doubleday, 1970), XLVI–XLVII. The passages involved are Ps 16:11; 21:5; 27:13; 30:6; 36:10; 56:14; 69:29; 116:8–9; 133:3; 142:6 and Pr 4:22; 8:35–36; 12:28; 15:24. Generally the term *ḥayyîm* denotes physical life, earthly happiness, or spiritual felicity (BDB, 313 a, b). But Dahood claims that the "philological break-through" for the equation *ḥayyîm* = "eternal life" is afforded by the synonymous parallelism found in the Ugaritic poem, the Legend of Aqhat: "Ask for life eternal (*ḥym*) and I will give it to you; immortality (*blmt*) and I will bestow it upon you" (2 Aqhat VI.26–27). Altogether, Dahood finds forty or so Old Testament texts that explicitly affirm or imply a belief in immortality and resurrection (*Psalms. III, XLVI–LI*). For two different evaluations of Dahood's proposals, see B. Vawter, "Intimations of Immortality and the Old Testament," *Journal of Biblical Literature* 91 (1972): 158–71. For a more positive evaluation, see E. Smick, "The Bearing of New Philological Data on the Subjects of Resurrection and Immortality in the Old Testament," *Westminster Theological Journal* 31 (1968): 12–21.

[11]A recent lengthy article by L. J. Greenspoon, entitled "The Origin of the Idea of Resurrection" (in *Traditions in Transformation. Turning Points in Biblical Faith*, ed. B. Halpern and J. D. Levenson [Winona Lake, Ind.: Eisenbrauns, 1981], 247–321), argues that the Old Testament belief in the bodily resurrection of the dead arose from ideas connected

with the motif of Yahweh as Divine Warrior and that this concept of resurrection was first expressed in the ninth century B.C. (ibid., 319).

[12]On this question see R. Martin-Achard, *From Death to Life. A Study of the Development of the Doctrine of the Resurrection in the Old Testament* (ETr. by J. P. Smith) (Edinburgh: Oliver and Boyd, 1960); R. H. Charles, *Eschatology. The Doctrine of a Future Life in Israel, Judaism and Christianity*, 2d ed. (New York: Schocken, 1963 [= 1913]), 1–166; E. F. Sutcliffe, *The Old Testament and the Future Life* (London: Burns, Oates & Washbourne, 1946).

[13]On "Hebrew Words for the Resurrection of the Dead," see an article with this title by J. F. A. Sawyer, *Vetus Testamentum* 23 (1973): 218–34. In references to BDB, I follow the useful convention of B. Einspahr (*Index to Brown, Driver & Briggs, Hebrew Lexicon* [Chicago: Moody, 1976]), of citing the page number and quadrant where the Hebrew word appears in the *Lexicon*, **a** indicating the upper half and **b** the lower half of the left-hand column, and **c** indicating the upper half and **d** the lower half of the right-hand column.

[14]Johnson, *Vitality* (see n. 1), 95.

[15]Not all are agreed that Isaiah is referring to a corporeal resurrection. Some take the "dead" or "dead bodies" to be the nation in captivity whose return to the land of promise (= resurrection) was shortly to occur. Others allege that the interpretation we have espoused is explicitly contradicted by v. 14 ("They are dead, they will not live; those departed spirits will not rise"). There, however, the prophet is asserting that Israel's oppressors will not arise to launch further attacks on the nation.

[16]*The Second Isaiah* (Oxford: Clarendon, 1964), 244.

[17]Cf. Martin-Achard, *Death* (see n. 12), 152.

III: Immortality and Resurrection in Intertestamental Judaism

[1]Four standard treatments of the Jewish literature of this period may be mentioned. P. Hoffmann, *Die Toten in Christus*, 2d ed. (Münster: Aschendorff, 1960), 81–155; G. W. E. Nick-

elsburg, Jr., *Resurrection, Immortality, and Eternal Life in Intertestamental Judaism* (Cambridge, Mass.: HUP, 1972); Nickelsburg, *Jewish Literature between the Bible and the Mishnah* (Philadelphia: Fortress / London: SCM, 1981); H. C. C. Cavallin, *Life after Death. Paul's Argument for the Resurrection of the Dead in 1 Cor 15. Part I. An Enquiry into the Jewish Background* (Lund: Gleerup, 1974).

²See Cavallin, *Life* (see n. 1), 76.

³The classification that follows reflects the careful and exhaustive analysis of Cavallin (see n. 1) and the references are drawn from the works cited in n. 1.

⁴There is a notorious disagreement between Josephus and Hippolytus regarding Essene conceptions of the afterlife. Josephus ascribes to them a pronounced belief "that bodies are corruptible and that the matter they are made of is not permanent but that souls will endure immortal forever" (*War* 2. 154; cf. *Ant.* 18.18), whereas Hippolytus asserts that "they confess that the flesh also will rise and that it will be immortal, just as the soul is already immortal" (*Refutations* 9.27), although he incongruously adds that when the soul has left the body it will rest in the "isles of the blessed." Nickelsburg (*Resurrection*, 167–69; see n. 1) and Cavallin (*Life*, 69–72; see n. 1) have adduced convincing reasons for preferring the testimony of Josephus. The Qumran community, which flourished during the two centuries before A.D. 70, was probably a branch of the Essenes. Some scholars (e.g., A. Dupont-Sommer and J. van der Ploeg) find in *Hymns of Thanksgiving* 3:19–23 a reference to the immortality of the souls of the faithful Covenanters which at death ascend to the celestial regions where they join "the eternal Assembly" and enjoy "communion with the congregation of the Sons of Heaven." Belief in the immortality of the soul has eclipsed belief in a future resurrection of the body, of which there is no explicit trace in the scrolls from Qumran (cf. Josephus's description of the Essenes cited above). However, fragments of the book of Daniel have been found, so the Qumranites must have been aware of the doctrine of the resurrection (see 4QPsDn 38–40). Indeed J. T. Milik notes that, in contrast with ortho-

dox Jewish burial practices, the heads of the deceased were
placed toward the south so that upon resurrection they
would be facing north where the Essenes believed paradise
was located (*Ten Years of Discovery in the Wilderness of
Judaea* [London: SCM, 1959], 104). K. Schubert may well
be right in affirming that the resurrection is presupposed
rather than explicitly taught in the documents from Qumran,
the emphasis being on "realized eschatology" ("Die Ent-
wicklung der Auferstehungslehre von der nachexilischen bis
zur frührabbinischen Zeit," *Biblische Zeitschrift* 6 [1962]:
202–4). Certainly the righteous enjoy eternal life already in
this life, although its consummation belongs to the next
world (1QS 11:7–9; CD 3:20; 1QH 4:21–22; 7:22–25). Be it
the immortality of the soul or the resurrection of the body
that was believed in at Qumran, the perpetuity of the future
state (at least of the community) is stressed, so that immortality as deathlessness seems to have been one aspect of
the expectation of the Covenanters (1QS 4:6–8; cf. 4:11–
14).

5See further on this paragraph, Cavallin, *Life* (see n. 1), 99–100,
166–70.

6P. Volz (*Die Eschatologie der jüdischen Gemeinde im neutes-
tamentlichen Zeitalter* [Tübingen: Mohr, 1934], 249–55; cf.
117–21) finds three basic views concerning the nature of the
resurrection in Jewish literature: "the reanimation of old
bodies," "the reunion of the old body and the old soul,"
and "the re-embodiment of preserved souls" (ibid., ix).
These three views he traces (respectively) to a materialistic,
a materialistic-spiritual, and a spiritual anthropology. He locates the religious motive behind the emphasis on the body
and its restoration in the necessity for the maintenance of
personal identity, and the religious motive behind the stress
on the spirit and its embodiment in a new corporeality in
the need for divine perfection and freedom from sin.

7On "The Doctrine of the Resurrection of the Dead in Rabbini-
cal Theology," see A. Marmorstein, *American Journal of
Theology* 19 (1915): 577–91; also S. Lieberman, *Texts and
Studies* (New York: Ktav, 1974), 235–70; Cavallin, *Life* (see
n. 1), 171–86; and SB IV.2, 1172–98.

IV: "Raisings" in the Gospels (and Acts)

[1]On Jewish mourning customs, see A. Edersheim, *The Life and Times of Jesus the Messiah* (Grand Rapids: Eerdmans, 1971 [= 1886]), 1:555-56; *Sketches of Jewish Social Life* (London: Religious Tract Society, 1876), 169-70; SB 1:521-23.

[2]For a detailed discussion of the literary parallels of this miracle (viz. 1Ki 17:8-24; Pliny, *Natural History* 26.15; Philostratus, *Life of Apollonius of Tyana* 4.45), see M. J. Harris, " 'The Dead are Restored to Life': Miracles of Revivification in the Gospels," in *Gospel Perspectives. Volume 6. The Miracles of Jesus*, ed. D. Wenham and C. L. Blomberg (Sheffield: JSOT, 1986), 299-303.

[3]Edersheim, *Life* (see n. 1 above), 1:555-56.

[4]The other three accounts are Lk 8:40-42, 49-56; Ac 9:36-42; 20:7-12.

[5]The historical setting of the miracle is not immediately obvious. According to Mark and Luke it occurred at some point after Jesus had returned to Capernaum on the western shore of the Sea of Galilee (Mk 5:21) following the healing of the demoniac at Gerasa (Mk 5:1-21; Lk 8:26-40). In the first gospel, however, it takes place immediately after the conversation in Matthew's house regarding Jesus' eating with sinners (Mt 9:9-13) and his disciples' failure to fast (Mt 9:14-17). No serious divergence between the accounts need be postulated, for if we assume (i) that the Gerasa/Gadara incident occurred between the calling of Matthew (Mt 9:9) and the meal held in his house (Mt 9:10-17); and (ii) that all three gospel writers have naturally associated Matthew's call and the meal in his house in topical fashion, placing them either earlier than (thus Mk and Lk) or after (thus Mt) the Gerasa incident, the apparent difficulty disappears and Matthew's setting for the miracle can be accepted simply as being more precise than that of Mark and Luke. See the useful discussion of D. A. Carson, "Matthew," in *The Expositor's Bible Commentary. Volume 8*, ed. F. E. Gaebelein (Grand Rapids: Zondervan, 1984), 221, 229. On this view Jairus entered Matthew's house in order to make

his request (cf. Mt 9:10, 18) and Jesus "got up" from the meal and followed Jairus (Mt 9:19).

[6]For a discussion of the features of the story that are distinctive of one or more Evangelist, see M. J. Harris, "Miracles of Revivification" (see n. 2 above), 307–9.

[7]Matthew omits the messenger scene and therefore telescopes Jairus's statement "My daughter is at the point of death" (Mk 5:23) and the messengers' announcement, "Your daughter has died" (Mk 5:35) into the one declaration, "My daughter has just now died. But come and lay your hand on her and she will come to life" (Mt 9:18).

[8]Apart from the fact that in the Lazarus episode we are confronted by another ostensible miracle of reanimation—and at that, reanimation four days (not shortly) after death—two main difficulties have been raised by those who question the Evangelist's historical accuracy in this story: the silence of the three Synoptic Gospels regarding the miracle, and the apparent discrepancy between John and the other three Evangelists concerning the event that precipitated the plan of the chief priests and Pharisees to destroy Jesus. For a discussion of these two issues and of alternative explanations of the origin of the narrative, see Harris, "Miracles of Revivification" (see n. 2 above), 312–15.

[9]For a defense of this exegesis, see M. J. Harris, *Raised Immortal*, 211–14.

[10]Lk 7:12, 15 (the widow of Nain's son); Mk 5:35; Lk 8:49, 53, 55 (the daughter of Jairus); Jn 11:13, 14, 16, 21, 32, 37, 39, 44 (Lazarus).

[11]A. Plummer makes the interesting observation that nearly all the instances of raising the dead recorded in the Bible were performed for women—1Ki 17:23; 2Ki 4:36; Lk 7:12–13, 15; Jn 11:21, 32; Ac 9:41; Heb 11:35 (*A Critical and Exegetical Commentary on the Gospel According to S. Luke* [Edinburgh: T. & T. Clark, 1896], 198). The exceptions are the cases of Jairus's daughter (Mk 5:22–23, 40–42) and Eutychus (Ac 20:12), yet even here women were among the beneficiaries.

[12]F. J. Matera, *Passion Narratives and Gospel Theologies* (New York: Paulist, 1986), 116–17.

[13]For further discussion of the historicity of Mt 27:51–54, see D. Wenham, "The Resurrection Narratives in Matthew's Gospel," *Tyndale Bulletin* 24 (1973): 42–46.

[14]For a defense of this view (a full stop after *aneōchthēsan*, v. 52a), see J. W. Wenham, "When were the Saints raised? A Note on the Punctuation of Matthew xxvii. 51–3," *Journal of Theological Studies* 32 (1981): 150–52.

[15]Most English versions reflect this view, usually by placing a full stop or semicolon at the end of v. 52. So also R. H. Gundry, *Matthew* (Grand Rapids: Eerdmans, 1982), who espouses the view that "Matthew probably means that the saints stayed in their tombs for several days even though their bodies had been raised to life" (ibid., 576).

[16]This view construes "after his resurrection" (v. 53) with what follows ("they went into . . . ," *eisēlthon*. . .), not with what precedes ("when they had come out/they came out . . ." *exelthontes*. . .), and is reflected in GOODSPEED, BARCLAY, and NIV. So also H. A. W. Meyer, *Critical and Exegetical Hand-Book to the Gospel of Matthew* (ETr. by P. Christie et al.) (New York: Funk and Wagnalls, 1884), 512.

V. Resurrection *from* the Grave: Verifiable History

[1]A. Schlatter, *Paulus, der Bote Jesu*, 2d ed. (Stuttgart: Calwer, 1956), 405.

[2]For a history of the interpretation of the resurrection of Christ, see D. P. Fuller, *Easter Faith and History* (Grand Rapids: Eerdmans, 1965); P. de Haes, *La Résurrection de Jésus dans l'Apologétique des Cinquante Dernières Années* (Rome: Gregorian University, 1953); R. Nìebuhr, *Resurrection and Historical Reason* (New York: Scribner's, 1957); G. O'Collins, *Jesus Risen* (New York: Paulist, 1987), 1–98; and more briefly, J. E. Alsup, *The Post-Resurrection Appearance Stories of the Gospel Tradition* (Stuttgart: Calwer, 1975), 19–54; C. F. Evans, *Resurrection and the New Testament* (London: SCM, 1970), 170–83; H. G. Geyer, "The Resurrection of Jesus Christ: A Survey of the Debate in Present Day Theology," in C. F. D. Moule (ed.), *The Significance of the Message of the Resurrection for Faith in*

Jesus Christ (London: SCM, 1968), 105–35; J. J. Smith, "Resurrection Faith Today," *Theological Studies* 30 (1969): 393–419; R. C. Ware, "The Resurrection of Jesus. I. Theological Orientations; II. Historical-Critical Studies," *Heythrop Journal* 16 (1975): 22–35, 174–94; C. Brown, "The Resurrection in Contemporary Theology," in *NIDNTT*, 3:281–302.

³E.g., R. Bultmann, *Theology of the New Testament. Volume 1* (London: SCM, 1952), 31.

⁴For a vigorous, scholarly defense of the authenticity of the relevant synoptic predictions, see H. F. Bayer, *Jesus' Predictions of Vindication and Resurrection* (Tübingen: Mohr, 1986).

⁵See the discussion of this issue in M. J. Harris, *Raised Immortal*, 14–16.

⁶C. H. Dodd, *Historical Tradition in the Fourth Gospel* (Cambridge: CUP, 1963), 143.

⁷"The Empty Tomb as History," *Christianity Today*, 28 March 1975, 5 (= p. 631).

⁸See M. J. Harris, *Raised Immortal*, 9.

⁹A list of forty-seven such scholars is found in W. L. Craig's fine article, "The Historicity of the Empty Tomb of Jesus," *New Testament Studies* 31 (1985): 67 n. 88.

¹⁰The most recent detailed defenses of the historicity of the empty tomb are found in E. L. Bode, *The First Easter Morning* (Rome: Pontifical Biblical Institute, 1970), 151–75; W. L. Craig, *The Son Rises: The Historical Evidence for the Resurrection of Jesus* (Chicago: Moody, 1981), 45–90; and his subsequent briefer treatment in *Knowing the Truth about the Resurrection* (Ann Arbor, Mich.: Servant, 1988), 63–86; see also n. 9; but see also the brief statement by R. H. Stein, "Was the tomb really empty?" *Themelios* 5 (1979): 8–12. A recent marshaling of the arguments against the historicity of the empty tomb tradition is found in L. Geering, *Resurrection—a Symbol of Hope* (London: Hodder, 1971), 28–69, whose view is critiqued by G. O'Collins, *The Easter Jesus* (London: Darton, 1973), 98–100, and more generally, 38–45, 90–97.

[11]Those who deny that Paul had any knowledge of the empty
   tomb tradition include R. Bultmann, *History of the Synoptic
   Tradition* (Oxford: Blackwell, 1963), 290; H. Grass, *Oster-
   geschehen und Osterberichte* (Göttingen: Vandenhoeck &
   Ruprecht, 1956), 173; P. Badham, *Christian Beliefs about
   Life after Death* (London: Macmillan, 1976), 33–35, 37. For
   a contrary view, see J. Mánek, "The Apostle Paul and the
   Empty Tomb," *Novum Testamentum* 2 (1957): 276–80.

[12]*The Historical Evidence for the Resurrection of Jesus Christ*
   (New York: Putnam's, 1907), 193–94.

[13]See, e.g., T. J. Thorburn, *The Resurrection Narratives and
   Modern Criticism* (London: Kegan Paul, 1910), 183–85;
   W. L. Craig, *The Son Rises: Historical Evidence for the
   Resurrection of Jesus* (Chicago: Moody, 1981), 36–40.

[14]*The Anastasis: the Resurrection of Jesus as an Historical
   Event* (Shipston-on-Stour, Warwickshire: Drinkwater, 1982),
   1–2, 38–45, 71, 85–86, 130–32 (the quotations are from
   pp. 2 and 71 respectively).

[15]E.g., K. Lake, *The Historical Evidence for the Resurrection of
   Jesus Christ* (New York: Putnam's, 1907), 251–52; P. Gard-
   ner-Smith, *The Narratives of the Resurrection* (London: Methuen, 1926), 134–39.

[16]The plurals ("they took him down [*kathelontes*] . . . they laid
   him [*ethēkan*] . . .") may be generalizing or nonspecific, like
   the expression in English, "some people took him
   down . . ." Alternatively, the reference could be to Joseph
   and Nicodemus who, as inhabitants of Jerusalem and Jewish
   leaders (Ac 13:27), carried out the task of burying Jesus
   (Lk 23:50–53; Jn 19:38–42) and so allayed general Jewish
   anxiety (at least in the case of Jesus) that crucified victims
   should not remain on the cross on the Sabbath (Jn 19:31).

[17]Representatives of this general approach to the empty tomb
   narratives include R. Bultmann, *Synoptic Tradition* (see
   n. 11), 287, 290; H. Grass, *Ostergeschehen* (see n. 11), 85–
   87, 92–93, 173–85; L. Geering, *Resurrection* (see n. 10),
   43–59.

[18]E.g., H. Grass, *Ostergeschehen* (see n. 11), 176–77, 179–80.
[19]Ibid., 185.

[20]"Un rescrit impérial sur la violation de sépulture," *Revue His-torique* 163 (1930): 241–66.

[21]This is the translation of F. F. Bruce, *New Testament History* (Garden City, N.Y.: Doubleday, 1971), 391. See the discussions of this edict in Bruce, 300–303; A. Momigliano, *Claudius the Emperor and His Achievement*, 2d ed. (Cambridge: Heffer, 1961), 35–37, 100–101 (but cf. ix); E. M. Blaiklock, *The Archaeology of the New Testament* (Grand Rapids: Zondervan, 1970), 75–83.

[22]"The Shroud of Turin and its Significance for Biblical Studies," *Journal of the Evangelical Theological Society* 24 (1981): 47–54.

[23]Ibid., 53–54; cf. *Verdict on the Shroud* (Ann Arbor, Mich.: Servant, 1981), 155–57.

[24]"Shroud" (see n. 22), 54.

[25]The information in the next three paragraphs is drawn from an article entitled "Debunking the Shroud of Turin," *Time*, 24 October 1988, 81.

[26]Ibid.

[27]See G. R. Habermas in *Did Jesus Rise from the Dead? The Resurrection Debate*, ed. T. L. Miethe (San Francisco: Harper & Row, 1987), 119–20.

[28]The literature on the Shroud is immense. Perhaps the best brief pre-1988 article is by Virginia Bortin, "Science and the Shroud of Turin," *Biblical Archaeologist* 43 (1980): 109–17. A lavishly illustrated article may be found in *National Geographic* 157 (1980): 730–53 ("The Mystery of the Shroud," by K. F. Weaver). The Shroud's history is documented by I. Wilson, *The Shroud of Turin* (Garden City, N.Y.: Doubleday, 1978), who also ventures the hypothesis that the Shroud's three-dimensional image has preserved for posterity "a literal snapshot" of Jesus' Resurrection (ibid., 211). But compare his considerably more cautious judgment in his 1986 volume, *The Mysterious Shroud* (Garden City, N.Y.: Doubleday), 136–37. The most provocative pre-1988 challenges to the Shroud's authenticity as the burial cloth of Jesus are probably those of J. Nickell, *Inquest on the Shroud of Turin* (Buffalo, N.Y.: Prometheus, 1983) and R. A. Wild, "The Shroud of Turin—Probably the Work of a

14th-Century Artist or Forger," *Biblical Archaeology Review* 10 (1984): 30–46; see also his reply to respondents in the same journal, 10 (1984): 20, 22. For the post-1988 situation, see D. Sox, *The Shroud Unmasked* (Basingstoke, England: Lamp, 1988). Sox, an Episcopal priest, was at one time General Secretary of the British Society for the Turin Shroud.

VI: Resurrection *in* a Transformed Body: Verifiable History

[1]Beginning at v. 6 of 1Co 15 there is a change of construction—from subordinate clauses introduced by "that" (*hoti*) to principal clauses. "Then he appeared . . . Then he appeared . . . Last of all he appeared . . ." (vv. 6–8). This change suggests that the pre-Pauline tradition ends at v. 5. If this is so, Paul found in the traditional formula a reference to one individual (Cephas; cf. Lk 24:34) and one group ("the Twelve") to whom Jesus appeared, and added two further individuals (James and himself) and two further groups (the five hundred brethren and "all the apostles").

[2]These verses are parenthetical and form a "flashback," with the Greek aorist being equivalent, as is quite often the case, to the English pluperfect: "But to their amazement there had been a great earthquake; for an angel of the Lord had descended from Heaven, and had come and rolled back the stone, and was sitting upon it. His appearance was like lightning, and his raiment white as snow. For fear of him the guards trembled violently, and became like dead men" (WEYMOUTH). This last sentence could also be rendered ". . . had trembled . . . and had become . . ." For a defense of this view, see J. N. D. Anderson, *A Lawyer Among the Theologians* (London: Hodder, 1973), 143–44 and n. 107; J. Wenham, *Easter Enigma* (Exeter: Paternoster, 1984), 77–78.

[3]E.g., Gospel of Peter 35–49; Gospel of the Hebrews *apud* Jerome, *De Viris Illustribus* 2.

[4]This suggested order of appearances assumes that the adverbial expressions in 1Co 15:5–8 (viz. "then . . . then . . . then

. . . then . . . last of all") point to a chronological sequence. For a defense of the view that Jesus appeared in *both* Galilee, *and* Jerusalem, against those who see these locations as theological symbols and those who believe that all the appearances occurred in either Jerusalem or Galilee, see M. J. Harris, *Raised Immortal*, 51–53.

[5]Lk 24:34; Jn 20:11–17; 1Co 15:5a, 7a.

[6]Mt 28:9–10, 16–17; Jn 21:1–2; 1Co 15:5b, 7b.

[7]1Co 15:6; cf. Ac 13:31.

[8]E.g., Mt 28:16–17.

[9]E.g., Mt 28:9–10; Jn 20:11–17.

[10]Jn 20:11–17.

[11]Mt 28:16–20.

[12]E.g., Lk 24:33, 36.

[13]Lk 24:13–15.

[14]Jn 21:1–22.

[15]Jn 20:19–29.

[16]E.g., Mt 28:9–10; Jn 20:14–17.

[17]E.g., Lk 24:13–31; Jn 21:4–22.

[18]Jn 21:4.

[19]Lk 24:13–15, 28–29.

[20]Jn 20:19–23.

[21]Mt 28:16–20; Lk 24:44–49; Jn 20:23, 29; Ac 1:3, 6–8; 10:42.

[22]Lk 24:13–27.

[23]Jn 21:9–13.

[24]Lk 24:41–43; Ac 1:4; 10:41.

[25]The two verbs Paul uses in v. 3 (*paralambanō*, "receive," corresponding to the Hebrew verb *qibbēl; paradidōmi*, "hand on," corresponding to the Hebrew *māśar*; see SB 3:444) are technical terms for the receipt and handing on of tradition.

[26]E.g., P. Rassinier, *Debunking the Genocide Myth* (Los Angeles: Noontide, 1978); A. R. Butz, *The Hoax of the Twentieth Century* (Torrance, Calif.: Institute for Historical Review, 1976).

[27]For a careful discussion of this question, see L. Swidler, *Women in Judaism: the Status of Women in Formative Judaism* (Metuchen, N.J.: Scarecrow, 1976), 115–16.

²⁸See, e.g., J. Weiss, *Earliest Christianity* (New York: Harper, 1959 edition of 1937 translation), 1:26-31.

²⁹This general position is represented by H. Grass, *Ostergeschehen und Osterberichte* (Göttingen: Vandenhoeck & Ruprecht, 1956; later editions unavailable), 233-49; G. W. H. Lampe, in G. W. H. Lampe and D. M. MacKinnon, *The Resurrection: A Dialogue* (London: Mowbray, 1966), 20-21, 30-31.

³⁰See, e.g., M. C. Perry, *The Easter Enigma* (London: Faber, 1959), 188-96. But in his later book *The Resurrection of Man* (London: Mowbray, 1975), Perry is much more cautious (see, e.g., p. 72).

³¹LSJ, 1245, under *horaō* II. 4.b; BDF, §§ 313, 101 under *horaō*; BAGD, 578 under *horaō* 1.a. delta. See the detailed discussion in M. J. Harris, *Raised Immortal*, 46-47.

³²Lk 24:34; Ac 9:17; 13:31; 26:16a; 1Co 15:5-8; 1Ti 3:16.

³³This latter would seem to be the position of J. A. Schep, *The Nature of the Resurrection Body* (Grand Rapids: Eerdmans, 1964), 107-79 ("a glorified body of flesh," 145; cf. 226, "a body of glorified flesh," with regard to the believer's resurrection body).

³⁴E.g., M. J. Harris, *Raised Immortal*, 53-55, 56-57.

³⁵E.g., H. B. Swete, *The Life of the World to Come* (New York: Macmillan/London: SPCK, 1917), 50-51.

³⁶R. H. Fuller, *The Formation of the Resurrection Narratives* (London: Macmillan, 1971), 173, 185.

³⁷Leicester/Downers Grove, Ill.: IVP, 1987.

³⁸Ed. D. Wenham et al. (Sheffield: JSOT, 1980-86).

³⁹Almost all scholars agree that Mark's gospel originally ended at 16:8. See M. J. Harris, *Raised Immortal*, 14-16.

⁴⁰This translation is taken from E. Hennecke, *New Testament Apocrypha*, ed. W. Schneemelcher (London: SCM, 1963), 2:647-48.

⁴¹Hennecke, *Apocrypha* (see n. 40), 1:185-86.

⁴²B. M. Metzger, *A Textual Commentary on the Greek New Testament* (New York: United Bible Societies, 1971), 122.

⁴³M. R. James, *The Apocryphal New Testament* (Oxford: Clarendon, 1924), 181-86.

[44]Cf. C. F. D. Moule, *The Phenomenon of the New Testament* (London: SCM, 1967), 10–20. He observes that "the birth and rapid rise of the Christian Church . . . *remain an unsolved enigma for any historian who refuses to take seriously the only explanation offered by the Church itself*" (ibid., 13).

[45]*The Jesus of History* (London: SCM, 1927), 188–89.

[46]That the believers at Troas had gathered on Sunday evening, not Saturday evening, "to break bread" (Ac 20:7) is apparent from the fact that the "morrow" after "the first day of the week" was marked by "daybreak," not sunset (Ac 20:7, 11).

VII: Objections to the Resurrection as Verifiable History

[1]E.g., J. Knox, *The Church and the Reality of Christ* (New York: Harper, 1962), 16, 60–77. The bases of this view are subjected to rigorous criticism by P. Carnley ("The Poverty of Historical Scepticism" in *Christ, Faith and History*, ed. S. W. Sykes and J. P. Clayton [Cambridge: CUP, 1972], 165–89) who contends that "it is not legitimate to argue that faith cannot be based on any historical judgments or must be *totally* independent of historical research and autonomous, because *no* historical judgment is *ever* justifiably claimed with certainty" (ibid., 189).

[2]R. Bultmann, in *Kerygma and Myth* (ed. H. W. Bartsch [London: SPCK, 1961]), 1:39. According to Bultmann, the Resurrection is "an attempt to convey the meaning of the cross" (ibid., 38) so that "faith in the resurrection is really the same thing as faith in the saving efficacy of the cross" (ibid., 41).

[3]On this whole issue see the judicious observations of A. Richardson, *History, Sacred and Profane* (London: SCM, 1964), 184–217; and more briefly G. E. Ladd, *I Believe in the Resurrection of Jesus* (Grand Rapids: Eerdmans/London: Hodder, 1975), 16–28.

[4]The "discrepancies" are set out fully in E. L. Bode, *The First Easter Morning* (Rome: Pontifical Biblical Institute, 1970), 6–24; see also the chart in G. E. Ladd, *Resurrection* (see

n. 3), 80–82. Both these authors defend the historicity of
the Resurrection.

[5]*The Resurrection of Jesus of Nazareth* (London: SCM, 1970),
156; cf. 71–74. According to Marxsen the Resurrection was
not an objective event of the past, but is an "interpretative
statement . . . an inference derived from personal faith"
(ibid., 138), one of several possible interpretations—exaltation is another—of the historical fact that the cause or
purpose of Jesus did not die with his death. "He still
comes today" in any who believe in his cause. To come to
faith, to participate in the ongoing work of Jesus (viz. reli-
ance on God and service of one's neighbor), is the real
miracle of the Resurrection (ibid., 77–78, 125–26, 147–48).
" 'Jesus is risen' simply means: today the crucified Jesus is
calling us to believe" (ibid., 128).

[6]*Livy, Books XXI and XXII* (London: Macmillan, 1931), 194–95;
see also his appendix "On the Route of Hannibal" (ibid.,
307–15).

[7]M. Grant, *Nero, Emperor in Revolt* (New York: American Her-
itage, 1970), 152.

[8]On this topic, see J. N. D. Anderson, *A Lawyer Among the
Theologians* (London: Hodder, 1973), 107–11, 142–49;
C. L. Blomberg, "The Legitimacy and Limits of Harmoniza-
tion," in *Hermeneutics, Authority and Canon* (ed. D. A.
Carson and J. D. Woodbridge (Grand Rapids: Zonder-
van/Leicester: IVP, 1986), 139–74; and his book *The Histor-
ical Reliability of the Gospels* (Downers Grove/Leicester:
IVP, 1987), 2–12, 113–96. The standard treatments are by
H. Merkel, *Die Wiedersprüche zwischen den Evangelien.
Ihre polemische und apologetische Behandlung in der Alten
Kirche bis zu Augustin* (Tübingen: Mohr, 1971), and *Die
Pluralität der Evangelien als theologisches und exegetisches
Problem in der Alten Kirche* (Bern/Las Vegas: Lang, 1978).

[9]For instance, it would be totally illegitimate to try to harmonize the accounts of Jesus' baptism, in which Matthew
(3:17) has the voice from heaven saying "This is my beloved Son" while Mark (1:11) and Luke (3:22) have "You
are my beloved Son," by suggesting that Jesus was bap-

tized on two different occasions or that the heavenly voice spoke twice on one occasion.

[10]Compare, for example, the efforts of H. Latham, *The Risen Master* (Cambridge: Bell, 1917), 225–29 (and the explanatory notes thereon, 229–41); G. D. Yarnold, *Risen Indeed* (London: OUP, 1959), 7–8, 44–47, 81–82, 121–23, 126–27; J. Lilly, "Alleged Discrepancies in the Gospel Accounts of the Resurrection," *Catholic Biblical Quarterly* 2 (1940): 98–111; and most recently, J. Wenham, *Easter Enigma. Do the Resurrection Stories Contradict One Another?* (Exeter: Paternoster, 1984).

[11]The task of reconciling the accounts is made unnecessarily difficult for some scholars by their arbitrary treatment of the narratives. Perhaps the best illustration of this is the way some handle the plural "we do not know" (*ouk oidamen*, Jn 20:2) in a passage that mentions Mary Magdalene alone. The plural must be significant since in v. 13 the same Mary uses the singular "I do not know" (*ouk oida*). But against this, see E. L. Bode, *Easter* (see n. 4), 73–75, 84.

[12]This reconstruction assumes that Luke (24:1–9) is dependent on a non-Markan tradition which recounted the visit of a second group of women to the tomb. For a defense of this view, see M. J. Harris, *Raised Immortal*, 23–24. The view is held, *inter alios*, by B. F. Westcott, *The Gospel according to St. John* (London: Clarke, 1958 reprint of 1880 ed.), 288; H. Latham, *Master* (see n. 10), 226; N. Geldenhuys, *Commentary on the Gospel of Luke* (London: Marshall, 1950), 627.

VIII: Resurrection *to* Glory at God's Right Hand: Item of Faith

[1]The point of the regulation of Deuteronomy was to set limitations on the practice of hanging the body of an executed criminal on a tree or wooden post as a public warning of the dire consequences of committing a crime that incurred the death penalty. The restriction was that the body had to be taken down and buried at sunset "because a hanged

man is under God's curse" (Dt 21:23), being a lawbreaker
who had, in effect, cursed God. As it was formulated, the
regulation also applied to a person who was hung up alive,
that is, crucified.

[2]On this theme, see R. N. Longenecker, *The Christology of
Early Jewish Christianity* (London: SCM, 1970), 63–82. It is
not necessary to interpret Ac 2:36 as meaning that Jesus
actually became Messiah (for the first time) at his resurrection, since: (i) the context describes Jesus as "a man ac-
credited for you [as Messiah] by God with mighty works,
wonders and signs which God did through him" (Ac 2:22),
a man whose death was "in accordance with God's definite
plan and foreknowledge" (Ac 2:33); (ii) Lukan references to
the earthly Jesus as Messiah (Lk 2:11, 26; 4:41; 9:20; 24:26,
46; Ac 4:27) cannot be simply dismissed as anachronisms.

[3]See M. J. Harris in *NIDNTT* 3:1188–89.

[4]"Resurrection of Jesus Christ," *ZPEB* 5:83.

[5]On the use of Psalm 110 in the New Testament, see D. M.
Hay, *Glory at the Right Hand: Psalm 110 in Early Christianity* (New York: Abingdon 1973); and W. R. G. Loader,
"Christ at the Right Hand—Ps cx. 1 in the New Testament," *New Testament Studies* 24 (1977–78): 199–217. According to Hay, the various functions of the psalm in the
New Testament may be grouped into four main categories:
to express exaltation to the right hand of God; to support
certain Christological titles (Lord, Son of Man, Son of God,
Son of David); to affirm the subjection of powers to Christ;
to depict Jesus' intercession and priesthood (ibid., 9–10,
155). In a word, the psalm was used "to articulate the
supreme glory, the divine transcendence, of Jesus, through
whom salvation was mediated. It was primarily used as a
symbol not of his saving work but of his ultimate status.
Indeed, a brief reference to Ps 110.1b could simply mean:
Jesus is God's messiah" (ibid., 155).

[6]The Epistle to the Hebrews emphasizes the death and exaltation of Jesus rather than his resurrection, because these two
aspects of Christ's priestly work correspond to the two
principal actions performed on the Day of Atonement—the
shedding of the sacrificial blood and its presentation inside

the sanctuary. Yet, in addition to the one explicit reference to the Resurrection (Heb 13:20), this event is implied in Christ's conquest of the prince of death (Heb 2:14), in his having a life that is beyond the reach of death (Heb 7:16, 25), and in the fact of his exaltation (Heb 1:3; 8:1; 10:12; 12:2) and eternal heavenly high priesthood (Heb 5:6; 7:17; 8:1).

7J. Jeremias comments, "Matt. 28:18 means that the prophecy that the Son of Man would be enthroned as ruler of the world [Da 7:14] was fulfilled in the resurrection" (*New Testament Theology* [London: SCM/New York: Scribner's, 1971], 310).

8That Jesus' exaltation occurred at his resurrection is recognized by the majority of New Testament scholars. See, for example, A. Oepke, *TDNT* 1:370; W. Künneth, *The Theology of the Resurrection* (London: SCM, 1965), 129–30, who regards the Exaltation as a theological interpretation of the resurrection of Jesus; W. Michaelis, *TDNT* 5:356; J. Jeremias, *Theology* (see n. 7), 310; G. E. Ladd, *I Believe in the Resurrection of Jesus* (Grand Rapids: Eerdmans, 1975), 127; L. Goppelt, *Theology of the New Testament*, vol. 1 (Grand Rapids: Eerdmans, 1981), 237–38; J. F. Maile, "The Ascension in Luke—Acts," *Tyndale Bulletin* 37 (1986): 45–48, 55–56.

9W. Künneth, *Resurrection* (see n. 8), 129.

10Sometimes the phrase "at the right hand" renders the expression *ek dexiōn*, as in Ps 109:1 (LXX) and the New Testament citations of this verse (e.g., Mt 22:44; Mk 12:36; Ac 2:34; Heb 1:13) or in allusions to the verse (e.g., Mk 14:62; Ac 7:55–56). Sometimes it renders *en dexia*, the form preferred by Paul (Ro 8:34; Eph 1:20; Col 3:1), the author of Hebrews (Heb 1:3; 8:1; 10:12; 12:2), and Peter (1 Pe 3:22). In Ac 2:33 and 5:31 *tē dexia* probably means not "at/to the right hand" (locatival dative, BDF, § 199) but "by the right hand" (instrumental dative, BAGD, 174 under *dexios* 2.a; 851 under *hypsoō* 1.); cf. Ps 117:16 (LXX), "The Lord's right hand has exalted me."

11For a discussion of the time of the Ascension, in particular the common view that John 20 and Luke 24 place the Ascension on the evening of Easter Day, see M. J. Harris, *Raised Immortal*, 89-91, where the conclusion is reached (ibid., 90) that there is nothing in either John 20 or Luke 24 that precludes a considerable interval, such as that posited in Acts 1:3, between the Resurrection and the Ascension. The silence of two witnesses should not be given precedence over the testimony of one witness—particularly when Luke 24 and Acts 1 come from a single pen.

[12]Evidences are not in themselves "proofs," but are pointers to some reality. When the reality to which the evidences point is accepted, those evidences become "convincing proofs" (*tekmēria*, Ac 1:3). But the reality behind the evidences may be accepted independently of the historical evidences. Correspondingly, however compelling the evidences may be, the individual may reject the reality to which they testify. Imagine, for example, that we were confronted with the autograph copy of the certificate of Jesus' death written by Pilate. We would remain unconvinced by this conclusive piece of evidence if we *wanted* to believe that Jesus never existed. So too, even if we had access to an affidavit sworn by the legal consultant of the Sanhedrin or by the president of the society of pathologists in Jerusalem to the effect that Jesus of Nazareth rose from the dead, this evidence would never become a "convincing proof" if we were convinced on *a priori* grounds that a dead man could never return to life.

IX: The Resurrection of Believers (1)

[1]For a careful exegesis of the Pauline passages relevant to this theme, see R. B. Gaffin, Jr., *The Centrality of the Resurrection* (Grand Rapids: Baker, 1978) who prefers to describe the two temporal stages or installments of the believer's resurrection by the "inward-outward," "invisible-visible" antithesis rather than by a "spiritual-physical" contrast (ibid., 60-62, 67-68).

[2]For a discussion of passages in Paul's earlier letters (e.g., Ro 6:1-11; 2Co 4:10-11; 13:4; Gal 2:19-20; Php 3:10) where

the thought of being "raised with Christ" is present in embryonic form, see M. J. Harris, *Raised Immortal*, 102–4.

[3]For a convincing defense of the view that the antecedent of *en hō* ("in which" or "in whom") is "baptism" (v. 12), not "Christ" (v. 8), see G. R. Beasley-Murray, *Baptism in the New Testament* (London: Macmillan, 1962), 153–54.

[4]*Die Eschatologie des Paulus* (Göttingen: Vandenhoeck & Ruprecht, 1893), 206; cf. 113, 188, 269.

[5]Thus R. Bultmann, *Theology of the New Testament*, vol. 1 (London: SCM, 1952), 198.

[6]R. H. Gundry, *Sōma in Biblical Theology* (Cambridge: CUP, 1976/Grand Rapids: Zondervan, 1987), 165–66. "The *sōma* denotes the physical body, roughly synonymous with 'flesh' in the neutral sense" (ibid., 50).

[7]J. A. Schep, *The Nature of the Resurrection Body* (Grand Rapids: Eerdmans, 1964), 179.

[8]W. J. Sparrow-Simpson, *Our Lord's Resurrection* (Grand Rapids: Zondervan, 1964 [= 1909], 2d ed.), 168.

[9]M. Green, "Why the Resurrection Matters," *Christianity Today*, 17 March 1989, 32. "Bodies" in 1Cor. 15 are defined as "forms in which the self can be expressed" (ibid.).

[10]Those who regard the spiritual body as basically a fleshly body often qualify Paul's affirmation in various ways: "[works of] flesh and blood"; "flesh and blood [alone/without the Spirit/apart from the Spirit]"; ". . . cannot inherit [until sanctified/changed/rendered incorruptible]"; "flesh and blood cannot inherit [but may be inherited by] the kingdom of God"; only the kingdom, but not resurrection, is withheld from "flesh and blood." But if "flesh and blood" simply refers to mortal man, man in his mortality, no qualification of Paul's absolute statement is necessary.

[11]E. L. Mascall, *Christian Theology and Natural Science* (London/New York: Longmans, Green and Co., 1956), 18.

[12]Cf. W. G. Kümmel in H. Lietzmann, *An Die Korinther I. II*, 4th ed. (Tübingen: Mohr, 1949), 195 (the continuity is not physical or substantial, but historical); C. K. Barrett, *A Commentary on the First Epistle to the Corinthians* (London: Black, 1968), 373 ("The same historically continuous

. . . *ego* makes use successively of two different kinds of body").

13E.g., Augustine, *Enchiridion* 84–91; Aquinas, *Summa Theologica*, Supplement, QQ. 79–85; M. C. Tenney, *The Reality of the Resurrection* (Chicago: Moody, 1972 [= 1963]), 170–72; E. L. Mascall, *Christian Theology* (see n. 11), 16–23. Only if we follow Origen's distinctive terminology can we hold to a strict identity between physical and resurrection bodies. He distinguished the "material substratum" (*to hylikon hypokeimenon*) of the body, which is perpetually changing, from the "distinctive form" (*to charaktērizon eidos*) of the body, which never changes. The "form" (*eidos*) is the principle of energy that guarantees the body's identity, viz. "seminal reason" (*logos spermatikos*). The earthly body and the heavenly body have a precisely identical "form" (*In Psalmos Commentarii* 1.5; *De Principiis* 2.10.3; 3.6.6) (J. N. D. Kelly, *Early Christian Doctrines*, 2d ed. [London: Black, 1960], 471–72; cf. 477).

14E.g., Aquinas, *Summa Theologica*, Supplement, Q.80.5. On this subject C. Hodge makes these poignant remarks: "Everything in the organization or constitution of our bodies designed to meet our present necessities, will cease with the life that now is . . . If blood be no longer our life, we shall have no need of organs of respiration and nutrition. So long as we are ignorant of the conditions of existence which await us after the resurrection, it is vain to speculate on the constitution of our future bodies. It is enough to know that the glorified people of God will not be cumbered with useless organs" (*Systematic Theology. Volume III* [Grand Rapids: Eerdmans, 1965 (= 1873)], 780).

15H. Bavinck, *Gereformeerde Dogmatiek* (Kampen: Kok, 1918), 4:776 (as cited by J. A. Schep, *Body* [see n. 7], 195).

16E.g., A. H. Strong, *Systematic Theology* (London: Pickering and Inglis, 1907), 1020.

17J. A. Schep, *Body* (see n. 7), 195–96.

18E.g., G. E. Ladd, *I Believe in the Resurrection of Jesus* (Grand Rapids: Eerdmans, 1975), 129.

19See O. Cullmann, *Immortality of the Soul or Resurrection of the Dead?* (London: Epworth, 1958), 48–57.

20A punctiliar sense ("fall asleep") is probable in 1Co 7:39; 15:6, 18, 20, 51; 1Th 4:14–15. In 1Th 4:13 *tōn koimōmenōn* may as easily mean "(concerning) those who, from time to time, fall asleep," as "those who are asleep." Similarly, in 1Co 11:30, *koimōntai hikanoi* may denote a (repeated) occurrence ("not a few are falling asleep," *obdormiunt*) and not a state ("several are sleeping," *dormiunt*). R. Bultmann (*TDNT* 3:14 n. 60; cf. SB 3:634; F. Nötscher, *Altorientalischer und alttestamentlicher Auferstehungsglauben* [Würzburg: Becker, 1926], 314) observes that both *hoi kekoimēmenoi* and *hoi koimōmenoi* simply mean "those who have passed away" (similarly BAGD, 437 under *koimaō* 2.b, "those who have fallen asleep"). Outside Pauline usage, only where a present form of the verb is used, in reference to physical sleep (viz. in Mt 28:13; Lk 22:45; Ac 12:6), must a linear sense be given to this verb.

21"Some Remarks on the GYMNOS in 2 Cor. 5:3," in *Studia Paulina in honorem Johannis de Zwaan* (Bohn: Haarlem, 1953), 207. The best recent defense of the traditional view of the intermediate state is by J. W. Cooper, *Body, Soul, and Life Everlasting* (Grand Rapids: Eerdmans, 1989), who argues that Scripture teaches both the functional integration of human life and a disembodied intermediate state. For a detailed examination of the relevant New Testament texts, see K. Hanhart, *The Intermediate State in the New Testament* (Franeker: Wever, 1966).

22For proponents of this view and a fuller indication of their arguments, see M. J. Harris, *Raised Immortal*, 98–101, 255–56.

23W. D. Davies, *Paul and Rabbinic Judaism*, 2d ed. (New York: Harper, 1955), 314–20.

24D. E. H. Whiteley, *The Theology of St. Paul* (Oxford: Blackwell, 1964), 260.

25E.g., T. F. Torrance, *Space, Time and Resurrection* (Grand Rapids: Eerdmans, 1976), 102; F. F. Bruce, *1 and 2 Corinthians* (London: Oliphants, 1971), 204; *Paul, Apostle of the Heart Set Free* (Grand Rapids: Eerdmans, 1977), 312 and n. 40.

[26]On this individual-corporate oscillation of perspective, see the article by C. F. D. Moule, "The Influence of Circumstances on the Use of Eschatological Terms," *Journal of Theological Studies*, new series 15 (1964): 1–15, especially 7, 10.

[27]Paul's twofold use of "naked" (*gymnos*) in 1Co 15:37 and 2Co 5:3 is inconclusive evidence in the discussion. In the former passage the adjective describes the seed without the clothing of the blade and the ear or, at most, mortal man without the spiritual body. In the latter it probably denotes the ideal of disembodiment espoused by certain gnosticizing Corinthians and rejected by Paul, not an intermediate state of physical disembodiment feared by him (see further M. J. Harris, *Raised Immortal*, 138–39, 219–26).

[28]Even if the Christian dead are thought of as in some sense "sleeping," the two concepts of sleep and communion are not mutually exclusive, for one could argue that where a predominantly corporate eschatology finds expression (as in 1Th 4 and 1Co 15) Paul views the whole company of departed Christians as "sleeping" in Christ as they await the Consummation, while in passages (such as 2Co 5 and Php 1) which embody essentially individual eschatology he describes the individual believer as enjoying communion with Christ during the interim state.

[29]London: Chapman, 1967.

[30]"Le mystère Pascal et la résurrection des chrétiens d' après les épîtres pauliniennes," *Nouvelle Revue Théologique* 79 (1957): 337–54.

X: The Resurrection of Believers (2)

[1]The close correspondence between Paul's description of the believer's spiritual body and his depiction of the resurrected Christ suggests that he derived his picture of the glorified state of the believer principally from his vision of Christ outside Damascus. But other factors may also have contributed to the emergence of his concept of the spiritual body: the idea of a transformed resurrection body as expressed in Jewish circles in the pre-Christian era (see chapter III.B); the dominical saying concerning the immortal nature of the

resurrection body (Lk 20:36), possibly known to Paul
through Luke; Paul's knowledge of the circumstances of the
resurrection appearances of Christ (1Co 15:5–7; cf. Gal
1:18–19); and the objections constantly levelled by cultured
Greeks against the idea of a bodily resurrection, which
forced Paul to elucidate his view of the resurrection state.

[2]Ex 23:16, 19; Lev 23:10; Nu 18:8, 12; Dt 18:4; 26:2, 10; 2Ch
31:5; Ne 10:37.

[3]There is a weighty textual variant in Ro 8:11b. Instead of
"through his Spirit" (*dia* with the genitive case), which
points to the agency of the Spirit (cf. 1Co 6:14), some early
and reliable manuscripts read "because of his Spirit" (*dia*
with the accusative). This would specify the ground of believers' resurrection and introduce the idea of the suitability
of the resurrection body as a home for the Spirit or of the
inevitability of resurrection given the indwelling of a life-giving Spirit.

XI: The "General Resurrection"

[1]The New Testament portrays "judgment," in both its senses,
as a present reality (e.g., Jn 3:18–19; 9:39; 12:31; Ac 5:1–
10; 12:23; 13:11; Ro 1:18–32; 1Co 5:3–5; 11:29–32) as well
as a future event (Mt 12:41–42; Jn 12:48; Ro 2:16; 2Ti 4:1).
In comparison with the inescapability and finality of divine
judgment, the precise time of its occurrence is incidental,
be it at death or at the Parousia (2Th 1:5–10; Heb 9:27).
Calendrical concern is as misplaced with regard to the time
of the judgment as it is in connection with the time of the
Parousia. The New Testament stresses repentance and read-
iness for judgment (Lk 13:1–5; 1Jn 2:28; Rev 2:5). And the
certainty of future accountability to Christ creates the desire
to please him and yet also a profound awe of him as the
divine assessor (2Co 5:9–11).

[2]Similarly Mt 19:29; 25:34–40; Mk 10:17, 21; Lk 18:29–30; Jn
6:40, 54; Ac 4:2, 12; Ro 6:5, 8, 23; Heb 2:10; 1Pe 1:3–9;
1Jn 2:24–25; 5:11, 20; Rev 2:7, 10–11.

[3]*Christian Beliefs about Life after Death* (Macmillan: London,
1976), 90–94 (the citation is from p. 91).

⁴Cf. J. Baillie, *And the Life Everlasting* (London: OUP, 1934), 228–37 (who speaks of "development in fruition," 234); U. Simon, *Heaven in the Christian Tradition* (Rockcliff: London, 1958), 227–36; and especially B. H. Streeter, "The Life of the World to Come," in *Immortality* by B. H. Streeter et al. (Macmillan: London, 1917), 131–66.

⁵On the possibility that 1Co 15:22–24 contains allusions to a "resurrection to judgment," see M. J. Harris, *Raised Immortal*, 173, 175. With regard to the time of this resurrection, it would seem that Jn 5:28–29 and Ac 24:15, which suggest *prima facie* that there is a single resurrection involving both the righteous and the unrighteous, should be interpreted in the light of Rev 20:4–6, which explicitly places the resurrection of unbelievers ("the rest of the dead") at the end of the millennium, with the resurrection of believers ("the first resurrection") at its beginning. See further *Raised Immortal*, 178–80.

⁶The destinies of the rich man and Lazarus are fixed and irreversible (Lk 16:23, 25–26), yet it is the intermediate, not the final, state that is being depicted, for life on earth continues (vv. 27–29) and resurrection and judgment lie in the future (vv. 27–31).

⁷That the concept of "destruction" (*apōleia*) (Mt 7:13; Php 3:19; Heb 10:39; 2Pe 3:7; Rev 17:8, 11) or "perishing" (*apollusthai*) (Jn 3:16; 10:28; Ro 2:12; 1Co 1:18; 15:18; 2Co 2:15; 2Pe 3:9) does not imply annihilation is clear from the use of the verb "perish" (*apollusthai*) in Jn 11:50; Ac 5:37; 1Co 10:9–10; Jude 11.

XII: Resurrection and Creation

¹In this passage (1Co 15:20–28) "kingdom" (v. 24) would seem to incorporate both the rational and the irrational universe, for *ta panta* (vv. 27, 28 *bis*) refers to "the universe in its totality" and *panta* (v. 27 *bis*) clearly has the same meaning.

²On the need to avoid oversystematizing New Testament eschatological statements, see the important article by C. F. D. Moule, "The Influence of Circumstances on the Use of Es-

chatological Terms," *Journal of Theological Studies*, new
series, 15 (1964): 1–15.

XIII: The Transformation of the Living

[1]There appear to be only two ways of avoiding this conclusion.
One is to claim that since the living are "raised" at the
Parousia from a state of mortality by the putting on of
immortality (cf. 1Cor. 15:53–54), they do not forfeit full
participation in Christ's bodily resurrection, so that although
omnes quidem resurgemus ("all of us indeed shall rise,"
1Co 15:51 Vulgate) are not Paul's words, the sentiment they
express is Pauline (thus A. Jones, "The Problem of the
Vulgate Reading in 1Cor. 15:51," *Scripture* 2 [1947]: 47).
The other way is to assert that "the transformation of the
living is a dying, but correspondingly the resurrection of the
dead is also a transformation" (A. T. Nikolainen, *Der Auferstehungsglauben in der Bibel und ihrer Umwelt* [Helsinki:
Annales Academiae Scientiarum Fennicae, 1944–46], 2:200).

XIV: Resurrection, Immortality, and Eternal Life

[1]London: Epworth, 1958, 5. This essay is reprinted in *Immortality and Resurrection*, ed. K. Stendahl (New York: Macmillan, 1965), 9–53 and is a translation of "Immortalité de
l'âme ou résurrection des morts?" first published in
Mélanges offerts à Karl Barth (Basle: Reinhardt, 1956),
126ff.

[2]E.g., W. Temple, "The Idea of Immortality in Relation to Religion and Ethics," the 1931 Drew Lecture on Immortality
reprinted in *Resurrection and Immortality*, ed. C. S. Duthie
(London: Bagster, 1979), 8–9; W. Strawson, *Jesus and the
Future Life* (Philadelphia: Westminster, 1959), 210.

[3]E.g., J. Macquarrie, *Principles of Christian Theology*, 2d ed.
(London: SCM, 1977), 362; cf. the comments of I. T. Ramsey, *Freedom and Immortality* (London: SCM, 1960), 142–
46.

[4]Recent writers who have recognized that resurrection and immortality are not incompatible notions include R.

Aldwinckle, *Death in the Secular City* (London: Allen, 1972), 82–100, especially 87–88, 99–100; M. Wiles, *The Remaking of Christian Doctrine* (London: SCM, 1974), 125–46, especially 137; C. K. Barrett, "Immortality and Resurrection," the 1964 Drew Lecture on Immortality reprinted in *Resurrection*, ed. C. S. Duthie (see above, n. 2), 68–88, especially 86; H. A. Wolfson, "Immortality and Resurrection in the Philosophy of the Church Fathers," the 1956 Ingersoll Lecture on "The Immortality of Man" reprinted in *Immortality*, ed. K. Stendahl (see above, n. 1), 54–96, especially 95–96; M. J. Harris, *Raised Immortal*, especially 209–40.

[5]J. B. Payne, for example, claims that "though man was not mortal prior to his probation, God had willed that, as a reward for passing the test, he should gain permanent immortality by eating of its fruit (3:22)" (*The Theology of the Older Testament* [Grand Rapids: Zondervan, 1962], 216; cf. 444).

[6]For the distinction between "immortable" and "immortal," see F. S. M. Bennet, *The Resurrection of the Dead* (London: Chapman and Hall, 1929), 1–53.

[7]L. Morris tentatively proposes that scientific and theological considerations can be harmonized if we regard death in its biological aspect as being "at one and the same time . . . completely natural and completely unnatural." We must take seriously "man's original constitution as being in a special relation both to God and to nature. Is it too much to imagine that this closeness to God and this primacy over nature found expression in forces of a spiritual character which kept the natural tendency to bodily decay in check? The entrance of sin so radically altered the situation that fleshly dissolution could no longer be held at bay, and thus death became inevitable" (*The Wages of Sin. An Examination of the New Testament Teaching on Death* [London: Tyndale, 1954], 12).

[8]Cf. A. B. Davidson, *The Theology of the Old Testament* (Edinburgh: T. & T. Clark, 1904), 439–40: "Man so far as we can gather from the narrative in Genesis, was made neither mortal nor immortal. He was not made so that he *must*

die, for the narrative represents him surrounded by the
means of living forever; nor was he so made that he *could
not* die, for the event has too clearly shown the reverse.
He was made capable of not dying, with the design that by
a free determination of his activity rewarded by God's fa-
vour, he should become not capable of dying."

[9]For a fuller discussion of the issues in this section, see M. J.
Harris, *Raised Immortal*, 191–94.

[10]F. W. Beare, however, is more confident on this point. "The
new life of the Christian believer . . . springs from 'incorruptible seed,' in that it is of God's sowing and is inherently immortal . . . The immortality of the Christian . . . is
the property of the new life which he receives by the creative act of God" (*The First Epistle of Peter*, 3d ed. [Ox-
ford: Blackwell, 1970], 111). O. Cullmann, too, dates the
gaining of immortality at the time of conversion (*Immortality of the Soul or Resurrection of the Dead?* [London: Epworth, 1958], 17), as does C. H. Dodd (*The Epistle of Paul
to the Romans* [London: Hodder, 1932], 126), but neither
scholar cites a scriptural passage in support.

[11]*The Christian in the Theology of St. Paul* (London: Chapman,
1967), 191–202, 223.

[12]Support for this conclusion comes from 2Pe 1:4 where, although the term immortality is not used, its positive and
qualitative aspect of immediate participation in the divine
nature is mentioned. Through the fulfillment of God's "mag-
nificent and precious promises" concerning the second advent of Christ (2Pe 1:16; 3:4, 9–10, 12), those who have
escaped from the world's corruption by their baptismal re-
nunciation of sin will become sharers of the divine nature.
"In other words," comments J. N. D. Kelly, "they will
enter into true union with God, participating in His glory,
immortality and blessedness" (*The Epistles of Peter and of
Jude* [New York: Harper, 1969], 301–2). Kelly sees clearly
what some commentators have failed to notice—that here
we have futurist, not realized, eschatology. Immediate and
full participation in the divine nature is a future gift (cf. Ro
5:2), not a present reality.

[13]"By immortality of the soul is meant the infinitely prolonged existence of that center of awareness to which the term 'I' refers" (W. L. Reese, *Dictionary of Philosophy and Religion. Eastern and Western Thought* [New Jersey: Humanities, 1980], 247).

[14]"Christian theologians have defended the soul's immortality (in a Platonic sense of immortal subsistence) on several grounds: 1. being immaterial and indivisible by nature, the soul is independent of the body and indestructible; 2. only a future life can bring to the necessary fruition the capacities and endowments of human nature and can rectify present inequalities and injustices; 3. the instinctive, universal and persistent belief of mankind that there is life after death argues for its reality" (M. J. Harris, "Immortality," in *New Dictionary of Theology*, ed. S. B. Ferguson, D. F. Wright, and J. I. Packer (Leicester/Downers Grove, Ill.: IVP, 1988), 333. To deny the *natural* immortality of the soul is not to deny that the soul survives death but it is to deny that it is preexistent or naturally divine.

[15]In biblical thought, life is not equated with mere existence and death with nonexistence, for both life and death are modes of existence (cf. L. Berkhof, *Systematic Theology* [Grand Rapids: Eerdmans, 1979 reprint of 1949 edition], 668).

[16]For a detailed discussion of the passages mentioned in this paragraph, see M. J. Harris, *Raised Immortal*, 209-32.

[17]A. Corell (*Consummatum Est* [London: SPCK, 1958], 142) has suggested that John deliberately avoided the technical terms for immortality "in order to emphasize that *zōē* is not a metaphysical or philosophical term but a purely religious one: life with Christ; life with God. This is particularly clear in 3:36, where the opposite to life is the wrath of God." Or it may be that John recognized "immortality" to be a term that includes the idea of immunity to physical death, and since the believer was still liable to physical death (Jn 11:25), immortality could not describe the present as well as the future experience of believers.

XV: Resurrection Formulas: Credal and Biblical

[1]J. T. Darragh, *The Resurrection of the Flesh* (New York: Macmillan/London: SPCK, 1921), 275-83.

²Thus, J. A. Schep, *The Nature of the Resurrection Body* (Grand Rapids: Eerdmans, 1964), 225–26. "Whenever the early Church Fathers and Creeds speak of the resurrection 'of the flesh,' they mean by 'flesh' man's flesh-body. The word 'flesh' is employed to safeguard the truth against spiritualizing interpretations" (ibid., 229). But, significantly, Schep admits that "from a formal point of view the traditional expression of the Creed may be called a misnomer. The word 'flesh' denotes here the substance of the body; whereas it is not the flesh-substance as such, not the crude, unorganized matter that will be raised, but *man in his flesh-body*" (ibid., 226).

³J. T. Darragh, *Resurrection* (see n. 1), 51, 154; L. Boliek, *The Resurrection of the Flesh* (Grand Rapids: Eerdmans, 1962), 120–43; G. C. Berkouwer, *The Return of Christ* (Grand Rapids: Eerdmans, 1972), 192–94. It is of particular significance that the two most detailed treatments in English of the history of the credal formulation "the resurrection of the flesh" (viz. Darragh and Boliek) both affirm that in this phrase "flesh" denotes the whole person, body and soul, and not the fleshly body as opposed to the incorporeal soul.

⁴J. Ratzinger, "Resurrection of the Body." B. Theological, in *Sacramentum Mundi*, ed. K. Rahner et al. (New York: Herder, 1970), 5:341.

⁵J. N. D. Kelly, *Early Christian Creeds*, 2d ed. (London: Longmans, 1960), 296.

⁶Darragh, *Resurrection*, 224 and n. 1.

⁷P. H. Menoud, *Le Sort des Trépassés* (Neuchâtel: Delachaux, 1966), 15.

⁸J. Heller, "The Resurrection of Man," *Theology Today* 15 (1958): 223; M. C. Perry, *The Resurrection of Man* (London: Mowbrays, 1975); O. Schilling, "Resurrection," in *Bauer Encyclopedia of Biblical Theology*, ed. J. B. Bauer (London: Sheed and Ward, 1970), 763 ("the formulation 'resurrection of the flesh' could be taken to imply 'resurrection of the man' involving a new formation of the body in the sense of a new creation of the material element in the human substance").

[9]C. R. Bowen, *The Resurrection in the New Testament* (New York/London: Putnam's, 1911), 76.

[10]See the discussion above (chap. IX.C.2) for these two views.

XVI: The Distinctives of the Christian View of Resurrection

[1]See references in A. Oepke, *TDNT* 1:369.

[2]Citing the "imprisonment-release" scheme (as in *Phaedo*) and the "transmigration-reincarnation" scheme (as in *Republic* and *Laws*), J. B. Skemp observes that it is impossible to construct from the Platonic dialogues an internally consistent scheme of doctrine regarding the fate of the soul (*The Greeks and the Gospel* [London: Carey Kingsgate, 1964], 80-81).

XVII: Conclusion

[1]Verses relevant to the content of this paragraph include: Mt 16:18; 28:20; Jn 1:9; 14:2-3, 16, 18, 26; 16:7-11; Ac 2:32-33, 47; 5:30-31; Ro 8:34; 10:13; 1Co 1:2; 15:24-28; Col 1:17-18; 1Th 4:13-18; Heb 1:3; 2:18; 4:15; 7:25; 9:28; 1Jn 2:1; Rev 1:5; 5:10.

[2]Mk 4:41; 5:15, 33; 9:6, 32; 10:32; 11:18.

[3]Mt 28:17b reads "But some [of the Eleven—see BDF, 131 § 250; BAGD, 549-50 under *ho* I.2] doubted." The doubt was not blatant disbelief but a wavering hesitation (*distazō*). On this occasion what was doubted was not the possibility of resurrection or the fact that Jesus had risen (although there had been such doubts among the Eleven earlier—Lk 24:11, 37-41; Jn 20:27). Far less did they doubt the propriety of worshiping the risen Jesus (see Mt 14:33). What happened was that some of the Eleven apparently failed to recognize Jesus (cf. Lk 24:37; Jn 20:14), perhaps because they had remained some distance from him (note "he came forward [*proselthōn*] to them," Mt 28:18a).

[4]We may compare the explicit or implied rebuke of persons who were worshiping someone other than God, found in Ac 10:25-26; 12:21-23; 14:8-18; Rev 19:9-10; 21:8-9.

PART 2

A RESPONSE TO DR. NORMAN L. GEISLER

XVIII

The Antecedent of the Controversy:
The Bishop of Durham Affair

At 2:30 A.M. on Monday, July 9, 1984, lightning struck the southern end of the south transept roof of York Minster, the majestic Gothic cathedral that is the pride of York in the north of England. The raging fire that broke out reduced to ashes the exquisitely crafted oak vaulting and cracked the glass windows, including a priceless sixteenth-century window of some 8,000 separate panes. Yet the inferno was contained. Only the roof of the south transept was gutted; most of the Minster remained intact.[1] Said Dr. Robert Runcie, the Archbishop of Canterbury, after visiting the scene later that day, "It seems miraculous that the fire was so confined."

But not everyone was disposed to see a divine miracle in the containing of the fire. Many saw the lightning as a sign from heaven of divine disapproval at the consecration, three days previously, of Dr. David E. Jenkins as the new Bishop of Durham.[2] A correspondent to *The Times* (London) made the comment: "'Just lightning,' says the Bishop [of Durham] dismissively. To those as old-fashioned as I, lightning is the wrath of God."[3] Religion was once more a topic of excited conversation throughout the British Isles.

Why did so many people up and down Britain react to the fire by wondering whether God had personally intervened to register his displeasure with the new appointment? It was because Dr. Jenkins had scandalized multitudes of people both inside and outside the church during previous months by

his offhand comments, often made into a journalist's micro-
phone or before a TV camera, that seemed to call into
question two cardinal doctrines of the Christian faith—the
Virgin Birth and especially the resurrection of Christ. For
instance, in a television program broadcast on April 29, 1984,[4]
he said "If I might be allowed to say so, I wouldn't put it past
God to arrange a virgin birth if he wanted, but I very much
doubt if he would, because it seems to be contrary to the way
in which he deals with persons and brings his wonders out of
natural personal relationships." And on the Resurrection: "It
doesn't seem to me, reading the records as they remain in
both the gospels and what Paul says in 1 Corinthians, that
there was any one event which you could identify with the
Resurrection."

Response to informal remarks such as these was predict-
able. The media relished the prospect of an ongoing dispute
within the established church. Some theologians in the
universities spoke of academic freedom and appealed to the
consensus of all "enlightened biblical scholars" (a species of
"academic terrorism," as Dr. Henry Chadwick aptly puts it).
But to the majority of Christians these expressions of doubt
and these reinterpretations of traditional doctrines, coming as
they did from a senior bishop in the Church of England, were
profoundly disturbing. Nor was the bishop's influence restricted to the British Isles. I have heard of Muslim intellectuals in Sri Lanka and skeptical high school seniors in
Australia who appealed to a doubting bishop in England to
justify their own unbelief.

Another cause of frustration for many members of the
Church of England were the circumstances surrounding the
consecration. In spite of multitudes of individual protests and
an official delegation of clergymen received at York, along
with a nationwide petition bearing 12,500 signatures and
requesting that the consecration be delayed or canceled, the
Archbishop of York, Dr. John Habgood, decided to proceed

with the installation, although no statute prevented him from refusing the Crown's appointee.

And so the ceremony took place in York Minster before a crowd of more than 2000 on Friday, July 6, with the customary "pomp and circumstance" and with two brief interruptions by protesters during the service. Then, "on the third day" (by Western, not biblical, reckoning) lightning struck the cathedral and the fire ensued.

Some months later, after I had participated in a BBC Radio 4 program with the bishop and others at Auckland Castle in Durham (the bishop's residence), I became convinced that his views were being unfairly represented in the press and that the differences between his view and biblical teaching about the Resurrection were not being carefully defined. At the same time consternation was growing among "ordinary believers" within and outside the Church of England: if a bishop could not be trusted to express and defend the historic truths of Christianity, what would become of the church? Yet they could turn to no authoritative source that treated the bishop fairly and yet also unashamedly compared his views with Scripture.

I was not a member of the Church of England, but I was at that time Warden of Tyndale House, a biblical research library in Cambridge, England. This community of academics is committed to the defense of the faith as well as to the scholarly study of the Scripture from an evangelical perspective. Given the urgency of the need, I decided to postpone the academic writing project on which I was working and prepare a reply to the bishop. It was my prayer that Christians in Britain and throughout the Commonwealth who had been unsettled by the adverse publicity given to orthodoxy over recent months might be reassured of the certainty of the Resurrection and that those outside the faith might be introduced to the truth and reality of the risen Lord.

First I carefully summarized the bishop's views in detail, quoting extensively from five books he had written over the period 1965–76 and supplementing these statements by four more recent, popular sources. Then I undertook an appraisal of his views in the light of New Testament teaching. And so it was that in April 1985 Paternoster Press published my thirty-two-page booklet, *Easter in Durham*.[5] It was reviewed in at least thirty-eight publications in six countries.

A word of explanation may be needed about the apparently strange title of the booklet. In technical religious language in Britain, a bishop is known by the name of the city where he officially resides. In this parlance, "Durham" refers to the Bishop of Durham, not the city of Durham. So my title means "The View of the Resurrection in the writings of the Bishop of Durham," not "An Easter Holiday in the City of Durham"!

The preface to the booklet was contributed by the Bishop of London, Dr. Graham Leonard, widely known and respected as a staunchly conservative theologian. Significantly, he is the third-ranking bishop in the Church of England, after the Archbishop of York and before the Bishop of Durham: thus the order is Canterbury, York, London, Durham.

His preface read as follows.

> The present controversy over the Resurrection of Our Lord is of cardinal importance for the proclamation of the Christian Gospel. The New Testament portays the Resurrection as the event through which the work of Jesus on the cross bore fruit in what it describes as a new creation. To bear first-hand witness to the Resurrection was the first duty of the Apostles and the evidence that Jesus was raised in body, mind and spirit is set out in detail.
>
> As Dr. Murray Harris makes clear in his excellent study, the ultimate point at issue is the authority of the Bible as a source of divine revelation and "the touchstone of Christian doctrine, the bar at which all belief which claims to be Christian must be tested."
>
> To reduce the Resurrection to nothing more than an experience in the minds of the disciples is not only to challenge the authority of the Scriptures. It is also to

challenge what they reveal about God. In the Bible he is both Creator of the universe and its Redeemer. It is significant that in his magisterial exposition of the Gospel in the Epistle to the Romans St. Paul begins with an affirmation of God as Creator before writing of what he has done in Christ. By the Resurrection man and the physical world, of which he is an integral part, are given a new potential and become capable of expressing the divine glory. Death and decay result in no more than the recycling of matter. In the Resurrection matter is given an ultimate place in God's design.

To see the Resurrection as no more than a spiritual experience is to abandon the biblical view and to pronounce a decree absolute between spirit and matter. Such an attitude conflicts both with the biblical teaching and, being based on an outdated positivism, with the modern scientific understanding of man as a psychosomatic unity. The deep and rich objective mystery of recreation in Christ, which calls for the fullest exercise of all our faculties if we are to be grasped by its meaning, is replaced by a bloodless and subjective experience.

Dr. Harris's study is a model of how Christians should contend for "the faith once delivered to the saints." With courtesy and fairness, he allows the Bishop of Durham to speak for himself and directs his creative criticism towards what the Bishop has actually written or said. Dr. Harris has done us a great service and I commend his study warmly.

Much of the booklet is a rejoinder to specific views held by the Bishop of Durham and therefore is not directly relevant to the present situation, but of undoubted relevance is my response to his central affirmation that the resurrection of Jesus (1) was a series of events demonstrating the "livingness" of Jesus and experienced by the disciples of Jesus, not a single event experienced by Jesus himself; and (2) was a personal resurrection, but not a bodily resurrection, so that there was and is no resurrection body of Jesus apart from "the body of Christ," the church.

The essence of my response to the bishop is found in my "Conclusion," which is here given in full.

In all his writings Bishop Jenkins has consistently argued that Jesus' resurrection was God's act of perpetuating the presence and power of Jesus among his disciples after his death. Jesus rose, not bodily, from the grave, but spiritually (although none the less really), in the minds of the disciples. The basic flaw of such a view is that it confuses the nature and the effect of the resurrection. The disciples' emerging conviction that Jesus "was in fact not dead and finished, but alive and purposefully active" (*Glory*, p. 32),[6] was not itself the resurrection of Jesus but the result of the resurrection. According to the New Testament the resurrection of Jesus was his bodily and permanent emergence from death in a transformed state, and his exaltation to God's right hand. When the empty tomb and appearances of Jesus had made it clear that he had been reanimated and transformed, faith in the risen Jesus was born in his followers. We must never lose sight of the necessary distinction between the resurrection fact and the resurrection faith. "If Christ has not been raised, your faith is futile" (1 Cor.15:17): first the fact, then the faith. The disciples' faith in the risen Jesus derived its validity from the prior fact that Jesus rose from the dead.

What the Bishop offers us, then, is a sophisticated reinterpretation of the resurrection of Jesus. But it is not simply the case that a familiar theme has undergone an insignificant transposition of key. The tune itself is forfeited in this musical re-arrangement which cannot therefore be regarded as an acceptable interpretation of the New Testament score. What is in effect denied by the Bishop's views is (1) an Easter event that was experienced by Jesus himself, (2) a tomb that was empty because of the actual revival of the buried Jesus of Nazareth, (3) an individual existence of the risen Jesus in a spiritual body apart from his relation to the Church; and (4) a future resurrection of the unrighteous leading to their banishment from the divine presence.

But above and beyond these four specific doctrinal aberrations of the Bishop, there lurks the fundamental question of the nature of divine revelation and the authority of Scripture as a witness to and source of that revelation. One looks in vain through the Bishop's writings to find any expression of the traditional view that God's special revelation is his self-disclosure in Jesus Christ and also in the Scriptures. Rather, "in its biblical and Christian form (or better, forms), the idea of revelation implies that men (some particular men, that is) have been enabled to form ideas, impressions and insights about the nature and possibilities of themselves and of the world under the particular guidance or influence of God" (*Man*, p. 72).[7] In keeping with this relativistic view of revelation, the Bishop sees his own theological writing as an exercise in experimental thought (*Glory*, pp. 21, 24, 117).[8] This explains why he frequently disclaims finality for his views, "these wonderings and wanderings of mine" as he expresses it in his 1969 "Easter meditation" on the resurrection (*Questions*, p. 141).[9] And in his most recent book (1976) he confesses at one point, with disarming frankness, "I am afraid of my arguing because it might be false and be so wholly a matter of fantasy and refusal to face realities that it is one more contribution to the confusing and misleading of human beings" (*Contradiction*, p. 78).[10] Precision of doctrine, he contends, is neither possible nor desirable. Thus a person may be regarded as a Christian who regards Jesus merely as a great moral teacher and a divine agent who leads people to God ("Credo"),[11] or who holds the resurrection of Jesus to be symbolic, not factual (*Questions*, p. 136).[12] It comes as no surprise, therefore, that although the Bishop's writings are punctuated at irregular intervals by allusions to biblical passages, Scriptural references or citations are exceedingly rare. The reader scarcely gains the impression either that "Holy Scripture contains all things necessary to salvation" (Article 6 of the Thirty-Nine Articles of Religion) or that it is one role of a Christian theologian to expound and defend its teaching.

In his views about the resurrection of Jesus, the Bishop has clearly failed to do justice to biblical teaching. Whatever assessment be made of his orthodoxy in other areas of belief, in this crucial area that is central to the Christian faith his views do not conform to the testimony of the New Testament in several important regards.

Perhaps the most effective way for the reader to gain a feeling for those times in 1984–85 and an impression of evangelical reaction to my booklet will be for me to reproduce two of the more colorful reviews.

The first is by Dr. Peter Graves, Lecturer in German at Leicester University, England.

It did not need a bolt of lightning setting fire to one of England's finest cathedrals to bring the name of David Jenkins to public attention. Even before this spectacular postscript to his installation as Bishop of Durham he had made a name for himself as a turbulent priest, not only stirring up a great deal of theological controversy but also voicing colourful opinions on matters of the day such as the miners' strike or the government's economic policies. Indeed, so outspoken were his views and so flamboyant his manner of expressing them that even the popular press devoted space to what one columnist called "the war of Jenkins' mouth."

Whatever the merits of his political pronouncements it is his beliefs in the area of theology and doctrine that are likely in the long run to be of more lasting influence, and among these his views on the resurrection have attracted the greatest publicity (the doubting bishop seems to be second in newsworthiness only to the adulterous vicar). It has not always been easy, however, to disentangle the substance of his convictions from the misrepresentation of which he has often complained or the ear-catching phrases to which he himself seems particularly addicted (the "conjuring trick with bones" being possibly the most notorious). In his book *Easter in Durham* Dr. Murray Harris, the Warden of Tyndale House, has sought to clear away the fog by distilling David Jenkins' statements on the resurrection from his books, articles and TV and radio broadcasts, and presenting them in cool and concise form under a number of headings covering different aspects of the subject. What emerges is a belief that identifies the resurrection primarily as a work of God on the consciousness of the disciples rather than on the dead body of Jesus: "God enabled some men to perceive the lasting significance of the shape of Jesus' personality"; over a period of time they underwent "the experienced discovery of his risenness" and thus came to the awareness of "a new living of Jesus." Jesus is now "a distinctive, living and personal activity," embodied in the Church, working for "the establishment, development and liberation of human identity." This process, essentially communal in nature, will be consummated in the Kingdom of God when "we shall all be perfected through the perfections of one another."

Dr. Harris then proceeds, succinctly but incisively, to compare David Jenkins' interpretation of the resurrection with the biblical revelation. He points out that in Scripture the resurrection of Jesus is located, not in the subjectivity of the first believers, but in the objective reality of an event that took place on a particular day in history. In addition, the resurrection denotes more than just the continuation of "the shape of Jesus Christ" but principally a physical miracle involving the bodily resuscitation, albeit in a transformed and exalted form, of the Jesus of Nazareth who walked this earth. He rejects David Jenkins' equation of Christ's risen body with the Church, because it implicitly denies the reality of our Lord's separate and individual resurrection body, and he dismisses the bishop's universalism on the grounds that the Bible foresees a resurrection not only to life but also to judgment.

Some of the arguments deployed by Dr. Harris are of course familiar from such books as *Who Moved the Stone?* or J. N. D. Anderson's *Evidence for the Resurrection,* but what is striking here is not so much their application to the views of one particular individual but the effect produced by juxtaposing the arguments of Dr. Jenkins and the evidence of Scripture. The former, robbed of the exuberance with which their progenitor communicates them on television, appear fragile, strained and attenuated, whereas the scriptural witness carries the conviction and dynamism and indeed logical persuasiveness, that turned the world upside down in the first place. One wonders, for instance, whether the early Christians would have had quite the effect that they did if, instead of affirming that "God has raised this Jesus to life, and we are all witnesses of the fact" (Acts 2:32), they had come with the proposition of Jesus' "livingness on the other side of his death."

Easter in Durham is written with an admirable restraint, and there is no more than the merest hint that Dr. Jenkins may not be fulfilling his ordination pledge to believe, expound and teach the doctrine of the Christian faith "which is revealed in the holy Scriptures." Yet that is the clear implication of this study. No-one would dispute the Bishop's right to hold, and to propagate, the views that he does, and one imagines that he must have been a stimulating university teacher. But it is one thing to address provocative, even outrageous, remarks to a lecture-room of sophisticated students trained in the discernment of abstract concepts. It is quite another when those same statements, couched in terms that positively invite the slick headline, are uttered by a senior representative of the Anglican Church and hence supposedly a guardian of the orthodox faith.

It is mischievously tempting to assume that the display of celestial fireworks which accompanied Bishop Jenkins' installation must have been a mark of divine displeasure, but it seems unlikely that the God of the New Testament works that way (if York, why not Auschwitz?). It is rather the responsibility of those who find the views currently espoused in Durham both inadequate and injurious to refute them by measured and lucid argument. Dr. Harris has shown us, in exemplary fashion, how that may be done.[13]

The second review comes from the pen of Dr. Robert P. Gordon, Lecturer in Hebrew and Aramaic at the University of Cambridge.

After his initial leap into theological controversy last year Dr. David Jenkins, bishop of Durham, was reported as having promised to lie low and keep quiet for a while, and for that we may be thankful! Who knows what heresies he might otherwise have stirred up during the period of "silence"! Still, the fact remains that Dr. Jenkins was busy muddying the water at a time when thousands of his fellow-Anglicans and others were working and praying for a revival of Christian faith in godless England. At the least there is a touch of historical irony here. What was the Holy Spirit doing in 1984? Hardly sending out such contradictory signals as are represented by Durham and York on the one hand and by "Mission England" on the other.

The "Jenkins Affair" presents orthodox Christians, and especially orthodox Christian scholars, with a familiar problem. How should one react to yet another denial, from within the fold, of cardinal Christian doctrines? It has happened so often; so what's new? Is it worth taking any notice? We have also to keep in mind that the theological balloonist of this particular moment thinks that doctrine is and must ever be imprecise in what it affirms about our condition and prospect. So should one take a sledge-hammer to a wisp of cotton wool? Most Christians, and especially those with strong pastoral or evangelistic concerns, will almost automatically feel that suitable responses should be made to the kind of challenge to traditional belief that the present controversy offers. And they are surely right.

In addition to his stated recreational interests of music, reading and walking (*Who's Who* [1984]), Dr. Jenkins seems to be making a hobby of trying to take a rise out of the Easter message, hence the title of Murray J. Harris's timely *Easter in Durham*. Dr. Harris, warden of Tyndale House, Cambridge, is not just any old evangelical fish eager for a nibble; he has already published an important volume entitled *Raised Immortal: Resurrection and Immortality in the New Testament* (1983) and is therefore unusually well-qualified to enter the present debate. Since the wide media coverage of Dr. Jenkins's utterances carries with it the usual problem of knowing what exactly someone has said and in what context, Dr. Harris first attempts to establish what has been said—or written, for good use is made of several books published by Dr. Jenkins before the present controversy blew up. The statements thus collected are then examined in the light of the evidence and teaching of the New Testament. Dr. Harris is always courteous—coming from the evangelical side this could well confuse the bishop—but never short of rigorous, and the result is an impressive restatement of a fundamental article of Christian belief.

It is in the nature of things that Dr. Jenkins is not always easy to pin down. To be fair, his prose is usually a class above the "colourless-green-ideas-sleep-furiously" brand, but there are many staging posts on the way to that *ultima Thule*. Not surprisingly, for one driven to abstraction, the suffix "ness" has a role to play ("risenness," "livingness"); Dr. Harris jocularly coins a usage of his own ("rising-ness"), which shows that he can play theology with the best of them.

The point at issue between Drs. Jenkins and Harris is that for the former the Resurrection does not mean the event of the first Easter morning, but a series of experiences whereby the disciples were convinced that their Lord was "not finished." So, of the two main ways of referring to the r(a)ising of our Lord from the dead in the New Testament, the bishop shows a preference for the elliptical "God raised Jesus," as being less likely to inhibit with objective or historical constraints. On this showing, the gulf between the New Testament and the bishop's reinterpretation of it yawns very wide indeed, and we may be grateful to Dr.

Harris for making the issue so clear. It is also noted that,
for Dr. Jenkins, the expression "the body of Christ" has
now but one significance, viz. the church, "the place where
Jesus is embodied now." At this point (p. 21) Dr. Harris is
led to wonder whether the bishop believes in a *personal*
resurrection of Jesus, let alone a physical one. Things are
particularly foggy here, and one wonders whether Dr.
Jenkins really intends going that far. For if the "resurrection" of Jesus means, for example, that members of the
human family will enjoy "the fullness of the life of God in
unimpeded relations with him and with one another" (cf.
Harris, p. 27), can resurrection be anything less than
personal for the church's Lord?

And so on. If the New Testament is "the bar at which all
belief which claims to be Christian must be tested" (p. 9),
then Dr. Jenkins has a lot of work still to do. But there is
another problem here, for, as Dr. Harris notes in his
Conclusion, there is little in what the bishop says to suggest
that "God's special revelation is his self-disclosure in Jesus
Christ and also in the Scriptures" (p. 32). (This is certainly
how it works out in practice, even if there are positive-
sounding statements in, for example, *Guide to the Debate
about God* [1966], which is another of Dr. Jenkins's
publications.) In particular, by his abandoning of the
Scriptures—which is what his demythologizing effectively
involves—the bishop tacitly acknowledges that, of the
three representative groupings in the first century—Jews,
Greeks and Christians—only the Christians got it wrong
about the Resurrection. The Jews denied it as historical
fact, and the Greeks had as much difficulty with the
concept, on scientific and philosophical grounds, as do
most thinking people nowadays. Christians down the
centuries have, however, been inclined to answer contemporary Sadduceeism along the lines of *Matthew 22:29*. In
point of fact the issue is more fundamental than that of the
authority of Scripture, in that it concerns the whole
question of God's activity in relation to this world—the
inspiration and authority of Scripture being but one aspect
of this. (So much is implied in the Bishop of London's

warmly commendatory foreword to Dr. Harris's pamphlet.) The point is often made that a miraculous event like the Resurrection is "not accessible to historical investigation" and therefore has to be treated differently from ordinary history. But in the case of the Resurrection—as distinct from, say, the Virgin Birth—this is not the whole story, of course, and Christians have commonly held that, inspiration apart, the New Testament witness to the Resurrection of our Lord provides a kind of historical evidence which is both open to investigation and capable of leading the sincere inquirer to the recognition of Jesus Christ as Son of God and Saviour. It is all the more regrettable, then, that Dr. Jenkins has gone so far in the opposite direction; and it is highly appropriate that Dr. Harris gives us a summary of that same evidence. For no amount of harping on the "livingness" of Christ can change the fact that the New Testament is disembowelled when the Resurrection on the third day is seen as a mistaken inference on the part of the apostles and prophets of the church.

The theologian who would be Christian cannot, in any case, get away from "special event," be his picture of Christ ever so human. Is a perfect, sinless adult life lived on this earth any less remarkable than the Resurrection? ("His character was more wonderful than the greatest miracle" [Tennyson, I believe].) Or is this also negotiable? That impeccable life was more than a little "accessible to historical investigation," as the late John Robinson clearly saw: "Positive sinlessness is attributed to Jesus, for theological reasons, within the lifetime of many who could have contradicted the Christian claim if the credibility gap had been too great. There are limits, first, to what you can persuade yourself to, then to what you can get away with, and still more to what you can assert without even having to defend" (*The Human Face of God* [1973], p. 98).

If one of the effects of theological controversy is sometimes to call forth notable restatements of "the faith once delivered to the saints," then Dr. Harris is to be thanked

and congratulated on taking his place in that noble tradition.[14]

In the course of my reply to the bishop I made several
affirmations that bear directly on the current controversy.

Page 16:

Against Professor Jenkins' insistence that it was the disciples'
settled conviction about Jesus' "risenness" that God caused,
we would urge that it was the reanimation and transformation
of a buried corpse.

Page 17:

But unlike the Bishop, we would regard the resurrection as
being principally a physical miracle rather than a purely
psychological or spiritual miracle.

Pages 17–18:

While the revival and metamorphosis of Jesus of Nazareth
after his crucifixion and burial are open to historical enquiry,
his exaltation to the right hand of God is a tenet of faith that is
not susceptible to historical investigation.

Page 20:

But the evidence of the New Testament demands we affirm
that the resurrection of Jesus was both personal and bodily.
The risen Jesus was precisely the same person as Jesus of
Nazareth . . . Jesus' resurrection body was not a fresh
creation of God, a "creation out of nothing."

Since the physical body of Jesus that had been buried had
gained, as the result of a resurrection transformation, the
properties of a spiritual body, we cannot say that the
resurrected Jesus had precisely the same body as Jesus of
Nazareth. That on which God worked in effecting a resurrec-

tion transformation was nothing other than the buried body of Jesus, but the outcome was that the same person occupied a different dwelling, so to speak. There had been a metamorphosis of his body.

Page 21:

If the actual body of Jesus was raised and transformed, there was no "trick" involving the removal of a corpse to produce an empty tomb.

Page 23:

To Jews of the first century A.D., any idea of a resurrection shortly after death involved the emptying of a tomb or grave, the revival of the physical body. . . . No one could be regarded as resurrected while his corpse lay in a tomb.

Page 25:

In their preaching both Peter (Acts 2:24–32) and Paul (Acts 13:34–37) insisted that the resurrection occurred before the body of Jesus began to decompose: whereas King David's body did "see corruption," God did not allow "his Holy One" to "see corruption." Such insistence is relevant only if Jesus' actual body was resurrected.

Page 31:

According to the New Testament the resurrection of Jesus was his bodily and permanent emergence from death in a transformed state, and his exaltation to God's right hand. When the empty tomb and appearances of Jesus had made it clear that he had been reanimated and transformed, faith in the risen Jesus was born in his followers.

What is in effect denied by the Bishop's views is . . . a tomb that was empty because of the actual revival of the buried Jesus of Nazareth.

From these *verbatim* excerpts any reader may see that I unequivocally affirmed in 1985, as I always have and will, the literal, physical resurrection of Jesus from the dead. No fair reading of *Easter in Durham* allows for any other interpretation. This, then, will prompt not a little astonishment that I should now be accused by Dr. Norman L. Geisler of denying the physical resurrection of Jesus. In his four articles on this issue (one in 1987 and three in 1989), Dr. Geisler has virtually ignored *Easter in Durham,*[15] although he has had a copy since October 1986. In his recent book he summarizes parts of *Easter in Durham* (*Battle,* 100–102) but, significantly, not one of the passages cited above that explicitly refer to the "reanimation" or "resuscitation" or "revival" of Jesus' body is ever quoted or even referred to in his book or in any of his publications. It would seem that when Dr. Geisler wishes to argue a particular case, he is willing, on occasion, to turn a blind eye to evidence that compromises or undermines his case.

But how did the whole controversy come about? What were the charges leveled by Dr. Geisler? What has been the reaction of Trinity Evangelical Divinity School and the Evangelical Free Church of America to these charges? In our next chapter we shall seek to answer these questions.

XIX

The History of the Controversy

For several years prior to 1985, Trinity had been investigating the possibility of launching a Ph.D. program with an emphasis in systematic theology. It was recognized that one ingredient in any such venture was to secure the services of additional teachers of international experience. And so it was that in December 1985 Trinity offered me an endowed chair as Professor of New Testament Exegesis and Theology.

I had already served two terms at Trinity, during the academic year 1967–68 while I was pursuing doctoral studies at the University of Manchester, and from 1971–78 when I was (ultimately) Professor of Biblical Greek and New Testament. I came to Trinity as a specialist in Pauline theology and the grammar of biblical Greek.

It is the procedure at Trinity to interview prospective faculty members with thoroughness. There are routine interviews with all the members of the particular department, with a faculty subcommittee, with the administration, and with a committee of the board of directors. Because I had already been a faculty member at Trinity for eight years, they felt such a series of interviews unnecessary in my case. However, I requested that all the normal procedures be followed, and Trinity was happy to comply with this request, particularly since some questions about my views on eschatology had arisen on one occasion during my previous time at Trinity. As a result of all these interviews, I was invited to rejoin the faculty, an invitation I gladly accepted.

On my arrival in the United States, I found awaiting me a letter from Dr. Geisler (dated August 11, 1986) that welcomed me on my return and inquired about three matters:

> Specifically, I am interested in whether you still hold that:
> 1. Paul changed his view on when the saints receive their resurrection bodies.
> 2. Paul changed his view on the nature of the resurrection body (as to whether it was material, physical).
> 3. There is no numerical or substantial identity between the pre and post resurrection body (bodies?) of Jesus.

To these questions I replied (October 9, 1986) as follows:

> Regarding your questions:
> On #1, see *Raised Immortal* p. 256 n. 5 (last sentence) which indicates a change of view on my part from the *Tyndale Bulletin* article.
> #2, I have never held!
> On #3, see the enclosed booklet *Easter in Durham*, *passim*, esp. 20f. Again you are crediting me with a view I have never held. Sadly, some person or persons are spreading erroneous (and malicious) rumours. As the booklet demonstrates, I have been at the forefront of demonstrating from the NT that the tomb of Jesus was empty and that the resurrected Lord was none other than the crucified Nazarene (= "numerical or 'substantial' identity").

After we had spoken together at length during a conference in Dallas in November 1986, Geisler prepared an initial draft of an article entitled "An Examination of the View of Murray Harris on the Resurrection Body," and in the best scholarly tradition, sent it to me for my comments. "I believe that your response and clarification of your view will be a helpful dialogue" (February 20, 1987). To this I replied (April 22, 1987):

> It is my considered opinion that nothing beneficial would be gained by the publication of the article, since . . . there are many serious misrepresentations of my views in the article;

and later (May 12, 1987) I wrote:

> Regarding the misunderstanding and misrepresentation of my views in your article, let me simply observe that they are too numerous and serious to warrant the time involved in any attempt to rectify them, especially since I have just embarked on a 20-volume series . . .

> It is my request . . . that you not seek a publisher for the article but rest content in the knowledge that I have taken careful note of your observations and am grateful for your critique.

A modified and expanded form of the article appeared in due course under the title "The Apologetic Significance of the Bodily Resurrection of Christ."[1]

In subsequent correspondence with me (November 2, December 8, December 17, 1987), Geisler repeatedly asked the question, "Do you now believe that Christ's resurrection body was a literal, physical body?" While firmly believing that the same physical body of Jesus that had been buried was raised from the dead, I was reluctant to answer with an unqualified "Yes" because the resurrection body of Jesus clearly had properties that were not true of a mortal, physical body. How can we affirm that Jesus' resurrection body was simply "a literal, physical body" such as we mortals now have? So my answer to him (December 25, 1987) was "Yes and No," and I cited a comparable instance in the life of Jesus when he refused to answer a simple question ("Is it lawful to pay taxes to Caesar, or not?") with either a "Yes" or a "No" (viz. Mk 12:13–17). To this Geisler replied (in a later letter, February 8, 1988), "To this day you have not given a clear and unequivocal answer to a straight-forward clearly understandable question."

In that letter of December 25, 1987, I made two further important points.

> For the third time I affirm my wholehearted and enthusiastic belief in the personal and bodily resurrection of Jesus Christ, as well as my total commitment to and belief in the two relevant EFC [Evangelical Free Church] affirmations, viz. that "He [Jesus Christ] arose bodily from the dead" (Article II, 3) and "We believe in the bodily resurrection of the dead" (Article II, 12).

The second point was a positive statement of what I believe, written, in a time-honored scholarly tradition, in one long sentence of classical Greek, within the format of an ancient papyrus letter. In translation the letter reads thus:

> Murray, to Norman, brother in Christ, greetings. If you are well, it would be splendid; I, for my part, am well.

> In reference to those who attempt to deny that after his resurrection Christ appeared to his disciples in another form, I shall affirm this specific fact—that I have always believed that since he is the firstfruits of those who have fallen asleep and the guarantee and pledge of the resurrection of the deceased righteous who will be raised immortal, Jesus of Nazareth himself actually rose from the dead in a spiritual body, for the body that is to be does not share in "flesh and blood," a point clearly made by Paul the apostle of the resurrected Jesus Christ in the passage about resurrection from the dead [1Co 15:35–50]; and is seated at the right hand of the Majesty on high in bodily form, as Paul clearly indicates in the passage about Christ's lordship [Col 2:8–3:4].

> Farewell.[2]

In the period just preceding the Evangelical Free Church's Annual Conference (June 20–24, 1988) there were two mailings to pastors: one from Dr. Geisler (June 1, 1988), specifying at length the grounds for his accusations against me and against the Free Church leadership for their handling of the matter; and one (May 9, 1988) from Dr. Thomas A. McDill, president of the denomination, outlining the stages of "due process" that had been followed and commenting, "I have reminded Dr. Geisler that Dr. Murray Harris is not accountable to him—he is accountable to Trinity Evangelical Divinity School and the Evangelical Free Church of America." He adds, "It is interesting to note that Dr. Geisler has not been an active member of an Evangelical Free Church for more than nine years (he retains membership in an Illinois Free Church though he lives in Dallas) and has not attended nor transferred his membership to the Free Church in Dallas."

One of the most significant documents in the whole controversy was an open letter (June 14, 1988) from Dr. Gleason L. Archer to Dr. Geisler that was distributed by the Free Church leadership to delegates at the conference. Its significance is twofold. First, in his role as an outstanding evangelical Old Testament scholar and author, Dr. Archer has gained a worldwide reputation as an unsurpassed champion of orthodoxy. Second, he was closely associated with Dr. Geisler when they were colleagues at Trinity in the 1970s and a question arose about my views. The letter deserves to be reproduced in full.

> Dear Norm:
>
> In response to your request for the promised article by Murray Harris on the bodily resurrection of Christ, reported to have been published in the TEDS organ, "VOICES." I made search and enquiry this morning at the School. What I discovered was that there has been a bit of delay in getting this issue to the printer, and so no one has received it at all. What confuses the picture is that Murray did contribute an article on Christian stewardship in a fairly

recent issue; but fine as the article is, it has no bearing on the Resurrection.

I therefore prevailed upon the young lady who prepares final copy for the printer, and I secured a photocopy of "Raised—Never to Die Again" by Murray J. Harris, and I am happy to send you a xerox copy of this by express mail. As I do so, I would like to comment that I could find no statement in these columns with which I could not heartily agree. He affirms (as you and I surely would affirm): "Our Lord . . . was not merely given a new lease on physical life when His Father raised Him to life. As Scripture describes it, He has a 'glorious body' (Phil. 3:21) and He lives 'by the power of an indestructible life' (Heb. 7:16)."

It may be observed that there is little analysis given as to the nature or properties of the resurrection body of our Lord in this short article. But as I turned to his 1985 discussion in "Easter in Durham," I find that this matter is dealt with in a very perceptive and discriminating way. For example, on p. 16 of that work we read: "Against Prof. Jenkins' insistence that it was the disciples' settled conviction about Jesus' 'risenness' that God caused, we would urge that it was the reanimation and transformation of a buried corpse." Further on he states (p. 17): "But unlike the Bishop, we would regard the resurrection as being principally a physical miracle rather than a purely psychological or spiritual miracle." This sounds to me like a forthright affirmation of the literal, physical nature of Christ's resurrection body.

Murray then goes on to say (p. 17): "In its full Christian sense, resurrection signifies more than mere resuscitation, the regaining of the life forfeited through death. It also involves transformation, the alteration and enhancement of the properties of the physical body." A careful study of the post-resurrection appearances of our Lord can hardly lead to any other conclusion than this. He goes on to say: "Jesus was no longer bound by material or space limitations (e.g., John 20:19, 26), his essential state was one of invisibility and therefore immateriality (Luke 24:31, 36) and he could materialize and therefore be localized at will (Luke 24:39–40; John 20:27). . . The resurrection marked Jesus' entrance upon a spiritual mode of existence, or, to borrow Paul's expression, his acquisition of a 'spiritual body' (1 Corinthians 15:44).'' At this point I have a bit of misgiving about concluding that our Lord's resurrection body was or is essentially immaterial—which is what Murray seems to be saying here. The term "spiritual body" to my mind implies a different sort of material than that which we humans now possess in our physical bodies, but rather it suggests a different kind of material that possesses capabilities and characteristics far superior to our own.

At any rate, however we might like to speculate upon the exact nature of a "spiritual body," it is quite clear that Dr. Harris takes literally the record of Christ's display of His body as material, touchable, and capable of such a physical function as eating. On p. 24 he states: "When Jesus appeared he was not only seen but also heard (Luke 24:25–27; John 21:15–18; Acts 1:3) and touched (Matthew 28:9; cf. Luke 24:37–40; John 20:25, 27). To assure his disciples of his reality he even took food (Luke 24:38–43)." This sentence clearly excludes a concept of immateriality in its usual sense, and affirms that the touching of the nailprints and the ingesting of bread and fish literally took place just as the Evangelists record.

In closing I would say that we all must wrestle with an element of mystery in our efforts to understand exactly what properties and abilities our Lord manifested in His post-resurrection appearances. This stems partly from that basic rule of cognition, that we learn by proceeding from the known to the unknown. When we deal with what is completely *sui generis* like Christ's glorified body, we inevitably fall short of complete comprehension, and must treat with all charity a brother theologian who is doing his best to formulate what he finds in attempting to bring into focus the data of Scripture. But I must at the same time confess that I have seldom, if ever, read a more lucid, persuasive and uplifting discussion of this entire resurrection theme than Murray Harris has produced in this stirring rejoinder to the antisupernatural interpretation of the Bishop of Durham.

The 104th Annual Conference of the Evangelical Free Church of America was held June 20–24, 1988, on the campus of Biola University, La Mirada, California. On Wednesday afternoon, June 22, at the meeting of the Ministerial Association, three hours were given over to a discussion of the charges brought against me by Dr. Geisler. Rev. Michael P. Andrus, chairman of the association, began proceedings with a review of the history of the controversy. This was followed by a twenty-minute presentation by Dr. Geisler, outlining the reasons why, as a member of the Ministerial Association, he had pressed the charges. In his contribution to the formal discussion as Academic Dean of the Divinity School, Dr. Walter C. Kaiser, Jr., suggested that here was a case of two brothers in Christ agreeing on essentials but speaking of resurrection and the resurrection body at two different levels—one (Geisler) concerned about apologetics and therefore favoring the expression "literal, physical resurrection," the other preferring the biblical expressions "the resurrection of the dead" and "spiritual body." Dr. Kenneth M. Meyer, President of the Divinity School, then spoke, questioning whether it was appropriate for one man to continue to make allegations when so many competent persons had considered the matter and declared me orthodox. Finally, the President of the Free Church, Dr. Thomas A. McDill, emphasized the care he had taken to ensure that the proper procedures had been followed in dealing with the charges. He observed that many different persons (about 60) and committees (9) over many months had been involved in examining me and my views in connection with my reappointment to Trinity, nomination for tenure, and the present charges. Yet everyone had been satisfied that my views were well within the Free Church's doctrinal position. Confronting the audience with a challenge, Dr. McDill, who was a candidate for a fifth term as president of the denomination, said, "Don't vote for me tomorrow [as president], if you don't vote for me today [against Geisler]!" A vigorous discussion followed, in which more than twenty persons spoke from the floor. At that meeting, Dr. John Vawter, Senior Pastor of Wayzata Evangelical Free Church in Minneapolis, made the following motion, which was passed by a vote of about 500 to 10.

> We restate our appreciation of and trust in Dr. McDill, Dr. Meyer, and Rev. Andrus and decide this afternoon to affirm their conclusions as to the orthodoxy of Dr. Murray Harris's view of the resurrection.[3]

By Thursday Geisler had distributed hundreds of copies of a *formally printed* leaflet entitled "Trinity Prof Denies Physical Resurrection," which contained seven one-sentence quotations from various places in my book *Raised Immortal* but no quotations from my *Easter in Durham*. The leaflet concluded:

> These assertions constitute a clear denial of the physical, material nature of the resurrection body taught in the Bible (John 20:17, 27; Luke 24:29, 40, 42) and as held by the framers of the Free Church doctrinal statement.
>
> We cannot allow our doctrinal statement to be diluted on this crucial doctrine. We must take a firm stand on the literal, physical nature of the resurrection body.

Dr. Geisler was personally confronted by Dr. McDill, Dr. Meyer, and Rev. Andrus, among others, for distributing his leaflet.

On the final day of the conference, Friday, June 24, the motion that had been passed overwhelmingly by the Ministerial Association was reported to the two thousand delegates in attendance. At this point the official report of the conference continues:

Since the Association's statement on the matter, Rev. Andrus reported that a document stating "Trinity Prof Denies Physical Resurrection" was being circulated by the person making the accusations. Rev. Andrus stated his belief and that of the ministers that the document is a deliberate distortion of the truth, encouraged conferees to talk with their pastor or with denominational leaders in dealing with the matter and to pray for the individual who has brought these charges.[4]

As the conference was concluding, a resolution was moved by Rev. Samuel Kostreva III, Pastor of the Lodi Evangelical Free Church, Wisconsin, and Dr. Geisler's son-in-law.

"Whereas: We affirm the Evangelical Free Church's emphasis and effort in maintaining doctrinal purity; and Whereas: There is some question over the nature of Christ's resurrection body;
Be it Resolved: That we affirm Articles III.C and L. of the Articles of Incorporation of the Evangelical Free Church of America, where it states that 'He arose bodily from the dead' and 'We believe in the bodily resurrection of the dead,' to exclude all views that maintain that the resurrection body is by nature immaterial and non-physical."

The moderator declared the resolution out of order because it placed parameters which are not stated in the Articles of Incorporation. . . . A delegate questioned whether or not the Committee on Ministerial Standing had already dealt with this issue. In response, Dr. McDill reported the following:

"The Committee on Ministerial Standing discussed this at a meeting when it was first brought to our attention, and a thorough investigation was made concerning the views of Dr. Murray Harris. We were satisfied that they were well within our doctrinal statement and that they were well within orthodoxy. This was communicated to the Committee on Ministerial Standing; it was communicated to the pastors of the Evangelical Free Church of America; it was debated at length in the ministerial session last Wednesday;

and a whole system has been set in place for such an examination, including a system prior to the hiring of a faculty member, as well as when that faculty member seeks tenure. So the system has worked, is working and has examined his view in light of the doctrinal statement. We have an excellent statement by Dr. Murray Harris which I will be happy to read to the conference."

A delegate asked if delegates would be told whether the church believes that Jesus physically rose from the dead or not.

In response, Dr. McDill stated, "There has been full investigation of the allegations against Dr. Murray Harris. Dr. Harris affirms very clearly, without equivocation, our doctrinal statement and signs it each year that he believes in the bodily resurrection of Jesus Christ. The information that has been circulated on the grounds here, I hate to tell you, is very false and misleading, but that's true. I want to read you the statement that Dr. Murray Harris has written as of June 17, 1988:

'Dear Dr. Meyer: I am happy to reaffirm that I believe that our Lord rose from the dead in the actual physical body he possessed before his death, but that as a result of his resurrection, there was an alteration and enhancement of the properties of that physical body so that He now possesses what Paul calls a spiritual body (1Cor. 15:44–49) or a glorified body (Phil. 3:21). Before the resurrection the body of Jesus was mortal (Mark 15:37, Col. 1:22). Through the resurrection the body of Jesus became immortal (Romans 6:9, Hebrews 7:16, Revelation 1:18)."[5]

The resolution brought by Pastor Kostreva was "nearly unanimously defeated by the entire Conference."[6]

The conference ended June 24. During the week of July 5, Free Church pastors received a mailing from "Norman Geisler Quest Ministries" in Dallas, which included a two-page statement by Dr. Geisler, "Why I Left the Evangelical Free Church Ministerial," a one-page "Evidence for Physical Nature of the Resurrection Body," and the one-page leaflet

"Trinity Prof Denies Physical Resurrection" that had already been made available at the conference.

On August 31, 1988, the office of Trinity's Academic Dean, Dr. Walter C. Kaiser, Jr., sent out the following news release.

Early in 1987, Dr. Norman Geisler, at the time a faculty member of Dallas Theological Seminary, invited Dr. Murray Harris, Professor of New Testament at Trinity Evangelical Divinity School, to respond to an article that he had just written critiquing Dr. Harris' views on the nature of the resurrected body of our Lord. Dr. Harris declined to accept this invitation saying "nothing beneficial would be gained by the publication of the article, since there are many serious misrepresentations of my views in the article . . ." and since his "unswerving adherence to inerrancy" was also a matter of record. Nevertheless, Dr. Geisler has continued to press his charges.

Dr. Harris had been nominated for tenure at the seminary while these charges were being made. The Academic Dean instructed the faculty committee of the Senate (Dr. Barry Beitzel, Associate Dean and chairman of the committee, Dr. Kenneth Kantzer, Dr. Walter Liefeld, Dr. David Hesselgrave) specifically to include these charges in their in-depth examination of the candidate.

Dr. Kenneth Kantzer, Dean Emeritus and Director of TEDS's Ph.D. Program, submitted a written summary of this investigation for the Senate and for the Board of Directors of TEDS as they voted on Dr. Harris' tenure review. In part the review reads: "On the resurrection of the body, Paul did not speak wrongly in 1 Thess. 4 and 1 Cor. 15, only in II Cor. 5 to correct an earlier erroneous view. Rather, he spoke the truth in all three passages, but they are looking at the resurrection of believers from a different perspective . . . The passages do not conflict."

On the nature of the believer's resurrection body, the report added "that he [Dr. Harris] sees it not as a resurrection of the same substantial body as we had at death. That is, the same atoms as are in our body at death need not compose the resurrection body. Yet we look forward not to a disembodied existence, but to an existence in the new and heavenly body. In the case of Christ's resurrection body, our Lord in several instances demonstrated the reality of his body, as in the eating of fish and appearing to the disciples as a corporeal being, though in other instances he possessed the ability in his body to pass through solid walls."

Subsequent to this review, a committee of the school board, a committee of the Evangelical Free Church of America, and a meeting with Dr. Thomas McDill (president of the EFCA) and Rev. Howard Matson (representing the Ministerial Board of the EFCA) also interviewed Dr. Harris on issues involved in the charges of Dr. Geisler along with many other standard tests used in the prescribed tenure review process of TEDS and the EFCA.

All these matters were fully aired at the Annual Conference of the EFCA in June, 1988, at La Mirada, CA. After a three hour discussion of the ministerial of the EFCA and a forty-five minute synopsis at the annual meeting on June 24, 1988, Dr. Harris was fully absolved of all charges made in the numerous written complaints by Dr. Norman Geisler, now associated with Liberty University in Lynchburg, VA.

In a letter he wrote August 26, 1988, to a Free Church pastor, Dr. Donald A. Carson, Professor of New Testament at Trinity, comments:

The most disturbing aspect of this entire affair, in my view, is that stories are still being circulated that there has been some kind of cover-up. In fact, the Administration had Murray examined by an appropriate faculty committee once again, and by a committee of the ministers of the Free Church, with full input from the head office in Minneapolis. On every point Murray has come out smelling like a rose. This is scarcely a cover-up! What is *not* appropriate is for the Administration to let Norman Geisler come in and question Murray personally. He is not to be placed in a position where his views and his views alone serve as the criterion for who is and who is not orthodox! The result is that Professor Geisler must now circulate endless stories about the incompetence or lassitude of the various committees, and so forth. All I can say is that when people as conservative as myself, as Gleason Archer, as Paul Feinberg, as well as several of the ministers on the Free Church committee all come to exactly the same conclusion, it takes a bit of cheek on Professor Geisler's part to insist that they are all wrong, or that there has been a cover-up!

On January 10, 1989, I addressed a meeting of the Ministerial Institute attended by about 200 pastors, outlining my view of the resurrection of Christ and then dealing with questions for about ninety minutes. In a subsequent letter, the chairman of the Ministerial Association, Rev. Michael P. Andrus, wrote me as follows:

I want to express my sincere appreciation, plus that of our Ministerial Board and our pastors, for the superb presentation you gave to our Ministerial Institute on Tuesday afternoon, January 10. I saw that session as possibly laying to rest any lingering doubts for the pastors in attendance, and it exceeded my greatest expectations.

In 1989 the Evangelical Free Church Conference was held at Carthage College in Kenosha, Wisconsin, from June 18–22. No reference was made to the controversy at the meeting of the Ministerial Association, but on the final day of the conference itself Dr. Geisler's son-in-law, Rev. Samuel Kostreva III, requested a transcript of the taped proceedings of the 1988 conference. It was explained to Pastor Kostreva that such tapes are never transcribed and that the secretary's minutes, as found in the yearbook of the denomination, are the official record of annual proceedings.

From this historical review of the controversy it is clear that the official position of the Evangelical Free Church of America and of Trinity Evangelical Divinity School is that:

(1) I have been fully absolved of all charges of unorthodoxy with regard to my view of the resurrection;

(2) my view is "well within" orthodoxy and the Doctrinal Statement of the Free Church;

(3) Dr. Geisler's published statements of my view are inaccurate and misleading;

(4) the whole issue should be regarded as closed.

XX

The Exegetical Issues in the Controversy

Before we begin any detailed discussion of the event we call the resurrection of Jesus Christ, it is appropriate for all of us reverently to stand back, slip off the shoes of our human pride, and remember that the ground under our feet is indeed sacred. For even when we have tried our utmost to understand rightly all the New Testament narratives that describe this unparalleled event, we must confess our inability as mere mortals fully to penetrate the mystery of Christ's resurrection to immortality. "Do not be afraid any more!" said the risen Christ to the apostle John. "I am the First and the Last, and the everliving One—for indeed I underwent death, but now I am alive forever and ever" (Rev 1:17–18). Nor should we ever forget that the Resurrection itself was without witnesses: certain people were privileged to see the risen Christ but not Christ rising. Even the testifying angels themselves were not witnesses of the actual event. Matthew's account (28:1–7) clearly implies that Jesus had risen prior to the descent of "the angel of the Lord" and his removal of the stone from the mouth of the sepulcher. The angelic testimony was not "I have just seen him rise," but "he has already risen, as he said he would" (Mt 28:6). The Resurrection was too sacred an event to be witnessed by either human or angelic eyes. Such sublime mystery should arouse our reverent worship.

A series of questions will serve to highlight the main exegetical issues in the controversy.

A. Is the testimony of the New Testament about the resurrection body of Jesus relatively uncomplicated or extraordinarily complex?

We would suggest that the data are extraordinarily complex. It has become customary to group the statements of the four gospels and Acts on this matter into two categories.

1. Materialistic statements

Mt 28:9	"They [probably Mary the mother of James, and Salome] came up to him, clasped his feet and worshiped him."
Lk 24:15	"Jesus himself overtook them and began to walk along with them."
Lk 24:39	"Look at my hands and my feet and you will see that it is I myself. Touch me and understand, because a ghost does not have flesh and bones, as you see I have."
Lk 24:43	"He took it [a piece of broiled fish] and ate it before their eyes."
Lk 24:50–51	"He led them out to the vicinity of Bethany, lifted up his hands, and gave them a blessing. And as he was in the act of blessing them, he departed from them and was taken up into heaven."
Jn 20:20	"He showed them his hands and his side."
Jn 20:27	"Then he said to Thomas, 'Put your finger here and look at my hands. Reach out your hand and place it in my side.'"
Ac 1:4	"And while he was eating with them . . ."
Ac 10:41	". . . to us . . . who ate and drank with him after he rose from the dead."

In addition to these specific verses, there is the general testimony of the Evangelists that Jesus engaged in the normal human activities of walking (e.g., Mt 28:18; Lk 24:15, 28, 50) and talking (e.g., Mt 28:9–10, 18–20; Lk 24:17, 25–27). He was recognized by his followers when he appeared to them after his resurrection because of such individual features as his tone of voice (Jn 20:16), his bodily movements (Lk 24:30–31, 35), and the marks of the crucifixion (Lk 24:39–40; Jn 20:27). When he appeared, Jesus stood on *terra firma*, was not suspended in the air; his body was solid, not ephemeral, and tangible, not immaterial.

2. The nonmaterialistic statements

Lk 24:31	"He disappeared from their sight."
Lk 24:36	"While they were still reporting this, Jesus himself stood among them."
Lk 24:44	"This was the meaning of my words which I spoke to you while I was still with you."
Jn 20:19	"Although the doors were locked for fear of the Jews, Jesus came and stood among them."
Jn 20:26	"Although the doors were locked, Jesus came and stood among them."
Ac 1:3	". . . appearing to them at intervals over the course of forty days."
Ac 10:40–41a	"God raised him up on the third day, and permitted him to become visible, not to all the people, but to us. . . ."

In his classic work, *Our Lord's Resurrection*, W. J. Sparrow-Simpson characterizes such statements concerning the "ethereal and intangible state"[1] of Jesus' resurrection body in the following manner.

It is obviously implied in the narrative that He dwells with them no more as He used to do in the days of His ministry; but somewhere, none knows where, apart in an unseen world. They never know when or where to find Him, or

> how long He will stay. Nor is it possible to detain Him as it
> was in former days. His coming and His going are alike
> unexpected; and His entrance is as mysterious and inexpli-
> cable as His manner of vanishing out of sight. And when
> He appears among them His appearance is sometimes
> greatly changed. His intimate companions can fail to
> recognise . . . He comes in different forms at different
> times . . . He seems to do nothing like an ordinary human
> being. "What was natural to Him before seems now
> miraculous; what was before miraculous is now natural."[2]

Not a few writers despair of reconciling these apparently
contradictory sets of data. How could one and the same body
retain all of its material components and physical characteristics, and yet not be immediately recognized, appear and
disappear at will, and pass through solid objects? To some,
such a union of matter and spirit seems incomprehensible, if
not a contradiction in terms. On the other hand, many others
believe that any attempt to reconcile these data is misguided,
since the increasingly materialistic viewpoint that is evident as
one moves from Matthew or Mark to Luke and John indicates
that this earthly, physical emphasis in the accounts is a late,
unreliable tradition that was designed to protect the infant
church from the influence of the Docetists, who taught that
the human body of Jesus was not real, either before or after
the Resurrection.

But we may reject all such solutions to the dilemma as being
both unnecessary and unorthodox. The resurrected Jesus did
not simply have a material body, indistinguishable in form and
function from other human bodies, so that the nonmaterialistic
emphasis is a later accommodation to spiritualized Greek
thought. Nor was the risen Jesus pure Spirit, permanently
immaterial and intangible, with the materialistic emphasis of
the narratives a defense against Docetism.

We must not neglect either set of information. But we must
also recognize that any effort we make to accommodate both

sets of data in some statement is a hypothetical solution, lacking finality and authoritativeness.

There seem to be at least five such hypotheses. All may be deemed possible and permissible; no one solution is more "orthodox" than another. In reality we are dealing here with one of the ultimate mysteries of the universe—the relation of matter or "body" to spirit—so that all these hypotheses are at best accommodations to human language.

(1) Jesus' resurrection body was basically "material" or "fleshly" but either was capable of temporary dematerialization or had nonmaterial properties.[3]

(2) His body was customarily "immaterial" or "nonfleshly" but was capable of temporary materialization.[4]

(3) His body was matter "spiritualized," matter "wholly and finally subjugated to spirit."[5]

(4) His body was composed of "glory" (cf. Php 3:21), regarded as its "material" or "substance."[6]

(5) His body was in the process of transition from the material to the spiritual during the forty days of appearances.[7]

Each of these solutions seeks to take seriously the whole complex range of facts about Jesus' risen body presented by the New Testament. This being so, none can be dismissed as unorthodox. The difference between them stems largely from their emphasis, either on the materiality of the resurrection appearances or on their nonmaterial features.

The two sections that now follow (viz. B and C) are controversial. Let me stress that we are not dealing with the nature of the Resurrection itself—its reality is assumed—but with the arguments that may be brought forward in support of one of the hypotheses mentioned above regarding the nature and characteristics of Jesus' resurrected body. Not all readers may be fully persuaded by our exegesis of the relevant biblical texts, which themselves are open to more than one interpretation, but hopefully they will permit and appreciate a spirited defense of the hypothesis that "His body was customarily 'immaterial' or 'nonfleshly' but was capable of temporary materialization" (#2 above). This will afford me the opportunity of spelling out, in far more detail than was possible in *Raised Immortal*, a very brief section (one page out of 275!) that included the following summary sentence: "This suggests that after his resurrection *his essential state was one of invisibility and therefore immateriality*" (p. 53).

B. Was the risen Jesus "customarily invisible"?

These two terms should be carefully defined. *Customarily* here means "in his normal or customary state of being," and *invisible* signifies "not visible to the human eye" (*Raised Immortal*, 58; similarly 54, 57). The question therefore becomes: "In his customary mode of existence after the Resurrection, was Jesus visible to the human eye?"

To begin with, we must emphasize that the reality of his resurrection appearances is not in question here: they were real, personal, physical, literal, material. The issue is: Did those appearances exhibit Jesus in his customary state of being during the forty days?

To grapple with these questions, we must examine in some detail the texts cited under A.2. above, along with the relevant data from Paul's letters and the verbal form ὤφθη (*ōphthē*).

1. The Lukan material

a. Luke 24:31

Most English versions render the relevant part of this verse, "And he vanished out of their sight" or "And he disappeared from their sight." Literally, it reads: "And he became invisible [ἄφαντος ἐγένετο, *aphantos egeneto*] from them

[= to their eyes]." A. R. C. Leaney simply translates it "And he became invisible to them."[8] The sense cannot be diluted to "he departed from them" (διέστη ἀπ' αὐτῶν, *diestē ap' autōn*, Lk 24:51).[9] This phrase "to become invisible" is found only here in the whole Greek Bible.[10] I. H. Marshall observes, "He becomes invisible (ἄφαντος) once he has been recognized. . . . It is as a supernatural visitor that the risen Jesus is portrayed."[11] And H. A. W. Meyer comments, "Luke intends manifestly to narrate *a sudden invisible withdrawal effected through divine agency.*"[12]

b. Luke 24:36

A sudden, unannounced appearance "from nowhere" at the "psychological moment" is depicted by Luke's statement that "while they were still reporting this [the Emmaus encounter with Jesus], Jesus himself stood among them." Even after he had given them his reassuring greeting, "Peace be with you" (24:36b), they were still startled, frightened, troubled, and doubtful (24:37–38), doubtless because of his supernatural mode of arrival and because they imagined that he was a ghost (24:37b).

c. Luke 24:44

"Then he said to them, 'This was the meaning of my words which I spoke to you *while I was still with you*: everything written about me in the Law of Moses, the prophets and the psalms must be fulfilled.' " There is no ambiguity of sense in the italicized clause; all English translations understand it this way. "My words" refers back to Jesus' repeated teaching that the Son of Man must suffer in Jerusalem and then be raised on the third day in accordance with the Scriptures (Lk 9:22, 44; 17:25; 18:31–33; 22:37), teaching that his disciples failed to understand at the time (Lk 9:45; 18:34).

The "you" of 24:48–49 ("you are witnesses . . .") shows that the "you" of 24:44 ("with you") includes all the disciples who were involved in these final events (24:36–53) and not only the two disciples to whom he spoke of his suffering and glory (24:25–27). "While I was still in your company" (σὺν ὑμῖν, *syn hymin*) therefore refers to the period before the crucifixion and resurrection. The orientation of Jesus' remark is the past, not the future: "my words which I *spoke*." Speaking now, after his resurrection but before his ascension, Jesus says "while I *was* with you." During his earthly ministry Jesus was constantly in the company of his disciples, so that he could say, "I have spoken these things to you, while I *am* still with you" (Jn 14:25).[13] But between his resurrection and ascension Jesus was no longer constantly "with" them.[14]

d. Acts 1:3

"After his suffering he presented himself to them [the apostles] with many convincing proofs that he was alive, appearing to them from time to time during forty days." Although the verb translated "appearing" (ὀπτανόμενος, *optanomenos*) is not itself frequentative in sense ("appearing from time to time/intermittently"), the present tense in which the verb is found here has such an iterative meaning. Following in the wake of the Greek Father Chrysostom, who interpreted the text to mean "from time to time during forty days,"[15] are three modern classical scholars, the first two being translators.

R. F. Weymouth:	". . . appearing to them at intervals during forty days."[16]
C. H. Rieu:	"He had appeared to them at various times over a period of forty days."[17]
F. F. Bruce:	"Over a period of forty days between his resurrection and ascension Jesus appeared at intervals . . ."[18]

Grammatical authorities agree on this point.[19] We conclude that the appearances of Jesus occurred at intervals. If he did not appear continuously, but only intermittently, we may say he was not customarily visible to the human eye.

e. Acts 10:40

Several modern translations have caught the precise import of this remarkable verse:

NASB: "God raised Him up on the third day, and granted that He should become visible."

NAB²: "God . . . granted that he be visible."

J. Munck: "God . . . let him appear visible."[20]

NEB: "God . . . allowed him to appear."

The crucial phrase (ἐμφανῆ γενέσθαι, *emphanē genesthai*) means "to become visible" (BAGD, 257, under ἐμφανής; but cf. 193 under δίδωμι) and is used only here and in Romans 10:20. The latter passage is a quotation of Isaiah 65:1 where the tolerative *niph'al* has the sense "I allowed myself to be inquired of" (GK, § 51c), "I revealed myself" (NIV; BAGD, 257, under ἐμφανής). Accordingly, since the adjective ἐμφανής refers principally to what is "visible to the eye" and was commonly used in Greek literature of the gods appearing among humans in bodily form (LSJ 549, under ἐμφανής), Acts 10:40 may mean "God permitted him [Jesus] to make himself accessible to the sight of . . ." It is true that our phrase can describe knowledge that is "made known," but here it is a person who became visible, not some fact about that person that became known. On each occasion Jesus appeared after his resurrection, God was graciously permitting him temporarily to come into visibility.

2. The Johannine material
(John 20:19, 26)

Both of these verses contain the statement "Jesus came and stood among them." Two separate appearances of Jesus are involved. In one case (20:19–23), taken by almost all scholars to be the same incident as related in Luke 24:36–43, Thomas is absent (20:24); in the other (20:26–29), he is present. In each episode John seems to emphasize that in spite of the fact that[21] the doors[22] were locked, Jesus "came and stood among them." Precisely how Jesus entered, we are not told; John simply says he "came." But his mode of entry must have been unusual, for if Jesus had entered through the door and walked toward them, his disciples may have been "frightened," but they would not have been "startled" as well (Lk 24:37 RSV). We do not read that the doors opened "of their own accord," as the iron gate of the prison did for Peter (Ac 12:10), nor is there any indication that Christ used his supernatural power to unlock the doors, so it is safe to assume that they remained locked throughout the encounter. The abnormality of his entry was that it was not by the door, as they would have expected, and it was without warning. That is, Jesus was invisible to them immediately prior to his arrival "in their midst." M. C. Tenney sums up the matter in this way.

> As mysteriously as Jesus had disappeared from the supper at Emmaus [Lk 24:31] He reappeared in the chamber at Jerusalem [Lk 24:36; Jn 20:19]. Since He could not have entered by the door, the only reasonable alternative, which John evidently purposed to imply, is that Jesus penetrated the walls of the room *and became visible*.[23]

These two Johannine texts, then, seem to imply that Jesus' appearances were incursions from the invisible world into the visible.

3. The Pauline material
(1 Corinthians 15:5–8)

In this passage Paul gives a list of appearances of the resurrected Jesus, three involving a group (the Twelve, 500 brethren, "all the apostles") and three involving individuals (Cephas = Peter, James, Paul). Given the information we find in the gospels about other resurrection appearances, no one wishes to claim that Paul regarded his list as exhaustive; indeed, the neat stylized pattern of "threes" suggests the opposite. But the fact remains that this is a list of distinct, isolated events. If Jesus had been living with his disciples after his resurrection on a continuous basis, as he had been before his death, there would be no place for such a list of appearances as evidence of the reality of his resurrection. All that would be relevant would be a list of the places where Jesus was seen. Combining all of the New Testament information, we discover that Jesus appeared eleven times prior to his ascension (*Raised Immortal*, 51), and did so, "over the course of many (= forty) days" (Ac 13:31; cf. 1:3)! There may have been other appearances, but the fewness of the number of appearances enshrined in early Christian traditions argues decisively against the continuous visibility of Jesus during the forty days. The conclusion is inevitable that Jesus was generally not visible to human beings between his resurrection and ascension.

4. The verbal form ὤφθη (ōphthē)

This is another point in our discussion where some technicality is unavoidable.

The form ὤφθη (ōphthē) is the third person singular of the aorist indicative passive of ὁράω (horaō), "see." In Attic Greek it generally has a true passive sense "he was seen"[24] and the person who sees or perceives is expressed by ὑπό (hypo, "by") with the genitive. But in Hellenistic Greek (the

Greek of the New Testament) the aorist passive forms of ὁράω (*horaō*) regularly have an intransitive sense, so that ὤφθη means "he appeared," "he became visible," and the accompanying dative denotes the person to whom the "appearance" was made, not the person by whom someone "was seen."[25]

We may classify under five headings the eighteen uses of this aorist passive in the New Testament when it applies to persons, as opposed to things (five instances).[26]

(1) of God (1x): Acts 7:2, of God's "coming" to Abraham with a revelatory word (Ge 12:1, 7) (cf. W. Michaelis, *TDNT* 5:333 and n. 93).

(2) of angels (4x): Luke 1:11; 22:43; Acts 7:30, 35. Here the verb certainly means "came into visibility."

(3) of Moses and Elijah (3x): Matthew 17:3; Mark 9:4; Luke 9:31. Here departed human beings reappeared on earth and became visible to human onlookers.

(4) of Moses (1x): Acts 7:26, of Moses "coming on the scene."

(5) of the risen Christ (9x): Luke 24:34; Acts 9:17; 13:31; 26:16a; 1 Corinthians 15:5, 6, 7, 8; 1 Timothy 3:16.

Our crucial question now is: when Christ "appeared" to various persons after his resurrection, which of the first four categories affords the nearest parallel?

The difficulty with finding a parallel in Acts 7:26 (#4), as Geisler does ("Physical," 155), is that ὤφθη is never used in any of the four gospels to describe an action of Jesus prior to his death. If this verbal form in fact simply described a movement "from a place where one is not seen to a place where one is seen" ("Physical," 155; *Battle*, 112), it is incomprehensible that no gospel writer ever used the word in this sense when the gospels are replete with notices of Jesus' movements—not to speak of the movements of others. Category #2 affords a doubtful parallel, for angels are bodiless spirits (Heb 1:14) whereas the risen Jesus was not. Our options are therefore reduced to #1 and #3.

Many find the closest parallel to Christ's appearances in the Old Testament references to God's presence with human beings to reveal himself and his will (#1). In the Greek Old Testament (LXX), ὤφθη is used "when God came forth out of hiddenness and addressed people in order to establish a bond with them. Hence, e.g., it was recounted in Genesis 12:7: 'Then the Lord appeared to Abram, and said . . .' "[27] In particular, in the LXX ὤφθη regularly renders the reflexive *niph'al* of the Hebrew verb *rā'âh* ("see") which is used about twenty-eight times to describe God's appearing to man, "he let himself be seen."[28] Certainly the New Testament emphasizes the initiative of Jesus in granting appearances: "Jesus revealed himself" (Jn 21:1, twice); "he presented himself alive . . . appearing" (Ac 1:3). But there remains the important difference that when God "appeared" he did not become visible (cf. Ex 33:20, 23),[29] whereas when Christ "appeared" he was really seen. In his resurrection state Christ has what God does not have—a "spiritual body."

At the transfiguration of Jesus (#3), we read that two heavenly visitors, Moses and Elijah, "appeared" to Jesus, Peter, James, and John. No one of the three Evangelists who describe this event indicates the bodily form in which these two Old Testament figures appeared, but both had long since departed from the earth—Moses by death, Elijah by "translation"—so that their reappearance to earth-bound human beings meant that they emerged from a realm that is invisible to man. The parallels with the appearances of Jesus are clear: an appearance to unsuspecting earthlings by human beings from the other side of the grave. Yet the focus of the gospel narratives is on Jesus transfigured and the voice from heaven witnessing to his Sonship rather than on Moses and Elijah

appearing. That is, the idea of revelation is associated, not
with their appearance, but with the person of Jesus.

From this discussion of the meaning of ὤφθη we conclude
that there are no precise parallels to the resurrection appearances of Jesus; they are in a category of their own, events that
are unprecedented in religious history. Yet the use of the term
ὤφθη in reference to God in the Greek Old Testament,
reflected in Acts 7:2, suggests that when Jesus "appeared," it
was for the purpose of self-disclosure, so that "he appeared"
implies "he revealed himself" (Jn 21:1, twice). Also, it was
entirely at his own initiative, so that "he appeared" implies
"he let himself be seen."[30] Moreover, in the case of angels
and of Moses and Elijah at the transfiguration of Jesus, we
have explicit precedent (seven New Testament instances) for
"he came into visibility" as a perfectly legitimate meaning of
ὤφθη. Correlating these data with the implications of the
Lukan, Johannine, and Pauline texts considered above, we
may confidently affirm that when we translate ὤφθη as "he
appeared," the implication is "he became visible at his own
initiative for the purpose of revealing himself and his will."[31]

5. Conclusion

A variety of texts and considerations leads us to conclude
that during the forty days between his resurrection and
ascension Jesus was normally not visible to mortal eyes. He
was not living with his disciples, constantly in their company,
but then suddenly disappearing from their sight for brief
periods. He was no longer with them on a permanent basis
(Lk 24:44), so that the beginning of each appearance is
invariably mentioned but rarely the disappearance (Lk 24:31 is
the only instance apart from the accounts of his ascension in
Lk 24:51 and Ac 1:9–11). What remains remarkable are his
appearances rather than his disappearances. A person's
instantaneous coming into sight "from nowhere" is an
emergence out of invisibility into visibility. As much is

indicated by Luke's pair of technical and complementary phrases, "to become visible" (ἐμφανὴς γενέσθαι, *emphanēs genesthai*, Ac 10:40), "to become invisible" (ἄφαντος γενέσθαι, *aphantos genesthai*, Lk 24:31). Lest it be thought that this is a highly unusual and "unorthodox" view, we may cite three conservative writers, acknowledged defenders of orthodoxy, two of the last century, one of this, who express themselves in a similar way. Commenting on "the corporeity for the risen Redeemer," J. J. van Oosterzee (1867) declares that it was "the same body, but with entirely different properties . . . endowed with the property of becoming now visible, and now invisible, in submission to the dictates of a more powerful will."[32] With regard to Luke 24:44 F. L. Godet (1870) remarks that "the expression: *while I was yet with you*, is remarkable; for it proves that, in the mind of Jesus, His separation from them was now consummated. He was with them only exceptionally; His abode was elsewhere."[33] And later, on Luke 24:50–53: "Like the high priest when, coming forth from the temple, he blessed the people, Jesus comes forth from the invisible world once more, before altogether shutting Himself up within it, and gives His own a last benediction."[34] Finally there is G. E. Ladd (1975), who maintains that the resurrection appearances "were momentary appearances of the invisible, risen Lord to the physical sight and senses of the disciples."[35] "Jesus' dead body was raised into the immortal, eternal life of the world of God, which is invisible to mortal eyes, unless it makes itself visible."[36] His appearances meant "that Jesus, who was with them but invisible, made himself visible to their physical senses."[37]

C. Was the risen Jesus "customarily immaterial"?

Again, a precise definition of terms is needed. As before, *customarily* here means "in his normal or customary state of being"; "immaterial" has the sense "not having the same

material components as comprise the earthly, human body."
The question then is: "In Jesus' customary mode of existence
after the Resurrection, was his body composed of 'flesh and
bones' (Lk 24:39) and therefore tangible?"

Once more, an introductory disclaimer is in order. The
reality of Jesus' body when he appeared to various persons is
not the issue here: that body clearly consisted of "flesh and
bones" (Lk 24:39) at such times, since he could be seen,
touched, and handled. The question is: "Was such a material
body constantly his during the forty days?"

These questions may be approached from several direc-
tions.

1. If the resurrection of Jesus involved his exaltation to the
   right hand of God, his resurrection appearances were from
   heaven and were in his "body of glory" (Php 3:21), which
   cannot be equated with his "body of flesh" (Col 1:22).

2. The gospels record three instances of his passing through
   what, to any material body, was a material obstruction.

3. If, in his resurrected state, Jesus was normally invisible to
   the human eye, it follows that he also usually lacked a
   fleshly form, for a person who customarily cannot be seen
   (rather than simply is not seen) must at the times of his
   invisibility be both intangible and immaterial.

4. If Jesus had a fleshly body continuously throughout the
   forty days: (i) Where was he when he was not appearing?
   (ii) Why did his disciples show no concern for his physical
   needs?

5. The appearances of Jesus, which were real and material,
   were designed to convince his disciples of the reality of his
   personal identity as the resurrected Jesus of Nazareth, not
   the physical nature of the resurrection body.

Let us take up each of these points in turn.

1. The exaltation of Jesus was God's act of raising Jesus on high by giving him a position of unparalleled honor and universal authority at his right hand. In early Christian teaching, no sharp distinction was drawn between the resurrection and the exaltation of Jesus. While the two were regarded as separate occurrences, each involved the other. Nowhere is this more clearly seen than in the first recorded sermon in the book of Acts. "It was this Jesus whom God raised up to life, and of that fact we are all witnesses. Being therefore [οὖν, oun] exalted by the right hand of God . . ." (Ac 2:32–33). We find a similar resurrection-exaltation pattern in Pauline and Petrine texts (Ro 8:34; Eph 1:20; 2:6; Col 3:1; 1Pe 1:21). Moreover it is the risen Jesus, not yet ascended, who says, "All authority in heaven and on earth has been given to me" (Mt 28:18) and "Was it not necessary for the Messiah to undergo these sufferings and then enter into his glory?" (Lk 24:26). All these texts suggest that the Exaltation took place at the Resurrection rather than after the Ascension.[38] Also it is interesting that in Hebrews, where there is only one explicit reference to the Resurrection (13:20), the author often speaks of Jesus' exaltation (1:3, 13; 8:1; 10:12; 12:2), as if the two terms were virtually interchangeable. See further chapter VIII.B.3 above.

If this is so, we must conclude with W. Milligan, W. Michaelis, F. F. Bruce, L. Goppelt[39] and many others, that the appearances of the risen Lord were from heaven; from heaven, where Jesus had already assumed his position as God's plenipotentiary. His form of embodiment in heaven Paul calls a "body of glory" or "a glorious body" (Php 3:21). There is a remarkable parallelism and contrast between this phrase, "his glorious body" (τῷ σώματι τῆς δόξης αὐτοῦ, tō sōmati tēs doxēs autou), and the phrase "his fleshly body," found in Colossians 1:22 [ἐν] τῷ σώματι τῆς σαρκὸς αὐτοῦ,

[*en*] *tō sōmati tēs sarkos autou*). The latter phrase refers to the physical body of Jesus, which was suited to earthly conditions and, in comparison with the heavenly body, lacked glory (δόξα, *doxa*) (1Co 15:43). The former phrase refers to the spiritual body of Jesus, which is adapted to its heavenly environment and, in comparison with the earthly body, lacks that "flesh and blood" (σὰρξ καὶ αἷμα, *sarx kai haima*) which cannot inherit the kingdom (1Co 15:50).

But these resurrection appearances were certainly not successive reincarnations of Christ, for the exalted Lord is not pure spirit but is permanently embodied. "All the fullness of deity dwells in him in bodily form" (Col 2:9), where, we must note, Paul wrote σωματικῶς (*sōmatikōs*), "in bodily form," not σαρκικῶς (*sarkikōs*), "in fleshly form."

2. Wilbur M. Smith has observed that "the body of Christ was able to pass through obstructions of matter; through the grave clothes and through the sepulcher, without the stone having been rolled away, and through the walls of the room in which the disciples were assembled on Easter Sunday night."[40]

It is particularly from the fourth gospel's account of the discovery of the "empty" tomb that we learn that the tomb was not completely empty: the body had gone, but the grave clothes remained. When "the other disciple" (John himself) saw that the tomb was open and empty and perceived the significance of the burial clothes, he "believed" (Jn 20:8). What prompted his faith was not only the presence of the clothes—no grave robbers had been at work—but also their position. The linen wrappings that had encircled the body had collapsed under the weight of the aromatic spices embedded in their folds, and the headcloth that had passed over his head and under his chin was not lying flattened like the linen wrappings but remained twirled up in its folds, turbanlike, in a place by itself, where Jesus' head had lain (Jn 20:6–7).[41] Jesus' body had miraculously passed through the graveclothes, leaving them undisturbed. He had not needed someone to unwind the strips of linen to set him free, as Lazarus had before him (Jn 11:44).

In a similar way, the stone that sealed off the entrance to the tomb was not removed to let Jesus emerge but to let the disciples enter. If Jesus had come out of the tomb through its entrance, once the stone had been removed by the angel of the Lord, we would have expected Matthew to describe the action and features of the risen Lord rather than those of the angel, and the reaction of the guards to Jesus rather than to the angel (see Mt 28:2–4[42]). In all four gospels there are witnesses of the tomb already empty, but no witnesses of the tomb being emptied. At some unspecified time before the earthquake and arrival of the angel, Jesus had risen and "passed through" the walls of the sealed tomb without disturbing the stone in front of the entrance or alerting the guard of soldiers.

We have already considered (B.2 above) the two occasions on which Jesus appeared in the midst of his disciples when the doors were locked (Jn 20:19–23 = Lk 24:36–43; and Jn 20:26–29). The phrase "because of their fear of the Jews" (Jn 20:19) shows that the doors were not merely "closed," but "shut" in the sense of "locked" or "barred" (see *BAGD*, 434, under $\kappa\lambda\epsilon\acute{\iota}\omega$). In each case John says that Jesus "came and stood among them" (Jn 20:19, 26). "Came" need denote no more than "arrival on the scene," but although it does not point to either horizontal or vertical movement, it does imply penetration of the room.

How are we to explain these three instances of a body penetrating another solid object? It is inadequate to propose that the risen Jesus was omnipresent,[43] so that no "penetration" was actually involved, for the New Testament "localizes" Jesus in heaven, not on earth, after the Ascension (e.g., Ac 1:11; 1Th 4:16; Heb 8:1), if not also after the Resurrection, and it is unthinkable that he was omnipresent only during the forty days. Admittedly, recognizing that matter is a form of energy, modern physicists would be reluctant to deny the hypothetical possibility that one material object could penetrate another, given the necessary alignment of atoms; from any perspective such alignment would certainly be miraculous. But neither can the explanation be ruled out of court that at the moment before "impact," if not generally before any appearance, the body of Jesus was nonmaterial.

3. Whenever Jesus appeared to his disciples, he was visible to their naked eye. As many as were present on each occasion actually saw him. Moreover, those who saw him could handle him, if they chose to or were invited to do so (Mt 28:9; Lk 24:39; Jn 20:17, 27). That is, when he was visible he was also tangible and therefore material. But the corollary of this is that when he could not be seen by the human eye, he could not be touched by the human hand, and any human "body" that is intangible must also not be fleshly or material.

4. If the resurrected Jesus had a physical, material body all the time during the forty days, we may be permitted to ask with due reverence: Where was Jesus when he was not appearing? (We have suggested that his appearances were incursions from the right hand of God in heaven—see C.1 above). If he was in Jerusalem or Galilee, did he make himself invisible for prolonged periods, or was he in hiding? If he mixed freely with his disciples and others, why are only isolated appearances recorded? It is remarkable that his appearances were so unpredictable and irregular; his disciples could never assume that he was exactly where they had last seen him. After his resurrection no one asked him "Where are you staying?" as some had asked him earlier (Jn 1:38). When he was invited by the two disciples at Emmaus, "Stay with us, for it is nearly evening and the day is almost over," we read that "he went indoors to stay with them" (Lk 24:29) but his

"stay" was brief—only for the beginning of a meal—for "he disappeared from their sight" (Lk 24:30–31).

Luke 8:2–3 refers to the women among Jesus' followers "who provided for him out of their means" (Lk 8:3). It must be significant that we do not read of any effort by such women or by the Twelve to provide for his ordinary human need of shelter and food, once he had risen from the dead. The best explanation of this remarkable silence on the part of his disciples—which in other circumstances would have amounted to utter indifference—is that they realized he had entered a different form of existence, one in which the normal human requirements of food and shelter were no longer "needs." This is consonant with his having a nonmaterial body that was not dependent on material means for its sustenance and well-being.

5. If the risen Jesus did not normally have a physical body such as we know it, why did he sometimes carry out ordinary human acts such as eating or invite or permit some persons to touch and handle him? The crucial point is that each such act or invitation or permission is linked with the need for his disciples to be assured that he was the same Jesus whom they knew and loved, and not a mere apparition, some ghostly representation of an absent Jesus. Not surprisingly, when Jesus suddenly appeared among the disciples (Lk 24:36 = Jn 20:19), they at first imagined he was a bodiless spirit who had returned from the unseen world and assumed a visible form as a ghost (Lk 24:37). To calm their fears and assure them of his identity, he invited them to look at the scars from his crucifixion and thus know "that it is I myself," to handle him and so understand that he was no bodiless spirit (Lk 24:39). Then, because they were "still disbelieving for sheer joy and were lost in wonder," he asked for something to eat (Lk 24:41), not to satisfy his hunger or

meet his physical needs, but to reassure them of his reality.

It is an established principle of learning that the new can be appreciated and understood only by means of, and in relation to, the old. As the possessor of a "spiritual body," which had remarkably different properties from any "body" the disciples already knew, Jesus faced the challenge of proving his reality and introducing his disciples to a phenomenon beyond their experience and imagination. This he did, in part, by the familiar act of eating (Lk 24:42–43). Luke emphasizes the evidential purpose of Jesus' action by noting that he ate "before their eyes," "in front of them" (ἐνώπιον αὐτῶν, enōpion autōn, Lk 24:43).

Consequently the material "flesh and bones" that Jesus had during this encounter with his disciples were not integral to his "spiritual body" but had been assumed temporarily, but none the less really, for evidential reasons, as accommodations to the understanding of his disciples. With regard to the statement of Jesus that "a spirit does not have flesh and bones, as you see that I have" (Lk 24:39), G. E. Ladd comments that "these words need not be taken to be a description of the actual material composition of Jesus' body, but are intended as a proof of Jesus' corporeity."[44] And I. H. Marshall: "It is true that for Paul 'flesh and blood shall not inherit the kingdom of God' [1Co 15:50], and that for Luke 'a spirit has not flesh and bones as you see that I have' [Lk 24:39], but they are writing from different perspectives, Paul considering the existence appropriate to heavenly life, and Luke that appropriate to a heavenly being appearing on earth and confirming the reality of His identity."[45]

And so we conclude our discussion of two controversial aspects (B. and C. above) regarding the resurrection body of Jesus by proposing that in his normal or customary bodily state after the Resurrection, Jesus was neither visible to the human eye nor composed of "flesh and bones."

This cannot be dismissed as an uncommon view among

evangelical writers. Apart from the work of J. A. Schep, *The Nature of the Resurrection Body*, which views Christ's resurrection body as one of glorified flesh, there has been no serious discussion of these issues among evangelicals during the last twenty-five years. So one must turn to two classic treatments by evangelicals of an earlier generation for support of the approach adopted here. I should mention that my view was arrived at independently of these scholars, as a result of reflection on the biblical texts.

(1) In *The Gospel of the Resurrection*, B. F. Westcott writes:

> Christ sought (if we may so speak) to impress on His disciples two great lessons, that He had raised man's body from the grave, and that He had glorified it. Nor can we conceive any way in which these truths could have been conveyed but by appearances at one time predominantly spiritual, at another predominantly material, though both were alike real. For the same reason we may suppose that the Lord took up into His Glorified Body the material elements of that human body which was laid in the grave, though . . . true personality lies in the preservation of the individual formula or law which rules the organisation in each case, and not in the actual but ever changing organisation, which may exist at any moment. (111–12)

> A little reflection will shew that the special outward forms in which the Lord was pleased to make Himself sensibly recognisable by His disciples were no more necessarily connected with His glorified Person than the robes which He wore. (112 n.1)

(2) But the most detailed and sophisticated view comes from the pen of W. J. Sparrow-Simpson, author of *Our Lord's Resurrection* and *The Resurrection and the Christian Faith* that first appeared in 1911 as *The Resurrection and Modern Thought*, as well as the standard article that summarizes his views, "Resurrection of Christ" in *A Dictionary of Christ and the Gospels*, edited by J. Hastings. Sparrow-Simpson insists

that the resurrection body, whether of Christ or of believers, is "material," in the sense that it is a formal vehicle or organ for the self-expression of the personality,[46] but, existing normally under heavenly conditions, it is not a fleshly organism of solid flesh and bones.

> The resurrection body of Christ may be viewed in two ways; first, in its own intrinsic nature as it is in its normal condition; and secondly, in that state which it may adopt for purposes of self-manifestation. (*Our Lord's Resurrection*, 168)

> The Evangelists are concerned with the historic manifestations of the Risen Christ, St. Paul with the intrinsic nature of the resurrection body. The former describe the body of Christ during the temporary periods in which its presence was ascertainable by the senses; the latter considers the body as it is in itself. (*DCG*, 2:509)

> If we say that our Lord being normally intangible, inaudible, invisible, existing in a purely unearthly state, did nevertheless assume solidity, and make Himself tangible, audible, visible, for evidential and instructive purposes, and so temporarily bring Himself within range of our earthly organisations, we have an explanation which does justice to all the facts. (*Our Lord's Resurrection*, 170)

> We believe that this pneumatical body of Christ did temporarily assume such conditions of tangibility and visibility as to bring His "subtle corporeity," for evidential and instructive purposes, within the range of our "grosser corporeity." (*DCG*, 2:509)

One might also note here that my view as set out in B. and C. above has been adopted, with due acknowledgment, by a leading British evangelical systematic theologian, Dr. Peter Toon, in his 1984 study *The Ascension of Our Lord*, 12–15, 19 n. 1, 20 n. 6. On page 14 he writes: "After his [Jesus'] resurrection, his essential state is that of invisibility and immateriality, but he had the power to come into visibility."

D. What does the phrase "like the angels" signify in Matthew 22:30; Mark 12:25; Luke 20:36?

This phrase occurs in Jesus' response to the question posed by the Sadducees regarding the resurrection state. They had tried to confound Jesus by a *reductio ad absurdum* regarding a woman who had married seven times: "Now then, at the resurrection which of the seven will have her as wife, since all of them were married to her?" (Mt 22:28). But their hypothetical question showed that they were laboring under a misconception about the future life. They imagined that it was simply an indefinite extension of present relationships, merely the continuation of earthly life in a new setting. Jesus diagnosed their error as being their failure to understand the general tenor of the Scriptures as well as the power of God to effect a resurrection transformation in accord with his covenantal promises (Mt 22:29). "At the resurrection, people will neither marry nor be given in marriage; rather, they will be like the angels [ὡς ἄγγελοι, *hōs angeloi*] in heaven" (Mt 22:30; similarly Mk 12:25).

We should note, first of all, that this is said of the righteous dead, "those who are considered worthy of taking part in that age and in the resurrection from the dead" (Lk 20:35), not of Jesus himself. Nowhere in the New Testament is the earthly or the heavenly state of Jesus likened to that of angels. In the period between the two Testaments there was intense interest among Jews in the role of angels as mediators between God and the world. Since Philo, the first-century A.D. Jewish philosopher and exegete, often depicts the *Logos* ("Word") as an angel, it would have been tempting for a Jewish Christian of the Dispersion to view the Incarnate Word as an angel,[47] more than human yet less than divine. Against any such misconception that could lead to the worship of angels (cf. Col 2:18), the writer of Hebrews insists on the full deity and true humanity of Jesus, both during his earthly life and in his heavenly state. He is superior to angels as the Son of God

(Heb 1:4–14) and as the Son of Man (Heb 2:5–18). This ever-present danger of a heterodox view of the person of Jesus accounts, at least in part, for the absence in the New Testament of any suggestion of similarity between angels and the earthly or heavenly Jesus.

"Like the angels in heaven" (Mt 22:30b). It is clear what this comparison does not mean. The righteous will not become sexless, for sexual identity is essential to personality, and personality is not destroyed but enhanced by the resurrection. Nor are they to be bodiless, for the very term "resurrection" implies a bodily state. Nor does the comparison signify simply that they will be in heaven; this would require a different word order, "in heaven, like the angels [are]." The Lukan parallel (20:36) actually omits "in heaven."

On the positive side, we may confidently affirm that the simile contains at least two elements. First, in all three synoptic gospels our phrase follows immediately after a reference to marriage. Jesus is saying that in the eternal state, marriage (here symbolized by the contracting of new marriages) will have no more role to play than it does among the angels who have neither sexual passions nor procreative powers (unless they forsake their "proper domain" and "indulge in unnatural lust"; cf. Jude 6–7; 1En 12:4; 15:4–7). The point of Jesus' answer becomes clear in Luke's expanded statement: the resurrected dead will not marry "for [γάρ, gar] they cannot die any more" (Lk 20:36). The marriage relationship, which involves procreation, will be unnecessary then, for the human race will not be depleted by death. When death is absent, the need for the perpetuation of humankind through marriage will have disappeared. This is not to say that existing earthly husband-wife relationships will be destroyed or that the resurrection state obliterates any distinction between male and female. Rather, resurrection means transformation into a glorious state, comparable to the angelic, in which preoccupation with God, not with other human beings, becomes the focus of existence.

The parallel in Luke supplies the second point of the comparison. Not only will the redeemed become preoccupied with God rather than with marriage and human relationships in general. They also will become immune to decay and death, just as the angels are. "They cannot die any more, because [γάρ, *gar*] they are equal to angels" (ἰσάγγελοι, *isangeloi*, Lk 20:36). Resurrection leads to immortality. The resurrected righteous are no longer mortal, because they now share the angelic condition of deathlessness.

This much we can say with assurance. But to judge from Jewish texts that reflect first-century A.D. traditions about the afterlife, it is quite probable that being "like the angels" also means: (i) being "spiritual" in the sense of having no sexual passions or procreative powers (1En 15:4, 6–7); (ii) having deep joy (1En 104:4); (iii) having a direct vision of the heavenly world, a privilege presently denied to mortals (2Ba 51:8); and (iv) being clothed in the garments of glory and life that never wear out (1En 62:16).

E. Did the resurrected Jesus appear to unbelievers?

There can be no denying the fact that Jesus appeared to certain of his disciples who initially refused or were hesitant to believe that they were looking at and listening to Jesus alive from the dead (e.g., Lk 24:10–11; Jn 20:25, 27). A resurrection appearance was no guarantee of immediate belief, for sometimes it prompted fear and uncertainty (Lk 24:37–38) or doubt (Mt 28:17), at least temporarily. But our concern here is with the broader question of his appearance or nonappearance to those who made no claim to be his disciples.

The records suggest there were only two unbelievers to whom Jesus appeared. One was his brother James, apparently an unbeliever during Jesus' ministry (Mk 6:3; Jn 7:5). It would seem that he was brought to faith through an individual appearance of Jesus (1Co 15:7), for he and his brothers are numbered among the 120 disciples gathered in Jerusalem after the Ascension (Ac 1:14–15). The other was Saul of Tarsus, the archenemy of the infant church, one of three persons to have a post-ascensional appearance (Ac 9:3–6, 27; 1Co 9:1; 15:8; for Stephen, see Ac 7:55–56; for John, Rev 1:12–16). Since both James and Saul became disciples of Jesus, we may conclude that Jesus appeared only to believers or those destined to become believers. Or we could say that prior to his ascension, Jesus appeared only to persons who had known him previously.

With regard to the soldiers guarding the tomb of Jesus, there is no evidence that they even overheard the angel's message to the women, far less were witnesses when Jesus met the women (Mt 28:1–10). We have suggested above (n. 42) that verses 2–4 of Matthew 28 are parenthetical. In this case the guards had fled from the tomb before the women arrived. This is confirmed by the fact that none of the other three gospels mentions the guards when recounting the women's arrival at the tomb.

All this accords with our earlier discussion of the visibility of the risen Jesus and the explicit statement of Peter in Acts 10:40–41: "God raised Him up on the third day, and granted that He should become visible, not to all the people, but to witnesses who were chosen beforehand by God" (NASB). On this E. F. Harrison rightly remarks that "Peter freely acknowledged that there was no appearance of the risen Lord to the general public."[48] Any person present at the crucifixion could have seen Jesus die, but no person could be guaranteed in advance of a sight of the risen Jesus. He appeared to whom he chose, when he chose. It was God who granted this privilege to certain individuals, on the initiative of Jesus. During Paul's encounter with the exalted Lord outside the city of Damascus, only Paul saw Jesus; his traveling companions saw only the bright light, not Jesus (Ac 9:7, 27; 22:9, 14; 26:13–14, 16). True, this was a resurrection appearance that occurred after Christ's ascension. But nevertheless it shows that there were some people who did not see the resurrected

Christ at the same time he was appearing to another person. His appearances were selective.

We may well ask why Jesus did not appear to the general public or to such notable persons as Herod Antipas or Caiaphas or Pilate. Surely such an appearance would have convinced them that he was indeed the Son of God or the Messiah. The apologetic value of such strategic appearances would seem to be enormous. Why, then, were these opportunities "overlooked"?

But appearances of this sort, whether to the general public or to individuals, would not guarantee belief. The people at large had already rejected the testimony of Moses and the prophets regarding the Messiah as well as the testimony of Jesus about himself, so that an earlier word of Jesus is apposite. "If they do not listen to Moses and the prophets, neither will they be convinced even if someone rises from the dead" (Lk 16:31). And, we may ask, if the disciples themselves, who had the benefit of Jesus' predictions about his rising and the experience of his presence for three years, were at first disbelieving when he appeared, what would have been the reaction of the people at large? To a person who is unwilling to be convinced, no type of evidence is compelling and everything may be explained away. Moreover, it was not Jesus' method of winning followers to provide dramatic signs in order to coerce faith (Mk 8:11–12; Lk 23:8). "He had refused the demand for a sign from heaven, when the Pharisees challenged Him to give one. He had worked no miracle before Herod. What the suffering Christ had refused to do, the triumphant Christ abstained from doing."[49]

Our discussion of the principal exegetical issues in the controversy has ended. What has become apparent is that all of the questions relate solely to the nature of Christ's glorified body. We have always steadfastly maintained the central truth that Jesus arose from the dead in the same body, though now glorified, in which he had lived and died, and that consequently his tomb was empty (apart from the grave clothes).

XXI

The Theological Issues in the Controversy

It is, of course, somewhat arbitrary to distinguish between exegetical and theological issues, for any sound theology is based on careful exegesis. But we shall be dealing in this chapter with the broader issues of interpretation that are less directly related to the exegesis of particular texts. As in chapter XX, it will be helpful to bring each issue into clear focus by posing a crucial question.

A. In what sense is the resurrection body "spiritual"? What are its other characteristics?

In 1 Corinthians 15:44 Paul describes the body of the resurrection as "spiritual" ($\pi\nu\epsilon\nu\mu\alpha\tau\iota\kappa\acute{o}\varsigma$, *pneumatikos*) and thereby coins the expression "spiritual body" ($\sigma\hat{\omega}\mu\alpha$ $\pi\nu\epsilon\nu\mu\alpha$-$\tau\iota\kappa\acute{o}\nu$, *sōma pneumatikon*). What does this Greek adjective signify?

First, we need to be clear what it does not mean. *Spiritual* does not mean "composed of spirit," as though "spirit" were some heavenly substance or the "Spirit" were conceived of in material as well as personal terms. "Made of spirit" would be expressed in Greek by $\dot{\epsilon}\kappa$ $\pi\nu\epsilon\acute{\nu}\mu\alpha\tau o\varsigma$ (*ek pneumatos*; see BAGD, 235 under $\dot{\epsilon}\kappa$ 3.h.). Nor does the adjective mean "ethereal" or "immaterial." "Spirit" and "matter" were not opposites for Paul. Or again, although what is described as "spiritual" is often also "supernatural," this is not the

significance of the word. The Greek word ὑπερκόσμιος
(hyperkosmios), "supernatural," "supramundane," is not
found in the New Testament, being a late Greek word used by
writers of the fifth and sixth centuries A.D. (see LSJ, 1865).[1] If
Paul had wished to speak of the "supernatural body," he
would have used the expression τὸ σῶμα τὸ ὑπὲρ φύσιν (to
sōma to hyper physin) (cf. Ro 1:26).

Since Greek adjectives ending in -ikos denote an ethical or
dynamic relation, not a material one,[2] pneumatikos means
"animated by the spirit" or "controlled by the spirit." This
"spirit" refers either to the Holy Spirit or to the human spirit
as transformed by the divine Spirit. Perhaps the latter is more
probable in light of the contrasted expression, "physical [or
psychical] body" (σῶμα ψυχικόν, sōma psychikon, 1Co
15:44), which means "animated by the [human] soul" (ψυχή,
psychē) or "controlled by the [human] soul."

So, then, the spiritual body is a form of embodiment that is
permanently revitalized by, and fully responsive to, the
Christian's perfected spirit or God's Holy Spirit. Perhaps Paul
intended both of these senses. If so, we may say that in the
resurrection state the believer will have a body enlivened by
and responsive to his or her redeemed spirit which in turn will
be completely amenable to the power and guidance of God's
Spirit.

What other descriptions does Paul give of the resurrection
body? A comparison of 1 Corinthians 15:35–50 and 2 Corinthians 5:1 yields five more features. It is:

(1) *provided by God* (1Co 15:38; 2Co 5:1, "from God").
Conceived of as an edifice, the resurrection body has God as
its architect and builder.

(2) *imperishable* (1Co 15:42b, 50, 52–54; 2Co 5:1, "eternal," "permanently durable"). Because it is constantly
renewed by the Holy Spirit, the spiritual body cannot perish.
No longer will human beings be characterized by physical
decay.

(3) *glorious* (1Co 15:43a; cf. Php 3:21). Because it is

completely suffused with the Spirit, the spiritual body is glorious (cf. 1Pe 4:14). No more will human existence be marked by physical indignity.

(4) *powerful* (1Co 15:43b). Because it is permanently energized by the Spirit, the spiritual body is powerful. Humankind will be forever delivered from physical weakness. In 1 Corinthians 15:42b–43 Paul is affirming that in place of an earthly body that is always characterized by physical decay, indignity, and weakness, the resurrected believer will have a body that is incapable of deterioration, beautiful in form and appearance, and with limitless energy and perfect health. Gone too will be the ugly taint of sin and the frustrations of spiritual powerlessness.

(5) *heavenly* (1Co 15:40, 47–49; 2Co 5:1, "in heaven"). The natural habitat of the spiritual body, the native land of the resurrected believer, is heaven.

As we turn to the Gospels, we discover two further features. The first we have already expounded (chapter XX.D. above): the heavenly body will be *angel-like*, that is, immortal and without sexual passions or procreative powers. The second and final characteristic arises from our earlier discussion concerning the materiality of Christ's risen body (chapter XX.C. above) and deserves more extensive treatment.

It has never been my view that the risen Jesus is "purely spiritual" in the sense that he ceased to be embodied or became "pure spirit" as a result of the Resurrection. As I expressed this point in 1980:

> The Resurrection did not convert Jesus into "pure spirit." It was more than "the triumph of his 'personality' or 'soul' over the death of his body."[3] In his resurrection Jesus is "life-giving spirit" (1Co 15:45) in the sense that his is a form of corporeality in which the spirit is supreme, unfettered by time and space and constantly generating new somatic and spiritual life. (*Raised Immortal*, 57)

"A form of corporeality in which the spirit is supreme," that is, a spiritual body. It is this supremacy of the spirit in the resurrection body that allows Paul to depict Jesus' resurrection state as "spirit" (1Co 15:45; 2Co 3:18; and perhaps 1Co 6:17; 1Ti 3:16) while never relinquishing his belief that that state was also "bodily" (Col 2:9). Both before and after his resurrection Jesus was "body-spirit," but only after his resurrection did he possess a "spiritual body."

It will thus be clear how my view differs radically from one which postulates that at the Resurrection Jesus returned to his pre-incarnate state as a purely spiritual Being. To highlight the differences, it may be helpful to sketch the hypothesis of Leslie D. Weatherhead, the British preacher, psychologist, and prolific author. In his book *The Resurrection of Christ in the Light of Modern Science and Psychical Research*, Weatherhead proposes that under the immense power of his spirit, Jesus set in motion, as he was dying, processes by which the molecular structure of his material body was altered so that it evanesced or evaporated while in the tomb, escaped through the crevices of the tomb in gaseous form, and then dispersed "to the four winds of heaven" (43–55, 79–80). Jesus "was thereafter free from physical imprisonment. He was once more a Spirit" (80) and became omnipresent (82). His appearances were not hallucinations but "apparitions" (in the technical sense) (66–79, 83–84). He appeared to his disciples in a spiritual or etheric form "which had the same effect on human senses as a physical one" (50) but "which only had the *appearance* of matter and the *appearance* of sound, reaching the brain centres of sight and sound and touch by routes other than those of the sensory nervous system" (47).

Nor have I ever expressed the view that the resurrection body of Christ was simply immaterial. It was "*customarily immaterial*" in the sense that in *his customary mode of existence* during the forty days, he did not have a material body of "flesh and bones" (see chapter XX.C. above). But when, on occasion, he chose to appear to various persons in a material form, this was just as really the "spiritual body" of Jesus as when he was not visible or tangible. The resurrection of Jesus was not his transformation into an immaterial body (as Prof. Geisler imagines I believe[4]) but into a "spiritual body" which could be expressed in an immaterial or a material mode, a nonphysical *or* a physical form.[5] In each instance it was his body and was "spiritual," so that he was not guilty of deception when he affirmed, "See my hands and my feet, that it is I myself" (Lk 24:39). As opposed to angels who by nature are disembodied spirits (Heb 1:14) yet can materialize (Heb 1:7), the risen Jesus is a permanently embodied Spirit who, during the forty days, occasionally became visible to human eyes and palpable to human touch. After the forty days, when his appearances on earth were ended, Jesus assumed the sole mode of being visible to the inhabitants of heaven but having a nonfleshly body.

It will thus be clear that I am using the terms *material* and *immaterial* in a popular, not a philosophical, sense. In reference to bodies, *material* means "physical" or "fleshly," and *immaterial* means "nonphysical" or "nonfleshly." But from a philosophical standpoint, any kind of human body, whether physical or spiritual, is "material" in the sense that it has a particular "form" behind which lies "substance" or "matter." Diagrammatically, we might express our conclusion as shown on the chart on page 406.

From the Gospels, then, we can deduce that one property of the resurrection body is the ability to become visible and tangible to earthlings under terrestrial conditions.

B. Will the bodily resurrection of believers be precisely the same as the resurrection of Jesus?

By the use of a picturesque analogy Paul makes clear in 1 Corinthians 15 the intimate relationship between these two resurrections: "Christ has been raised from the dead, the firstfruits of those who have fallen asleep" (1Co 15:20; cf. 15:23).

Resurrection body of Jesus during the forty days from an earthly perspective

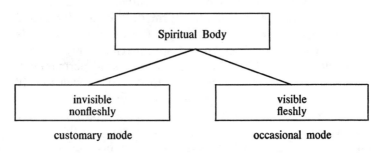

customary mode   occasional mode

Resurrection body of Jesus after the forty days from a heavenly perspective

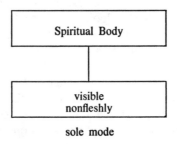

sole mode

In the Old Testament the firstfruits were the initial part of the annual production of grain, wine, oil, and sheared wool that was offered to God to acknowledge that he owned all the produce of the field and flocks and to thank him for his generous provision.

Twin ideas are suggested by the analogy: unity and

distinction. The firstfruits were part of the harvest (unity) yet not the whole harvest (distinction).

1. Unity

As the first part of the harvest, the firstfruits were representative of the whole harvest. To affirm Christ's resurrection is to affirm the resurrection of "those who belong to Christ" (1Co 15:12, 20, 23). To deny their resurrection is to deny his (1Co 15:13, 15–16). Each implies the other. Paul cannot conceive of the firstfruits without the full harvest any more than he can think of the full harvest without the firstfruits. "As is the man of heaven, so will be those who are of heaven. . . . We shall bear the image of the man of heaven" (1Co 15:48–49).

There are two Pauline texts that go one step further and see the future resurrection of believers so closely linked with the past resurrection of Christ that they suggest that when Christ rose bodily from the grave the resurrection of the dead began, or, in an ideal or anticipatory sense, actually took place. In Romans 1:4 Paul asserts that "as a result of the resurrection of the dead" Jesus Christ was decisively declared to be the Son of God. Paul must be thinking mainly of Christ's own resurrection *from the dead*, but his general expression "of the dead" (= "of dead persons") suggests that he viewed the resurrection of all believers as ideally achieved when Christ rose. Then there is 1 Corinthians 15:21: "Since by a man came death, by a man came also the resurrection of the dead." The resurrection of the dead was involved in the resurrection of Christ so that resurrection is not simply a future possibility but a present reality.

2. Distinction

The very term "*first*fruits" implies priority in time. Firstfruits were gathered before the remainder of the "harvest" was ripe or mature or had been gathered. Using a military metaphor, Paul names two "orders" or "ranks" that are related by succession: "Each in his own rank—Christ the firstfruits, then, at his coming, those who belong to Christ" (1Co 15:23). As Paul expressed it in his speech before Herod Agrippa II, Christ was "the first to rise from the dead" (Ac 26:23), never to die again (Ro 6:9). Moreover, when Jesus Christ is described as "the firstborn of the dead" (Rev 1:5) and as "the firstborn from the dead" (Col 1:18), the thought is not only that he was the first person ever to rise from the dead with immortal life but also that he enjoys a supreme status, a superior rank, as the first and most important part of a series.

At this point we may usefully broaden our discussion to include all the similarities and differences between his resurrection and ours. Clearly, the similarities we enumerate are linked with the "unity" just discussed, and the differences with the idea of "distinction."

1. Similarities

   a. with regard to the resurrection body

Characteristic	Christ	Believers
(1) spiritual	1Co 15:45	1Co 15:44
(2) from God	Ro 8:11	1Co 15:38; 2Co 5:1–2
(3) imperishable	Ro 6:9	1Co 15:42, 50, 52–54; 2Co 5:1
(4) glorious	2Co 4:6; Php 3:21a	1Co 15:43a; Php 3:21
(5) powerful	Php 3:10, 21b	1Co 15:43b
(6) heavenly	1Co 15:49; 1Th 4:16	1Co 15:40, 47–49; 2Co 5:1

If Paul had been asked to give an abbreviated answer to his own question, "With what kind of body do they come?" (1Co 15:35), which he answers at length in 1 Corinthians 15:42–50, he would doubtless have replied "With a body like Christ's!"

Christ now is what redeemed man will be. The glorified Christ is the firstfruits of perfected humanity.

b. with regard to resurrection in general

(1) its cause

On two occasions in the Corinthian letters (1Co 6:14; 2Co 4:14) Paul affirms that God will display his life-giving power by raising dead believers just as he raised the Lord Jesus. It is the same God who raised Christ from the dead who will imbue with resurrection life the mortal bodies of believers (Ro 8:11). His resurrection and ours may be traced to an identical cause—the creative power of God.

(2) its nature

	Christ	Believers
reanimation	Mk 16:6; Ro 8:11; 14:9	Jn 5:28–29; Rev 20:4
transformation	Lk 24:31; Ac 1:3	1Co 15:42–43, 51–54
exaltation	Ac 1:9–11; 2:32–33; 5:30–31	1Th 4:17; 2Ti 2:12

(3) its results

immortality	Ro 6:9; Rev 1:18	1Co 15:42, 52–54
possession of a glorified body	Php 3:21	1Co 15:42–44, 49; Php 3:21
residence in heaven	Ac 3:20–21; Eph 1:20; 1Th 4:16	2Co 5:8; 1Th 4:17; Php 1:23

2. Differences

Whether we view the resurrection of Christ as the cause, the pledge, or the pattern of believers' resurrection,[6] there need not be a precise identity between the two. Basic similarities do not exclude significant differences.

Several of these differences stem from the distinctiveness of

Christ's person and work. Although believers first acquire immortality through their resurrection (1Co 15:53–54), when Christ rose from the grave he regained the immortality that he had surrendered when he became "obedient to death" (Php 2:8; Rev 1:18). Only of Christ can it be said that he "became a life-giving spirit" (1Co 15:45) through his resurrection, or that his coming to life vindicated him as the suffering Son of Man (Lk 24:26, 46) and established him as the prince of life and conqueror of death (Ac 2:24–28; Rev 1:18). Only of Christ is it true that resurrection meant his designation as "Son of God in power" (Ro 1:4) and as universal Lord and Judge (Ac 17:31; Ro 14:9; Eph 1:20–21). And only Christ needed to reappear on earth to convince his disciples that he had indeed risen from his tomb and was the all-sovereign Lord.

One other difference calls for attention. We have seen that the term *firstfruits* itself implies that the full harvest will occur at a later time. In other words, while Christ was raised "on the third day" (1Co 15:4), his people experience their resurrection on the Last Day. This leads to a difference of great importance. In the case of Christ, resurrection some thirty-six or so hours after his death preserved him from decaying in the grave (Ac 2:27–31; 13:34–37), whereas the bodies of believers who die before the second advent of Christ are not spared dissolution. When Christ rose on the third day, the flesh and bones of his body were still intact; when believers rise on the Last Day, their bodies in most cases will long since have disintegrated, either through cremation or through natural processes after burial.[7]

Given the fact of the empty grave of Christ, we may insist on an "identity" between the body that was crucified and buried and the body that was raised, provided we bear in mind two points. First, all human bodies are in a continuous state of flux, so much so that the molecular composition of our bodies is completely changed during a seven-year cycle. After death change continues, but now it is the process of cellular breakdown. When Jesus rose from the dead, the process of decomposition which began when he died was halted and completely reversed. God did not permit his Holy One to experience final dissolution (Ac 13:37).[8] So the bodily "sameness" in the case of Christ was not complete, but relative. Second, dramatic changes had taken place in his body as a result of his rising, so that it could now be described as "glorious" (Php 3:21) and immortal (cf. Heb 7:16; Rev 1:18).

But does the concept of "resurrection," of "rising up," compel us to believe that in the case of believers who die, the scattered fragments of their decomposed or cremated bodies will be miraculously reassembled to assume once more the form they had at the time of their death, prior to being transformed into the likeness of Christ? Let it be said immediately that such a miracle, though stupendous, would be less dramatic than the initial creation of matter, for that was "out of nothing."

As he grapples with this issue in his book *The Reality of the Resurrection*, M. C. Tenney cites the intriguing case of Roger Williams.

> When the body of Roger Williams, founder of the Rhode Island colony, was exhumed for reburial, it was found that the root of an apple tree had penetrated the head of the coffin and had followed down Williams' spine, dividing into a fork at the legs. The tree had absorbed the chemicals of the decaying body and had transmuted them into its wood and fruit. The apples, in turn, had been eaten by people, quite unconscious of the fact that they were indirectly taking into their systems part of the long-dead Williams. The objection may therefore be raised: How, out of the complex sequence of decay, absorption, and new formation, will it be possible to resurrect believers of past ages, and to reconstitute them as separate entities?[9]

To resolve this dilemma, Tenney aptly turns to Paul's analogy of the seed in 1 Corinthians 15:36–38. His answer to the quandary deserves to be quoted in full.

> When a grain of wheat is dropped into the ground, its husk quickly decays, and even the live core disintegrates. The life of the seed, rather than its material substance, provides the continuity of existence. As the rootlets begin to grow, they draw nourishment from the earth, and by the chemistry of sun and rain the small seed soon becomes a large plant. The plant bears no external resemblance to the seed, nor is the bulk of its tissue drawn from the seed; nevertheless, the continuity is undeniable. There is persistence of type, because a given seed will always produce its own kind. Identity of type is not incompatible with discontinuity of substance.
>
> Continuity of individuality is assured by the persistence of the personality, which God will reclothe with a body. Jesus' statement, "all that are in the tombs shall hear his voice, and shall come forth; they that have done good, unto the resurrection of life; and they that have done evil, unto the resurrection of judgment" (Jn 5:28–29), assumes the preservation of individuality, since those that have been buried will be restored to life. The restoration, however, is not a reconstitution of the original body that was interred, but a new structure patterned on the resurrection body of Christ. "As we have borne the image of the earthy, we shall also bear the image of the heavenly" (1Co 15:49).[10]

Tenney, who was for many years Dean of Wheaton College Graduate School, is certainly not alone in maintaining this view of the resurrection of believers. It is no exaggeration to say that the majority of theologians, whatever their view of Scripture and revelation, hold a similar view. True, others may use different terminology in describing the relationship of the "spiritual body" to the physical body. Some speak of "continuity of corporeal life" (G. B. Stevens),[11] "somatic identity" (M. E. Dahl),[12] "continuity of person and personality" (G. E. Ladd),[13] "identity of form if not of substance, as the grain on the stalk is the same in kind, though not numerically the same, or composed of the same particles, as the seed out of which it springs" (A. B. Bruce),[14] identity of occupant but not of dwelling (C. R. Bowen),[15] or historical continuity, with the same "I" inhabiting first an earthly, then a heavenly body (W. G. Kümmel).[16] Common to all these proposals is the insistence that *for Christians* the continuity between the earthly and heavenly bodies is personal, not material.

To conclude: our final difference between the resurrection of believers and of Jesus is this. In his case there was, to use another Tenney phrase, "continuity . . . of substance"[17] as well as identity of person. In their case there will be "continuity of human personality" but "discontinuity of substance."[18] (It is of not inconsiderable interest that Dr. Harold Lindsell, who supplied the front cover recommendation for Dr. Geisler's recent book, wrote a similar recommendation for the Moody Press edition of Dr. Tenney's book, although that book expresses a quite different view than that espoused by Dr. Geisler.)

C. Is the glorified Jesus still "in the flesh"?

Basic to Christianity is the truth that the eternal Word "became flesh" (Jn 1:14). "Flesh" here refers to complete and genuine human existence, the possession of a human body and soul. In the womb of Mary the eternal Son of God assumed human form and identity, he became "incarnate" ("enfleshed," from the Latin *in carne*, "in the flesh"; see 1Ti 3:16; 1Jn 4:2; 2Jn 7). As a result, during the earthly life of Jesus there was nothing that is true of man as man that was not also true of Jesus, except that he was without sin. He was fully human, both in physical form and in personal experience—for example, he needed food and sleep for energy; he felt both joy and pain.

Was this humanity jettisoned at the Resurrection? Did Jesus cease to be fully human when he rose? Certainly not. The "flesh" he assumed at his conception was glorified at the Resurrection, so that Christians now have in heaven a merciful High Priest who is able to sympathize with our weaknesses precisely because he himself shared in our nature of "flesh and blood" (Heb 2:14, 17–18; 4:14–15; 6:19–20).

This comforting doctrine of the permanent humanity of Christ finds specific expression in both Paul and John.

"In him [Christ] there dwells the whole fullness of deity in bodily form" (Col 2:9). The two crucial terms are the verb κατοικεῖ (*katoikei*), "dwells," and the adverb σωματικῶς (*sōmatikōs*), "in bodily form," "embodied," "bodily." In Greek these two words are not side by side, as the translation "dwells embodied" (NEB) might suggest. Their separation points to two distinct affirmations:

(1) that the complete fullness of the Godhead dwells (timeless present tense) in Christ eternally;

(2) that this fullness now permanently resides in the incarnate Christ in bodily form.

It is true that before the incarnation the fullness did not dwell in Christ "in bodily form," but it is not true that prior to the incarnation the fullness of the Godhead did not reside in him. In this way Paul implies both the eternal deity and the permanent humanity of Christ.

"There is one God and one mediator between God and men—a man, Christ Jesus" (1Ti 2:5). For Paul, the mediatorial work of Christ did not cease when he "gave himself as a ransom for all" (1Ti 2:6) but continues at the right hand of God as he intercedes for his people (Ro 8:34). In both roles— as Redeemer and as Intercessor—he represents people before God and so is properly a mediator. He performs both functions as a man. When Jesus rose from the grave, and later when he ascended into heaven, it was as a man, with a glorified body. So far from ceasing to be fully human when he rose and ascended, Jesus then embodied in his own person the full potential and ultimate destiny of glorified humanity.

Hidden away in the Johannine corpus is a trio of fascinating texts that relate to the Incarnation.

Jn 1:14   "The Word *became* flesh."

1Jn 4:2   "Every spirit who confesses Jesus Christ as
            having come in the flesh comes from God."

2Jn 7   "For many deceivers have gone out into the
            world, people who do not confess Jesus Christ
            as *coming* in the flesh."

The verbs underlined are in three different tenses in Greek,
reflecting differing emphases regarding the Incarnation.

In John 1:14, the aorist ("became flesh") emphasizes the
Incarnation as a past fact, a historical event (cf. 1Jn 5:6). The
perfect participle in 1 John 4:2 (ἐληλυθότα, *elēlythota*,
"having come in the flesh") stresses the ongoing effects and
permanent consequences of Christ's coming in the flesh. Then
in 2 John 7 the present participle (ἐρχόμενον, *erchomenon*,
"coming in the flesh") points to that past fact as a timeless
truth;[19] the mark of "the deceiver" and "the antichrist" is the
denial of the coming of Jesus Christ in the flesh. In these three
verses, taken together, John assures us that the
"enfleshment" of the Son of God is not only a historical fact
but also a permanent fact; the incarnation is irreversible. The
implication is that, as our advocate before the Father (1Jn
2:1), Jesus Christ retains the full humanity he assumed in the
Incarnation. But "in the flesh" in 1 John 4:2 and 2 John 7
must be understood in the same sense as "flesh" (σάρξ, *sarx*)
in John 1:14—of an embodied human being. (For the range of
meanings of *flesh*, see chapter XV.A.1.)

In the Incarnation the Son of God became what he was not
(viz. "flesh"), without ceasing to be what he was (a divine
Being). In the Resurrection he assumed what he did not have
(viz. a "spiritual body"), without losing what he already had
(a truly human nature and form). The glorified Jesus is still "in
the flesh."

D. What should be the church's confessional formula—the resurrection of the flesh, or of the body, or of the dead, or from the dead, or of the person, or of man?

At the outset we should bear in mind that whatever formula is chosen, it describes principally, if not exclusively, a future resurrection, not the past resurrection of Christ.

There are forty-two uses of the noun *resurrection* (ἀνάστασις, *anastasis*) in the New Testament, always in reference to resurrection from the dead (apart from Lk 2:34). Often the noun is qualified by a word or phrase. Sometimes this qualification denotes a result—"the resurrection that leads to life . . . the resurrection that leads to judgment" (Jn 5:29) (cf. BDF, § 166). Sometimes it describes a place— "resurrection from [the realm of] the dead," "resurrection from among the dead" (e.g., Lk 20:35). But usually the qualifying word refers to people, those who are raised, whether "the dead" (e.g., Ac 17:32), "the just" (Lk 14:14; Ac 24:15), or "the unjust" (Ac 24:15).

It will be clear that most of the proposed qualifications of the word *resurrection* listed in our question are in fact not found in Scripture. So our treatment of these options may conveniently proceed under three headings: credal formulations, biblical expressions, phrases without credal or biblical precedent.

Why not be satisfied with the simple affirmation, "I believe in the resurrection"? Is further definition really necessary? It is. If we add a qualification, it serves the useful purpose of reducing the likelihood of misunderstanding. True, the qualifying phrases themselves can be and have been misunderstood, but this is no reason to question their value, which is twofold. First, they all exclude the view that it is only the spirit that is "raised"; resurrection cannot be equated with the Greek notion of the natural immortality of the soul. Second, because any Christian view of resurrection assumes that it amounts to more than the resuscitation of corpses and the return to an unchanged physical life on earth, the very notion of resurrection implies change: "the dead will be raised immortal" (1Co 15:52). What the various qualifications all do, is to stress the continuity, however it be defined, between the pre- and post-resurrection states, against the backdrop of this change, this assumed discontinuity. *Alter et idem*, "other, yet the same," was the way the Latin Fathers used to put it. Τοῦτο, οὐ τοιοῦτο, *touto, ou toiouto*, "this [body], but not such as it was," was the similar sentiment of the Greek Fathers.

But if all of the suggested qualifications clearly distinguish resurrection from the immortality of the soul and serve to emphasize the continuity between Now and Then, which is to be preferred and why?

1. Credal formulations

a. *the resurrection of the flesh (carnis resurrectio; σαρκὸς ἀνάστασις, sarkos anastasis)*

This phrase gained early dominance in both the Western and Eastern regions of the church, owing to its apologetic value in countering Docetism on one side and gnostic spiritualism on the other, and its vigorous defense by apologists of the early church such as Athenagoras and Tertullian, both of whom wrote a treatise "On the Resurrection." After the Council of Constantinople (A.D. 381), the credal formula "the resurrection of the dead" came to be preferred by the Eastern church because of its biblical origin. But until the time of the Reformation the creeds of the West spoke only of "the resurrection of the flesh."[20]

There is no unanimity among the defenders of this phrase as to the meaning of *flesh* as used here. Some would follow J. A. Schep[21] and take *flesh* to mean the material components, the substance, of the body, the fleshly body as distinct from the soul.

Some of the difficulties attaching to this view may be mentioned.

(1) Schep himself draws attention to the fact that

> from a formal point of view the traditional expression of the Creed may be called a misnomer. The word "flesh" denotes here the substance of the body, whereas it is not the flesh-substance as such, not the crude, unorganized "matter" that will be raised, but *man in his flesh-body*.[22]

> Though the expression "the resurrection of the flesh" is not found in Scripture and does not adequately formulate the biblical truth, it should be retained in view of the spiritualizing tendencies abounding in our modern world.[23]

(2) The dramatic change occurring at the resurrection (see Php 3:21) is reduced to the addition of new properties and functions to an earthly body or even becomes simply "a tremendous change regarding the conditions of its existence."[24]

(3) If *flesh* refers to material elements, which material elements are to be raised? Not only are the body's material particles dispersed by the processes of nature after burial or cremation, but they are, like all matter, themselves constantly changing. And why should the particular material particles of which a physical body is composed at the time of death, as opposed to those of earlier years or of the time of one's birth, form the nucleus of the resurrection body?

(4) Why does there need to be material and anatomical identity between the physical and the spiritual body, if, in the resurrection state (as Schep observes), "not only the sexual but also the digestive function of the human body will cease"?[25] It seems out of keeping with God's way of acting, for an eternal resurrection body to retain forever the useless relics of a former earthly body.

But not all writers take *flesh* in the formula "the resurrection of the flesh" to mean the physical components of the earthly body. J. T. Darragh proposes that it means the whole

man, "complete human nature," "full and complete humanity,"[26] while W. Bieder suggests "the person himself."[27] And
no less an authority in matters of historical theology than
Cardinal Joseph Ratzinger, the Vatican Prefect of the Sacred
Congregation for the Doctrine of the Faith, contends that *caro*
("flesh") in the phrase *resurrectio carnis* signifies the human
world,[28] so that the credal formula would refer to the general
resurrection. In any one of these three senses, the formula is
unobjectionable.

   b. *the resurrection of the body* (*resurrectio corporis*;
σώματος ἀνάστασις, *sōmatos anastasis*)

In this formulation, *body* could mean "physical body," in
which case "body" = "flesh" = material elements of the
earthly body. But it could also refer to "man in his total
being," as both body and spirit.

The nearest the New Testament comes to speaking of "the
resurrection of the body" is when the verb *raise* is associated
with the term *body* (Mt 27:52; 1Co 15:35, 44). The latter verse
is fascinating, for however we translate it, it suggests or
actually says that what is raised is a spiritual body!

   (1) "It [the body that is sown] is raised a spiritual body"
        (NASB, NIV, NAB[2]), "It is raised as a spiritual body"
        (NEB).
   (2) "It rises a spiritual body" (Twentieth Century New
        Testament; MOFFATT).
   (3) "A spiritual body is raised up" (C. K. Barrett;[29]
        similarly WEYMOUTH), "It is a spiritual body that is
        raised" (GOODSPEED).
   (4) "The raising is of a spiritual body" (E. B. Allo[30]).

That is, from one viewpoint the New Testament teaches the
resurrection of the spiritual body.[31]

2. *Biblical expressions*

   a. *the resurrection of the dead* ([τῶν] νεκρῶν, [tōn] nekrōn)

This expression is both biblical (e.g., Mt 22:31; Heb 6:2) and credal (the dominant form in the Eastern churches). In the creeds "the dead" are deceased persons, both the just and the unjust, but in Scripture sometimes the phrase refers to the general resurrection (e.g., Ac 17:32), sometimes to the resurrection of believers alone (e.g., 1Co 15:42).

b. *the resurrection from the dead* (ἐκ νεκρῶν, *ek nekrōn*)
This construction, found only four times in the New Testament (Lk 20:35; Ac 4:2; Php 3:11; 1Pe 1:3), always refers to the resurrection of believers, never to the resurrection of unbelievers. "From the dead" means "from the realm of the dead" or "from death" (if "the dead" is a case of "concrete for abstract"), or possibly "from the total company of the deceased" (since the expression is used only of the resurrection of believers).

Like all biblical concepts, these two expressions can be easily misunderstood or willfully misinterpreted. "Resurrection of the dead" could be taken to mean the eternal survival of those who once died but are now disembodied spirits, or the reanimation of corpses. Similarly, "resurrection from the dead" could be conceived of as the rescue of immortal souls from the underworld. But just because misunderstanding is possible or misinterpretation has occurred is not sufficient reason for discarding biblical phrases.

3. *Phrases without credal or biblical precedent*

a. *the resurrection of the person*
P. H. Menoud has vigorously defended this formulation on the grounds that it avoids all ambiguity and faithfully represents the teaching of the New Testament.[32] Indulging in some broad (and misleading) generalizations, he distinguishes between three competing views of the End: Greek eschatology, which involves the immortality of the soul and deliverance from embodiment; Jewish eschatology, which focuses on the resurrection of the flesh and the eternal nature of corporeality;

and Christian eschatology, that may be summed up as the resurrection of the person and the redemption of corporeality itself.[33]

b. *the resurrection of man*

On occasion a preference for this formula has been expressed,[34] usually because of the ambiguity of the terms *flesh* and *body*. But it has an obvious drawback: it is not some generic "man" that is to be raised, nor an amorphous "mankind," but individual persons. Like the abstract terms *flesh* and *body*, the word *man* makes resurrection seem generic rather than individual.

Five reasons may be given for preferring the confession, "I believe in the resurrection of the dead."

(1) This formulation is both biblical and credal, which is not true of any of the alternatives. The phrase "the resurrection from the dead" is biblical but not credal, and occurs only four times in the New Testament as opposed to eleven occurrences of "the resurrection of the dead."

(2) In the church at large, and within evangelical circles, two views have been held, and are held, with regard to the relation of the physical body to the spiritual body. One view argues for continuity of both person and "substance," and is epitomized in the phrase "the resurrection of the flesh." The other position contends for continuity of person but discontinuity of "substance." Since no ecumenical council of the church ever defined the nature of the resurrection body of believers, a formulation of Christian belief in the resurrection that accommodates both these views is to be preferred. "The resurrection of the dead" does precisely that.

(3) Resurrection marks victory over death. Since the terms *resurrection* and *death* are virtual opposites, their juxtaposition in the formula "the resurrection of the dead" highlights the victory of God and Christ in abolishing the "last enemy" (1Co 15:26, 54–57).

(4) Of all the proposed qualifications of the term *resurrection*, only the expression "of the dead" is personal in

reference and plural in form, the others being generic and singular. Yet, in its essence, resurrection involves people who are eternally related to God and one another in the holy city, New Jerusalem.

(5) If "the dead" is ambiguous, "the flesh" is much more so. Does it refer to the material envelope of the soul, or to the fleshly, muscular parts of the body that cover the bones, or to the physical body in its totality, or to the person as a whole, spirit and body, or to humankind? What is more, because of Pauline usage, where *flesh* often denotes the physical body as dominated by sin, the term has come to have many negative connotations, a situation which does not obtain with "the dead," which simply refers to those who have died.

E. Was the ascension of Jesus a visible ascent into heaven? If the exaltation of Jesus occurred at the time of his resurrection, what was the significance of his ascension?

Luke's narratives of the Ascension in Luke 24:50–51 and Acts 1:9–11 can and should be interpreted literally. It was a real Jesus of "flesh and bones" (Lk 24:39) who was taken up before the eyes of his disciples. Acts 1 focuses special attention on the visibility of Jesus' withdrawal: "before their very eyes . . . from their sight" (v. 9), "looking intently" (v. 10), "looking into the sky . . . in the same way you have seen him go" (v. 11) (NIV). Where Jesus went is expressed by a single Greek phrase (εἰς τὸν οὐρανόν, *eis ton ouranon*), which is repeated four times in verses 10–11. In the first two instances (v. 10 and v. 11a) the phrase means "into the sky," not "into heaven," for mortal man cannot gaze into heaven. But the reassurance given to the "men of Galilee" by the "two men dressed in white" was that Jesus had in reality been taken up "into heaven" (v. 11b; also Lk 24:51) and would return (from heaven) in the same way they had seen him go "into heaven" (v. 11c). This distinction between the two possible meanings of the Greek phrase is found in several English translations—WEYMOUTH, GOODSPEED, NEB, NASB, NIV, NAB[2]. "In the same way" (v. 11) implies personally and visibly, and might also suggest "in a cloud" (cf. v. 9), the cloud being a divine vehicle and a symbol of the divine presence (Mt 17:5; 24:30; Lk 21:27; Rev 1:7).

Of the eleven verbs used in the New Testament to describe this final departure of Jesus,[35] undoubtedly the most picturesque term is the verb ὑπολαμβάνω (hypolambanō), which means "take up by getting under," as when a dolphin "takes up" its rider or a father stoops down to give his child a ride on his shoulders. Weymouth's rendering catches the sense perfectly: "a cloud closing beneath Him hid Him from their sight" (Ac 1:9). Precisely where Jesus "went," once the cloud had caught him away from the gaze of his disciples, is not stated, but Paul's statements that he "ascended higher than all the heavens" (Eph 4:10) and is seated "in the heavenly realms" (Eph 1:20; 2:6) make it clear that "heaven" cannot be located directly above the vicinity of Bethany (Lk 24:50), the locality of the Ascension. We can merely affirm the paradox that Jesus resides in "heaven," in the immediate presence of a God whom "the heavens, even the highest heaven, cannot contain" (1Ki 8:27).

We have already reviewed the New Testament evidence that led us to the conclusion that when Jesus rose from the grave he was exalted to God's right hand (chapter XX.C.1. above). If this be so, what was the purpose and meaning of his visible ascent into heaven at the end of the forty days of appearances?[36]

The Ascension vividly dramatized Christ's earlier exaltation to God's right hand. It was a parable acted out for the benefit of the disciples as a visual and historical confirmation of a spiritual reality. In this sense it was comparable to the removal of the stone from the tomb (Mt 28:2) and the eating of a piece of broiled fish (Lk 24:42–43). Each was an act of divine condescension performed for the benefit of Jesus' disciples. The angel of the Lord rolled back the stone to let the disciples in, not to let Jesus out. Jesus ate the broiled fish, not because his resurrection body needed material sustenance, but in order to convince his followers that he was not a ghost (Lk 24:37). Similarly, Jesus ascended into the skies and was enveloped in a cloud, not in order to reach heaven but to dramatize the fact that God had exalted him to a position of preeminence in heaven. Christ's ascension to the Father no more necessitated actual spatial movement "upward" than the Incarnation required actual motion "downward," since the heaven that Christ left and returned to is not located directly "above" any single point on the earth.[37] What more dramatic way was there for Jesus to reinforce his teaching about his being "lifted up" to universal dominion (Mt 28:18; Jn 12:32) than by being slowly elevated before the very eyes of his disciples and enclosed within a cloud, the symbol of the divine presence?

Other aspects of the significance of the Ascension may be more briefly mentioned. First, it marked the end of Christ's appearances on earth. Without a dramatic, visual symbol of the end of the period of earthly appearances, the disciples would doubtless have continued to hope for further encounters with their risen Master. Whereas his previous withdrawals from view had been sudden (e.g., Lk 24:31 RSV, "he vanished out of their sight"), this departure was slow and therefore distinctive: "he was [slowly] taken up" (ἀνεφέρετο, *anephereto*, imperfect, in the midst of aorists, Lk 24:51), "as they were gazing intently into the sky while He was departing . . ." (Ac 1:10 NASB). Moreover, it was a withdrawal upward.

Second, it marked the end of that phase of the earthly history of Jesus which began with his incarnation. Once Jesus had gone to his Father, his disciples no longer visibly saw him (Jn 16:10) and the era of seeing and believing was ended. From now on, to believe was to "see," until the second phase of Jesus' direct involvement in human history began with his

Parousia (Ac 1:11). So it was that the Ascension marked the beginning of the church age, the era of faith.

Third, Christ's ascension was a natural result of his resurrection. When Jesus was raised from the dead, he received a spiritual body whose natural habitat was heaven. A permanent return to heaven was therefore in keeping with his heavenly embodiment.

Fourth, Christ's "going away" to his Father was a necessary prelude to the coming of the Spirit (Jn 16:7). As long as Jesus was continuing to appear to his disciples, the Spirit could not come, for the Spirit mediates the presence of an *absent* Lord.

Fifth, the Ascension points to the final destiny of believers. When Christ ascended into heaven, he ascended as "the man, Christ Jesus" (1Ti 2:5), taking with him the humanity he had assumed when he became incarnate. God's plan is not to obliterate human nature but to redeem and glorify it. Assumption to heaven is the destiny of redeemed humanity.

XXII

Reflections on the Controversy

Until the publication of this present book I have been the silent partner in this controversy. For his part, Dr. Geisler has published four articles and a book, has written two letters to the editor which have appeared in *Christianity Today*,[1] has sent out two mailings and a "Resurrection Survey" to pastors of the Evangelical Free Church of America, reported on the matter in his own publication *Quest News and Notes*, and spoken on the issue across the United States. In spite of this flurry of activity, I would have continued to maintain my silence were it not for the fact that Dr. Geisler has leveled certain accusations against Trinity Evangelical Divinity School and the Evangelical Free Church of America. At that point, as a faculty member of Trinity for eleven years, I felt I had no option but to rally to their defense, just as Trinity and the Evangelical Free Church have supported me wholeheartedly throughout this affair.

In chapter XIX, reference was made to a letter (dated May 12, 1987) I wrote Prof. Geisler, seeking to dissuade him from publishing his projected article.

> Regarding the misunderstanding and misrepresentation of my views in your article, let me simply observe that they are too numerous and serious to warrant the time involved in any attempt to rectify them, especially since I have just embarked on a 20-volume series . . .

In 1987 I was unwilling to respond in print to Dr. Geisler because I felt it would be an unprofitable exercise and because I was under no obligation to answer questions raised by a single individual to whom I was not accountable. But what I was not willing to do in 1987, I now do in 1990 because the matter has been made even more public through the publication of a book and because it now involves an institution and a denomination, not simply an individual.

The present chapter, then, breaks a three-year public silence and affords me an opportunity to do two things—to document some of the misrepresentations in Dr. Geisler's writing, and to attempt to set the whole controversy in perspective. Up to this point in my response there has been little specific interaction with Dr. Geisler's views. The matters discussed under "Issues in the Controversy" (chapters XX and XXI), however, have all been determined by questions he has raised. Now we may turn to particular points, and it will become clear to the reader that detailed interaction at an earlier stage in part 2 was impossible and inappropriate because of the misrepresentation of my views found in Dr. Geisler's writing. To interact with his response to these misrepresented views would not have been profitable. Alternatively, to correct his understanding of my views at every point would have been an imposition on the reader's patience.

It may be helpful to repeat here the abbreviations of Dr. Geisler's writings found under "List of Abbreviations" (see chart on p. 429).

Concerning the titles of his articles, one notes the movement from "Bodily Resurrection" to "Physical Resurrection" or "Resurrection of the Flesh." He regards the three expressions as synonymous (*Battle*, 31–32, 40, 51–65). Oddly enough, however, of the four chapters in his endnotes that have the heading "Bodily Resurrection," three bear the title "Physical Resurrection" in the Table of Contents and at the beginning of each chapter. What is of particular interest in this regard is the finding of J. T. Darragh in the standard work in

English on the history of the doctrine of the resurrection of humankind, entitled *The Resurrection of the Flesh*. He observes that the expression "physical resurrection" is "never used by any Latin or Greek Father"[2] and "is not a Christian expression at all. The very point of the resurrection of the body is that it is non-physical though real. S. Augustine, S. Leo, S. Gregory, and the whole line of Greek Fathers labour to distinguish between the Christian idea of the spiritual body and the resuscitation of the physical body."[3]

"Bodily"	:	"The Apologetic Significance of the Bodily Resurrection of Christ," *Bulletin of the Evangelical Philosophical Society* 10 (1987): 15–37.
"Battle"	:	"The Battle for the Resurrection," *Fundamentalist Journal* (March 1989): 12–15.
"Physical"	:	"The Significance of Christ's Physical Resurrection," *Bibliotheca Sacra* 146 (1989): 148–70.
"Flesh"	:	" 'I Believe . . . in the Resurrection of the Flesh,' " *Christian Research Journal* 12 (1989): 20–22.
Battle	:	*The Battle for the Resurrection* (Nashville: Nelson, 1989).

A. Misrepresentations

1. By misquotation

a. Presumably because it can be easily misunderstood, Dr. Geisler seems to dislike the translation "spiritual body" for σῶμα πνευματικόν (*sōma pneumatikon*) in 1 Corinthians 15:44 and prefers to render it "supernatural body" ("Physical," 152–54; *Battle*, 108–11) (see the discussion above, chapter XXI.A). He cites the RSV in support ("Physical," 156; but not in the earlier "Bodily," 25). But neither the 1946 nor the 1952 edition of the RSV has this translation. A check of eighteen major English translations reveals that none uses the word *supernatural* in 1 Corinthians 15:44, while sixteen have *spiritual*. In the same connection, when he cites BAGD (1957 edition) concerning the meaning of this phrase *sōma pneumatikon* ("Physical," 153; *Battle*, 109–10), he makes the misleading suggestion, by supplying "supernatural body" in square brackets *within* the quotation, that BAGD actually proposes this meaning. In fact, all this authority says is: "That which belongs to the supernatural order of being is described as πν.: accordingly, the resurrection body is a σῶμα πν." (685 in 1957 edition, 679 in 1979 edition).

b. In two important places Dr. Geisler cites the views of W. Michaelis, author of the substantial and influential article on the ὁράω (*horaō*, "see") word group in the New Testament (*TDNT* 5:315-82).

(1) Michaelis	Geisler's citation
TDNT 5:356	"Physical," 155 (= "Bodily," 24 = *Battle*, 112)
"Inasmuch as it is a mark of ὁράματα that they **do not occur in a reality** which can be perceived by the natural senses (→352), the fact that the appearances do not belong to this category suggests that they occur in a reality to which ὁράματα do not belong and which is characterized by the antithesis of ὅραμα and ἀληθές in Ac. 12:9,→ 359."	"Michaelis notes that appearances 'occur in a reality' which can be perceived by the natural senses.' "

Dr. Geisler's "citation" may give the general import of Michaelis's complex statement, but it is not what Michaelis "notes." Moreover, Michaelis holds two views that are anathema to Geisler. "We are thus to think of the appearances between Easter and the ascension (certainly in Ac. and hence in Lk., but also in the Synoptists generally) as appearances of the risen Lord from heaven" (*TDNT*, 5:356), and "It must be regarded as a reflection of the inaccessibility of transfigured corporeality to human sight that in some stories the risen Lord

is not immediately recognised because He has the garb of a
travelling stranger (Lk. 24:15f.) or an unknown gardener (Jn.
20:14f.)" (*TDNT*, 5:359 n. 214).

(2)	Michaelis	Geisler's citation
	TDNT 5:357	"Physical," 158 n. 37 (= "Bodily," 27 = *Battle,* 115)
	"Hence **he [Paul]** would reckon the ὀράματα of Ac. 9:10; 16:9f.; 18:9 among ὀπτασίαι or ἀποκαλύψεις, but would distinguish them **thereby** from the Damascus experience."	"As Michaelis correctly notes about visions, **the New Testament** **always** 'distinguish[es] them from the Damascus experience.' "

This "citation" of Michaelis is found at the end of a
footnote in which Geisler argues against my view that Acts
26:19 refers to Paul's Damascus experience, yet Michaelis
himself advocates my position (*TDNT*, 5:357, twice), along
with virtually all commentators on Acts 26:19!

c. On two occasions in *Battle*, Prof. Geisler refers to and
cites from an article by J. Jeremias, " 'Flesh and Blood cannot
inherit the Kingdom of God,' " *New Testament Studies* 2
(1956): 151–59.

(1)	Jeremias	Geisler's citation
	NTS 2 (1956): 158	*Battle,* 123
	"To this view of the Pauline eschatology we must oppose the simple assertion that it is wrong to assume that the sentence 'Flesh and blood cannot inherit the kingdom of God' **is speaking** of the resurrection. **It speaks** rather of the change of the living at the parousia."	"After careful exegesis of the passage, he concludes that 'the sentence "flesh and blood cannot inherit the kingdom of God" **does not speak** of the resurrection **of the dead** but rather of the change of the living at the Parousia.' "

Here arbitrary changes have been made in the citation,
although the general sense is retained.

(2) Jeremias	Geisler's citation
NTS 2 (1956) 157	*Battle*, 184
"It must be said that the **misunderstanding** of the first half of I Cor. xv. 50: 'Flesh and blood cannot inherit the kingdom of God' as speaking of the resurrection has played a disastrous role in the New Testament theology of the last sixty years until the present day."	"The source of the mischievous view of an immaterial resurrection body . . . is identified by Joachim Jeremias as E. Teichmann. . . . Jeremias says that '**a misunderstanding on this issue** has played a disastrous role in the New Testament theology of the last sixty years until the present day.' "

In this case Dr. Geisler has applied Jeremias's statement about the "disastrous role" to a totally different "misunderstanding."

d. In "Physical," 154 = "Bodily," 23 = *Battle*, 111 Dr. Geisler cites J. D. G. Dunn (*NIDNTT*, 3:707) in support of his view of the general meaning of the adjective πνευματικός (*pneumatikos*, "spiritual"). But Dunn is referring simply to the meaning of the neuter plural noun as used in two particular Pauline passages (Ro 15:27 and 1Co 9:11) and classifies 1 Corinthians 15:44 under category (a) of Pauline usage (*NIDNTT*, 3:706), not (c), as Dr. Geisler's citation would suggest.

e. In an attachment to a letter of June 1, 1988, addressed to Free Church ministers, entitled "Professor Murray Harris and the Resurrection Body," and again in *Battle* (31, 147), Dr. Geisler misquotes both of the brief Free Church articles he cites.

Original	Geisler's citation
"He **arose** bodily from the dead"	" 'He [Jesus Christ] **rose** bodily from the dead . . . ' "
"We believe in the bodily resurrection of the dead."	" 'We believe in the bodily resurrection of **all** the dead'."

Here the misquotations may not alter the intent of the original, but, sad to say, these and other such inaccuracies betray a lack of attention to words and a lack of concern about the accurate representation of others' views.

2. By distortion

On numerous occasions I am credited with views which I have in fact never held or expressed in writing, and emphatically disown.

View Attributed	Place where claim made
a. That the resurrection body of Christ was invisible and intangible	"Bodily," 15–16; "Physical," 163
b. That Christ's resurrection body was not "the same" as the body laid in the tomb	"Bodily," 17, 32; "Flesh," 20; *Battle*, 99, 104
c. That there was no material continuity between the pre- and post-resurrection embodiments of Christ	"Bodily," 31; "Physical," 170 n. 65; *Battle*, 99, 193 n. 13
d. That Jesus did not rise in a literal/physical/material body or "in the flesh"	"Bodily," 31; "Physical," 169, 170; "Flesh," 20, 21; *Christianity Today*, December 9, 1988, p. 9; *Battle*, 99, 102, 105, 107, 162, 194 n. 18; but see "Physical," 157 n. 34
e. That a miracle was needed for Christ's resurrection body to become visible	"Bodily," 27; "Physical," 150, 155, 157 n. 34; *Battle*, 96.
f. That the resurrection body of Jesus was angel-like	"Bodily," 33; *Battle*, 99.
g. That the resurrection of Christ and of believers is in an immaterial body	"Bodily," 28, 30, 33–34; "Physical," 150, 152 n. 20; 167, 169; *Battle*, 97, 101, 102, 104
h. That the resurrection of Christ was not a historical event that occurred in time and space	*Battle*, 25, 64, 99, 105–7, 178, 184; but cf. 100

i. That the resurrection appearances were tantamount to visions	"Bodily," 27; "Physical," 157 and n. 34; *Battle*, 200 n. 14
j. That the adjective *spiritual* means purely immaterial	"Bodily," 23; "Physical," 154
k. That a spiritual body cannot be seen	"Bodily," 27; "Physical," 157–58

3. By omission

a. In chapter XVIII, I drew attention to Dr. Geisler's neglect of my booklet *Easter in Durham* in which there are multiplied affirmations of my belief in the literal, physical resurrection of Christ. He was given a copy of this booklet in October 1986 and refers to it in an unpublished and privately circulated article he wrote in 1987, but in none of his published writing on this matter does he ever quote or even refer to one of the simple, unambiguous statements about the "reanimation" or "resuscitation" or "revival" of Jesus' body, statements which are reproduced in chapter XVIII.

In chapter XIX I reproduced in full a letter written by Dr. Gleason Archer to Dr. Geisler that was distributed to delegates at the 1988 annual Conference of the Evangelical Free Church of America. I find it to be most interesting that, having read the same booklet, *Easter in Durham*, Dr. Archer chooses to cite in his letter my reference to the Resurrection (i) as God's causing "the reanimation and transformation of a buried corpse" (*Easter in Durham*, 16) and (ii) "as being principally a physical miracle rather than a purely psychological or spiritual miracle" (*Easter in Durham*, 17).

b. This selective citation of material is also particularly evident in the one-page document, "Trinity Prof Denies Physical Resurrection," which was sent out by "Norman Geisler Quest Ministries." It contains seven one-sentence quotations from five separate pages of *Raised Immortal*, quotations that are removed from their explanatory contexts. One can imagine how indignant Paul would have felt if he had ever read a headline such as "Christian Theologian Denies Monotheism," that was based on a portion of 1 Corinthians 8:5, "There are many gods and many lords." And yet Dr. Geisler himself admits, "According to Harris, Jesus' physical body was resurrected, but the resurrected body itself was not one of flesh or material substance" ("Physical," 157 n. 34). Significantly this sentence is omitted in an almost identical footnote in *Battle* (200 n. 14).

c. Dr. Geisler again and again refers to my "suggestion" that after Jesus' resurrection, "his essential state was one of invisibility and therefore immateriality" (*Raised Immortal*, 53). What was implied by this summary statement has been discussed in chapter XX. The crucial phrase, of course, is "essential state," which I used in the sense, "customary mode of existence." Let me quote from my fuller explanation in chapter XXI above. "The Resurrection of Jesus was not his transformation into an immaterial body . . . but into a 'spiritual body' which could be expressed in an immaterial *or* a material mode." Often Dr. Geisler employs the word "essentially" (*Battle*, 37, 96, 113, 114, 200 n. 14) or supplies the misleading paraphrase "by nature" (*Battle*, 96, 99, 104, 105). But he often omits even this word in his description of my view and consequently leads the reader to imagine that I believe that Jesus was raised in a purely immaterial body ("Bodily," 28, 30, 33–34; "Physical," 150, 152 n. 20, 167, 169; *Battle*, 97, 101, 102, 104). Notice, for example, the subtle shift from "essentially immaterial" to "immaterial" in the following quotation.

> An essentially immaterial resurrection "body" is no more proof of Christ's bodily resurrection than is an angelic manifestation a proof that it [*sic*] once died in a physical body and was resurrected. Resurrection in an immaterial body is no proof that Christ conquered death of the material body (cf. 1Cor. 15:54–56). In brief, an immaterial resurrection body is not evidentially different from no resurrection body at all. ("Bodily," 33–34)

4. By ignoring my clear distinction between the resurrection of Christ and the resurrection of believers in certain respects

On page 109 of *Raised Immortal* I wrote:

> There are certain differences between the two categories of resurrection. Christ was raised "on the third day" (1Cor. 15:4), while his people experience resurrection on the Last Day. . . . In the case of Christ, resurrection on the third day preserved him from decaying in the grave (Acts 2:27, 31; 13:34–37) whereas the bodies of believers who die before the second advent are not spared dissolution.

Such differences prevent our applying to the resurrection of Christ all that may be said of the resurrection of believers. (See chapter XXI.B. for a full discussion of the unity and distinction between the two resurrections.)

As a result of overlooking this explicit distinction, Dr. Geisler applies to Christ's resurrection various statements I have made about believers' resurrection. For example, because I argue that there is no identity between the molecular structure of the physical and spiritual bodies of believers (*Raised Immortal*, 125–30), he arrives at two erroneous conclusions. One is that "Harris explicitly denies that Jesus was resurrected in the flesh" ("Bodily," 31, citing *Raised Immortal*, 124–26) and the other is that "Harris argues there is no material continuity between the pre-resurrection and post-resurrection embodiments of Christ" ("Physical," 170 n. 65 = "Bodily," 31, citing *Raised Immortal*, 126, and adding "cf./see also" 54–56, which deals with the material nature of Christ's resurrection appearances; *Battle*, 99, 193 n. 13). Similar, false transfers are made in "Bodily," 33; "Physical," 152 n. 19, 160–61; *Battle*, xix–xx, 64, 97, 99.

These, then, are examples of the more serious misrepresentations of others' views and my own views found in Dr. Geisler's writing.

B. Observations on some of Dr. Geisler's methods of argumentation

1. Through the misrepresentation of others' views, he creates "straw men," who are then demolished

Ample instances of these misrepresentations with regard to my own views have been mentioned above (A.1–4). With the misrepresentation in hand (so to speak), Dr. Geisler can argue as follows, if we may cite but one example ("Flesh," 20, 22).

(1) Harris believes Jesus' resurrection body was a "second embodiment."
(2) But Jesus claimed to have the same body in which he died.
(3) Therefore, according to Harris, Jesus must have lied.

Where he does not or cannot cite any proponent of a view he is opposing, Dr. Geisler simply says:

> These critics also argue that Jesus' sovereignty over His appearances indicates that He was essentially invisible, and made Himself visible only when He wished to do so. In this connection *they note* that Jesus did not appear to unbelievers, *supposedly indicating* that He was not naturally visible to the naked eye (*Battle*, 117, emphasis mine).

Then he proceeds to show that Jesus did appear to some unbelievers (*Battle*, 117–18), as I also have argued (*Raised Immortal*, 49–50; and see above, chapter VI.A.1).

2. He creates evidence to establish a point

Four examples of this procedure must suffice.

a. Being concerned that Paul never uses the term *flesh* (*sarx*) of the resurrection body (cf. *Battle*, 41), he tries to create the necessary evidence in this manner.

> While Paul said that corruptible "flesh and blood" cannot inherit the kingdom of God (1Cor. 15:50), nevertheless, he affirmed that Christ rose in *incorruptible* human flesh (*sarx*, Acts 2:31; 1Cor. 15:42) ("Battle," 14).

In this one sentence there are no fewer than three simple errors of fact.

(1) In Acts 2:31 it is Peter, not Paul, who is speaking.
(2) In 1 Corinthians 15:42 Paul is discussing the resurrection of believers, not the resurrection of Christ.
(3) What Acts 2:31 "affirms" is that Christ's flesh did not see corruption, not that Christ rose in human flesh (which is at best an inference). *Sarx* in this verse refers to "flesh" that is potentially corruptible.

b. Wishing to establish conclusively that Jesus did appear to unbelievers, Geisler claims that "He [Jesus] appeared to His unbelieving brothers (see John 7:5)" (*Battle*, 117). The evidence he cites is 1 Corinthians 15:7 (the appearance to James) and Jude 1 (which simply reads "Jude, a servant of Jesus Christ and brother of James"). The appearance to James is unquestionable, but evidence is simply lacking of his appearance to Joses, Judas, or Simon (see Mk 6:3).

c. So eager is Geisler to retroject the idea of a "resurrection of the flesh" into New Testament times, that on one occasion he actually speaks of "the apostolic confession of 'the resurrection of the flesh'" ("Flesh," 21).

d. In his desire to have my most recent article confirm his understanding of my view of the resurrection, Geisler writes as follows:

Even though this tiny article ["Raised . . . Never to Die
Again," *Voices* 14 (1988): 12–13] is *barely over one page*,
it contains the following: (1) Jesus' body before the
resurrection was material . . .(2) Resurrection changed
Jesus' body into an immaterial body. . . . Unlike His
previous physical body, the resurrection body was an
immaterial or "*glorious body*" (p. 13) . . . (3) The appearances of Christ after His resurrection are not mentioned. In
this two-page article there are no references to post-
resurrection appearances, although there is one to John's
vision in Revelation 1. (*Battle*, 102–3, emphasis mine)

In reality the article was a simple, brief comparison of Jesus'
resurrection to immortality with the resurrection of Lazarus to
the mere continuation of physical life. Never is the term
immaterial used. And what could my nonreference to Jesus'
appearances in "this tiny article" possibly signify?

3. He hints at "guilt by association"

Consider the following examples.

a. Unlike Jehovah's Witnesses, Harris does not believe
    the physical body was changed into gases or preserved
    somewhere as a memorial (*Battle*, 97; similarly "Physi-
    cal," 152 nn. 19, 20; *Battle*, 162).

b. Some have argued in favor of an immaterial resurrec-
    tion body on the grounds used by the old Socinian (*sic*)
    that a physical resurrection body would imply "a
    crassly materialistic view of resurrection according to
    which the scattered fragments of decomposed corpses
    were to be reassembled . . ." (*Battle*, 120, citing [out
    of context] *Raised Immortal*, 126).

c. If Paul had preached to Greeks on Mars Hill that
    believers were raised in an invisible, immaterial form
    while their physical bodies were still in the grave, his
    listeners would not have mocked him (see Acts 17:32).
    This view would not have been substantially different

from their own belief in the immortality of the immaterial person (*Battle*, 105).

d. It is an established scholarly custom to use footnotes to
refer to proponents of views that are similar to, or
different from, those defended in the text, as well as to
refer to scholars who support the views expressed. For
reasons unknown, Geisler ignores this scholarly convention, for he assumes that to cite a scholar or a view in a
footnote is to concur with that scholar or that view.
Accordingly he arbitrarily attributes to me the view of J.
G. Davies regarding "Factors leading to the Emergence of
Belief in the Resurrection of the Flesh." These "factors"
are converted by Geisler into "reasons given by Harris
(from J. G. Davies) for explaining the illegitimacy of belief
in the 'resurrection of the flesh'" (*Battle*, 97). Or again,
after he has misrepresented my view about the "transhistorical" *aspect* of the Resurrection, Geisler observes
(in a footnote): "In support of his statement here, Harris
quotes *people like* Reginald Fuller, Emil Brunner, J.
Moltmann, and others who call the resurrection 'meta-
historical' or the like" (*Battle*, 199 n. 16; emphasis mine).

C. The extent of our common ground

In writing on the theme of resurrection and immortality in
Raised Immortal, I sought to accommodate all the relevant
biblical data and not deny any of it. Inevitably, when we set
ourselves a task such as this and are investigating a topic such
as Christ's resurrection, we soon discover that we are probing
a mystery that defies human understanding and mocks human
language. It therefore comes as no surprise for us to learn that
there has never been unanimity in the church concerning the
nature and properties of the resurrection body nor any
statement on the matter issued by an ecumenical council of
the church. The community of believers has been content to

affirm "the resurrection of the flesh" or "the resurrection of the dead" or "the resurrection of the body." Both Dr. Geisler and I would happily affirm all three confessions, although partially disagreeing over the implications of each confession. Perhaps the greatest difference between us is that while I prefer to express my understanding of the resurrection in biblical terminology such as "the resurrection of the dead" and "the spiritual body," Geisler opts for terminology such as "the resurrection of the flesh" and "the supernatural body" which he believes excludes misinterpretations of biblical truth.

On three points that are particularly germane to any discussion of the nature of the resurrection body, I wholeheartedly agree with Geisler, although we would make different use of each point.

(1) "It is obvious that Jesus' resurrection body was not a normal physical body" ("Physical," 156 n. 32).

(2) "It is unnecessary to the orthodox view to believe that the same before-death particles will be restored in the resurrection body" (*Battle*, 120).

(3) "The resurrection body does not need the same particles in order to be the same body" (*Battle*, 121; similarly 174–75, 195 n. 23).

The points at issue between us seem relatively inconsequential when we review the breadth of our common ground. To borrow two sentences from my Introduction, we both believe (if I rightly understand Geisler's view) that,

> by God's miraculous act, the same body of Jesus of Nazareth that had been placed in the tomb after his crucifixion, was raised from the dead on the third day and transformed, so that the tomb was left empty and the risen Lord appeared in person to his disciples over the course of forty days and is now at the right hand of God in his immortal "body of glory." At the End, believers too will

be raised from the grave in spiritual bodies to enjoy eternal life in the presence of God.

Perhaps it was because he realized how much we have in common in these essentials that in 1988 Geisler rejected the idea that my views were heretical, preferring to call them unorthodox (although most dictionaries define *heretical* as "not orthodox").[4] But in 1989 he writes with dark innuendos.

There is a Trojan horse inside the Christian camp. A new battle has broken out, and the enemy is on the inside, not the outside. Theological termites are eating at the foundational pillar holding up the superstructure of Christian truth. ("Battle," 12).

The Trojan horse is within and the dynamite has been placed. The battle for the resurrection has begun (*Battle*, xx).

First Satan suggested "The Bible is true, but do not take it literally." Now he suggests, "Christ rose from the dead but not in a literal body" (*Battle*, 22).

D. Dr. Geisler's competence in Greek

Reluctantly one is compelled to make a comment about Dr. Geisler's ability to handle Greek, since in numerous places he makes confident assertions about what a particular word or expression in Greek may or may not mean. On page 153 of his *Bibliotheca Sacra* article ("Physical") he refers to the Greek words σῶμα πνευματικός (*sōma pneumatikos*). This, of course, should be σῶμα πνευματικόν (*sōma pneumatikon*, "spiritual body"), since σῶμα (*sōma*, "body") is neuter in gender. That this was no slip of the pen or oversight in proofreading is clear from the fact that this basic error is repeated three times on the one page, on one occasion actually being attributed by Geisler to the standard New Testament Greek Lexicon by Bauer-Arndt-Gingrich (685, 1957 edition), although earlier (p. 151) he reproduced correctly W. Pannenberg's explicit reference to a *sōma pneumatikon*. Some reader must have brought these errors to Geisler's attention for they are not repeated in identical material in *Battle* (109–10), although he remains uncertain whether the lexical form of the Greek word for "spiritual" is *pneumatikos* (*Battle*, 109, 110) or *pneumatikon* (*Battle*, 204). However, Geisler has now introduced several further errors: "the perfect participle tense in Greek" (*Battle*, 34), "the active mood" (*Battle*, 112), "the usual word for 'vision' is *orama*, not *horao*" (*Battle*, 200 n. 6), "the Greek aorist passive tense" (*Battle*, 200 n. 7).

Given these facts, people must be forgiven for questioning the validity of any appeal that Dr. Geisler makes to technicalities of Greek usage. But perhaps the most disturbing fact of all is that in his most technical treatment of our subject, the *Bibliotheca Sacra* article entitled "The Significance of Christ's Physical Resurrection," when he actually quotes an "authority" on some technical matter of Greek meaning or usage, he usually misrepresents that authority, either (1) by misquotation, or (2) by omitting to mention that the authority disagrees with him on the central point under discussion.

(1) p. 153   :   BAGD (685 in 1957 edition) is misquoted in that the translation "supernatural body" is arbitrarily supplied by Dr. Geisler. And he erroneously supplies σῶμα πνευματικός.
    p. 154   :   NIDNTT 3:707 (see above A.1.d.).
    p. 155   :   TDNT 5:356 (see above A.1.b.).
    p. 158 n. 37 :   TDNT 5:357 (see above A.1.b.).

(2) p. 155   :   BAGD (581 in 1957 edition) is quoted thus: "Arndt and Gingrich point out that the word [the passive of ὁράω] is used 'of persons who appear in a natural way.' " But this authority classifies the appearances of the risen Christ (the concern of Dr. Geisler) under the heading "Mostly of beings that make their appearance in a supernatural manner . . ." (581 in 1957 edition, 578 in 1979 edition).
    p. 155   :   TDNT 5:356 (see above A.1.b.).

p. 158 n. 37   :   TDNT 5:357 (see above A.1.b.).
p. 162   :   BAGD (530 in 1957 edition) is quoted to show
                    that "the word 'form' ($\mu o\rho\phi\acute{\eta}$) can mean simply
                    an 'outward appearance'." But this authority
                    gives the meaning of $\mu o\rho\phi\acute{\eta}$ in Mark 16:12 (the
                    verse in question) as "(in a different) form"
                    (530 in 1957 edition, 528 in 1979 edition).

Against these instances should be set the three occasions on which Prof. Geisler accurately represents the views of others on some technical matter of Greek usage: page 165 and note 46 (BAGD); the quotations of R. H. Gundry on page 166; page 169 note 64 (J. R. W. Stott).

It is sadly true that one can be confident of Geisler's accuracy in citing or summarizing a person's view only when he is expressing his own (although he himself misquotes the titles of both of his principal articles on this issue—*Battle*, 193 n. 1).

E. Dr. Geisler and the "consensus of the faithful"

Recent events on the U.S. theological scene have focused attention on the critical need for Christian leaders to be accountable to their colleagues or superiors. But it would seem that there is an even more important and complementary issue at stake—the submission of Christian leaders to those to whom they are accountable. Now no Protestant would want to claim that any branch of the church or group of believers is infallible in their judgment. But an individual believer who finds himself fighting a lone-handed battle against those whom he regards as brothers and sisters in Christ does well to take stock of his isolated situation and the cause for which he is striving.

Norman Geisler had a right to register his concerns regarding the views of a professor who teaches at the seminary of the denomination in which he maintains his credentials. But it is fair to say that the Divinity School and

Free Church leadership were disappointed and grieved when Geisler short-circuited "due process" by appealing directly to Free Church pastors. In addition, Geisler was unwilling to accept the unanimous verdict of the Divinity School faculty and board of directors and the virtually unanimous verdict of the ministerial and the General Conference that my view of the resurrection was orthodox and well within the Doctrinal Statement of the Free Church. The charges brought by Geisler were in fact not sustained by one person out of the sixty or so who were involved in my reappointment to Trinity, my application for tenure, or the examination of my views about the resurrection. And, as far as the Board of the Ministerial Association is aware, not one Free Church pastor out of more than 1800 (other than Dr. Geisler's son-in-law, Rev. Samuel Kostreva III, and now his former colleague, Dr. Robert D. Culver) has spoken publicly in Dr. Geisler's defense. Does not the "consensus of the faithful" outweigh a one-man theological commission?

F. Conclusion

Any future historian of evangelicalism or of the Evangelical Free Church of America will note, with not a little amazement, a consummate paradox. It is the paradox that the person who championed the cause of orthodoxy regarding the resurrection of Christ on behalf of conservative Protestants in the United Kingdom and Commonwealth in 1985 was two years later, without having written any more on the topic, accused of unorthodoxy in precisely the same area by a Christian apologist in the United States. And inevitably that historian will raise the question: What motivated Dr. Geisler to try to convert what should have remained a private, intramural discussion about the nature of the resurrection body into a public *Battle for the Resurrection*, especially when he was playing the part of "one man against the world"? That Geisler himself is aware of this "conversion" seems evident from the change from his earlier mailings ("Professor Murray Harris and the Resurrection Body," "Evidence for Physical Nature of the Resurrection Body") to the more recent title of his book, *The Battle for the Resurrection.*

No battle for the resurrection has begun among evangelicals, nor is one even brewing. In May 1989 several hundred leading evangelical biblical scholars and theologians met for a three-day conference that was designed to identify distinctive "evangelical affirmations" and to isolate areas of current concern in evangelical belief and practice.[5] A broad range of denominations and theological outlook was represented but not once in the nineteen formal papers or responses was mention made of a concern about the erosion of belief in the resurrection within evangelical ranks. It would seem that Dr. Geisler has mistaken an exegetical skirmish for a theological battle and an evangelical friend for an unorthodox enemy.

For my part, I would prefer to emphasize the extensive areas of agreement between Geisler and myself, our joint commitment to the thrilling and liberating truth that Jesus Christ rose from the grave in a transformed body to heavenly glory and cosmic dominion, and that believers in him will also rise from the dead and will share his glory and his rule.

From grave to glory: Jesus is Lord!

──── ENDNOTES TO PART 2 ────

**XVIII: The Antecedent of the Controversy:
        The Bishop of Durham Affair**

[1]For these details about the fire I am indebted to T. Harrison,
The Durham Phenomenon (London: Darton, Longman and
Todd, 1985), 1–2.

[2]The See of Durham is famous for several of its remarkably
gifted Bishops, such as the Biblical scholar Joseph Barbour
Lightfoot and the religious philosopher Ian T. Ramsey.
From 1979–84 Dr. Jenkins was Professor of Theology and
Head of the Department of Theology and Religious Studies
at Leeds University, England.

[3]Regarding the fire in York Minster, W. Ledwich (*The Durham
Affair*, Welshpool, Wales: Stylite Publishing, 1985, 37) observes that "it would obviously be impossible to say that it
was God's direct intervention; it would be equally wrong to
assert that it was not. We shall never know. The report
[BBC TV Weather Report, July 9, 1984] denied that there
was a storm over York that night, though lightning was
seen. And were there no lightning conductors? Another report [from the Radar Research Laboratory at Malvern]
shows that an isolated cell of rainfall moved rapidly over
the city early on the Monday morning. The report said, 'It
is surprising that it apparently produced such devastating
lightning' but nonetheless saw it as a plausible origin of the
bolt."

[4]"Credo" program, copyright London Weekend Television.

[5]Publication had been purposely delayed for a month in order
for me to solicit and benefit from the reaction of fifteen

leading evangelicals to my projected response to the bishop. Through the generosity of a friend of Tyndale House, 1300 complimentary copies of *Easter in Durham* were sent out to all the principal figures in the Church of England.

[6]*The Glory of Man* (London: SCM, 1967).

[7]*What is Man?* (London: SCM, 1970).

[8]See above, n. 6.

[9]*Living with Questions* (London: SCM, 1969).

[10]*The Contradiction of Christianity* (London: SCM, 1976).

[11]"Credo" program broadcast on April 29, 1984, copyright London Weekend Television.

[12]See above, n. 9.

[13]From the *University Staffs' Christian Fellowship Broadsheet* (Summer 1985): 43-45. Used by permission.

[14]From *Harvester* 64 (1985): 8-9. Used by permission.

[15]The only references to *Easter in Durham* are in "Bodily," 35 n. 16 (in connection with the properties of Christ's "spiritual body"), in "Physical," 157 n. 34; *Battle*, 200 n. 14 (in regard to my nonuse of the argument that the "resurrection appearances are called visions"), and in *Battle*, 100–102, (which summarizes portions of *Easter in Durham*) (see the text).

XIX: The History of the Controversy

[1]*Bulletin of the Evangelical Philosophical Society* 10 (1987): 15–37.

[2]The Greek text of the letter reads as follows.

Μούριος τῷ Νορμάνῳ τῷ ἀδελφῷ ἐν Χριστῷ χαίρειν. εἰ ἔρρωσαι, καλῶς ἂν ἔχοι· ὑγιαίνω δὲ καὶ αὐτός.

Τοὺς τὸν Χριστὸν ἐν ἑτέρᾳ μορφῇ τοῖς μαθηταῖς αὐτοῦ ὀφθῆναι μετὰ τὴν ἔγερσιν ἀρνήσασθαι ἐπιχειροῦντας, ἐγὼ ὁμολογήσω αὐτὸ τοῦτο ἵνα ἀεὶ πιστεύω ὅτι ὢν ἀπαρχὴ τῶν κεκοιμημένων, ἐχέγγυόν τε καὶ ἀρραβὼν τῆς ἀναστάσεως τῶν θνητῶν δικαίων οἳ ἄφθαρτοι ἐγερθήσονται Ἰησοῦς ὁ Ναζωραῖος αὐτὸς ἀπὸ τῶν νεκρῶν ὄντως ἀνέστη, σῶμα πνευματικόν, τὸ γὰρ σῶμα τὸ γενησόμενον οὐ σαρκὸς καὶ αἵματός ἐστιν καθὼς ἐπὶ τῆς ἐξαναστάσεως τῆς ἐκ νεκρῶν, καὶ σωματικῶς ἐν δεξιᾷ τῆς μεγαλωσύνης ἐν ὑψηλοῖς ἐστιν

καθήμενος καθὼς ἐπὶ τῆς κυριότητος ὁ Παῦλος ὁ ἀπόστολος
τοῦ Ἰησοῦ Χριστοῦ τοῦ ἐγηγερμένου φανερῶς ἐμήνυσεν.
῎Ερρωσο.

[3]From the "Minutes and Reports of the 104th Annual Conference" in *By My Spirit: 1988–89 Yearbook, Evangelical Free
Church* (Minneapolis: Evangelical Free Church of America,
1988), 12c.

[4]Ibid.

[5]Ibid., 14c.

[6]From a letter to the TEDS Faculty (July 6, 1988) from the
President of the Divinity School, Dr. Meyer.

XX: The Exegetical Issues in the Controversy

[1]*Our Lord's Resurrection* (Grand Rapids: Zondervan, 1964 reprint of 1909 edition), 159.

[2]Ibid., 160–61 (no reference is given for his citation).

[3]This latter would seem to be the position of J. A. Schep,
Nature of the Resurrection Body (Grand Rapids: Eerdmans,
1964), 107–79 ("a glorified body of flesh," 145; cf. 226, "a
body of glorified flesh," of the believer's resurrection body)

[4]M. J. Harris, *Raised Immortal*, 53–55, 56–57; *Easter in Durham*, 17.

[5]C. Gore, *The Body of Christ. An Enquiry into the Institution
and Doctrine of Holy Communion*, 4th ed. (London: Murray, 1907), 127. "The risen body of Christ was spiritual . . .
not because it was less than before material, but because in
it matter was wholly and finally subjugated to spirit, and
not to the exigencies of physical life. Matter no longer restricted Him or hindered. It had become the pure and
transparent vehicle of spiritual purpose" (127). "The spirituality of the risen body of Christ lies not so much in any
physical qualities as in the fact that His material presence
is absolutely controlled by His spiritual will" (129).

[6]B. Weiss speaks of δόξα (*doxa*, "glory") as "the heavenly
light-substance of the resurrection body" (*Biblical Theology
of the New Testament*, Vol. 2 [ETr. by J. E. Duguid] [Ed-
inburgh: T. & T. Clark, 1883], 60).

[7]H. B. Swete, *The Life of the World to Come* (New York: Macmillan/London: SPCK, 1917), 50–51.

[8]*The Gospel According to St. Luke* (New York: Harper/London: Black, 1958), 290.

[9]A. Plummer rightly notes that "it is very unnatural to take ἐγένετο with ἀπ' αὐτῶν and make ἄφαντος adverbial: 'He departed from them without being seen'" (*A Critical and Exegetical Commentary on the Gospel according to S. Luke* [Edinburgh: T. & T. Clark, 1896], 557).

[10]A common poetic word, equivalent to the prose term ἀφανής (Heb 4:13), ἄφαντος is often used in Greek literature of the disappearance of gods. It derives from the verb ἀφανίζειν, to render invisible; (pass.) to become/be made invisible.

[11]*The Gospel of Luke* (Exeter: Paternoster, 1978), 898, citing Euripides, *Or.* 1496; *Hel.* 605–6; Virgil, *Aen.* 9:657; 2Mc 3:34 for the motif of supernatural disappearance.

[12]*Critical and Exegetical Hand-Book to the Gospels of Mark and Luke* (ETr. by R. E. Wallis et al.) (New York: Funk & Wagnalls, 1884), 580.

[13]Here a present participle (μένων, *menōn*) follows a perfect tense (λελάληκα, *lelalēka*); in Lk 24:44 a present participle (ὤν, *ōn*) follows an aorist tense (ἐλάλησα, *elalēsa*).

[14]"It must be remembered that Jesus, strictly speaking, *was* already *no more with them* (ver. 44), and that the miracle consisted rather in His appearing than in His disappearing" (F. Godet, *The Gospel of St. Luke*, vol. 2 [ETr. by M. D. Cusin], 5th ed. [Edinburgh: T. & T. Clark, 1870], 355).

[15]*The Nicene and Post-Nicene Fathers of the Christian Church* (ed. P. Schaff), Vol. XI. *Saint Chrysostom* (Grand Rapids: Eerdmans, 1956), 5. He points out that Luke uses διά (*dia*) with the genitive, not the simple accusative of "time throughout which."

[16]*The New Testament in Modern Speech* (Boston: Pilgrim/London: Clarke, 1902), 309.

[17]*The Acts of the Apostles* (Baltimore/Harmondsworth, Middlesex: Penguin, 1957), 35.

[18]*The Book of the Acts*, 2d ed. (Grand Rapids: Eerdmans, 1988), 31; similarly his *The Acts of the Apostles. The Greek Text*

with Introduction and Commentary, 2d ed. (London: Tyndale, 1952), 67.

[19]BDF, § 223 (1); A. Oepke, *TDNT* 2:66 n. 3; M. J. Harris, *NIDNTT* 3:1181.

[20]*The Acts of the Apostles* (revised by W. F. Albright and C. S. Mann) (Garden City, NY: Doubleday, 1967), 92.

[21]By its position in Jn 20:26 the phrase τῶν θυρῶν κεκλεισμένων is shown to be a concessive genitive absolute clause; and the parallelism between verses 19 and 26 (some 16 words are identical in Greek) suggests that this clause bears the same meaning in verse 19.

[22]Τῶν θυρῶν could be a generalizing plural (thus "the door [of the room]"), but more probably refers to the house-gate as well as the door of the room, or, conceivably, to two folding doors forming a gate.

[23]*The Reality of the Resurrection* (Chicago: Moody, 1972), 128 (italics mine).

[24]LSJ (ninth edition) 1245, under ὁράω II.4.b. Accordingly τὰ ὁρώμενα = τὰ ὁρατά, "things that are seen," "things visible."

[25]BDF, §§ 313, 101 under ὁράω; BAGD, 578 under ὁράω 1.a. delta; Turner, 58; W. Michaelis, *TDNT* 5:358. The verb ὀπτάνομαι, "appear" (found only in Ac 1:3 in the New Testament) is a "back–formation" from ὤφθην (MH, 382; cf. 214; BDF, § 101, under ὁράω).

[26]Applied to things, ὀφθῆναι usually means little more than γενέσθαι ("arose," "came on the scene"), as a comparison of Ac 2:2 (ἐγένετο ἄφνω) and Ac 2:3 (ὤφθησαν . . . γλῶσσαι) well illustrates. Similarly Ac 16:9; Rev 12:1, 3. But in Rev 11:19 ὤφθη must be rendered "was seen," since it follows ἠνοίγη.

[27]L. Goppelt, *Theology of the New Testament*, vol. 1 (Grand Rapids: Eerdmans, 1981), 235.

[28]See, BDB, 908, under *rā'âh* niphal 1.a.

[29]The appearances of God in the Old Testament did not include a visual presentation. Although Moses spoke to God "face to face" (Ex 33:11), he did not see his "face," "for man shall not see me and live" (Ex 33:20; cf. 33:23). Similarly, in the burning bush incident God appeared to Moses (Ex

3:2, 4, 16) but his face was not seen, for Moses "was afraid to look at God" (Ex 3:6) (W. Michaelis, *TDNT*, 5:331–33). "God does not become visible; He is revealed" (ibid., 369).

[30]This meaning of ὤφθη is proposed by BAGD, 576, under ὀπτάνομαι; F. F. Bruce, *1 and 2 Corinthians* (London: Marshall, Morgan & Scott, 1971), 140.

[31]That is, ὤφθη may well be a constative aorist rather than an ingressive aorist. Rather than indicating entrance upon the state of "being seen" (viz. "he came into visibility"), it may denote the whole process of coming into visibility, being seen, and speaking (Jesus always conversed with those to whom he appeared), conceived of as a single phenomenon (viz. "he appeared").

[32]*The Gospel of St. Luke*, vol. 2, ed. J. P. Lange (ETr. by S. Taylor [Edinburgh: T. & T. Clark, 1867]), 437.

[33]*The Gospel of St. Luke*, vol. 2, 5th ed. (ETr. by M. D. Cusin [Edinburgh: T. & T. Clark, 1870]), 359.

[34]Ibid., 366.

[35]*I Believe in the Resurrection of Jesus* (Grand Rapids: Eerdmans, 1975), 100.

[36]Ibid., 101.

[37]Ibid., 127.

[38]"The Ascension visually dramatized the unseen reality of Christ's exaltation to and by God's right hand which occurred through the Resurrection" (*Raised Immortal*, 93; and see 91–93 on the nature and significance of the Ascension).

[39]W. Milligan, *The Resurrection of Our Lord*, 3d ed. (London: Macmillan, 1890), 248 Note 11, 267 Note 38; W. Michaelis, *TDNT* 5:355–56, who cites his previous thorough investigation *Die Erscheinungen des Auferstandenen* (Majer: Basel, 1944), 73–96; F. F. Bruce, *The Book of Acts*, 2d ed. (Grand Rapids: Eerdmans, 1988), 37; L. Goppelt, *Theology of the New Testament*, vol. 1 (Grand Rapids: Eerdmans, 1981), 238.

[40]"Resurrection" in *Baker's Dictionary of Theology*, ed. E. F. Harrison et al. (Grand Rapids: Baker, 1960), 452; similarly, with regard to the graveclothes and the tomb, G. E. Ladd, *I Believe in the Resurrection of Jesus* (Grand Rapids: Eerd-

mans, 1975), 94, 96, 126, who prefers the expression "passed from" rather than "passed through." Smith does not address the question of the materiality of Jesus' risen body.

41In support of this interpretation of the position of the grave-clothes, see A. Feuillet, "La découverte du tombeau vide en Jean 20.3–10 et la Foi au Christ ressuscité," *Esprit et Vie* 87 (1977): 257–66, 273–84. For a similar view of an earlier date, see H. Latham, *The Risen Master*, 2d ed. (Cambridge: Bell, 1904), 40–44.

42These verses are parenthetical and form a "flashback," with the Greek aorist being equivalent, as is quite often the case, to the English pluperfect: "But to their amazement there had been a great earthquake; for an angel of the Lord had descended from Heaven, and had come and rolled back the stone, and was sitting upon it. His appearance was like lightning, and his raiment white as snow. For fear of him the guards trembled violently, and became like dead men" (WEYMOUTH). This last sentence could also be rendered ". . . had trembled . . . and had become . . ." For a defense of this view, see J. N. D. Anderson, *A Lawyer Among the Theologians* (London: Hodder, 1973), 143–44 and n. 107; J. Wenham, *Easter Enigma* (Exeter: Paternoster/Grand Rapids: Zondervan, 1984), 77–78.

43Thus R. C. H. Lenski, *The Interpretation of St. John's Gospel* (Minneapolis: Augsburg, 1961 [= 1943]), 1365–66, who speaks of "the divine omnipresence of which the human nature of Jesus partakes and which he exercised since his vivification in the tomb" (ibid., 1366).

44*I Believe in the Resurrection of Jesus* (Grand Rapids: Eerdmans, 1975), 98.

45"The Resurrection of Jesus in Luke," *Tyndale Bulletin* 24 (1973): 88.

46*DCG* 2:509; *Our Lord's Resurrection*, 167–68. Yet in his *The Resurrection and the Christian Faith* (415) he appears to use "material" in a semi-philosophical sense, where "matter" is the same as "substance," viz. that which underlies any organism.

47H. W. Montefiore, *A Commentary on the Epistle to the Hebrews* (New York: Harper/London: Black, 1964), 41.

48*Acts: The Expanding Church* (Chicago: Moody, 1975), 173.

49A. Plummer, *The Gospel According to S. Matthew* (London: Scott, 1909), 438.

XXI: The Theological Issues in the Controversy

1The word φυσικός (*physikos*), "natural," is used three times in the New Testament (Ro 1:26–27; 2Pe 2:12), but the compound ὑπερφυσικός (*hyperphysikos*), "supernatural," is found only in modern Greek, not in classical or Hellenistic Greek.

2MH, 359 § 146.8; 378 § 157.6(b). Thus σαρκικός (*sarkikos*) means "controlled by the flesh," "fleshly," while σάρκινος (*sarkinos*) means "made of flesh," "fleshy." There is no Greek word πνευμάτινος (*pneumatinos*), meaning "made of spirit."

3P. Badham, *Christian Beliefs about Life after Death* (London: Macmillan, 1976), 41.

4In an open letter of June 1, 1988, addressed to "Dear Fellow Free Church Minister": "If asked whether he [Harris] believes in the 'physical resurrection' he says yes, meaning that the physical body placed in the tomb was later 'resurrected' (that is, it was transformed into an immaterial body)" (p. 2).

5This view therefore differs from that of C. K. Barrett, who, commenting on Jn 20:19, maintains that "it is probable that John's motive . . . for mentioning that the doors were shut was to suggest the mysterious power of the risen Jesus, who was *at once* sufficiently corporeal to show his wounds and sufficiently immaterial to pass through closed doors" (*The Gospel according to St. John*, 2d ed. [Philadelphia: Westminster/London: SPCK, 1978], 568, italics mine; "at once" here clearly means "at one and the same time").

6See the discussion of this issue in *Raised Immortal*, 112–14.

7This assumes the traditional view that believers will receive their resurrection bodies at the Parousia. If, in fact, they receive them at death (see the discussion of these two op-

tions above, chapter IX.C.3.), there remains the difference
that Christ was raised on the third day, believers on the
day of their death; his grave was empty, theirs remains
"full," with the result that in their case there is no material continuity between the body buried and the body
raised. In *Raised Immortal* I always accommodated both
options (see e.g., ibid., 138, 196), although "inclining"
toward the "resurrection at death" position (ibid., 100).
This "inclination" Geisler converts into a "conclusion" or
a "contention" (*Battle*, 98, "Harris concludes"; 184, "Harris contends").

[8]Ps 16:9-10 reads "[9]Therefore my heart is glad and my tongue
rejoices; my body also will rest secure, [10]because you will
not abandon me to the grave, nor will you let your Holy
One see decay" (NIV). Verse 10 is cited by Peter in Ac
2:27, 31 and by Paul in Ac 13:35, 37 in reference to
Christ's resurrection. Does the psalm as cited in the New
Testament mean that God's Messiah would experience no
decay at all, or no ultimate decay? Probably the latter, for
three reasons. (1) The synonymous parallelism of Ps 16:10
suggests that the "decay" referred to may be the ultimate
dissolution brought about by decomposition in the grave.
(2) In all four citations of the verse, the negative is attached to the verb, not the noun. For instance, in Ac 2:31
we read οὔτε ἡ σὰρξ αὐτοῦ εἶδεν διαφθοράν ("nor did his
body see decay"), not οὔτε ἡ σὰρξ αὐτοῦ εἶδεν οὐδεμίαν
διαφθοράν ("nor did his body see any decay [at all]").
(3) In commenting on Ps 16:10 in Ac 13:34, Paul observes
that through his resurrection Christ was "no longer in danger of returning to decay," or, as Weymouth renders this
phrase, "never again to be in the position of one soon to
return to decay." That is, the Resurrection arrested and
reversed the natural process of putrefaction that begins after
death.

[9]*The Reality of the Resurrection* (New York: Harper,
    1963/Chicago: Moody, 1972), 170-71.
[10]Ibid., 171.
[11]*The Theology of the New Testament*, 2d ed. (Edinburgh: T. &
    T. Clark, 1911), 477.

[12]*The Resurrection of the Body* (London: SCM, 1962), 94.

[13]*I Believe in the Resurrection of Jesus* (Grand Rapids: Eerdmans, 1975), 129. Similarly S. H. Travis, *Christian Hope and the Future of Man* (Leicester: IVP, 1980), 115, "continuity of person," 116 n. 72, "continuity of personal identity."

[14]*St. Paul's Conception of Christianity* (Edinburgh: T. & T. Clark, 1896), 394.

[15]*The Resurrection in the New Testament* (New York: Putnam's, 1911), 100.

[16]Supplementary Notes in H. Lietzmann, *An die Korinther*. I. II. (Tübingen: Mohr, 1949), 195.

[17]The full quotation reads: "There was continuity both in appearance and in substance with the body that the disciples had previously known, yet the dynamics were changed." M. C. Tenney, *The Reality of the Resurrection* (New York: Harper, 1963/Chicago: Moody, 1972), 128.

[18]Ibid., 171. In his treatment of this problem (pp. 1018–20), A. H. Strong repeatedly speaks of a certain "physical connection" between the present body and the future body. But his conclusion highlights the difficulty of defending any degree of "continuity of substance." "What that physical connection is, it is vain to speculate. We only teach that, though there may not be a single material particle in the new that was present in the old, there yet will be such a physical connection that it can be said: 'the new has grown out of the old'; 'that which was in the grave has come forth'; 'this mortal has put on immortality' " (*Systematic Theology* [London: Pickering & Inglis, 1907], 1020; similarly his *Lectures on Theology* [Rochester: E. R. Andrews, 1876], 264).

[19]It is just possible that "coming in the flesh" refers to the second Advent (as in Ep. Barn. 6:9), but in this case we might have expected "in glory" instead of "in the flesh." Alternatively, the present participle could allude to the ongoing manifestation of the incarnate Messiah.

[20]On the use of these credal statements in the church, see L. Boliek, *The Resurrection of the Flesh* (Grand Rapids: Eerdmans, 1962), 13–82.

21*The Nature of the Resurrection Body* (Grand Rapids: Eerdmans, 1964), passim, especially 220–26.

22Ibid., 226.

23Ibid., 229.

24J. A. Schep, "Resurrection," in *ZPEB* 4:74.

25*Resurrection Body*, 214.

26*The Resurrection of the Flesh* (New York: Macmillan/London: SPCK, 1921), 154, 51 (respectively). Similarly L. Boliek, *The Resurrection of the Flesh* (Grand Rapids: Eerdmans, 1962), 129, "flesh" = man in his integral wholeness; (cf. 120–43); G. C. Berkouwer, *The Return of Christ* (Grand Rapids: Eerdmans, 1972), 194, "the whole man in his earthly existence."

27"Auferstehung des Fleisches oder des Leibes," *Theologische Zeitschrift* 1 (1945): 109.

28"Resurrection of the Body. B. Theological," in *Sacramentum Mundi*, ed. K. Rahner et al. (New York: Herder, 1970), 5:341.

29*The First Epistle to the Corinthians* (New York: Harper/London: Black, 1968), 369, 372.

30*Saint Paul. Première Épître aux Corinthiens*, 2d ed. (Paris: Gabalda, 1956), 423, 425.

31Except for "from the dead," all qualifications of the term "resurrection" would be classified as objective genitives— what is raised is "the flesh," "the body," "the dead," "man," "the person." But we may distinguish between that with which the resurrection begins, and that with which it ends, its outcome. That is, "the resurrection of the body" could refer to the physical body (the *terminus a quo* of the resurrection), or to the spiritual body (the *terminus ad quem* of the resurrection). In traditional usage, the phrase has referred to the earthly body, but 1Co 15:44 shows how appropriately it could be applied to the heavenly body.

32*Le Sort des Trépassés* (Neuchâtel: Delachaux, 1966), 60–61.

33Ibid., 14–15, 50 n. 1, 85–86.

34J. Heller, "The Resurrection of Man," *Theology Today* 15 (1958): 223; M. C. Perry, *The Resurrection of Man. Christian Teaching on Life after Death* (London: Mowbrays, 1975).

35See *Raised Immortal*, 86. If Rev 12:5 contains an allusion to the Ascension, the number of verbs would be twelve.

36P. Benoit has usefully distinguished two "moments" in the mystery of the Ascension: (a) an invisible ascent of Jesus to the Father's right hand, immediately after the Resurrection, marking his entrance into the invisible divine world; and (b) a visible display of this exaltation on the Mount of Olives, some forty days after the Resurrection. He reserves the technical term "Ascension" for this latter aspect (*Jesus and the Gospel* [New York: Herder, 1973], Vol. 1, 243–53; *The Passion and Resurrection of Jesus Christ* [London: Darton, 1969], 341–42).

37Useful comments on this point may be found in B. M. Metzger, "The Meaning of Christ's Ascension," in *Search the Scriptures*, ed. J. M. Myers et al. (Leiden: Brill, 1969), 124–26; and P. Toon, *The Ascension of our Lord* (New York: Nelson, 1984), "Appendix I: Cosmology and Theology," 115–18, where he distinguishes a theological "world view" reflected in statements about the fact and meaning of the Resurrection, Exaltation, Ascension, and Session of Jesus, from a cosmological "world picture" of a "three-decker universe."

XXII: Reflections on the Controversy

1October 21, 1988, p. 9 (responding to a report under "North American Scene," p. 56 in August 12, 1988, edition); December 9, 1988, p. 9.

2*The Resurrection of the Flesh* (New York: Macmillan/London: SPCK, 1921), 229.

3Ibid., 228.

4See his two letters to the editor in *Christianity Today*, October 21, 1988, p. 9, and December 9, 1988, p. 9. My views, as Dr. Geisler understands them, are "unusual," "unbiblical," "unorthodox," "illogical," and "unhistorical," but not heretical ("Bodily," 28, 30; "Physical," 167–70; *Battle*, 32, 50, 97, 104, 106–8, 173–74, 178, 189.

5The proceedings of this conference are available in a book edited by K. S. Kantzer and C. F. H. Henry, entitled *Evangelical Affirmations* (Grand Rapids: Zondervan, 1990).

── APPENDIX ──

TERMS DENOTING RESURRECTION IN THE NEW TESTAMENT

A. Nouns

1. **Anastasis**, forty-two New Testament uses, always (apart from Lk 2:34) in reference to resurrection from the dead. The word is often qualified by a word or phrase: (a) "of the dead" (*nekrōn*, e.g., Ac 17:32; or *tōn nekrōn*, e.g., 1Co 15:42); (b) "from the dead" ([*hē*] *ek nekrōn*, Lk 20:35; Ac 4:2; 1Pe 1:3; this construction is never used of unbelievers); (c) "of the just" (Lk 14:14; Ac 24:15); (d) "of life" (Jn 5:29); (e) "of the unjust" (Ac 24:15); (f) "of judgment" (Jn 5:29). Regarding (a), the use or nonuse of the Greek article with *anastasis* does not distinguish the Christian dead from all the dead (cf. BDF 133 § 254[2]), but contextual considerations seem to indicate that in Acts 17:32; 24:21 and Hebrews 6:2 a universal resurrection is in mind, while Matthew 22:31; Acts 23:6; 26:23; and 1 Corinthians 15:12, 13, 21, 42 allude to the resurrection of the just and Romans 1:4 primarily to the resurrection of Christ.
2. **Exanastasis,** one use in the Greek Bible (Php 3:11). It may simply be a stylistic variant of *anastasis* (see Zerwick 162 § 484), or Paul may be stressing the distinctive nature of the privilege accorded to believers (cf. Lk 20:35) or simply emphasizing the imagery of resurrection as "out from among [*ek*]" the dead.
3. **Egersis,** only New Testament use in Matthew 27:53 (on which see above, chapter IV.G.).

B. Verbs

1. **Anhistēmi**, "raise up," "rise up," the verbal equivalent of *anastasis*, used 107 times in the New Testament, fifteen times of Christ's resurrection, twenty-six times of the resurrection of others. Nonresurrection meanings therefore predominate (sixty-six out of 107 uses). (Statistics here and for *egeirō* below are from L. Coenen, "Resurrection," *NIDNTT*, 3:276, 280; C. R. Smith, *The Bible Doctrine of the Hereafter* [London: Epworth, 1958], 177).

2. **Egeirō**, "rouse," "rise up," matching the noun *egersis*, 143 New Testament uses. On fifty-three occasions it refers to the resurrection of Christ, on twelve occasions to the resurrection of others (of which ten occur in 1Co 15). Like *anhistēmi*, it may signify the raising of the dead to physical life (Mk 5:41; Lk 7:14) as well as to bodily resurrection life (1Co 15:42–44, 52). As with *anhistēmi*, the phrase "from the dead" (*ek nekrōn*; but note *apo tōn nekrōn* in Mt 14:2; 27:64; 28:7) is sometimes attached to this verb (twenty-two times, always in connection with Christ's resurrection).

3. **Exegeirō**, "raise up," found only twice (Ro 9:17; and of resurrection, 1Co 6:14).

4. **Synegeirō**, "raise with," three uses (Eph 2:6; Col 2:12; 3:1) where the prepositional prefix (*syn-*) points to similarity of action and identity of destiny. Christians are raised to new life, just as Christ was.

5. **Zaō**, "live," refers to Christ's resurrection (e.g., Ro 14:9a) or present resurrection life (e.g., 2Co 13:4a), reanimation (e.g., Mt 9:18), the acquisition of resurrection life (e.g., Jn 11:25), and the enjoyment of spiritual rejuvenation (e.g., Ro 6:11).

6. **Anazaō**, "come to life again," used once of spiritual resurrection (Lk 15:24), once of the revival of sin (Ro 7:9).

7. **Syzaō**, "live with," used twice of sharing Christ's resurrection (Ro 6:8; 2Ti 2:11).

8. **Zōopoieō**, "give life to," denotes the action of God in revivifying Christ (1Pe 3:18) or other dead persons (Jn 5:21a; Ro 4:17; 8:11; 1Co 15:22), or Christ's work of endowing his people with new spiritual or bodily life (Jn 5:21b; 1 Co 15:45).

9. **Syzōopoieō**, "make alive together with," used only in Ephesians 2:5 and Colossians 2:13, describing believers' acquisition of Christ's resurrection life.

10. **Anagō**, "bring up," used twice of Christ's resurrection (Ro 10:7; Heb 13:20).

11. **Ekporeuomai**, "go, come out," used once of the emergence of the dead from their graves (Jn 5:29).

C. Observations

1. It is not possible to discover a consistent theological distinction between *egeirō* and *anhistēmi*, viz. that the former term stresses the divine agency in Christ's resurrection while the latter term points to his own resurrecting power. In point of fact, the passive voice of *egeirō* may bear an intransitive sense, so that *ēgerthē* may, like *anestē*, mean "he rose" (BDF 42 § 78; Turner 57; Zerwick 74–75 § 231). This translation of *ēgerthē* (in passages such as Mk 14:28; 16:6; Ro 6:4, 9; 8:34; 2 Co 5:15) does not, of course, contradict the frequent New Testament assertions of the Father's role in raising Jesus (e.g., *egeirō*, Ac 3:15; Ro 10:9; 1Pe 1:21; *anhistēmi*, Ac 2:24, 32; 13:34), but it does show that the New Testament tradition that ascribes the Resurrection to Jesus' own power (a tradition climaxed in Jn 2:19–22; 10:18) cannot be deemed a late development. As in classical Greek and the LXX, so in the New Testament, these two verbs are often synonymous, as in Matthew 12:41–42 (see also Mk 5:41–42; 9:27, and compare Mt 16:21 and Mk 8:31, and Mt 17:23 and Mk 9:31).

2. If the prepositional prefix *ana* retains a spatial sense in the compound terms *anhistēmi* ("raise up") and *anastasis* ("a rising up"), it will denote the standing up erect of someone who has been in a prostrate or reclining position (on ledges or shelves in the case of a sepulcher) rather than a rising up out of the ground, since among first-century Jews caves or burial chambers were used more often than graves in the ground (but see Mt 27:7; Lk 11:44). But probably here we should think in temporal rather than spatial categories (*ana* may mean "again" as well as "up" in word composition), of a coming to life again after a period of death. As for the preposition *ek* in the phrase

ek nekrōn (which is not materially different from the Matthean *apo tōn nekrōn*), the idea conveyed will be not the emergence of bodies from their tombs (but note *ekporeuomai*, "come out" in Jn 5:29) but the rescue of persons from the realm of the dead (cf. the verb *exegeirō*, "raise up," and the noun *exanastasis*, "a rising up"), or from death (if "the dead" is a case of "concrete for abstract"). Never used of the resurrection of unbelievers, the phrase perhaps denotes the distinctiveness of the "resurrection that leads to [eternal] life" (Jn 5:29), "the resurrection of the just" (Lk 14:14). Christian resurrection is (to paraphrase the expression *ek nekrōn*) "out from the total company of the deceased." When one speaks of resurrection "from the grave" (as in this book's title), "the grave" signifies first the place of burial, whatever it be, and then, by metonymy, the realm of the dead. Cremation is simply an acceleration of the natural process of decomposition that begins at death and is associated with burial. In its basic sense, then, resurrection denotes a person's restoration to life after an interval spent in the realm of the dead.

3. We may distinguish five types of resurrection in New Testament usage:
   a. the past bodily resurrection of isolated individuals to physical life (e.g., Mk 5:41–42; Heb 11:35);
   b. the past bodily resurrection of Christ to immortality (e.g., Ro 6:9);
   c. the past spiritual resurrection of believers with Christ (e.g., Col 2:12);
   d. the future bodily resurrection of believers to immortality (e.g., Jn 5:29a; 1Co 15:52);
   e. the future personal resurrection of unbelievers to judgment (Jn 5:29b; Ac 24:15).

4. Resurrection should not be regarded as both an event and a process, for the present tense of verbs that denote the act of raising or rising is never found in the New Testament. Rather, it is an event leading to a state. The form *egēgertai* ("he is risen," the perfect passive of *egeirō*), used seven times in 1 Corinthians 15, implies the past event of Christ's resurrection ("he rose," *ēgerthē* or *anestē*) but highlights the present consequences of that event (note also the perfect *egēgermenon*

ek nekrōn, "risen from the dead," in 2Ti 2:8; cf. Ro 6:9; 2Co 13:4). Christians, too, as raised with Christ (Col 3:1), are now "alive from the dead" (Ro 6:13). "Resurrection with Christ" is not only union with Christ in his resurrection but also sharing his resurrection life at the present time. And in the future as well, the resurrection event leads to the resurrected state: "we shall be raised immortal" (1Co 15:52).

5. There are, we suggest, three levels of meaning in the concept of resurrection.

   a. In its most elementary sense, resurrection denotes resuscitation, the regaining of the physical life forfeited through death. We find this meaning in connection with the "raisings" recorded in the Gospels and Acts (Mk 5:22–24, 35–43; Lk 7:11–17; Jn 11:1–44; Ac 9:36–42; 20:7–12; probably Mt 27:52; and cf. Heb 11:35), and sometimes in reference to the future (Jn 5:29b; Ac 24:15; Rev 20:5).

   b. Generally, such resuscitation is implied, and resurrection emphasizes the change that occurs (e.g., 1Co 15:42b). Believers are "raised immortal" (1Co 15:52), which suggests that the transformation that results in immortality is coincident with the resurrection and in fact is part of the resurrection itself.

   c. A third element, that of exaltation, is usually involved. A person is revived, changed, and elevated. The raising up (of believers) is from the dead (resuscitation) in newness of life (transformation) into the presence of Christ (exaltation). This three-stage process applies to spiritual resurrection as well as to bodily resurrection. From their spiritual death Christians are raised up (Eph 2:1, 6) to new life (Ro 6:4) in the heavenly realm (Eph 2:6).

We conclude that although resurrection may occasionally denote mere restoration to life, in its distinctively Christian sense it also implies transformation and exaltation. In its full theological import, therefore, resurrection signifies the raising of persons from the dead to new and permanent life in the presence of God. Such a definition applies to the resurrection of Christ and to the spiritual and bodily resurrection of believers.

──SELECT BIBLIOGRAPHY──

This is restricted to books written in or translated into English. For relevant books in other languages, see Harris, *Raised Immortal*, 277–80; and for periodical literature, see Bode, *Easter*, 187–200, and Boliek, *Resurrection*, 144–48.

Alsup, J. E. *The Post-Resurrection Appearance Stories of the Gospel Tradition*. Stuttgart: Calwer, 1975.

Barth, M. and V. H. Fletcher. *Acquittal by Resurrection*. New York: Holt, Rinehart & Winston, 1964.

Bayer, H. F. *Jesus' Predictions of Vindication and Resurrection*. Tübingen: Mohr, 1986.

Benoit, P. and R. Murphy, eds. *Immortality and Resurrection*. New York: Herder, 1970.

Blomberg, C. L. *The Historical Reliability of the Gospels*. Downers Grove/Leicester: InterVarsity, 1987.

Bode, E. L. *The First Easter Morning*. Rome: Biblical Institute, 1970.

Boliek, L. *The Resurrection of the Flesh. A Study of a Confessional Phrase*. Grand Rapids: Eerdmans, 1962.

Bowen, C. R. *The Resurrection in the New Testament*. New York: Putnam's, 1911.

Brown, R. E. *The Virginal Conception and Bodily Resurrection of Jesus*. New York: Paulist, 1973.

Cavallin, H. C. C. *Life After Death. Part I*. Lund: Gleerup, 1974.

pCharles, R. H. *Eschatology. The Doctrine of a Future Life in Israel, Judaism and Christianity*. London: Black, 1899/New York: Schocken, 1963 [= 1913].

Clark, N. *Interpreting the Resurrection*. London: SCM, 1967.

Cooper, J. W. *Body, Soul, and Life Everlasting. Biblical Anthropology and the Monism-Dualism Debate. Grand Rapids: Eerdmans, 1989.

Craig, W. L. The Historical Argument for the Resurrection of Jesus During the Deist Controversy. Lewiston, New York/Queenston, Ontario: Mellen, 1985.

————— . The Son Rises: Historical Evidence for the Resurrection of Jesus. Chicago: Moody, 1981.

Cullmann, O. Immortality of the Soul or Resurrection of the Dead? New York: Macmillan/London: Epworth, 1958.

Dahl, M. E. The Resurrection of the Body. London: SCM, 1962.

Darragh, J. T. The Resurrection of the Flesh. New York: Macmillan/London: SPCK, 1921.

Durrwell, F. X., The Resurrection. New York/London: Sheed, 1960.

Duthie, C. S., ed. RND Immortality. London: Bagster, 1979.

Evans, C. F. Resurrection and the New Testament. London: SCM, 1970.

Evans, E. Tertullian's Treatise on the Resurrection. London: SPCK, 1960.

Fuller, D. P. Easter Faith and History. Grand Rapids: Eerdmans, 1965.

Fuller, R. H. The Formation of the Resurrection Narratives. New York/London: Macmillan, 1971.

Gaffin, R. B., Jr. The Centrality of the Resurrection. A Study in Paul's Soteriology. Grand Rapids: Baker, 1978.

Green, M. Man Alive! Downers Grove: InterVarsity, 1967.

Habermas, G. R. Ancient Evidence for the Life of Jesus: Historical Records of His Death and Resurrection. New York: Nelson, 1984.

————— . Resurrection of Jesus: An Apologetic. Grand Rapids: Baker, 1980.

Harris, M. J. Raised Immortal: Resurrection and Immortality in the New T London: Marshall, Morgan & Scott, 1983/Grand Rapids: Eerdmans, 1985.

Hooke, S. H. The Resurrection of Christ as History and Experience. London: Darton, 1967.

Jansen, J. F. The Resurrection of Jesus Christ in New Testament Theology. Philadelphia: Westminster, 1980.

Kennedy, H. A. A. *St. Paul's Conceptions of the Last Things*. 2d ed. London: Hodder, 1904.

Kesich, V. *The First Day of the New Creation. The Resurrection and the Christian Faith*. New York: St. Vladimir's, 1982.

Künneth, W. *The Theology of the Resurrection*. St. Louis: Concordia/London: SCM, 1965.

Ladd, G. E., *I Believe in the Resurrection of Jesus*. Grand Rapids: Eerdmans, 1975.

Lake, K. *The Historical Evidence for the Resurrection of Jesus Christ*. New York: Putnam's, 1907.

Lampe, G. W. H. and D. M. MacKinnon. *The Resurrection: A Dialogue*. Philadelphia: Westminster/London: Mowbray, 1966.

Lapide, P. *The Resurrection of Jesus: A Jewish Perspective*. Minneapolis: Augsburg, 1983.

Latham, H. *The Risen Master*, 2d ed. Cambridge: Bell, 1904.

Leckie, J. H. *The World to Come and Final Destiny*. Edinburgh: T. & T. Clark, 1918.

Léon-Dufour, X. *Resurrection and the Message of Easter*. London: Chapman, 1974.

Lincoln, A. T. *Paradise Now and Not Yet*. Cambridge: CUP, 1981.

Mahoney, R. *Two Disciples at the Tomb*. Bern: Lang, 1974.

Marxsen, W. *The Resurrection of Jesus of Nazareth*. Philadelphia: Fortress/London: SCM, 1970.

Miethe, T. L., ed. *Did Jesus Rise From the Dead? The Resurrection Debate*. San Francisco: Harper, 1987.

Milligan, W. *The Resurrection of Our Lord*. 3d ed. London: Macmillan, 1890.

Morison, F. *Who Moved the Stone*? Grand Rapids: Zondervan, 1958.

Moule, C. F. D., ed. *The Significanc of the Message of the Resurrection for Faith in Jesus Christ*. London: SCM, 1968.

Nickelsburg, G. W. E., Jr. *Resurrection, Immortality and Eternal Life in Intertestamental Judaism*. Cambridge: HUP/London: OUP, 1972.

s41R. *Resurrection and Historical Reason*. New York: Scribner's, 1957.

O'Collins, G. *The Easter Jesus*. London: Darton, 1973.

———— . *Jesus Risen*. New York: Paulist, 1987.

———— . *What Are They Saying About the Resurrection*? New York: Paulist, 1978.

Orr, J. *The Resurrection of Jesus*. London: Hodder, 1908/Grand Rapids: Zondervan, 1965 reprint.

Osborne, G. R. *The Resurrection Narratives: A Redactional Study*. Grand Rapids: Baker, 1984.

Pannenberg, W. *Jesus—God and Man*. Philadelphia: Westminster, 1968.

Perkins, P. *Resurrection: New Testament Witness and Contemporary Reflection*. New York: Doubleday, 1984/London: Chapman, 1985.

Perrin, N. *The Resurrection According to Matthew, Mark, and Luke*. Philadelphia: Fortress, 1977.

Perry, M. *The Resurrection of Man*. London: Mowbray, 1975.

Ramsey, A. M. *The Resurrection of Christ*. London: Bles, 1945.

Salmond, S. D. F. *Christian Doctrine of Immortality*. 2d ed. Edinburgh: T. & T. Clark, 1896.

Schep, J. A. *The Nature of the Resurrection Body*. Grand Rapids: Eerdmans, 1964.

Schwarz, H. *On the Way to the Future*. Minneapolis: Augsburg, 1972.

Shaw, J. M. *The Resurrection of Christ*. Edinburgh: T. & T. Clark, 1920.

Smith, R. H. *Easter Gospels*. Minneapolis: Augsburg, 1983.

Sparrow-Simpson, W. J. *Our Lord's Resurrection*. Grand Rapids: Zondervan, 1964 [= 1909, 2d ed.].

————. *The Resurrection and the Christian Faith*. Grand Rapids: Zondervan, 1968 [= 1911].

Stanley, D. M. *Christ's Resurrection in Pauline Soteriology*. Rome: Biblical Institute, 1961.

Stendahl, K., ed. *Immortality and Resurrection*. New York: Macmillan, 1965.

Swete, H. B. *The Appearances of our Lord after the Passion*. London: Macmillan, 1907.

Tenney, M. C. *The Reality of the Resurrection*. New York: Harper, 1963/Chicago: Moody, 1972.

Toon, P. *The Ascension of Our Lord*. New York: Nelson, 1984.

Torrance, T. F. *Space, Time, and Resurrection*. Grand Rapids: Eerdmans, 1976.

Travis, S. H. *Christian Hope and the Future of Man*. Leicester: InterVarsity, 1980.

Vos, G. *The Pauline Eschatology*. Grand Rapids: Eerdmans, 1953 reprint.

Weatherhead, L. D. *The Resurrection of Christ in the Light of Modern Science and Psychical Research*. London: Hodder/ Nashville, Abingdon, 1959.

Wenham, J. *Easter Enigma: Are the Resurrection Accounts in Conflict?* Grand Rapids: Zondervan, 1984.

Westcott, B. F. *The Gospel of the Resurrection*. 6th ed. London: Macmillan, 1888.

Wilckens, U. *Resurrection*. Edinburgh: Saint Andrew, 1977/Atlanta: Knox, 1978.

——Author Index——

──SUBJECT INDEX──

REFERENCE INDEX

(Boldface type indicates more detailed discussion)

OLD TESTAMENT

NEW TESTAMENT

INTERTESTAMENTAL AND OTHER JEWISH LITERATURE

OTHER ANCIENT AUTHORS AND WRITINGS

From Grave to Glory was typeset by the
Photocomposition Department of Zondervan Publishing House,
Grand Rapids, Michigan on a Mergenthaler Linotron 202/N.
Compositor: Susan A. Koppenol
Editors: Lori Walburg and Leonard G. Goss

*The text was set in 10 point Times Roman, a face
designed by Stanley Morison in 1931 for the* London
Times. *Times Roman is compact, economical, and
popular for bookwork. This book was printed on 50-pound
Spring Hill Vellum paper by Arcata Graphics / Kingsport,
Kingsport, Tennessee.*

124